1914:

Austria-Hungary, the Origins, and the First Year of World War I

Günter Bischof, Ferdinand Karlhofer (Eds.)
Samuel R. Williamson, Jr. (Guest Editor)

CONTEMPORARY AUSTRIAN STUDIES | VOLUME 23

UNO PRESS   *innsbruck* university press

Printed in the United States of America

Design by Allison Reu

Cover photo: "In enemy position on the Piave levy" (Italy), June 18, 1918
WK1/ALB079/23142, Photo Kriegsvermessung 5, K.u.k. Kriegspressequartier,
Lichtbildstelle Vienna
Cover photo used with permission from the
Austrian National Library – Picture Archives and Graphics Department, Vienna

Published in the United States by
University of New Orleans Press
ISBN: 9781608010264

Published and distributed in Europe
by Innsbruck University Press
ISBN: 9783902936356

UNO PRESS

*i*up

Contemporary Austrian Studies

Sponsored by the University of New Orleans and Universität Innsbruck

Publication of this volume has been made possible through generous grants from the Austrian Ministry of European and International Affairs through the Austrian Cultural Forum in New York as well as the Austrian Academic Exchange Service (ÖAAD). The Austrian Marshall Plan Anniversary Foundation in Vienna has been very generous in supporting CenterAustria at the University of New Orleans and its publications series. The College of Liberal Arts at the University of New Orleans and the *Auslandsamt* of the University of Innsbruck provided additional financial support.

*Dedicated to Charles S. Maier, Harvard University,
on the Occasion of His 75th Birthday*

Table of Contents

NON-TOPICAL ESSAYS

BOOK REVIEWS

Preface

Günter Bischof

Mark Trachtenberg has rightly suggested that the great French historian Elie Halévy summed up the origins of World War I in the Rhodes Lectures delivered at Oxford in 1929 only 15 years after the outbreak of the war in "a single but quite remarkable paragraph." Halevy wrote: "But everyone knew, who chose to know, that, whenever Austria declared war upon Serbia, Pan-Slavist sentiment would become too strong for any Russian government to resist its pressure. Everyone knew, who chose to know, that whenever Russia gave so much as a sign of declaring war upon Austria, Pan-German feelings would compel the German government to enter the lists in turn. It was likewise common knowledge that Germany, whenever she declared war upon Russia, was resolved not to tolerate the existence in the west of an army that was after all the second best army in Europe; that she would first march upon Paris and annihilate France as a military power, before rushing to back to the east, and settling matters with Russia." It was also clear that, in order to implement that plan, the German army felt it would have to march through Belgium. But "everybody understood that if ever the Belgian coast and the northern coast of France were to fall under the domination of Germany, Great Britain, feeling her prestige and her security in danger, would enter the war on the side of Belgium and France." War by August 1914 became virtually inevitable: "everyone knew, who wished to know, not only that European war was imminent, but what the general shape of the war would be."[1]

For the past 100 years some of the greatest historians and political scientists of the twentieth century have picked apart, analyzed and reinterpreted this sequence of events taking place within a single month

---

1. Marc Trachtenberg, *The Craft of International History: A Guide to the Literature* (Princeton: Princeton University Press, 2006), 31, summarizing and citing Halevy, "The World Crisis of 1914-1918: An Interpretation," first published in 1930, and reprinted in *The Era of Tyrannies: Essay on Socialism and War* (London: Allen Lane, 1967), 179.

in July/early August 1914, again and again, from the classic works of
Luigi Albertini, Fritz Fischer and Barbara Tuchman, and Jack Synder
onwards to Christopher Clark and Margaret Macmillan most recently.
The four years of fighting during World War I destroyed the international
system put into place at the Congress of Vienna in 1814/15 and led to
the dissolution of some of the great old empires of Europe (Austrian-
Hungarian, Ottoman, Russian). The 100th anniversary of the assassination
of the Austrian successor to the throne Archduke Francis Ferdinand and
his wife Sophie in Sarajevo unleashed the series of events described with
such economy by Halevy above. The assassination in Sarajevo, the spark
that set asunder the European powder keg, has been the focus of a veritable
blizzard of commemorations, scholarly conferences and a new avalanche of
publications dealing with this signal historical event that changed the world.
The July 1914 crisis has served as a ready-made paradigm for commentators
to analyze the current crisis in Ukraine/Crimea, unleashed by Ukrainian
"people power" on Majdan Square in February 2014, and culminating in
Putin's "Anschluss" of Crimea in late March. Once again well-informed
observers see Europe "sleep walking" towards disaster. Will Putin—the
"new czar" in the Kremlin—once again mobilize troops to intimidate
Russia's neighbors and thereby precipitate a much larger crisis?

Contemporary Austrian Studies would not miss the opportunity to make
its contribution to these scholarly discourses by focusing on reassessing the
Dual Monarchy's crucial role in the outbreak and the first year of the war.
The following essays by both senior and junior scholars summarize and
update the historiography of what has been known for a long time as well
as new and fresh approaches to research on the World War I era. Samuel
R. Williamson, Jr. who has spent a lifetime of scholarly engagement with
the Habsburg Monarchy's role in the origins of World War I, summarizes
the complex cycles of historiography on the events of July 1914 in Vienna
and Budapest. Based on British and Russian sources, Hannes Leidinger
presents a fresh view on Colonel Redl, the infamous spy in the Austrian
intelligence services who gave vital information about Austrian-Hungarian
operational war plans to Russia. Wolfram Dornik looks at the role Conrad
von Hötzendorf, the chief of staff of the Austrian-Hungarian Army, played
in unleashing the war and covering his tracks after the war as one of the
chief "war mongerers" in the Habsburg Monarchy before and in 1914. Based
on newly available personal diaries, Günther Kronenbitter returns to the
central part Count Leopold Berchtold, the Monarchy's Foreign Minister,
played in 1914 and his efforts to (not) remember too many details about
July 1914 decision making in Vienna after the war. Both von Hötzendorf

and Berchtold indulged in diluting and cover up their crucial roles played in July 1914 after the war—so issues of memory of the war enter the discussion in these essays.

A second section deals with aspects of both the military history in the first year of the war and the social and economic history on the home front. Richard Lein deals with the convoluted changing war plans of the chief of staff of the Austrian-Hungarian Army—as well as the lack of coordination with its German ally—and how these changes negatively affected the fortunes of the Army in the initial battles against Russia on the Galician frontlines in the East. Jonathan Gumz sheds light on the ill success of the Army on the Serbian front in the South and the resulting breaches in international rules of humanitarian warfare. Based on the memoir literature of common soldiers and officers, Jason Engle delves deeply into the *mentalité* and fighting spirit of the men on the frontlines. Peter Berger's essay on the increasingly social and economic chaos in the Empire's capital Vienna returns us to the home front. Gerhard Senft deals with the little-known aspect of the peace movement in the Monarchy and the conscientious objectors. The Habsburg armed forces construction of war heroes for propaganda purposes in producing domestic support of the war is the subject of Melanie Goll's spirited essay. Verena Moritz concentrates on the treatment of huge numbers of enemy prisoners of war and the breach of international law in the inhumane treatment of these POWs and the suspected civilians interned close to the frontlines of the war. Hans Petschar's stunning essay produces an impressive visual record of the predecessor to today's Austrian National Library's efforts to gather the rich record of war propaganda etc. for posterity. The Habsburg Monarchy's propaganda efforts and military record, including the perpetration of "war crimes", then, offer innovative contributions to World War I scholarship by a younger generation of scholars that are being made available to an international readership here.

Next to these "topical" essays dealing with the main theme of this CAS volume, we also present essays not related to main theme of this volume. These non-topical essays by younger scholars push the study of contemporary Austrian history into methodologically and topically new areas rarely covered by traditional scholarship. Marion Krammer and Margarethe Szeless are visual historians who are embarking on a large scale project on analyzing the vast record of the picture archives of the "United States Information Service" that was active in Austria for much of the post-World War II occupation decade. Their analysis of the work of the Japanese-American photographer Yoichi Okamoto, the chief of the USIS picture section and later principal photographer in Lyndon B. Johnson's White House, is a first result of this work. The consortium of Vienna historians Birgit Johler, Katharina Kober, Barbara Sauer, Ulrike Tauss, Joanna White have done remarkable work on the micro-history of the "Anschluss" in Vienna. They have reconstructed the history of the Jews that lived on one Vienna Street – the Servitengasse in the 9th district. They are trying to reconstruct the Jewish life of this street before March 1938, as well as their persecutions, dispersal and extinction during the Holocaust. They traced down and interviewed the survivors and try to keep their memory alive of those who perished. Such local histories of the "Anschluss" and its consequences give us a much more complete picture of the huge tragedy that befell the Jewish community of Vienna in World War II.

As always, book reviews and the annual summary and update of Austrian politics in 2013 complete this volume.

A number of people have been instrumental in making the completion of this collection possible. Samuel R. Williamson, Jr. has been instrumental in the conception and execution of the topical essays on World War I. As an eminent historian on the origins of World War I and the senior scholar in the Ango-American scholarly world of the Austrian Monarchy's role in the outbreak of the war, we are fortunate to have won him over as the guest editor of this volume. He has been deeply engaged in assessing and improving the individual manuscripts of the topical essays. His high professional standards and keen sense of the state of the art of the field have made this a much better volume than we could ever hoped it would be. Markus Habermann, the 2013/14 Austrian Ministry of Science Dissertation Fellow at UNO and PhD student in political science at the University of Vienna, worked hard on tracking every manuscript through both the copy-editing and proof-reading processes and towards final publication. Jen Hanks at UNO Publishing put her customary skills into copy-editing the individual manuscripts; Allison Reu skilfully type-set the final pdf of the volume. G.K. Darby and Abram Himelstein, the leadership team at UNO Press, have been hugely supportive to spirit this volume through to final publication. At CenterAustria Gertraud Griessner and Katrin Lisa Voggenberger conducted the Center's daily business with superb efficiency to allow the co-editor to work on managing the completion of the volume. Gertraud was also very helpful with proofreading the final copy. Inge Fink from the UNO Department of English has been forthcoming and quick as always in helping with translations of texts into English. Without the CenterAustria and UNO Publishing teams there would be no CAS series. At innsbruck university press Birgit Holzner was helpful with the final round of proof-reading and then producing the volume for the European market. Cooperating with her has become a big bonus in the production of these volumes. Hans Petschar and Marlies Dornik at the Picture Archives of the Austrian National Library in Vienna have been kind, quick and most helpful in helping us find the pictures to illustrate this volume and granted the righs for publication of the pictures in this richly illustrated volume. Richard Lein has produced a useful map for his esssay. Petschar has richly illustrated his own essay and so have Krammer/Szeless and Johler et al.. We are grateful to them all.

As always, we are happy in acknowledging our sponsors and supporters for making the publication of the CAS series possible at all. At the Universities of Innsbruck and New Orleans our thanks got to Matthias Schennach of the *Auslandsamt* as well as Christina Antenhofer and Marion Wieser in the New Orleans Office as well as Kevin Graves, the Acting Dean of the College of Liberal Arts at UNO, and Andrew Goss, the chair of the History Department. We are also grateful to *Rektor* Tilmann Märk and President Peter Fos for their support of the UNO – Innsbruck partnership agenda, including its publication series. At the Austrian Cultural Forum in New York Christine Moser and Christian Ebner have supported our work as has their "boss" Martin Eichtinger, the chief of the Cultural Division of the Austrian Ministry of European and International Affairs. In the Ministry of Science, Research, and Economics and its student exchange office Österreichischer Auslandsdienst (ÖAD), we are grateful to Barbara Weitgruber, Christoph Ramoser, Josef Leidenfrost and Florian Gerhardus. Eugen Stark, the outgoing executive secretary, and Markus Schweiger, the incoming executive secretary, Ambassador Wolfgang Petritsch, the board's chairman, as well as the board members of the Austrian Marshall Plan Foundation have been our strongest supporters for more than a decade now. It is a great pleasure and privilege to work with them all and acknowledge their unerring support of CenterAustria and its activities.

New Orleans, Louisiana, April 2014

Austria-Hungary
and the Origins of World War I

Arrival of the Successor to the Throne Francis Ferdinand with his wife Sophie in Sarajevo,
June 28, 1914, Photo Raoul Korty, KO 877-C,
Austrian National Library - Picture Archives and Graphics Department, Vienna

Austria and the Origins of the Great War: A Selective Historiographical Survey

Samuel R. Williamson, Jr.

On 28 July 1914 Austria-Hungary declared war on Serbia and began mobilization for Plan B against Belgrade. On Sunday, 2 August, Harvard historian Albert Bushnell Hart wrote in the *New York Times* that "Austrian Fear of Serb Empire is Real War Cause."Within days, Russia's mobilization converted that fear into a larger war.

Each of the warring governments moved to defend and explain its decision, with the Germans publishing a first set of diplomatic papers in early August. But the government in Vienna waited, finally releasing the *Austro-Hungarian Red Book* in February 1915. The small volume started with an introductory survey on Austro-Serbian relations after 1903 and included the publication of sixty-nine documents.[1] Then later in 1915 it issued another short volume of documents that chronicled relations with Italy, and a similar volume appeared in 1916 that covered relations with Romania until its entry into the war. Meanwhile, the government propaganda machinery defended the July 1914 decisions.[2]

But in preparation for the peace negotiations, the new socialist government in Austria in early 1919 took two defensive steps to defend itself in the peace negotiations. The Ballplatz authorized one of its officials, Roderich Gooss, to prepare a summary of key diplomatic documents with brief commentary on many of them. His work, *Das Wiener Kabinett und die Entstehung des Weltkrieges*, left little doubt that the monarchy, the old

---

1. Austria-Hungary, *Austro-Hungarian Red Book: Official English Edition with an Introduction* (New York: John C. Rankin, 1915); *Diplomatische Aktenstücke zur Vorgeschichte des Krieges* (Vienna: Staatsdruckerei, 1915). For a recent discussion of the publication of official documents during the war, see Annika Mombauer, *The Origins of the First World War: Diplomatic and Military Documents* (Manchester University Press, 2013), 1-15; on the German approach, Holger Herwig, "Clio Deceived: Patriotic Self-Censorship in Germany after the Great War," *International Security*, 12 (Fall 1987): 5-44.
2. Austria-Hungary, *Diplomatische Aktenstücke betreffend die Beziehungen Österreich-Ungarns zu Italien in der Zeit vom 20. Juli 1914 bis 23. Mai 1915* (Vienna: Staatsdruckerei, 1915) and *Diplomatische Aktenstücke betreffend die Beziehungen Österreich-Ungarns zu Rumänien in der Zeit vom 22.Juli 1914 bis 27. August 1916* (Vienna: Staatsdruckerei, 1916).

regime, had made a deliberate decision to avenge the murders at Sarajevo with military action against Serbia. Later in 1919, the Ballplatz released three small volumes of documents that started with June 28, 1914 and ended with documents from mid-August. This *Austrian Red Book* had 352 documents.[3]

Further, the new Austrian government authorized Alfred Francis Pribram, an internationally known professor of history at the University of Vienna, to comb the diplomatic archives for evidence about the secret prewar treaties. Pribram did just that and collected an impressive set of documents, first published in Vienna and Leipzig in 1920 as *Die politischen Geheimverträge Österreich-Ungarns 1879-1914*. Then Archibald Cary Coolidge of Harvard edited and published them as *The Secret Treaties of Austria-Hungary, 1879-1914* that same year.[4] Pribram did not stop there. He published a series of biographical sketches of key Habsburg decision makers including Emperor Franz Joseph, Archduke Franz Ferdinand, Count Alois Lexa von Aehrenthal, Count Leopold Berchtold, Baron István Burián, and Count Ottokar Czernin for the 1922 edition of the *Encyclopedia Britannica*. Then in 1923 he also published a small volume, *Austrian Foreign Policy, 1908-14*, based on the articles and lectures given in London, which briefly examined the outbreak of the war. His commentary left no doubt that Austria-Hungary had resolved to deal with the Serbian issue and had been a driving force for war. Nor did he conceal his own contempt for the assassinated archduke.[5]

Pribram's work did not end there. Encouraged for obvious reasons by the Germans to publish all of the relevant Habsburg documents on July 1914, which would shift the blame away from Germany to Vienna, the Austrian government agreed and in fact accepted some financial subsidy for such an effort.[6] Once again Pribram played a key role in selecting the documents, with

---

3. Roderich Gooss, *Das Wiener Kabinett und die Entstehung des Weltkrieges* (Vienna: Verlag L.W. Seidel und Sohn, 1919); Austria: Staatsamt für Äusseres, *Diplomatische Aktenstücke zur Vorgeschichte des Krieges 1914. Ergänzungen und Nachträge zum österreichisch-ungarischen Rotbuch*, 3 vols. (Vienna: Staatsdruckerei, 1919) and the English translation, *Austrian Red Book, Official Files Pertaining to Pre-War History*, 3 vols. (London: George Allen & Unwin, 1920).

4. Alfred Francis Pribram, *Die politischen Geheimverträge Österreich-Ungarns 1879-1914* (Vienna and Leipzig: W. Braumüller, 1920) and *The Secret Treaties of Austria-Hungary, 1879-1914*, ed. Archibald Cary Coolidge (Cambridge, MA: Harvard University Press, 1920).

5. Alfred Francis Pribram, *Austrian Foreign Policy, 1908-14* (London: George Allen & Unwin, 1923).

6. Ulfried Burz, "Austria and the Great War: Official Publications in the 1920s and 1930s," in *Forging the Collective Memory: Governments and International Historians Through Two World Wars*, ed. Keith Wilson (Providence: Berghahn Books, 1996), 178-91. Also see the still useful annotations in Mario Toscano, *The History of Treaties and International Politics* (Baltimore: Johns Hopkins, 1966), 126-39, 153-55, 417-26.

help from three other experts two of whom then prepared the documents for publication. The nine volumes, entitled *Österreich-Ungarns Aussenpolitik von der bosnischen Krise 1908 bis zum Kriegsausbruch 1914*, were released officially in early 1930 and contained 11,204 documents. The collection ended with a letter from Emperor Franz Joseph to Kaiser Wilhelm II dated August 1, 1914.[7] The first historian to use them in a limited fashion was Professor Bernadotte Schmitt whose two-volume study, *The Coming of the War 1914*, was essentially finished when the volumes were published.[8] The volumes, of course, came too late for use by Sidney Fay or Pierre Renouvin, but G. P. Gooch would use them extensively in his biographical sketches of Aehrenthal and Berchtold in *Before the War: Studies in Diplomacy*. Moreover, Luigi Albertini made extensive use of them as he prepared his monumental study on the outbreak of the war.[9]

The war had barely ended when a flood of memoir accounts and then assessments on the outbreak of the war and its conduct started to appear. Some were exculpatory such as the five volumes of former Chief of Staff Franz Conrad von Hötzendorf who blamed everyone but himself. Some were accusatory, such as the memoir of Julius Szilassy who savaged his old boss, Count Berchtold. Some accounts, including that by newspaper man Heinrich Kanner spared no one (often he cited articles he had written at the time in *Die Zeit*), while others added bits and pieces of detail about the Habsburg decision process and about the key personalities such as the Emperor Franz Joseph and Archduke Franz Ferdinand. Indeed, the old Kaiser enjoyed a sympathetic press while the *Thronfolger* was often excoriated.[10]

The fact that four of the key players in the decision process before the war were deceased—Franz Joseph, Franz Ferdinand, István Tisza, and Karl Stürgkh—meant there were gaps. Nor did Berchtold ever publish a full account, rather limiting himself to occasional responses to queries and to an article or two that revealed very little. The memoirs of Leon von Biliński,

7. Selected by Ludwig Bittner, Alfred Francis Pribram, Heinrich Srbik, and Hans Uebersberger and edited by Ludwig Bittner and Hans Uebersberger, *Österreich-Ungarns Aussenpolitik von der bosnischen Krise 1908 bis zum Kriegsausbruch 1914*, 9 vols. (Wien and Leipzig: Österreichischer Bundesverlag, 1930).
8. Bernadotte E. Schmitt, *The Coming of the War 1914*, 2 vols. (New York: Charles Scribner's Sons, 1930).
9. G.P. Gooch, *Before the War: Studies in Diplomacy*, 2 vols. (London: Longmans, Green, 1936-38); Luigi Albertini, *The Origins of the War of 1914*, trans. and ed. Isabella M. Massey, 3 vols. (Oxford University Press, 1952-57).
10. Franz Conrad von Hötzendorf, *Aus meiner Dienstzeit, 1906-1916*, 5 vols. (Vienna: Rikola Verlag, 1921-25); Julius Szilassy, *Der Untergang der Donau-Monarchie* (Berlin: Verlag Neues Vaterland, E. Berger, 1921); Heinrich Kanner, *Kaiserliche Katastrophenpolitik* (Leipzig: E.P. Tal & Co., 1922).

the Common Finance Minister, were written in Polish and never translated, but they were conspicuous in deliberately revealing little useful information about the July crisis.[11]

Unlike the full-throttled German effort to challenge the *Kriegsschuldfrage* verdict, the Austrian government with very limited means made no similar effort. Some Austrian historians wrote articles based on guarded access to archival sources, such as Rudolf Kiszling, for the *Berliner Monatshefte* but few focused precisely on the July crisis per se.[12]

During the 1930s Austrian and Hungarian historians were largely preoccupied by other political concerns. Still there were three revealing, almost indiscrete publications. Gina von Reininghaus published an account of her relationship with Conrad and many of his love letters to her. They shed embarrassing new information on a tangled part of Habsburg history. Conrad's former intelligence chief, August von Urbanski, wrote a biography of his mentor that sought to burnish the legacy but raised new questions about the commander's competency. Karl Bardolff, who would become a Nazi, wrote of his service as aide to Archduke Franz Ferdinand and in the process did not enhance public esteem for his former superior.[13]

Curiously, the most credible study of the Habsburg monarchy on the eve of war in 1939 came from a young American historian, E. C. Helmreich. In the late 1920s and early 1930s he interviewed Berchtold, Gottlieb von Jagow (the German Foreign Secretary), Friedrich Szápáry (the Habsburg ambassador to Russia and a senior Ballplatz official during the Balkan Wars), N. N. Schebeko (Russian ambassador to Vienna), and thanks to the help of Pribram gained access to the key files in the Kriegsarchiv in Vienna. *The Diplomacy of the Balkan Wars, 1912-1913* remains a valuable work and the best early example of the impact of the rich Vienna archives upon historical research.[14]

While Helmreich worked, so did Albertini who also interviewed many of the key players in the Vienna drama. But he did not work in the archives of any of the powers, though he apparently had some access to Italian records. In any event, his monumental work made full use of all of the

11. Leon von Biliński, *Wspomnienia i dokumenty 1846-1922*, 2 vols. (Warsaw: F. Hosick, 1924-25). On the omissions, see Sidney B. Fay, *The Origins of the World War*, 2nd ed. rev. (New York: Macmillan, 1930): II: 161-62.

12. E.g., Rudolf Kiszling, "Russlands Kriegsvorbereitungen im Herbst 1912 und ihre Rückwirkungen auf Österreich-Ungarn," *Berliner Monatshefte*, 13 (March 1935).

13. Gina Conrad von Hötzendorf, *Mein Leben mit Conrad von Hötzendorf* (Leipzig: Grethlein, 1935); August von Urbanski, *Conrad von Hötzendorf: Soldat und Mensch* (Vienna: Ulrich Mosers Verlag, 1938); Karl von Bardolff, *Soldat im alten Österreich* (Jena: Diederichs, 1938).

14. Ernst C. Helmreich, *The Diplomacy of the Balkan Wars, 1912-1913* (Cambridge, MA: Harvard University Press, 1938).

available published documents though the Serbian ones were of limited range and those of Italy still not published. Published in Italy during the Second World War, the work appeared in English as *The Origins of the War of 1914*.

The advent of the Second World War put an end to any serious research in Austria or Hungary on the role of the Habsburg monarchy and the start of the war. Nor did the war's end, with the divided occupation of both Austria and the city of Vienna, make things easier. But gradually some important historical work resumed. One of the most notable was Fritz Fellner's extraordinary edition of the diary of Josef Redlich who had been an important figure with access to almost all of the senior Habsburg officials, save the emperor and the archduke. Redlich chronicled his frequent meetings with Berchtold and Alex Hoyos and others, giving historians new insights into the tensions that existed among the ruling elite after the end of the Balkan Wars.[15]

The English translation of Albertini brought new attention to Austria-Hungary and the start of the war among American and British scholars but appears to have had less impact on German, Austrian, or Hungarian scholars. Then came Fritz Fischer's *Griff nach der Weltmacht* in 1961. Reviewed by Austrian scholars and with a wide impact on German scholarship, Fischer's study and his subsequent *Krieg der Illusionen* (1969) did not neglect Vienna's role in the July crisis. But his study and the work of his students put the attention on Berlin and the German role in pushing the Vienna government to war. In that sense his work reduced the impetus for Austrian historians to revisit the origins' question.[16] Already A. J. May's highly successful study of the Habsburg monarchy dealt with the July crisis almost as an afterthought, as did many Austrian textbooks, for instance, the one by Erich Zöllner, *Geschichte Österreichs: Von den Anfängen bis zur Gegenwart*. The details were recited but no extensive analysis and no use of any but familiar source materials. Two other volumes added more detail but remained general in their approach: Egon Corti and Hans Sokol penned a lengthy portrait of Franz Joseph and Kiszling added new details on Franz Ferdinand as he made use of papers in the Kriegsarchiv on the heir-apparent. These offered occasional pithy insights and some telling new details, though

---

15. Josef Redlich, *Schicksalsjahre Österreichs, 1908-1919: Das politische Tagebuch Josef Redlichs*, ed. Fritz Fellner, 2 vols. (Graz: Böhlau Verlag, 1953-54). Fellner helped to prepare a new edition of the diaries, with added personal material on Redlich, as *Schicksalsjahre Österreichs: Die Erinnerungen und Tagebücher Josef Redlichs, 1869-1936*, ed. Fritz Fellner and Doris A Corradini, 3 vols. (Vienna: Böhlau Verlag, 2011).

16. For a superb recent account of the impact of Fischer on Austrian historians and on their evolving views on July 1914, see Günther Kronenbitter, "Keeping a Low Profile: Austrian Historiography and the Fischer Controversy," *Journal of Contemporary History* 48(2): 333-49.

neither pretended to be the last word.[17]

Three developments in the late 1950s and early 1960s propelled new work on the monarchy and the outbreak of the war, though it would take time for this to be apparent. First, there was new access to the private paper collections of key participants in the life of the monarchy. The surviving children of Franz Ferdinand and Sophie agreed to make available, on a permission basis, access to the papers of the Archduke. Among the first to gain this access was Robert A. Kann, who had fled to the United States and whose study on nationalities in the empire remains valuable. From his access he wrote articles that explored the archduke's relationship with Kaiser Wilhelm II among others.[18] At almost the same time, the Berchtold family agreed to let Professor Hugo Hantsch have access to the Berchtold collection and diary. This access led to his thorough and very useful study, *Leopold Graf Berchtold: Grandseigneur und Staatsmann*, which appeared in 1963. Hantsch's analysis made possible an entirely different approach to Berchtold and helped to suggest why he was less a failure than some of his contemporaries believed.[19]

A second development also helped to reshape approaches to July 1914. In Britain the application of the fifty-year rule for access to government archives meant that researchers could explore topics long considered off-limits or unproductive. This new access was soon duplicated in Vienna where a host of researchers descended upon the Haus-, Hof-, und Staatsarchiv and the Kriegsarchiv for access to government records and even private paper collections. Soon works by Solomon Wank on Aehrenthal, Norman Stone on Conrad, Gunther Rothenberg on the Habsburg army, and the path breaking work of Francis Roy Bridge on Anglo-Austrian relations and on Habsburg foreign ministers opened new venues. The present writer would join this group in 1969, benefitting from their having opened the doors earlier. And a further important work also came from French historian, Jean-Paul Bled who wrote carefully and thoughtfully about Franz Joseph in a very useful biographical study of his long and complicated reign.[20]

---

17. Arthur J. May, *The Habsburg Monarchy, 1867-1914* (Cambridge, MA: Harvard University Press, 1951); Erich Zöllner, *Geschichte Österreichs: Von den Anfängen bis zur Gegenwart* (Vienna: R. Oldenbourg, 1961); Egon Corti and Han Sokol, *Der alte Kaiser: Franz Joseph I. vom Berliner Congress bis zu seinem Tod* (Graz: Verlag Styria, 1955); Rudolf Kiszling, *Erzherzog Franz Ferdinand von Österreich-Este: Leben, Pläne und Wirken am Schicksalsweg der Donaumonarchie* (Graz: Hermann Böhlau, 1953).

18. For a full collection of the articles, see Robert A. Kann, *Erzherzog Franz Ferdinand Studien* (Vienna: Verlag für Geschichte und Politik, 1976).

19. Hugo Hantsch, *Leopold Graf Berchtold: Grandseigneur und Staatsmann*, 2 vols. (Graz: Verlag Styria, 1963).

20. Solomon Wank, "The Appointment of Count Berchtold as Austro-Hungarian Foreign Minister," *Journal of Central European Affairs*, 23 (July 1963); Norman Stone, "Moltke-

At the same time Austrian archivists and students also displayed the impact of access to the archives, with Kurt Peball and Peter Broucek writing repeatedly about different aspects of military planning on the eve of war. Johann Allmayer-Beck joined their effort with *Die k.u.k. Armee, 1848-1914*. Austrian students began to benefit from the access to the archives.[21] Horst Brettner Messler wrote critically of Conrad's war plans and Wilhelm Deutschman did extensive work on the military impact of the Balkan Wars.[22]

In Hungary historians also were at work, with more freedom than might have been assumed under the Communist regime. Istvan Diószegi edited the July 1914 diary of Burián and then wrote an analysis of the influence of the so-called "Magyar clique" upon the formation of foreign policy. Equally impressive, Jósef Galántai wrote a critical assessment of the monarchy's foreign policy on the eve of war. And their works were joined by Gabor Vermes' detailed study of the career of István Tisza, having utilized many archival resources.[23]

Conrad: Relations Between the Austro-Hungarian and German General Staffs, 1909-1914," *The Historical Journal*, 9 (1966): 201-28, and *The Eastern Front, 1914-1917* (London: Hodder and Stoughton, 1975): Gunther Rothenberg, *The Army of Francis Joseph* (West Lafayette, IN: Purdue University Press, 1976); Francis Roy Bridge, *Great Britain and Austria-Hungary, 1906-1914: A Diplomatic History* (London: London School of Economics; Weidenfeld and Nicolson, 1972) and *From Sadowa to Sarajevo: The Foreign Policy of Austria-Hungary, 1866-1914* (London: Routledge & Kegan Paul, 1972); Samuel R. Williamson, Jr., "Influence, Power, and the Policy Process: The Case of Franz Ferdinand, 1906-1914," *The Historical Journal*, 17 (1974): 417-34; Jean Paul-Bled, *François-Joseph* (Paris: Fayard, 1987).

21. For instance, on Peball, see "Briefe an eine Freundin. Zu den Briefen des Feldmarschalls Conrad von Hötzendorf an Frau Walburga von Sonnleithner während der Jahre 1905 bis 1918," *Mitteilungen des Österreichischen Staatsarchiv*, 25 (1972): 492-503, and his edition of Conrad's *Private Aufzeichnungen: Erste Veröffentlichungen aus den Papieren des k.u.k. Generalstabs-Chef* (Vienna: Amalthea, 1977). On Broucek, see "Der Nachlass Feldmarschall Conrad und den Kriegsarchiv," *Mitteilungen des Österreichischen Staatsarchiv*, 28 (1975): 164-182. For the full extent of their efforts, see their bibliographic entries in Peter Broucek and Kurt Peball, eds., *Geschichte der Österreichischen Militärhistoriographie* (Vienna: Böhlau, 2000). Also Johann C. Allmayer-Beck, *Die k.u.k. Armee* (Vienna: Gütersloh Prisma Verlag, 1974).

22. Horst Brettner-Messler, "Die Balkanpolitik Conrad von Hötzendorf von seiner Wiederernennung zum Chef des Generalstabes bis Oktober-Ultimatum, 1913," *Mitteilungen des Österreichischen Staatsarchiv*, 20 (1967); Wilhelm Deutschmann, "Die militärischen Massnahmen im Österreich-Ungarn während der Balkankriege," 1912/13 (Dissertation, Vienna, 1965).

23. Istvan Diószegi "Aussenminister Stephan Graf Burián: Biographie und Tagebuchstelle," *Annales Universitatis Scientiarum Budapestinensis des Kolando Eötvös: Sectio Historica*, 8 (Budapest: Akadémiai Kiadó, 1966) and *Hungarians in the Ballhausplatz: Studies on the Austro-Hungarian Common Foreign Policy*, trans. Kornél Balás and Mary Boros (Budapest: Corvina, 1983); Jószef Galántai, *Die Österreichisch-Ungarische Monarchie und der Weltkrieg* (Budapest: Akadémiai Kiadó, 1979); Gabor Vermes, *István Tisza: The Liberal Vision and Conservative Statecraft of a Magyar Nationalist* (New York: East European Monographs, 1985).

In Vienna, however, no Austrian historian addressed anew the question of Austria-Hungary's role in the July crisis. Friedrich Würthle, a former government official, compiled an exhaustive collection of material on the assassination plot. His work, *Die Spur führt nach Belgrad*, echoed many of the findings of Vladimir Dedijer's *The Road to Sarajevo* but also dealt with decision making in Vienna during July. During the 1970s and 1980s Fellner wrote two important articles on aspects of the July crisis, but produced no longer work. His most comprehensive article on the July crisis, published in the 1990s, blamed Vienna for starting a local war and then accused Germany of converting it into a larger war. But again, his work did not exploit archival sources to any degree.[24]

In the meantime, the Austrian Academy of Sciences began its multivolume study of the Habsburg monarchy. In 1987 the fifth volume, *Die Bewaffnete Macht*, included important articles by Lothar Höbelt, Allmayer-Beck, and Walter Wagner on aspects of the military organization of Austria-Hungary. And then in 1991 Rudolf Jeřábek published a biography of Oskar Potiorek that carefully mined the archives for material that put the ill-fated governor-general into perspective, if not always in a flattering fashion. Also István Deák added still more detail about the Habsburg officer corps, with telling insights into the life and career patterns of the officers.[25]

In the early 1990s three works by Bridge, John Leslie, and the author offered the first overall assessment of the Habsburg decisions for war based upon extensive archival sources. Bridge's work tracked the diplomatic record in detail and his study also appeared in the multivolume series published by the Austrian Academy of Sciences. That by Williamson in 1991 drew upon work in all of the relevant archives, including those of the Common Finance Ministry, and described Berchtold's efforts to neutralize Tisza during the crisis. Leslie's long and important article surveyed the entire senior policy establishment in Vienna and Budapest, with pungent and

24. Friedrich Würthle, *Die Spur führt nach Belgrad: Die Hintergründe des Dramas von Sarajevo 1914* (Vienna: Fritz Molden, 1975) and also his *Dokumente zum Sarajevoprozess*, Ergänzungsband 9 (Vienna; *Mitteilungen des Österreichischen Staatsarchiv*, 1978); Vladimir Dedijer, *The Road to Sarajevo* (New York: Simon and Schuster, 1966). Fritz Fellner, "Die 'Mission Hoyos,'" [first published in 1976] and "Zwischen Kriegsbegeisterung und Resignation - ein Memorandum des Sektionschefs Forgách von Jänner 1915," [first published 1975] in Heidrun Maschl and Brigitte Mazohl-Wallnig (eds.), *Vom Dreibund zum Völkerbund: Studien zur Geschichte der internationalen Beziehungen, 1882-1919*. (Vienna: Verlag für Geschichte und Politik, 1994), 112-41 and 142-54, and his "Austria-Hungary," in *Decisions for War 1914*, ed. Keith Wilson (New York: St. Martin's Press, 1995), 9-25.
25. Adam Wandruszka and Peter Urbanitsch (eds.), *Die Habsburgermonarchie, 1848-1918*, vol. 5, *Die Bewaffnete Macht* (Vienna: Austrian Academy of Sciences, 1987); Rudolf Jeřábek, *Potiorek: General im Schatten von Sarajevo* (Graz: Verlag Styria, 1991); István Deák, *Beyond Nationalism: A Social and Political History of the Habsburg Officer Corps, 1848-1918* (Oxford: Oxford University Press, 1990).

incisive comments on the personalities.[26]

In 1993 Manfried Rauchensteiner broke the long Austrian silence with a massive study of Austria-Hungary, the July crisis, and the ensuing war. A careful student of military history, he explored both the diplomatic and the strategic planning process in the unfolding of the war. In his work he addressed key issues, did not shy from judgments about the leadership elite, and reminded readers of just how wrong Conrad had been in both his planning and his execution of the flawed plans. Almost simultaneously with Rauchensteiner's contribution came that of Graydon A. Tunstall, Jr., in his *Planning for War against Russia and Serbia: Austro-Hungarian and German Military Strategies, 1871-1914*. A thorough, detailed examination of the military planning. Tunstall left no doubt about the strategic dilemmas that confronted the planners and their misreading of the situation.[27]

The Habsburg naval efforts received periodic attention from historians. In the 1990s three of the most significant works appeared. First, Paul Halpern tracked the career of Admiral Anton Haus, the naval chief of staff, and an occasional participant in the key war-peace decisions. Then Lawrence Sondhaus and Milan Vego produced the first detailed analyses of Habsburg naval policy as it emerged in the decades before the war. The Habsburg navy became a significant factor in the war planning of their erstwhile ally, Italy, and in that of the French and British naval staffs. More easily funded than the army, not least because of the military contracts that went to both Austrian and Hungarian shipyards, the navy became the favorite of Archduke Franz Ferdinand in the same fashion that its German counterpart did for Wilhelm II.[28]

26. F.R. Bridge, *The Habsburg Monarchy among the Great Powers, 1815-1918*. (New York: Berg, 1990), 335-44, and John Leslie, "The Antecedents of Austria-Hungary's War Aims: Policies and Policy-Makers in Vienna and Budapest before and during 1914," in Elisabeth Springer and Leopold Kammerhold (eds.), *Archiv und Forschung: Das Haus-, Hof- und Staatsarchiv in seiner Bedeutung für die Geschichte Österreichs und Europas*. (Vienna: Verlag für Geschichte und Politik, 1993), 307-94, and "Österreich-Ungarn vor dem Kriegsausbruch: Der Ballhausplatz in Wien im Juli 1914 aus der Sicht eines Österreichisch-Ungarischen Diplomaten," in Ralph Melville, Claus Scharf, Martin Vogt, and Ulrich Wengenroth, eds., *Deutschland und Europa in der Neuzeit*. (Stuttgart: Franz Stei-ner, 1988), 661-84; Samuel R. Williamson, Jr., *Austria-Hungary and the Origins of the First World War* (New York: St. Martin's Press, 1991).

27. Manfried Rauchensteiner, *Der Tod des Doppeladlers: Österreich-Ungarn und der Erste Weltkrieg* (Graz: Verlag Styria, 1993); Graydon A. Tunstall, Jr., *Planning for War against Russia and Serbia: Austro-Hungarian and German Military Strategies, 1871-1914* (New York: East European Monographs, 1993). Also see the review of books on Austria-Hungary in Samuel R. Williamson, Jr. and Ernest R. May, "An Identity of Opinion: Historians and July 1914," *Journal of Modern History*, 79 (2007): 353-59.

28. Paul C. Halpern, *Anton Haus: Österreich-Ungarns Grossadmiral* (Graz: Verlag Styria, 1998); Lawrence Sondhaus, *Navalism, Industrial Development, and the Politics of Dualism* (West Lafayette, IN: Purdue University Press, 1994); Milan N. Vego, *Austro-Hungarian*

But perhaps the most important, thorough military study came from German historian Günther Kronenbitter and his blunt examination of the Habsburg army. Displaying a thorough mastery of both the archival sources and the relevant historical work, Kronenbitter brought his long meditations about Habsburg military leadership to bear on his analysis. He tracked the social composition of the officer corps, the ideological views of the army leadership, and then analyzed the confrontation of that leadership with the reality of their strategic situation. His analysis of the war-peace decisions faced by Conrad, the military, and the civilian elite add copious details to an understanding of the miscalculations made in Vienna (and Budapest) in the summer of 1914.[29]

Another set of insights came from Albert Pethö's extensive study of Habsburg intelligence operations before and during the war. He exploited the archival papers of Maximilian Ronge, sometime head of military intelligence, and of the relevant files of the general staff, along with existing printed materials. What emerged was a detailed analysis of almost every aspect of Habsburg intelligence operations before and during the war. The impact of Alfred Redl's treason upon Conrad's war plans is examined; he concludes that the colonel did reveal the attack plan against Russia and gave St. Petersburg valuable information about the monarchy's spy networks. But he also thinks that Conrad's impromptu shifts of troop locations in 1914 rendered much of the treasonous material of less value. He does not address the question of whether his information about attack plans on Serbia played any part in the disasters of August 1914. Pethö's section on the efforts to break ciphers is exceptionally revealing, a reminder that Vienna did not lag in these operations.[30]

Biographical studies of key Austrian figures have also appeared over the last two decades. Steven Beller and later Lothar Höbelt offered summary assessments of Emperor Franz Joseph, though neither added any new details of his role in the July crisis. Sondhaus produced a more detailed assessment of Conrad, one that incorporated the work of earlier criticisms of the general. He dealt with his relationship with Gina von Reininghaus

Naval Policy, 1904-1914 (London: Frank Cass, 1996).

29. Günther Kronenbitter, *"Krieg im Frieden": Die Führung der k.u.k. Armee und die Grossmachtpolitik Österreichs-Ungarns 1906-1914.* (Munich: Oldenbourg, 2003). Also see his essay, "The German and Austro-Hungarian General Staffs and their Reflections on an 'Improbable War,'" in *An Improbable War: The Outbreak of World War I and European Political Culture before 1914,* eds. Holger Afflerbach and David Stevenson (New York, Berghahn Books, 2007), 149-158; also see Samuel R. Williamson, Jr., "Aggressive and Defensive Aims of Political Elites: Austro-Hungarian Policy in 1914," *ibid.,* 61-74.

30. Albert Pethö, *Agenten für den Doppeladler: Österreich-Ungarns Geheimer Dienst im Weltkrieg* (Graz: Leopold Stocker Verlag, 1998).

and his controversial decision to go south against Serbia rather than north against Russia. A second new assessment, reviewed in this volume as well, comes from Wolfram Dornik and utilizes some of the available material in the Austrian archives. Dornik offers valuable perspectives on the opposition that Conrad received from his critics among the Hofburg elite. Further, his sober assessment of the personality and temperament of the chief of staff raise acutely the question of how any state could allow such a person to head its military forces. This assessment continues the earlier efforts that have consistently revised Conrad's reputation downward.[31]

A new biography of Archduke Franz Ferdinand by Jean-Paul Bled fills a major gap in the study of key personalities. Using the full range of archival material, Bled provides an incisive, compelling assessment of a man whose temperament always remained on edge and whose willfulness became an acute liability. The author of this essay has recently sought to define more precisely the role played by Berchtold in the decisions of July 1914. In this analysis, the decision points that confronted Berchtold are examined carefully. Further, Kronenbitter's essay in this volume adds still more information on Berchtold, all of which make his central role in the decision process more defined and important.[32]

The first decade of the new century has seen a momentous shift in interest. Now a series of Austrian historians are addressing issues of the Great War from a variety of angles. One example, with exemplary essays, *Glanz-Gewalt-Gehorsam: Militär und Gesellschaft in der Habsburgermonarchie (1800 bis 1918)*, dealt with military discipline, suicides inside the army, women at war, and the care of invalided soldiers, among other topics. A great deal of attention has focused on the issue of prisoners of war, both those of the monarchy held in Russia and the Russians held by the Habsburg forces. More recently, attention has shifted to intelligence issues and the July crisis itself, as seen in the work of Verena Moritz, Hannes Leidinger, and Gerhard Jagschitz. Their study of Maximilian Ronge adds new information on the central operation of Habsburg military intelligence, while the Moritz and Leidinger study on Colonel Alfred Redl revisit the impact and the myths

31. Steven Beller, *Francis Joseph* (New York: Longman, 1996); Lothar Höbelt, *Franz Joseph I. Der Kaiser und sein Reich. Eine politische Geschichte* (Vienna: Böhlau Verlag, 2009); Lawrence Sondhaus, *Franz Conrad von Hötzendorf: Architect of the Apocalypse* (Boston: Humanities Press, 2000); Wolfram Dornik, *Des Kaisers Falke: Wirken und Nach-Wirken von Franz Conrad von Hötzendorf*, with an afterward by Verena Moritz and Hannes Leidinger (Innsbruck: Studien Verlag, 2013).

32. Jean-Paul Bled, *Franz Ferdinand: Der eigensinnige Thronfolger*, trans. Susanna Grabmayr and Marie-Therese Pitner (Vienna: Böhlau, 2013); Samuel R. Williamson, Jr., "Leopold Count Berchtold: the Man Who Could Have Prevented the Great War," in *From Empire to Republic: Post World War I Austria*, eds. Günter Bischof, Fritz Plasser, and Peter Berger (New Orleans: University of New Orleans Press, 2010): 24-51.

surrounding the famous spy. And in the essays in this volume Moritz continues to examine, in more succinct form, the context for Redl's spying and offers an assessment of the impact of the information he conveyed. Dornik's biography of Conrad has an excellent bibliography that enumerates many of these newer studies. And of course the essays contained in this celebratory volume also reflect this new and revived interest in the last years of the monarchy.[33]

More contributions are just appearing. The several volumes that the Austrian Academy of Sciences plan for the July crisis and then the war will be of great importance. Further, Rauchensteiner has produced a monumental study on both the origins of the war and the conflict that followed. His *Der Erste Weltkrieg und das Ende der Habsburgermonarchie 1914-1918* is 1,223 pages long and contains extensive material from his earlier opus. But the author has conveniently divided the chapters into smaller sections and the study reads almost like a novel. Its clarity of presentation and its comprehensive research show on almost every page. He too shows a Berchtold determined not to show any weakness and to proceed against Serbia. The disastrous results of those decisions then occupy the rest of the study, an exemplary analysis of the juxtaposition of domestic politics and military strategy. Students will be using this study for years to come.[34]

Among the many other works that have appeared as the centenary of July 1914 approaches three stand out: two long and one short. Christopher Clark, *The Sleepwalkers: How Europe Went to War in 1914*, reframes the entire discussion of July 1914, away from concepts of guilt and responsibility to shared contributions to the disaster. He places special emphasis on the Serbian and Austrian roles in adopting dangerous policies, while suggesting that France and Russia were determined to protect Serbia at all costs. Germany's irresponsible actions are not ignored but set into context. The study by Konrad Canis, *Der Weg in den Abgrund: Deutsche Aussenpolitik, 1902-1914*, naturally focuses upon the German role but also places new emphasis on the aggressive behavior displayed by St. Petersburg after the First Balkan War. Far more succinct but well written and pithy, Annika

---

33. *Glanz-Gewalt-Gehorsam: Militär und Gesellschaft in der Habsburgermonarchie* (1800 bis 1918), eds. Laurence Cole, Christa Hämmerle, and Martin Scheutz (Vienna: Klartext, 2011); this study has an excellent set of references to military history. On espionage Verena Moritz, Hannes Leidinger, and Gerhard Jagschitz, *Im Zentrum der Macht: Die vielen Gesichter des Geheimdienstchefs Maximilian Ronge* (St. Pölten Residenz Verlag 2007) and Verena Moritz and Hannes Leidinger, *Oberst Redl: Der Spionagefall—der Skandal—die Fakten* (St. Pölten: Residenz Verlag, 2012).
34. Manfried Rauchensteiner, *Der Erste Weltkrieg und das Ende der Habsburgermonarchie 1914-1918* (Vienna: Böhlau Verlag, 2013).

Mombauer's *Die Julikrise: Europas Weg im Ersten Weltkrieg* summarizes much of the very recent studies on the way, while insisting that Germany and Austria-Hungary made the most crucial decisions that brought the war, though there is a nod to French and Russian actions in accelerating the crisis at the end. Taken together these three volumes, and many others that now appear almost weekly, show that historians are not neglecting the chance to once again visit the origins of the Great War.[35]

After a century, Austria-Hungary and its part in the origins of the First World War are now proving fertile fields for research. But there is still more to come for even the most recent new works, important though they are, have usually only touched one or two sets of archival sources when myriads of documents remain available. Almost certainly a few more private archival collections will emerge. This is a wonderful time and opportunity for historians of the Danubian monarchy, wherever based, to think grandly of the challenges that lie ahead.

For my part, I applaud them and wish them the greatest success.

---

35. Christopher Clark, *The Sleepwalkers: How Europe Went to War in 1914* (London: Allen Lane, 2012); Konrad Canis, *Der Weg in den Abgrund: Deutsche Aussenpolitik, 1902-1914* (Paderborn: Ferdinand Schöningh, 2011); Annika Mombauer, *Die Julikrise: Europas Weg im Ersten Weltkrieg* (Munich: C.H. Beck, 2013).

Alfred Redl in uniform, Pf 6924:C(1),
Austrian National Library - Picture Archives and Graphics Department, Vienna

The Case of Alfred Redl and the Situation of Austro-Hungarian Military Intelligence on the Eve of World War I

Hannes Leidinger[1]

Spy Mania

The "Redl Case" was a cause célèbre in 1913.[2] For a brief moment on the eve of the World War, the people living in a time marked by disturbing events did not pay attention to the rivalries between the great powers, the fight over colonial territory, and the bitter struggles on the Balkans. In the midst of all the crises and the expectations of new and possibly even greater armed conflicts, the public briefly focused on the "monstrous deeds" of a "black sheep" that symbolized the monarchy's moral decay. Along with other scandals in civil administration and the army, Redl's betrayal contributed to the picture of a crumbling, moribund Danube Monarchy.

This impression was further fuelled by other notorious espionage cases—such as the exposure of the spy network of the Russian military attaché in Vienna, Michail I. Zankevič, and especially the arrest of the spies Cedomil and Alexander Jandric—and by a general "spy mania" that characterized the period. Everybody expected a "great matching of powers," and strategists were obsessed with the idea of a preventive strike and a swift victory. As a result, there was great demand for information about the supposed enemies' military and political developments. More and more "traitors" and "enemy agents" were caught by "counterespionage specialists." The k. u. k. [imperial & royal] *Evidenzbureau*, the Danubian Monarchy's military intelligence service, noted an increase in espionage-related investigations, arrests, and court proceedings. Maximilian Ronge, a high-ranking intelligence officer and the last director of the Habsburg military intelligence service, wrote in 1930 that the number of suspects had risen from 60 in 1908 to 150 in 1909. In addition, he cited 300 espionage investigations for 1905 and 6,000 for

---

1. This essay has been translated from German into English by Inge Fink of the University of New Orleans' Department of English.
2. Ian Armour, Review. Georg Markus, "Der Fall Redl," in *Intelligence and National Security*, no. 2 (1987): 186.

1913. The records for arrests and court sentences present a similar picture: 32 arrests and four convictions in 1905, 530 arrests and 560 convictions in 1913.[3]

The scandal surrounding Chief of Staff Alfred Redl rode the crest of a wave of investigations and revelations, many of which indicated that trouble was brewing in certain regions. At the turn of the year 1913/14, British and French diplomats reported that Galicia was "infested" with Russian "spies." However, the representatives of the Western powers rated the "trials for high treason conducted by the Hungarian government," as they occurred in Marmaros Sziget, as counterproductive. These proceedings could only widen the gap between Austria and Russia, and they could serve as a stage for "Russophile" propaganda.[4]

Distrust dominated the relationship between the treaty partners in Vienna and Rome, and there was good reason for this. In 1902, Italian spies gave up all espionage against France and turned to the Habsburg Empire with renewed vigor. The Austrian news agents responded to the challenge. From 1908 on—and with greater success after 1912—the k. u. k. Evidenzbureau was determined to crack the Italian espionage code. This "clandestine skirmish" took place against the background of various border conflicts or "irredenta incidents," as well as a number of small espionage affairs.[5]

The alliance between Austria-Hungary and Romania was equally fragile. While the k. u. k. Chief of Staff Franz Conrad von Hötzendorf continued to speculate on the support of the Bucharest army, the Russian authorities knew the Romanian executive forces were on their side, including their secret service, the "Siguranta Generala Statului." Accordingly, the Austro-Hungarian "reconnaissance" of Russia proved rather difficult. The local police authorities regularly arrested k. u. k. agents, but they often looked the other way when Russian military attachés expanded their espionage network to Transylvania, Galicia, and Bukovina.[6] Along with Russia, Romania and Italy—despite their official dependence on Berlin and Vienna—fought a

3. Max Ronge, *Kriegs- und Industrie-Spionage* (Vienna: Amalthea 1930), 36, 66 und 394f.
4. British Embassy Vienna to Foreign Office, 16 February 1914 and 16 March 1914, Foreign Office 371/1898, The National Archives (TNA), London, FO 371/1898, No. 6952 and No. 11682; Hallier to French Ministry of War, 18 December 1913, Etat-major de l´armée de terre. Attaché militaire, Autriche-Hongrie 1911-1913, 7 N 1131, Nouvelles politiques, Service Historique de la Défense/Archives de l´armée de terre (SHD/AAT), Paris.
5. Günther Kronenbitter, *Krieg im Frieden: Die Führung der k. u. k. Armee und die Großmachtpolitik Österreich-Ungarns 1906-1914* (München: R. Oldenbourg 2003), 233; Holger Afflerbach, *Der Dreibund: Europäische Großmacht- und Allianzpolitik vor dem Ersten Weltkrieg* (Vienna: Böhlau 2002), 788f.
6. Albert Pethö, *Agenten für den Doppeladler: Österreich-Ungarns Geheimer Dienst im Weltkrieg* (Graz: Leopold Stocker 1998), 199.

"Cold War" through military intelligence, which anticipated overt military actions against the Danubian Monarchy.

Cooperation and Distrust

These developments bothered the intelligence officers of the Austro-Hungarian general staff because in the course of trying to improve communications with St. Petersburg since 1900, the Evidenzbureau had reduced intelligence activities in Russia. The intelligence posts, which in 1903 had a yearly budget of 20,000 koronas for their work "in the East," were cut to slightly over 6,000 koronas by 1906.[7] The status of the Austrian espionage network had decreased; fewer and fewer informants were willing to continue in the light of these budget cuts. Not only did their numbers dwindle, but the remaining employees even cooperated occasionally with the Russian representatives, for example during the Russian-Japanese war of 1904/5. The leaders of the Austrian army sanctioned further collaboration because they did not see the Russians, after their defeat in East Asia, as an immediate threat. Besides, the Austrians had already agreed to establish exchange programs with the Russians, and the future rivals in the "espionage duel" on the eve of World War I learned the "enemy's" language: The future head of the Razvedka post in Kiev, Michael Galkin, learned German in Upper Austria while Alfred Redl studied Russian in Kazan (Kasan).

Under these circumstances, Redl's betrayal may have originated in the relatively relaxed atmosphere of an "informal exchange of information" among "friends"— until bilateral relationships drastically deteriorated again and Chief of Staff Conrad von Hötzendorf demanded a revival of the weakened Russian "reconnaissance."[8]

The numerous espionage scandals could have benefitted Conrad. However, after the failed attempt to cover up the true reasons for Redl's suicide, vague suspicions prevailed. Russian diplomats in particular became the targets of this growing distrust, especially the "Russian consuls" in Lemberg and Prague, Alfred Redl's alleged "seducers."[9]

Such accusations marred the already difficult relationship between the Habsburg and Russian empires even further, even though, in this particular case, the "Czar's ambassadors" were soon found to be innocent. Reservations and prejudices against diplomats persisted, and the representatives of the other great powers had to work around them. Not surprisingly, Austrian

---

7. Heinz Höhne, *Der Krieg im Dunkeln: Die Geschichte der deutsch-russischen Spionage* (Bindlach: Gondrom 1993), 84.

8. Pethö, *Agenten für den Doppeladler*, 17f. and 237.

9. *Die Zeit*, 30 May 1913, 2 und 5 June 1913, 4; *Le Figaro*, 6 June 1913, 2.

security officials became suspicious when the British embassy in Sarajevo tried to get information about the Habsburg army's military operations in the Balkans.[10] The Austro-Hungarian foreign ministry hinted to the British military attaché Cuninghame that a "change at the top of 'His Majesty the King's consulate' in Sarajevo would be desirable."[11]

The Habsburg officials used the general mood after the exposure of the "Causa Redl" to justify getting rid of "unwanted foreigners" and tightening security against "enemy snoops." Even Britain's official representatives were urged to be especially judicious as a result. Commander Forbes, British consul in Prague, was not too pleased to hear, when he was on holiday in London, that during his absence military attaché Cuninghame had sought information about Habsburg troop movements and mobilization from those of his "employees who had Austro-Hungarian citizenship." Forbes thought Cuninghame's actions especially "incomprehensible at the present time." In effect, the Foreign Office noted on June 26, 1913 that "the Austrian authorities already suspected our embassy in Sarajevo" before the "revelations regarding Colonel Redl's suicide," which made the k.u.k authorities even more "impatient with everything that smacks of espionage." [12]

Changes

In the first few days after the exposure of the "master spy in the general staff," many demanded a radical reorganization of the Austro-Hungarian intelligence service. Several experts agreed that Redl's betrayal had "indisputably" caused "considerable damage."[13]

Detailed evidence for this is hard to find—even though there are numerous records that document the increased efforts to put a stop to the game of potential enemy "agents." It was the scandals of 1913 that caused the Budapest state police to improve "counterintelligence measures."[14] While the border patrols in the eastern part of the Habsburg Empire were already participating in the proactive *Kundschaftsdienst* [espionage service]—"K-

---

10. British Embassy Vienna to Foreign Office, 27 July 1913 and 7 July 1913, FO 371/1576, Austria-Hungary No. 29217 and No. 30968, TNA, London.
11. British Embassy Vienna to Foreign Office, 26 July 1913, FO 371/1576, Austria-Hungary No. 29217, TNA, London.
12. Foreign Office, 26 July 1913, 28 July 1913 and 30 July 1913, FO 371/1576, Austria-Hungary No. 29339, No. 29673 and No. 29876, TNA, London.
13. Hallier to French Ministry of War, 12 June 1913, Etat-major de l´armée de terre. Attaché militaire, Autriche-Hongrie 1911-1913, 7 N 1131, SHD/AAT, Paris. SHD/AAT, Kronenbitter, *Krieg im Frieden*, 237.
14. Ibid.

Dienst" for short—the reorganization of counterintelligence services, which involved tighter cooperation between civil and military authorities, reached its climax in May of 1914. Under the leadership of Maximilian Ronge, a special conference was dedicated to questions of counter-espionage. The interior ministries of Croatia-Slavonia and Bosnia-Herzegovina, as well as the head of the Vienna police, participated in the internal discussion, which lead to the establishment of a new central agency designed to help out the understaffed military intelligence service.[15] The cooperation to "exterminate enemy moles" thus rested heavily on police officers, which Ronge hoped to use in the centers of the enemy agents' network. He advocated becoming proactive over passively reacting to enemy attacks as the only sensible strategy in an era of "shadow wars" and "hollow peace." However, most of the Habsburg authorities opposed Ronge's ideas on account of the complications caused by the exposure of "civil spies" abroad.[16]

However, the measures to combat "treason" and "espionage" received new judicial support. As early as July 1913, Lieutenant-Colonel Hallier, the French military attaché in Vienna, reported that the House of Lords (*Herrenhaus*), in its "last session on June 26," spoke in favor of tighter espionage laws. The House of Representatives will probably support the decision, Hallier added, pointing out "that the suggested measures were not influenced solely by the Redl affair but also by a number of similar, albeit less significant, cases."[17]

The French representatives in Austria understood that it would not make any sense to make the "suggested changes" merely because of a scandal involving a former military intelligence officer. Consequently, Hallier started his communiqué by referring to similar parliamentary decisions in Russia and Germany.[18] The Hohenzollern rules in particular served as a model for the Austrian empire. In fact, the German legislature had recently discussed the behavior of journalists. The targeted new laws—in Berlin as well as in Vienna—advocated against "the indiscretions of the press," even though the legal part of the process was slowed down by the difficulties in

15.   Konferenz "Schaffung der Zentral- und Hauptstellen für den defensiven Kundschaftsdienst, May 18, 1914, Kriegsarchiv (KA)/Kriegsministerium (KM)/Präs. 1914 40-20/6, Österreichisches Staatsarchiv (ÖSTA), Wien.

16. Interministerielle Konferenz in Angelegenheit der Schaffung einer Zentralstelle für den defensiven Kundschaftsdienst, 30 April 1914 und Konferenz "Schaffung der Zentral- und Hauptstellen für den defensiven Kundschaftsdienst, 18 May 1914, KA/NL Ronge, B 126:1a, 496-500, ÖSTA, Wien beziehungsweise KA/KM/Präs. 1914 40-20/6, Österreichisches Staatsarchiv (ÖSTA), Wien.

17. Hallier to French Ministry of War, 4 June 1913, Etat-major de l´armée de terre. Attaché militaire, Autriche-Hongrie 1911-13, 7 N 1131, SHD/AAT, Paris.

18. Ibid.

formulating a precise definition of "treason."[19]

In Austria, the reorganization of the military intelligence service posed particular problems due to one specific trait of the k. u. k. espionage system. Unlike Germany, where several departments of the General Staff ran intelligence services and section IIIb was in charge of actually procuring information, the Austro-Hungarian Evidenzbureau united all of these tasks. The example provided by other governments more than the Redl affair prompted Austro-Hungarian general staff officers, as early as 1909, to suggest closing down the Evidenzbuerau.[20] They proposed reassigning the Bureau's employees to the war units of the operations office, where they would examine problematic cases. However, they envisioned a continuation of the intelligence service; Max Ronge was hoping to upgrade the espionage division to be part of the general staff office after the potential "dissolution of the Evidenzbureau."[21] However, this was not meant to be as Chief of Staff Conrad von Hötzendorf and heir-apparent Franz Ferdinand were increasingly at loggerheads with each other, which complicated the reorganization.[22]

The Extent of the Betrayal

For the longest time, nobody was exactly sure as to how significant the files were that Alfred Redl handed over to the Russians. The Russian author M. Mil'štejn claimed that Redl gave away the "Austria-Hungarian plans for a march on Russia," which led to preparatory maneuvers "in the Kiev military district."[23] As a result, the czarist Razvedka paid the "master spy" 50,000 koronas for "courtesies rendered," an enormous sum of money that reflected the significance of the material. August Urbański, who once headed the Evidenzbureau, stated in 1931 that such documents informed the enemy about the area "in which a probable enemy readied his forces for commencement" and "how the troops will be distributed." The acquisition of such materials has always been one of the "highest goals of military intelligence."[24] Consequently, the French military attaché Hallier wondered why, after "Redl's enormous betrayal," the Russians did not immediately

19. *Danzer's Armee-Zeitung*, 5 June 1913, 7.
20. Kronenbitter, *Krieg im Frieden*, 240.
21. Konferenz "Schaffung der Zentral- und Hauptstellen für den defensiven Kundschaftsdienst, 18 May 1914, KA/NL Ronge, B 126:1a, 519, ÖSTA, Wien.
22. Kronenbitter, *Krieg im Frieden*, 241.
23. M. Mil´štejn, Delo polkovnika Redlja, in: *Voenno-istoriceskij zurnal*, no. 1 (1966), 45-56, 48.
24. August Urbanski, Aufmarschpläne, in: *Weltkriegsspionage* (Munich: Justin Moser 1931), 85.

attack the Austrians. The "hesitation" of the Russians "in rather favorable circumstances" prompted him to draw the opposite conclusion in the middle of July of 1913: The Russians' failure to take action, he claimed, restored a "new kind of self-confidence to the "Austrian officer" because "he actually thought the Russian army incapable of launching an attack."[25]

Hallier's observations were not completely unjustified. However, they do not spring from new insights. Similar views of the k. u. k. military can be traced to earlier "espionage successes" of the Austro-Hungarian military intelligence, some of them barred by the statute of limitations. Since the 1880s, the Evidenzbureau had repeatedly acquired key documents with information about the Russian military districts and the general staff. In 1906 or 1908, it bought "the current Russian war plan" for 10,000 rubles, as well as information about their intentions to "move the troop concentration area behind the middle of the Weichsel."[26] How much influence and "power of suggestion" this information had on subsequent Austria-Hungary's military plans remains questionable. Until shortly before the first World War, the Austrians relied on the problems the Russians incurred during the Russian-Japanese war and the revolution of 1905, paying very little attention to the reserve divisions which had been financed with French money. Looking back, August Urbański concluded that the files about the Russian army that were acquired before 1908 had "a lasting effect, even though there were numerous indications that they were no longer fully accurate."[27]

Speculations on the Russian army's psychological state were also influential factors. During the tenure of Chief of Staff Blasius von Schemua, who temporarily replaced Conrad von Hötzendorf in 1911/12, the Austrians considered the Russian forces as "inferior on principle." Clichés about "the East" informed their views about the "Muscovites' lack of ability to defend themselves." Schemua opined that the "Russian national character was not disposed to fight," which would increase the Habsburg army's chance for success, and he continued that "our army, so different in national origin and character, has, in my opinion, much more attack spirit than the Russian army."[28]

Naturally, such opinions provoked skepticism at least among those who kept a "cool head." After sober evaluation and unemotional analysis of the existing data, comments about the "character traits" of potential opponents

25. Hallier to French Ministry of War, 12 June 1913, Etat-major de l'armée de terre. Attaché militaire, Autriche-Hongrie 1911-13, 7 N 1131, SHD/AAT, Paris.
26. Pethö, *Agenten für den Doppeladler*, 234.
27. Urbanski, Aufmarschpläne, 87.
28. Quoted in: Kronenbitter, *Krieg im Frieden*, 387.

appear as superfluous and inaccurate. As a result, Austria's relationship with Russia was rather unstable, based as it was on a combination of information, values, and prejudices. The opinions of the Austro-Hungarian army vacillated between over and underestimating the rival in the East. This also influenced the question as to whether the information acquired by the Evidenzbureau before 1908 was counterfeit or not.[29] Nobody could accurately estimate the extent of Redl's betrayal. It seemed clear that he had handed over secret files that could have given the enemy at least an approximate picture of the Austro-Hungarian forces and military plans, which would have been difficult to compile from legally obtainable information and informants' reports. It was equally clear that Redl had dealt a significant blow to the Austrian secret service, the extent of which was hard to calculate. All efforts to hush up the "monstrous affair" must be interpreted as attempts to control the damage.[30]

At the same time, we cannot exclude the possibility that the cover addresses and courier information found on Redl's desk provided an opportunity for the Austrian counter-espionage services to plant a lot of disinformation on the Razvedka.[31]

Mil'štejn, on the other hand, does not provide convincing evidence to support his claim that Redl handed over the Austro-Hungarian plans for a march on Russia. Apart from regulations concerning railroads and communications zones and from general information about the status of the Austro-Hungarian forces and a number of orders concerning Galicia, he had access to the mobilization regulations for the event of war with "R" (Russia) and "I" (Italy), as well as the complete "*Kriegs-Ordre de bataille*" (order of battle) for the Balkans and the partial plan for "R" and "I."[32]

This kind of information could have had quite an impact. As early as the 1870s, military encyclopedias already predicted the reorganization of the entire state in case of troop mobilization. The instructions and plans for this event covered many areas, especially the "organization of military forces" and the preparation for and transition to a "strategic concentration of military forces." To accomplish this as quickly as possible, "preparation for mobilization includes the concentration of mobile armies and the transportation of all reserve and occupation units to their destinations." The assembly of troops, as a "transition" and "concentration" of armed forces on

29. Pethö, *Agenten für den Doppeladler*, 388.
30. Ibid., 235.
31. Ibid.
32. Michail Alekseev, *Voennaja razvedka Rossii: Ot Rjurika do Nikolaja*. Kniga II (Moskva: Izdatel´skij dom "Russkaja Razvedka": 1998), 553; Erhebungsakten Oberst Redl, KA/ Evidenzbüro 1914, Kt. 3509, ÖSTA, Wien.

"a larger front," is thus closely connected with mobilization and the "*Kriegs-Ordre de bataille*" which "organizes the armed forces and assigns different troops to their units" at the "beginning of a military campaign.[33]

As a result, Alfred Redl was able to provide the Russian military with an invaluable amount of information by handing over the documents he had "worked" on. Besides, the claim that Redl, when he was chief of staff in Prague, only had access to documents about the local corps is false. As a high-ranking general staff officer, he had access to information outside of his immediate area of responsibility.[34] We cannot exclude the possibility that, under these circumstances, he handed over war plans for one or several war scenarios, yet we can only speculate as to whether it really did happen. But even without embellishing the case, Redl had delivered enough, especially if we consider that August Ubański's description applied to the Russian general staff as well: "Every general staff must be informed about the enemy's mobilization plans and the capacity of their railroads. This information allows the daily calculation of the enemy troop movements. Military intelligence services must not overlook any information that indicates the enemy's use of the territory."[35]

Given certain geographical and infrastructural conditions and the significant amount of material delivered by "top spies" like Alfred Redl, the Russian general staff, on the eve of World War I, had enough information about the Austrian army to cause some serious concern.

Russian Triumphs and Defeats

In the years before World War I, the central department of the Russian general staff in St. Petersburg (GUGS for short) mostly sought to fill in some gaps in their knowledge. They claimed that the Habsburg army's "battle order" was not complete yet, but that they were otherwise more than happy with the information they had.[36] In fact, GUGS possessed "most of the details concerning the mobilization of the Austro-Hungarian army, in the form of photographed originals." In May of 1913, shortly before Redl's exposure, the Russian army was well informed (as stated in writing) about "the concentration of the Austro-Hungarian army" and individual "k. u. k.

---

33. Verena Moritz/Hannes Leidinger, *Oberst Redl; Der Spionagefall, der Skandal, die Fakten* (St. Pölten: Residenz 2012), 225.
34. Cf. Hallier to French Ministry of War, 12 June 1913, Etat-major de l´armée de terre. Attaché militaire, Autriche-Hongrie 1911-13, 7 N 1131, SHD/AAT, Paris.
35. Urbanski, Aufmarschpläne, 87f.
36. Hauptverwaltung des Generalstabs der Russischen Armee (GUGS), Spionagematerialien zu Österreich-Ungarn, 1909-1913, f. 2000, op. 1, d. 2831, l. 60, 62, 72 und 164, Rossiskij Voenno-Istoriceskij Archiv (RGVIA), Moskau.

corps" in the event of a "war against Russia."[37]

In addition, it was clear that the files Alfred Redl had delivered contained up-to-date information, a fact confirmed by the Russian intelligence officer Aleksandr A. Samojlo, one of the "recipients" of the documents in question. Consequently, the claim made by some experts that the main damage to the k. u. k. monarchy was done by Redl between 1907 and 1910 (thus before 1913) is incorrect.[38] The most important documents clearly indicate the plans for the years 1913/14.[39]

The Russian files also indicate that Alfred Redl was seen as probably the most important but by far not the only "top spy" in Razvedka's employ. GUGS noted that in the spring of 1913, they had been informed about "the concentration of the Habsburg army" against the Russian empire by an "agent operating covertly, a Czech citizen and former officer, who had worked on mobilization plans." According to a note written the same year, the Russian military leadership had received "war plans" that had been "initiated by the Austro-Hungarian general staff" but "developed in Berlin."[40]

Obviously, the Hohenzollern kingdom had leaks as well. According to GUGS, the Razvedka's increased efforts (from 1905 on) to "shine a light through" the "two German kingdoms" bore fruit. An impressive amount of information arrived from Germany, particularly about the "eastern fortifications" on the Russian border. Sergeant Gustav Wőlkerling proved to be a particularly productive source, and he soon became so important to the Russian secret service that they forewent all direct contact so as not to endanger him.[41]

Hot information was transferred through cover addresses. Both Redl and Wőlkerling delivered files to middle men in Switzerland; they were then passed on to the military attaché in the Russian embassy in Bern, Dmitrij Gurko, who transmitted them to the final recipients in Russia.[42] Gurko, who also cooperated with the intelligence operations of the French captain Paul Larguier, was one of the key figures in the Europe-wide Razvedka network, which would find itself in severe trouble within a few months.

---

37. Hauptverwaltung des Generalstabs der Russischen Armee (GUGS), Spionagematerialien zu Österreich-Ungarn, May 1913, f. 2000, d. 2869, l. 279-283, RGVIA, Moskau.
38. Diether Degreif, *Operative Planungen des k. u. k. Generalstabes für einen Krieg in der Zeit vor 1914* (Wiesbaden: Wiku Verlag 1985), 163.
39. Alekseev, *Voennaja razvedka Rossii*, 553; Erhebungsakten Oberst Redl, KA/Evidenzbüro 1914, Kt. 3509, ÖSTA/Wien.
40. Hauptverwaltung des Generalstabs der Russischen Armee (GUGS), Spionagematerialien zu Österreich-Ungarn, May 1913, f. 2000, d. 2869, l. 279-285, RGVIA, Moskau.
41. Höhne, *Der Krieg im Dunkeln*, 68.
42. Ibid., 69.

After the discovery of incriminating evidence had forced the recall of the Russian military attachés in Vienna and Berlin in 1910/11, events followed each other in rapid succession after the turn of the year 1912/13. The k. u. k. Evidenzbureau informed their colleagues in the Hohenzollern army about an unknown man who temporarily lived in Vienna and who, among other things, offered mobilization orders for troops and fortifications in the German-Russian border regions for sale. The "suspect"—it turned out to be Wőlkerling—was finally arrested in February of 1913 after he had returned to Germany from a trip through Austria, France, and Switzerland.[43] The cooperation between IIIb and the Evidenzbureau intensified and, after some k. u. k. officers had helped decode some secret documents, eventually led to the "exposure of the traitor Alfred Redl." The shock caused by his exposure and his death almost caused the entire Russian intelligence system to collapse, a fact of which the general public was largely unaware. While the departure of the czarist military attaché in Vienna, Michail Zankevič, from Austria (a result of the Jandrić affair) had kept the news media busy for a good while, central Europe took very little notice of Razvedka's other defeats. Yet, some of these had very serious consequences: In October of 1913, the Russian military attaché Petr Assanovič in Stockholm stumbled on the "discovery" of a middle man; Gurko was exposed very soon after this. "Russia's gray eminence in Switzerland" was so hopelessly discredited that not even Italy wanted to employ him as a military diplomat.[44]

Preparing for an Emergency

In the context of the overall development of Russian espionage, the sensational Redl scandal showed the Razvedka's successes and setbacks. If we look at the "espied" materials and the Russian military plans based on them, a similar ambivalent picture emerges.[45] After all, they led to a major dispute between czarist officers: One group opposed the plan developed by General Quartermaster Grigorij N. Danilov in 1910, which largely ignored Austria. Danilov's primary target was the Hohenzollern troops in Eastern Prussia. The French embassy in Vienna referred to them in 1909, noting that an armed conflict between Berlin and Vienna on the one hand and Paris and St. Petersburg on the other hand could cause the Habsburg and Hohenzollern troops to attack and occupy Russian Poland. If major

---

43. Ibid., 105.
44. Ronge, *Kriegs- und Industrie-Spionage*, 68.
45. Cf. Hallier to French Ministry of War, 12 June 1913, Etat-major de l´armée de terre. Attaché militaire, Autriche-Hongrie 1911-13, 7 N 1131, SHD/AAT, Paris; Degreif, *Operative Planungen des k. u. k. Generalstabes*, 158, 210 und 214.

Russian forces were defeated in this region, Germany would have a chance to advance on the "Grande Nation." It was speculated that Wilhelm II's forces in the West would initially act defensively.[46]

In the spring of 1913, the armed forces came to a radically different conclusion. On March 9 of the same year, the British military attaché in Paris was absolutely sure that, if the Hohenzollern had to wage war on two fronts, they would first attack France, their "primary enemy," "with all their might."[47] The Russian military leaders expected pretty much the same scenario at the time. Based on the information provided by their intelligence service, especially the "war game" that had been developed in Berlin, they foresaw—months before Redl's exposure—the basic structure of the armed conflict at the beginning of World War I.[48] The military leaders in Paris adamantly pushed the Russians to arm themselves heavily and to plan their deployment of troops, all of which could facilitate a relief offensive in the East on behalf of the "Grande Nation." The French funded not only the formation of reserve units but also improved the Russian infrastructure, especially the railroad network. Contrary to the anticipations of Jakov G.Zilinskij, the Russian chief of staff, in 1911, the reorganization of the armed forces and the preparations for a potential mobilization proceeded more quickly than originally expected.[49]

In a similar fashion, the Zilinkij's officers turned away from Danilov's ideas more and more. In addition to designing plan "G" ("Germanjija"), which was based on the assumption that Germany would first attack Russia, Plan "A" ("Avstrija") was ready by May of 1912 in case the Hohenzollern army would target France. In October, Ziliniskij ordered further work on Plan "G," but he specified in a circular to military commanders that if war was to break out, "plan A would automatically come into effect." At the same time, another important decision was made: The area for troop concentration was moved to the west, which indicated that the Russian army was determined to hold the Weichsel line. Austro-Hungarian sources, for a long time, counted on weaker Russian units in the region or expected the Russian army to give up Kongress-Poland altogether. The Russian general staff knew about Austria-Hungary's strategic principles, largely because of information gathered by the Razvedka. The documents Redl had handed over, in particular, aided in planning and confirming Russian tactics, which

46. L´Autriche-Hongrie en cas de guerre franco-allemande, 6 May 1909, Etat-major de l´armée de terre. Attaché militaire, Autriche-Hongrie 1907-10, 7 N 1130, SHD/AAT, Paris.
47. Military Attaché France, 9 March 1913, FO 371/1744, TNA, London.
48. Hauptverwaltung des Generalstabs der Russischen Armee (GUGS), Spionagematerialien zu Österreich-Ungarn, May 1913, f. 2000, d. 2869, l. 283-285, RGVIA, Moscow.
49. Hallier to French Ministry of War, 24 Jan. 1913, Etat-major de l´armée de terre. Attaché militaire, Autrich-Hongrie 1911-13, 7 N 1131, SHD/AAT, Paris.

made it almost impossible for the k. u. k. army to reach its goals: An assault would have put the left wing of the Habsburg forces in Galicia face to face with a superior number of enemy troops, which would have made it impossible to support the north-eastern and eastern main thrust against the Russians. The success of the entire Austrian operation was thus more than questionable.[50]

In Vienna, however, the military authorities retained most of the existing plans for troop concentration. Strategic planners as late as 1914/15 speculated about reinforcement of the Russian units on the eastern border; at the same time, the papers drawn up by the military authorities in St. Petersburg show that the Russians planned to undercut Conrad von Hötzendorf's plans with massive troop reinforcements further to the west.[51] As a result, Austria-Hungary found itself in a dangerous strategic position before and immediately after the Redl affair. The Austrian military commanders' failure to make any changes to plan "R" at first was partially due to their underestimation of the potential damage. There was no shortage of critics, however. The consequences of a Russian breakthrough at the eastern border in the Tarnopol region raised some concern. It was said that the Austro-Hungarian forces in Galicia might be forced to retreat. According to an Evidenzbureau employee, the head of the secret service voiced serious concerns. August Urbański did not think that out-of-date Russian documents, acquired a long time ago, were an adequate base for strategic planning.[52] He thus advised the drawing-up of new plans based on a worst-case scenario. However, the operations office ignored his advice. In the meantime Urbański himself had stumbled upon the Redl affair in April of 1914, which ended his influence as an advisor.[53]

Changing Contexts

Despite these disclosures, we must ask if the undeniably difficult situation at the time of the Habsburg monarchy's most spectacular espionage case did not change immediately thereafter. In the course of 1913, the Vienna press reported improvements to the infrastructure and a reinforcement of troops in the Russian borderland.[54] In February of 1914, Helmuth von

---

50. Degreif, *Operative Planungen des k. u. k. Generalstabes*, 159f.
51. Ibid., 209f. und 212.
52. It is not clear if this opinion also applied to "reconnaissance results" regarding "the strategic situation of Russia" from 1911. In any case, information taken "confidentially" from the reports of the British military attaché in St. Petersburg supposedly became the basis for reworking the "battle order" and the plans for the concentration of Habsburg troops.
53. Degreif, *Operative Planungen des k. u. k. Generalstabes*, 207 und 213.
54. Hallier to French Ministry of War, 12 June 1913, SHD/AAT, Etat-major de l´armée de

Moltke, the German chief of staff, warned his Austrian colleague Conrad von Hőtzendorf that the Russians might strike sooner than expected and further to the West, possibly in the Weichsel area. Subsequently, Conrad's precautions were much closer to the strategies of the military leaders in St. Petersburg. Because he now expected a comprehensive Russian strike and a possible encirclement of the Austro-Hungarian forces around and east of Lemberg, the k. u. k. general staff considered both defensive and offensive measures in the region between Bug and Weichsel before the "ring" of the Russian army closed around the Austrian units in Galicia.[55]

While he also considered cooperations between the Habsburg and Hohenzollern units in these cases, Conrad displayed his trademark flexibility. He explained that one cannot rely on only one scenario because the enemy's main striking force could very well be in Vohynia and Podolia. Torn between the different options and trying to do prepare for all eventualities, Conrad decided on an "arced" distribution of troops and their "displacement to the left"—toward the middle and the West—over the original plan. These changes, recommended by the officers of the Austrio-Hungarian operations office as early as the winter of 1913/14, seemed to bother the Russians even sooner. As early as May 1913, after agents had reported a concentration of k. u. k. troops in the Cracow region, they wondered if the Austrians were redistributing their forces.[56]

In essence, Alfred Redl had barely been exposed before the military leadership initiated significant changes in their strategic plans. These included discussions about transferring the concentration area of the Austro-Hungarian army in Galicia. For a variety of reasons, some voices called for gathering the units of the Habsburg army on the San-Dnjestr-line, a plan that was abandoned again in the fall of 1913. In 1914/15, the "R" war plan specified eastern Galicia as the starting point of operations.[57]

However, the issue was not off the table. After a general-staff trip in 1913, Conrad was still hoping for support from the Romanians, who were to contain mostly czarist units in the Odessa military district and help protect eastern Galicia and Bukovina.[58] However, such considerations had to raise concerns at this particular point in time. When Austria-Hungary took the side of Bulgaria during the crisis in the Balkans, Bucharest took this as a hostile act, which made the idea of the Romanians' being brothers-in-arms

terre. Attaché militaire, Autriche-Hongrie 1911-13, 7 N 1131, SHD/AAT, Paris.
55. Degreif, *Operative Planungen des k. u. k. Generalstabes*, 214f.
56. Hauptverwaltung des Generalstabs der Russischen Armee (GUGS), Spionagematerialien zu Österreich-Ungarn, May 1913, f. 2000, d. 2869, l. 283-285, RGVIA, Moskau; vgl. Aufmarsch "R" 1914/15, Generalstab/Operationsbüro, Karton 687, ÖSTA/KA, Wien.
57. Aufmarsch "R" 1914/15, Generalstab/Operationsbüro, Karton 687, ÖSTA/KA, Wien.
58. Degreif, *Operative Planungen des k. u. k. Generalstabes*, 183-186 und 209.

with the Austrians extremely unlikely. To protect the exposed eastern wing of the Habsburg army in Galicia from "Russian encirclement" in the case of a Romanian sortie, the "transfer of the detrucking area" remained on the agenda. Concerned, Conrad wrote a detailed study "on the problem" in the spring of 1914. On July 1, 1914, he ordered that the "position of readiness in the Northeast" be revised according to the principles presented therein.[59]

The k. u. k. chief of staff was more concerned with the danger of relying on a single crisis scenario. Since the correspondence with Moltke regarding the transfer of Russian troops to the west, he had been afraid of overlooking alternatives in other issues as well. He believed that it was not enough to anticipate different "war scenarios." Instead, the different variations had to be calibrated with each other and prepared in a way that would make them "dovetail seamlessly with each other." What Conrad von Hötzendorf feared the most was a Russian strike at a time when the Habsburg units were heavily engaged in the Balkans.[60] He organized the Austro-Hungarian forces in the event of the "R" war after the sudden beginning of an armed conflict as follows: The so-called "B squadron," which would at first support the "Balkan minimal group," would be turned around and transferred to Galicia, where they would help out the "A squadron," which was "to fight against Russia under all circumstances."[61]

Failed Offensives

In truth, from July of 1914 on, hardly anything worked out the way the Austro-Hungarian army had hoped. Some "immutable facts" spoke against Austria from the very start. For one, Russia could rely on a much larger number of subjects. The Russian "human potential" could also be moved more quickly to the places where they were needed thanks to improved roads and railroads. This was essential as all European military leaders were hoping to save time and score quick victories. This was especially true for the Habsburg Empire. After all, the military's railroad experts believed that their own units would fall behind the "increasing numbers of Russians"

---

59. With regard to the transfer of the assembly position, I would like to refer to Lothar Höbelt, who believes that this measure had no bearing on the majority of the troops in the face of the "conditions of railroads" and that it was based more on the "loss of the federal cooperative Romania" than on the "Redl espionage affair." — Lothar Höbelt, "So wie wir haben nicht einmal die Japaner angegriffen": Österreich-Ungarns Nordostfront 1914/15, in Gerhard P. Groß, ed., Die vergessene Front. Der Osten 1914/15: Ereignis, Wirkung, Nachwirkung (Paderborn: Ferdinand Schöningh 2006), 87-120, hier 89f.

60. Degreif, Operative Planungen des k. u. k. Generalstabes, 205.

61. Manfried Rauchensteiner, Der Tod des Doppeladlers:. Österreich-Ungarn und der Erste Weltkrieg (Graz: Styria 1993), 114; Österreich-Ungarns letzter Krieg 1914-1918: Das Kriegsjahr 1914 (Vienna: Verlag der Militärwissenschaftlichen Mitteilungen 1930), 6f.

after the 15th day of mobilization. Another factor complicated matters for Conrad von Hötzendorf and his officers: The "B squadron" could not be easily redirected as soon as the conflict with Russia was certain. In essence, the Austrians were not as flexible as Conrad wanted them to be. Still, even until the end of July of 1914, he was very much committed to a Serbian campaign[62] even though the Habsburg units stationed in the region suffered a crucial defeat. Until August 24, 1914, they had been pushed back to their jump-off position. The news from Galicia was no better. Instead of remaining on the defensive and shifting back the area of concentration—as had been taken for granted until July of 1914—the Austro-Hungarian army commanders decided to launch an offensive from the border region.[63] The attack ended with a distressing loss of territory and Conrad's allegation that their German allies had deserted them.[64]

In the midst of these defeats, it remained unclear how much Alfred Redl's betrayal had contributed to them. Even the k. u. k. commanders were uncomfortable, if Max Ronge's records are to be believed: He claims that the military leaders in Teschen had requested the Redl file in 1915.[65] If one looks at the individual events of the "gambit campaigns," one can easily see the connections with the scandal of May 1913. For example, as the Austrians were battling the Serbs, some units of the "8th corps, whose chief of staff the "master spy" had been on his last assignment, showed signs of disintegration.[66] We must assume that the Serbs received useful information from their Russian "patrons" because of the attested cooperation between the Western powers and the Russians, which included the crisis regions in south-eastern Europe.[67] However, such a complicated exchange of information was not necessary. Russian documents confirm suspicions: Russia delivered its "espionage results" directly to Serbia and asked the

---

62. For a commentary from a military as well as a political perspective, see Höbelt, "So wie wir haben nicht einmal die Japaner angegriffen", 88f.

63. Rauchensteiner, *Der Tod des Doppeladlers*, 114-121 und 130; Hannes Leidinger/Verena Moritz, *Der Erste Weltkrieg* (Vienna: Böhlau 2011), 36f. The operations of the 3rd k. u. k. army brought negative consequences such as "forced arches and frontal attacks against a much stronger opponent." "Attack fever had turned into attack madness," states Anton Pitreich in his 1930 account see *Der österreichisch-ungarische Bundesgenosse im Sperrfeuer* (Klagenfurt: Kollitsch 1930), 118.

64. Martin Schmitz, Verrat am Waffenbruder? Die Siedlice-Kontroverse im Spannungsfeld von Kriegsgeschichte und Geschichtspolitik, in: *Militärgeschichtliche Zeitschrift* 67 (2008): 385-407, 385f.

65. Verena Moritz/Hannes Leidinger/Gerhard Jagschitz, *Im Zentrum der Macht: Die vielen Gesichter des Geheimdienstchefs Maximilian Ronge* (St. Pölten: Residenz 2007), 112.

66. Rauchensteiner, *Der Tod des Doppeladlers*, 130.

67. Télégramme déchiffré 1912, Correspondance politique et commerciale, 1896-1918, Autriche-Hongrie, Défense Nationale, Vol. IV, 1912-1914, Archives des Affaires étrangères, Archives de l´administration centrale à Paris/Affaires politiques (AAÉ, AAC/AP), Paris.

intelligence services of both countries to cooperate as closely as possible.[68] They more than complied. Naturally, Belgrade had precise information about the 16th k. u. k. corps in Sarajevo and Ragusa and passed on the battle orders of both units to St. Petersburg.[69] By contrast, the Russian intelligence correspondence does not mention the 8th corps. Our suspicions in this regard are thus mere speculation.

We can confidently deny that the "Redl affair" had any bearing whatsoever on the initial Austrian defeats against the Russians. Even though it looks as if the war plans for "R" had been heavily influenced by military intelligence, the "sensational case of betrayal," and the significant shortcomings of the Austro-Hungarian counter-espionage services, the calculations of the general staff changed as a result of political and military considerations by the turn of the year 1913/14 at the latest. In addition, the covert acquisition of classified information could only do so much, as many other cases indicate. The state of the infrastructure or the topographical and geographical conditions could not be changed at short notice, and some important information could be obtained by legal means. Karl Bornemann, who would later serve as brigadier general in the Austrian army and who had met Alfred Redl when he was a young lieutenant, put it as follows: The Russians were well acquainted with "established facts" such as the capacity of the railroads that connected the center of the Austrian Empire with its borders, and they knew about the "peacetime dislocation of the Austro-Hungarian forces." On the other hand, says Bornemann, the k. u. k. general staff had been revising instructions since the end of 1913, which included the transferal of troops to regions "much further west." Things did not happen the way the Austrians had wished because of their delayed "readiness for operations" and because of the difficulties involved in "directing" the "supernumerary units" in Serbia to the "north-eastern theatre of war." Naturally, Redl's betrayal "had no influence on this development of events."[70]

If we keep in mind the discussion concerning the transfer of the Austro-Hungarian concentration area to "the Russian front," we also gain a different perspective on the initial territorial losses in Galicia. Before 1914, they had been part of the strategic plan at least twice. In 1915, the lost territories were regained as the Habsburg and Hohenzollern troops "broke through" in Tarnów-Gorlice. A few month later, in the late fall of the same

68. Alekseev, *Voennaja razvedka Rossii*, 552.
69. Russischer Militärattaché in Belgrad an den Generalquartiermeister des Russischen Generalstabs, 29 Jan. 1912, f. 2000, op. 1, d. 2829, l. 42, RGVIA, Moskau.
70. Generalmajor d. R. Karl Bornemann to Dipl. Ing. Franz Schmidt, 13 February 1964, NL Bornemann, B 1041:79, ÖSTA/KA, Wien.

year, the Austrians conquered Serbia with German and Bulgarian help after Sofia had agreed to an alliance with Vienna and Berlin.[71]

However, the generals of Kaiser Wilhelm and Emperor Francis Joseph could only derive so much joy from their victories. The brief armed conflict they had hoped for had turned into a long "battle of material" with increasingly uncontrollable political, economic, and social repercussions. In the end, these events brought about the downfall of the monarchies in middle and Eastern Europe and the end of the Romanov, Hohenzollern, and Habsburg dynasties. Against this background, the plans made and discussions held before 1914 lose their significance, as do the actions and "faux pas" of Alfred Redl.

---

71. Leidinger/Moritz, *Der Erste Weltkrieg,* 36 und 39.

Conrad v. Hötzendorf studying maps, Pf 342:C(7), Photo Charles, Scolik, Jr.,
Austrian National Library - Picture Archives and Graphics Department, Vienna

Conrad von Hötzendorf and the "Smoking Gun": A Biographical Examination of Responsibility and Traditions of Violence against Civilians in the Habsburg Army

Wolfram Dornik[1]

To this day, one of the most controversial figures of the late Habsburg Empire is Franz Conrad von Hötzendorf, chief of the General Staff between 1906 and 1911 and again between 1912 and 1917.[2] The contentious commander, who is at least partly to blame for the ambivalent picture we now have of him, divided opinion through his words and deeds on both the military as well as other issues. Over the course of thousands of pages written in the final years of his life, he tried to present his life's work—which had come into criticism first after his dismissal and then even more after the collapse of the Danube monarchy in 1918—in the proper light.[3]

While there are a number of publications, including critical ones, on individual aspects of the life and work of Conrad von Hötzendorf, especially on his strategic and military views, only a few biographies have attempted to sketch a more complete picture. Lawrence Sondhaus set the standard in 2000 with his definitive work, *Architect of the Apocalypse.*[4] Thanks to Sondhaus' book, more recent studies on Conrad von Hötzendorf have been able to discuss issues such as his cult of the offensive and his social

---

1. This essay was translated from German into English by Mark Miscovich.
2. This paper is based on studies conducted as part of the "Beyond the Trenches" research project, which has been funded by the Austrian Science Fund (P23070-G15) at the Ludwig Boltzmann Institute for Research on the Consequences of War in Graz between 2011 and 2014.
3. On his role during the war, see the controversy already caused by Karl Friedrich Nowak's book *Der Weg zur Katastrophe* in 1919, as discussed in Wolfram Dornik, *Des Kaisers Falke. Wirken und Nach-Wirken von Franz Conrad von Hötzendorf*, mit einer Nachbetrachtung von Verena Moritz und Hannes Leidinger (Innsbruck: Studienverlag, 2013), 179-184. On his contemporary military critics (particularly Maximilian Csicserics von Bacsány and Alfred Krauß), Ibid., 183f.
4. Lawrence Sondhaus, *Franz Conrad von Hötzendorf: Architect of the Apocalypse* (Boston: Humanities Press, 2000).

56   Dornik: Conrad von Hötzendorf and the "Smoking Gun":
A Biographical Examination of Responsibility and Traditions of Violence against Civilians in
the Habsburg Army

Darwinist views.[5] But, there are a number of other aspects that still require further consideration. This paper focuses on three issues that have received too little attention so far. To what extent do the existing sources on Conrad von Hötzendorf allow us to reconstruct a biography of his development? To what extent can we trace a radicalization of the use of force, particularly against civilians, in the decisions of the chief of the General Staff? Can we even go so far as to accuse him of responsibility for the war crimes and violence against civilians at the outbreak of the war?

My hypothesis is that Conrad von Hötzendorf is largely responsible for the war crimes committed in Galicia and Bucovina as well as in Bosnia-Hercegovina and Southern Hungary in the summer and fall of 1914. These crimes can largely be attributed to his biographical background. But they are also a structural problem, one that was inherent to the self-image of the Habsburg Army and one that influenced Conrad himself in the course of his biographical development. It is further a problem that Conrad—as a high-ranking general, an instructor at the military academy, and chief of the General Staff—also helped perpetuate and create.

Shaping his own image for posterity

In retrospect, the written documents on Conrad von Hötzendorf yield a complex picture. The majority of autobiographical publications are from the first half of the 1920s, including, in particular, his five-volume defense of his career, *Aus meiner Dienstzeit* (1921-25), and a considerably shorter volume on his early military career, *Mein Anfang* (1925).[6] There are also the private notes (*Anthologien*), which were compiled and written in the final years of Conrad's life. Kurt Peball, the later director of the Austrian State Archives, published them in 1977.[7] These three publications are the most commonly used sources on Conrad von Hötzendorf in the secondary literature as well.

Several editions of his two most important military books, the two-volume *Zum Studium der Taktik* (1891) and *Die Gefechtsausbildung der*

5. See, for example, Dieter Hackl, "Der Offensivgeist des Conrad von Hötzendorf," diploma thesis, University of Vienna, 2009; Stefan Kazainschütz, "Biologie und Legitimation: Die Heterogenität des Biologismusdiskurses an der Schwelle zum 20. Jahrhundert. Dargestellt am Beispiel ausgewählter Personen," diploma thesis, University of Graz, 2008; Willibald Rosner, "Fortifikation und Operation: Die Sperre Lavarone-Folgaria," 2 vols., diploma thesis, University of Vienna, 2007.

6. Feldmarschall Conrad, *Aus meiner Dienstzeit 1906-1918*, 5 vols. (Vienna: Ricola Verlag, 1921-1925); Feldmarschall Conrad, *Mein Anfang: Kriegserinnerungen aus der Jugendzeit, 1878-1882* (Berlin: Verlag für Kulturpolitik, 1925).

7. Kurt Peball, ed., *Conrad von Hötzendorf. Private Aufzeichnungen: Erste Veröffentlichungen aus den Papieren des k.u.k. Generalstabs-Chef* (Vienna: Amalthea, 1977).

Infanterie (1900), had already been published during his active military service.[8] Additionally, Conrad's image has been significantly shaped by the publications of his students, his admirers, and his immediate surroundings. These were published from the outbreak of the war up to the second half of the 20th century.[9] They primarily deal with his military qualifications, but they discuss his private life as well.

In the Military Archives of the Austrian State Archives, there is a collection of private papers and documents consisting of 509 fascicles. Each fascicle contains between one and several hundred pages. The provenance and original compilation of these documents are not always clear from the existing indexes and catalogues of the state archives. However, they mainly consist of notes, drafts of documents, private and professional correspondence (originals as well as copies), documents relating to his publications (manuscripts, notes etc.), photo albums as well as sketches and drawings made by Conrad von Hötzendorf himself that have been handed down by his heirs. What is not clear is who contributed to the collection, when they did it, and how much they contributed. During Conrad von Hötzendorf's lifetime, for instance, his mother, his second wife, Virginia ("Gina") Conrad von Hötzendorf (née Agujari, and, after her first marriage, von Reininghaus), and particularly his aide-de-camp managed his documents, made copies, and took notes. After his death, his private papers and documents were divided and found their way to the Austrian State Archives through various channels. Other original documents or copies were purchased later at auctions.[10]

Despite these external influences, it can be assumed that Conrad von Hötzendorf paid very close attention to what should and should not be passed down to posterity. He planned to counter the large amount of unsupervised correspondence with his influential publications, which hardly any publication on the First World War or the July Crisis can dare do without. The problem with these sources, regardless of whether from his

8. Franz Conrad von Hötzendorf, *Zum Studium der Taktik*, 2 vols. (Vienna: L.W. Seidel, 1891). Franz Conrad von Hötzendorf, *Die Gefechtsausbildung der Infanterie* (Vienna: L.W. Seidel, 1900).

9. August von Cramon, *Unser österreichisch-ungarischer Bundesgenosse im Weltkriege: Erinnerungen aus meiner vierjährigen Tätigkeit als bevollmächtigter deutscher General beim k.u.k. Armeeoberkommando* (Berlin: Mittler, 1922). Karl Friedrich Nowak, *Hötzendorfs Lager* (Berlin: Fischer, 1916). Edith Gräfin Salburg, *Conrad von Hötzendorf. Der Preuße Österreichs: Ein Feldherrn-Roman* (Leipzig: Koehler, 1935).

10. See, for example, Kurt Peball, "Briefe an eine Freundin: Zu den Briefen des Feldmarschalls Conrad von Hötzendorf an Frau Walburga von Sonnleitner während der Jahre 1905 bis 1918," *Mitteilungen des Österreichischen Staatsarchivs*, Sonderdruck/vol. 25 (1972): 492-503. See also the catalogue entry on the bequest of Franz Conrad von Hötzendorf, A/B/C 1450, Österreichisches Staatsarchiv/Kriegsarchiv.

58   Dornik: Conrad von Hötzendorf and the "Smoking Gun":
A Biographical Examination of Responsibility and Traditions of Violence against Civilians in
the Habsburg Army

private papers and documents or those published by him during his lifetime, is the filtering done by Conrad von Hötzendorf himself. This editing extended from omitting certain information to endlessly repeating the same arguments to altering cited documents. His published works, therefore, present a challenge to constructing a biography of his development, since Conrad edited and revised the majority of them himself between 1920 and 1925. If one is interested in pinpointing the defining moments of Conrad's life, one must rely on the few sources that can be clearly dated to a specific time. In particular, documents of people from his immediate surroundings are especially important in this regard. This means drawing on the official correspondence of the General Staff and the Army High Command; the private papers and documents of his trusted subordinates, Rudolf Kundmann and Josef Metzger; and his foreign-policy counterparts, Count Alois Lexa von Aehrenthal and Count Leopold Berchtold von und zu Ungarschitz, as well as his military ones, Carl von Bardolff, Arthur von Bolfras, and Oskar Potiorek.[11] The records of Archduke Franz Ferdinand, Emperor Franz Josef, and Emperor Karl might provide some insight, too.[12]

Stages of a biographical escalation

This paper cannot and does not intend to recount all the stations of Conrad von Hötzendorf's life, but instead will outline the most important formative experiences and discuss them along important climatic points. His childhood and youth were shaped by his father, Franz, who had been wounded in the Revolution of 1848, and particularly by his mother, who instilled strict discipline and rigor in him. Throughout his life, he always referred to the important role his mother played in his upbringing, whereas his father did not figure prominently in his recollections. Because Conrad's father was thirty-two years older than his mother, his mother was interested in preparing him to take over as the breadwinner of the family. Though his mother envisaged a technical profession for Conrad, his father chose a

---

11. See, for this, in particular the private papers and documents of Count Alois Lexa von Aehrenthal or Count Leopold Berchtold von und zu Ungarschitz in the Austrian State Archives/House, Court, and State Archives as well as those of Rudolf Kundmann and Josef Metzger in the Austrian State Archives/Military Archives. Also, there are presumably other relevant files in private archives, such as the archive of the Reininghaus family, as well as the descendants of Conrad von Hötzendorf.

12.   Thus, the documents come from the *Militärkanzlei Seiner Majestät des Kaisers* (MKSM, Military Chancery of His Majesty the Emperor) as well as the *Militärkanzlei des Generalinspektors der gesamten bewaffneten Macht Erzherzog Franz Ferdinand* (MKFF, Military Chancery of the Inspector General of All the Armed Forces of Archduke Franz Ferdinand); additionally, these would also include the biographical publications on the above mentioned persons.

military career for him instead.[13]

His keen fascination with the natural sciences, a main focus at both the Cadet School in Hainburg and the Military Academy in Wiener Neustadt, would accompany Conrad throughout his life. An integral part of the discourse of the time was a strong faith in progress (*"Fortschrittsglaube"*). This led to the broad acceptance of social Darwinist arguments within military circles which made it easier to justify the existence of armies throughout Europe as well as expansionist foreign policy goals, an offensive approach in grand strategy, and arguments for the need for more and more natural resources. This ideology greatly influenced Conrad, as we can see from his early writings. The "struggle for existence" or the "eternal struggle to survive" only continued to increase during the course of his career and resulted in a distinct racial hierarchy.[14]

Based on this way of thinking, it was only "logical" to Conrad von Hötzendorf that he, as chief of the General Staff, would counsel preventive wars, for only a nation that "aggressively" pursued its goals would also achieve them. In a memorandum from November 15, 1911, he wrote:

> My fundamental view is that a nation must always pursue politics and therefore aggressive goals. For any nation that limits itself to merely maintaining what it has only makes a loss all the more inevitable, as its surrounding neighbors will seek to expand their dominion. Therefore, I am also of the opinion that it is a fiction to believe in a status quo. It is a fallacy to base a nation's politics and, what affects me more, its related military provisions on such an idea. Furthermore, I hold the view that in order to pursue one's own political development goals it is essential to hold off on the actions that are inevitable to achieve these goals until the conditions for them are most favorable, [...]. Moreover, I think that the only way to make the great costs of the armed forces worthwhile is by following the latter principle, [...] for it seems that this is the only way possible to maximize the preparations and thus the expenses of a particular action, [...] In particular, a nation, which, like the monarchy, is surrounded on all sides by potential enemies, can scarcely afford to be ready at any time and on all sides to strike against several enemies, possibly at the same time. I think that precisely a nation such as this must, more than

---

13. Dornik, *Des Kaisers Falke*, 14-27.
14. Dornik, *Des Kaisers Falke*, 45-47.

60   Dornik: Conrad von Hötzendorf and the "Smoking Gun":
A Biographical Examination of Responsibility and Traditions of Violence against Civilians in
the Habsburg Army

any other, work towards identifying its potential enemies in good time and must seek to defeat these one after the other, [...].[15]

Besides his emphasis on preventive war, another basic feature of Conrad von Hötzendorf's military thinking is the cult of the offensive. His thinking here was not only influenced by his extensive studies of the Austro-Prussian War of 1866 and the Franco-Prussian War of 1870/71 but also by his own wartime experiences. These were limited almost exclusively to "irregular" conflicts: the occupation campaign of 1878/79 and the uprising in Southern Dalmatia and Western Bosnia in the early 1880s. Both times, they faced guerilla bands as well as a hostile civilian population; both times, they had to maneuver in rough terrain, because moving on the main transportation routes made them an ideal target.[16]

Both experiences confirmed, in particular, two tenets of his thinking. First, that moving troops according to strategies created on the drawing board, regardless of the circumstances, put the regular troops at a serious disadvantage to the irregular ones. And second, that hesitating or proceeding according to service regulations, without any further thought, was an additional handicap on the regular troops.[17] Both deployments had also taught him that the local civilian population could not be trusted during a war. There was always the danger of them collaborating with the enemy. This reinforced in him the Austro-Hungarian army's skepticism (one that began long before 1848) of the nationalist movements within its own country in particular and the civilian population in general.[18]

Following this initial action in the field as a first lieutenant and a captain, his military career made huge strides. He became chief of the General Staff of the 11th Infantry Division in Lviv in 1883. Then he was assigned to the Operations Office of the General Staff in 1887. After that, he worked as an instructor and taught two classes of cadets at the Military Academy. Then he was assigned to the 93rd Infantry Regiment in Olmütz in 1892. He was the commander of the 1st Infantry Regiment in Troppau

---

15. Kopie des Memorandums des Chefs des Generalstabes an den Kaiser, 15 November 1911, Nachlass: Conrad von Hötzendorf, B/1450:67, Nr. 4350, Österreichisches Staatsarchiv/ Kriegsarchiv.

16. Dornik, *Des Kaisers Falke*, 40-45.

17. See, for this, for example, his study, commissioned by the General Staff, on a possible deployment in Bosnia-Hercegovina: Kopie des Berichts über Herzegowina von Conrad von Hötzendorf vom Frühjahr 1880, 23 March 1908, Nachlass: Conrad von Hötzendorf, B/1450:6, Österreichisches Staatsarchiv/Kriegsarchiv.

18. Walter Wagner, "Die K.(u.)k. Armee – Gliederung und Aufgabenstellung," in *Die Bewaffnete Macht*, aus *Die Habsburgermonarchie 1848-1918*, ed. Adam Wandruszka, and Peter Urbanitsch, vol. 5 (Vienna: Verlag der Österreichischen Akademie der Wissenschaften, 1987), 142.

from 1895 to 1899, before receiving command of the 55th Infantry Brigade in Trieste until 1903.

As the Austro-Hungarian commander in the Adriatic harbor, he was the highest military officer in the empire's most important "door to the world." Trieste was undergoing fundamental social changes at the time due to a growing industrial sector and its social and cultural heterogenic setting. Since the beginning of February 1902, the Lloyd stokers had been on strike to reduce working hours and to alter night work regulations. The situation stagnated for nearly two weeks and then began to escalate slowly due to the growing solidarity among other workers. On February 13, the police presence was increased and troops took up position. On February 14, shots were fired as soldiers attempted to stop a protest march from reaching the Piazza Grande, leading to the first casualties. As the situation remained tense on the following day and additional lives were lost to the use of military force, a state of emergency was declared and martial law was imposed. Reinforcements were requested from Ljubljana and Görz, with three battalions of the 27th Infantry Regiment and two of the 47th Infantry Regiment reinforcing the eight battalions of the 87th and 97th Infantry Regiments of the city garrison.[19] Suspicious labor leaders were arrested preemptively. The situation did not begin to calm until February 16. In total, at least a dozen people died and numerous civilians and soldiers were injured. Though the labor dispute of the Lloyd stokers was referred to arbitration on February 14, the situation had already developed its own uncontrollable dynamic. In the end, there was hardly any talk about the stokers' demands. The highly charged atmosphere was particularly fueled by the tense economic situation of the port city due to the high cost of living and food as well as enormous youth unemployment. The deployment of troops also contributed to poisoning the situation.[20]

In the Cisleithanian Imperial Council (*Reichsrat*) in Vienna, a heated debate on the actions of the law enforcement forces and the civil administration broke out shortly after February 14. The Social Democratic members of parliament found themselves alone, and the state of emergency

---

19. Together, the four regiments with the 3rd Calvary Brigade in Marburg/Maribor and the 3rd Artillery Brigade in Graz belonged to the 28th Infantry Division in Laibach/Ljubljana and were assigned to the 3rd Army Corps in Graz. See: *Schematismus für das kaiserliche und königliche Heer und für die kaiserliche und königliche Kriegs-Marine für 1902* (Vienna: k.k. Hof- und Staatsdruckerei, 1901).

20. On the order of events, see the press coverage on the official report Prime Minister Koerber delivered to Parliament during the debate on the imposition of the state of emergency, reported in the *Reichspost*, 19 February 1902, S. 5f. Since the respective files cannot be found in the records of the Office of the Prime Minister, it can be assumed that these were either destroyed in the fire of the Palace of Justice in 1927 or were returned to Italy on the basis of the Baden Agreement on Archives of 1926.

62   Dornik: Conrad von Hötzendorf and the "Smoking Gun":
A Biographical Examination of Responsibility and Traditions of Violence against Civilians in
the Habsburg Army

was extended for weeks. The rhetoric of class struggle left a clear mark on the press coverage. It was clear to the Social Democratic *Arbeiter-Zeitung* (Workers' Newspaper) that the "incompetent" Governor Count Leopold von Goess as well as Prime Minister Ernest von Koerber were responsible for the escalation. For the conservative *Reichspost* newspaper, the Social Democrats, who could not control the workers, the anarchists and the Italian irredentists, were to blame for the drama. The *Danzer's Armeezeitung* (Danzer's Army Newspaper), the officers' newspaper and mouthpiece of Archduke Franz Ferdinand, pointed quite rightly to the much too careless and frequent use of troops to assist the police since the 1880s. The officers' newspaper begins its report "On the Use of Military Armed Force in Trieste" by stating that "The bloody incidents in Trieste surely fill every soldier with deep regret. Yet that is our profession: to protect the state from without and within, in war as well as peace." After that, although the report goes on to criticize the excessive use of military troops to assist the police during times of social unrest, the paper is quick to point out that one of the main tasks of the army, now, is to maintain law and order.[21]

Conrad was not part of the public debate. What also stands out is that the military was treated quite leniently, even by the *Arbeiter-Zeitung*. Nevertheless, Conrad had made a name for himself in this critical situation, at least among leading circles, as someone who was not afraid to use armed force to crack down if worst came to worst. The Minister of War, Edmund von Krieghammer, thanked Conrad in a letter on February 27, 1902 and conveyed the Emperor's "highest satisfaction" that he "had been capable of taking those precautions which were necessary to restore peace and order with forethought, vigor, and confidence in light of the recent riots in Trieste."[22]

The heir to the throne—Franz Ferdinand, whose influence had continued to increase since the turn of the century—was probably also impressed. Conrad's publications not only caught his eye, but also his panache at the annual imperial maneuvers as the commander of the 8th Infantry Division in Innsbruck. At all the previous stages of his career, Conrad made sure to draw attention to himself through his vigor, practicality, camaraderie, and openness to reform. Franz Ferdinand was looking for a modernizer and offensive strategist who suited him as the successor for Friedrich von Beck-Rzikowsky, whose age was taking a heavy toll on him. It was also to

---

21. See, for this, the press coverage in the *Arbeiter-Zeitung*, 14 February to 7 March 1902; *Reichspost*, 17 - 20 February 1902; *Danzer's Armeezeitung*, 20 February 1902, 27 March, 1902.
22. Krieghammer an Conrad von Hötzendorf, 27 February 1902, Nachlass: Conrad von Hötzendorf, B/1450:508, Österreichisches Staatsarchiv/Kriegsarchiv.

Conrad's benefit that he was not considered to be one of Beck-Rzikowsky's men and thus the Emperor's too, but instead was associated with the legendary chief of general staff in the 1870s and early 1880s Baron Anton von Schönfeld. This was also the reason why he was finally chosen over Oskar Potiorek, who had been regarded as the logical successor.[23]

Strengthened by Franz Ferdinand's confidence in him, Conrad immediately went on the offensive in his new post in November 1906. As early as in his second memorandum, which was traditionally presented to the Emperor at the end of the year, he was already calling for preventive war in 1908. Despite the crisis over the annexation of Bosnia-Hercegovina, his preventive war proposal was not put into action, leaving Conrad practically traumatized. From this point on, he continued to repeat his proposals for a preemptive strike against Serbia and/or Italy, frequently pointing out the "missed opportunities" in 1908 and later on (for example, during the Italo-Turkish War of 1911/12). This not only turned the Emperor against him but also the heir to the throne, leading both of them to abandon him in 1911. Though he returned to his post as "chief" one year later at the height of the First Balkan War, the fact that they had not listened to him still hurt him. The situation was made even worse by the fact that the opportunity to take action was missed once again during the Second Balkan War in 1913.[24]

The period between July and December 1914 would prove to be another climatic point of his career. Although he had been working his whole life towards leading a war, Conrad often proved unable to deal with the pressure of the events in this situation and was, at times, no match for the task. The deployment of troops itself turned into a farce, which had nothing to do with the perfectly conceived war plans of the prewar period. The decision to activate War Plan "B" was based on false—some may even argue "naive"—assumptions, and shifting the mobile reinforcements of the B-Staffel to the northeastern theater of war resulted in a logistical disaster. The situation was further complicated by the fact that during the July Crisis Conrad had plans drawn up to push the deployment zone forward. These were then carried out on his orders, although the troops were not prepared for this change in plans and had to fight their first battles still tired from the prolonged march to the deployment zone. One disaster followed another. The Russian troops proved to be better prepared and advanced to their operational zone faster than expected, and the anticipated number of German troops could not be moved to the Eastern Front because the Schlieffen/Moltke Plan failed. What is more, Conrad's son Herbert was killed near Lviv in September, a

23. Dornik, *Des Kaisers Falke*, 47-57; Alma Hannig, *Franz Ferdinand: Die Biografie* (Vienna: Amalthea, 2013), 90-98.
24. Dornik, *Des Kaisers Falke*, 78-109.

64   Dornik: Conrad von Hötzendorf and the "Smoking Gun":
A Biographical Examination of Responsibility and Traditions of Violence against Civilians in
the Habsburg Army

painful personal loss. Also, Potiorek, his rival within his own ranks, failed in his attempt to crush Serbia. Thus, Conrad's personal and strategic position at the end of 1914 was more disastrous than he ever anticipated, and with that all the pre-war plans were obsolete. A completely different kind of war had to be waged: a war of position, a war in which civilians on the home front also had to help achieve victory on the front—a "total war" involving all of society. Paradigms that Conrad neither wanted nor could accept right up to the end of his career as well as his life.

The final step in the escalation of his biography was not his dismissal by Emperor Karl on March 1, 1917. On the contrary, he had been expecting this and looked forward to it with resignation. He now hoped to finally be granted his eagerly anticipated retirement, but the young Emperor also did not want to lose this symbol for the war against Italy. The "hawk" should at least maintain the threat of force on the mountain front; even if Conrad was no longer heard there like he would have liked to have been. The young Emperor had more confidence in others like Alfred Krauß, who worked the "Wonder of Karfreit."[25]

The real breaking point in Conrad's life came instead with the period of defeat and revolution, which extended for him from his final dismissal as chief of the army group in July 1918 to the founding of the Republic of German-Austria in November. The new order was established in the Peace of Saint Germain-en-Laye in September 1919. After the system he had defended during his active career had been swept away, the social constraints that had structured his thinking and utterances fell, too. Whereas before he never used to let himself have any doubts about the (self-proclaimed) supranational and non-denominational role of the military, his German nationalist, anti-democratic, anti-liberal, and anti-religious views became more radical, as the foundation for these had already been laid by his social Darwinist thinking. Until the final years of his life, he refused to accept the new Austria and envisioned salvation in a German federation, encompassing a vast area.[26]

This radicalization particularly finds expression in the posthumously published *Anthologien* as well as in the individual volumes of *Aus meiner Dienstzeit*. These documents should also be read with this in mind. They do not offer us an insight into the development of his thinking during his time as chief of the General Staff but rather provide a picture of his "look back in anger." To get an idea of this furious anger, consider what Conrad wrote about Russia in the *Anthologien*: "Hypocrisy, deceit, intrigue, and assassination were the methods used by these barely whitewashed Asians.

25. Dornik, *Des Kaisers Falke*, 169-175.
26. Dornik, *Des Kaisers Falke*, 175-179.

These are means to which our thinking is strictly opposed and, what stands out to me at the moment in my philosophical indifference, means that must fill us Germans, who feel so differently, with disgust."[27] Even if he and many of his colleagues of the General Staff basically underestimated Russia and the Russian Army, phrases such as "whitewashed Asians," "us Germans," and "disgust" would not have been found in any of his official documents or private letters before 1917.

"Fight Russophilism [...] with all available means"

While Conrad von Hötzendorf was not traumatized in the trenches of war but radicalized through an escalating series of formative events leading to the ultimate defeat in World War I, we now want to turn to the mistreatment of civilians at the beginning of the war, particularly in Galicia. The issue at hand is the following: What form does the question of responsibility take in this biographical context? How does Conrad von Hötzendorf justify his deeds in the particular situation or in hindsight? Is there any indication of self-criticism?

"Based on the increasing number of reports of treasonous Russophile activities in Galicia, order Op. No. 221 was issued to the 11th Army Corps to urge the City of Lviv to dissolve the Russophile associations and to make arrests. The seed that was allowed to grow rampantly in peace has now begun to sprout to the great disadvantage of our troops and military interests—only drastic measures could help now," argued Conrad in *Aus meiner Dienstzeit* the "necessary" harsh measures in the northeast of the monarchy from the perspective of the Army High Command. And even late in his life, the failed general vehemently defended the radical crackdown on "fellow," ostensibly "pro-Russian" civilians in Galicia.[28] Conrad's orders for the persecution of alleged "Russophiles" were based on Russian military materials, which never received any further clarification.[29]

The entire Ruthenian *intelligentsia* were held to be pro-Russian: They were treated according to the laws of warfare (*Standrecht*) or forcefully interned in Thalerhof (near Graz, Styria). The example of Galicia shows us that the army leadership collaborated with the Polish-dominated civil

---

27. Peball, *Conrad von Hötzendorf*, 245.

28. Feldmarschall Conrad, *Aus meiner Dienstzeit 1906-1918, 24.6.-30.9.1914: Die politischen und militärischen Vorgängen vom Fürstenmord in Sarajevo bis zum Abschluß der ersten und bis zum Beginn der zweiten Offensive gegen Serbien und Rußland*, vol. 4 (Vienna: Ricola, 1923), 331.

29. Befehl des k.u.k. operierenden Oberkommandos an das Evidenzbüro des k.u.k. Generalstabes, 14 October 1914, Kt. 3508, Nr. K-9154, Österreichisches Staatsarchiv/ Kriegsarchiv, Armeeoberkommando/Evidenzbüro.

66   Dornik: Conrad von Hötzendorf and the "Smoking Gun":
A Biographical Examination of Responsibility and Traditions of Violence against Civilians in
the Habsburg Army

administration. The statistical analyses of the deaths at the Thalerhof camp suggest that it was not the particularly pro-Russian population that was supposed to be neutralized but rather the "Ruthenian"/"Ukrainian" intelligentsia.[30] This reflected less an immediate security need than a long-term ethnic conflict, in which the army leadership allowed itself to be instrumentalized for the purposes of local ethnic hegemony.[31]

Not only was Galicia put under military control, but also Bosnia-Hercegovina, Bačka, Croatia, Dalmatia and Bucovina were affected, as was later the Italian-inhabited areas behind the front in the southwest of the monarchy. Thousands of people were forced to flee or were put into internment camps, where their freedom depended on the assistance of influential persons.[32] Within the Habsburg monarchy, but also in neutral and enemy states, the case of Cesare Battisti became very prominent. Battisti, who was a member of the Cisleithanian Imperial Council (*Reichsratsabgeordnete*), joined the Italian army as a volunteer shortly after Italy entered the war. In July 1916, he was captured by Austro-Hungarian soldiers and sentenced to death in a hasty military trial. The picture of the dead body, with the grinning executor and onlookers, was spread as propaganda to discourage traitors. But a few days later, the publication and sale of this picture were banned because the grotesque picture was water on the propaganda mills of the enemies, who used this as proof of the barbarism of the Habsburg *soldatesca*.[33]

Apart from this famous case, we have no clear picture of how many people in the monarchy were sentenced to death in military trials and were finally executed or shot on the spot. In his research on military cases in Tyrol between 1915 and 1918, Oswald Überegger has shown that there was a certain degree of restraint on the part of the authorities and a desire to reduce the sentences. Therefore, we can assume that most of the executions took place at the beginning of the war in the Southeast (Bosnia-Hercegovina, South Hungary) and the Northeast (Galicia, Bucovina) of the monarchy. Ukrainian deputies reported in parliamentary debates 30,000 dead civilians, a figure doubted by many experts. Hannes Leidinger has

---

30. I would like to thank Mag. Katharina Stampler for providing me with her unpublished research results, which she presented in a doctoral candidates' colloquium at the University of Graz on 12 December 2008.

31. On the camp in general, see Georg Hoffmann/Nicole-Melanie Goll/Philipp Lesiak, *Thalerhof 1914-1936: Die Geschichte eines vergessenen Lagers und seiner Opfer* (Herne: Schäfer, 2010).

32. On the use of military jurisdiction in the southwest of the monarchy, see Oswald Überegger, *Der andere Krieg: Die Tiroler Militärgerichtsbarkeit im Ersten Weltkrieg* (Innsbruck: Wagner, 2002).

33. Anton Holzer, *Die andere Front. Fotografie und Propaganda im Ersten Weltkrieg* (Darmstadt: Primus Verlag, 2007), 249-253; Überegger, Der andere Krieg, 366-386.

presented evidence showing that at least 630 Galicians were hung or shot during the first year of the war. But these represent only the official cases in the files of the High Command.[34] Manfried Rauchensteiner estimates that 5,000 death sentences were handed down in Galicia and Bucovina alone, although he points out that only a part of the condemned were probably executed. Eyewitness reports of rows of hanged men in the trees lining Galician streets lend credence to these figures.[35] Hautmann estimates that up to 5,000 death sentences were passed in the monarchy on the basis of the state of emergency regulations during the war.[36]

On enemy territory, the Austro-Hungarian troops did not treat civilians with any more decency. In Serbia and Montenegro, civilian hostages were taken and shot in cases of open resistance to the occupying troops. Particularly during the initial fighting, there was widespread fear of Serbian guerilla fighters ("*Komitadjis*") and the *Kriegsnotwehr* (martial law imposed in defense of the nation) was often enforced.[37] Even during the counterinsurgency operations in the Ukraine between May and October 1918, the Austro-Hungarian troops killed at least 880 civilians, insurgents and "criminals" as part of searches for weapons and ammunition ("*Strafexpeditionen*"). This is surprising, considering that the troops of the Central Powers were not stationed there as occupying forces but rather as friends sent there to help the Kiev government remain in power. And these people were killed, although the military operations officially ended in April, and there were still valid agreements with the Ukrainian authorities on legal action in the case of resistance.[38]

With his call for "drastic measures" against the "Russophile Ruthenians," Conrad joined the choir of those responsible military officers who made or implemented the decisions at the time. For instance, there is also Maximilian Ronge, who, after the Alfred Redl scandal, rose to become a key figure in the military secret service of the Habsburg monarchy.[39] After

34. Hannes Leidinger, '*Der Einzug des Galgens und des Mordes*': Die parlamentarischen Stellungnahmen polnischer und ruthenischer Reichsratsabgeordneter zu den Massenhinrichtungen in Galizien 1914/15, zeitgeschichte 33, no. 5 (September/Oktober 2006): 235-260 (245).

35. Manfried Rauchensteiner, *Der Erste Weltkrieg und das Ende der Habsburgermonarchie* (Vienna: Böhlau Verlag, 2013), 273-276.

36. Hans Hautmann, "Todesurteile in der Endphase der Habsburgermonarchie und im Ersten Weltkrieg," in Claudia Kuretsidis-Haider/Heimo Halbrainer/Elisabeth Ebner, eds., *Mit dem Tode bestraft: Historische und rechtspolitische Aspekte zur Todesstrafe in Österreich im 20. Jahrhundert und der Kampf um ihre weltweite Abschaffung* (Graz: Clio, 2008), 15-38.

37. Jonathan E. Gumz, *The Resurrection and Collapse of Empire in Habsburg Serbia, 1914-1918* (New York: Cambridge University Press, 2009), 27-61.

38. Wolfram Dornik et al., *Die Ukraine zwischen Selbstbestimmung und Fremdherrschaft 1917-1922* (Graz: Leykam, 2011), 235.

39. See, for this, also the statements made by Maximilian Ronge as quoted in Leidinger, "*Der Einzug des Galgens und des Mordes*," 247, 253. For a biography of Ronge, see Verena

68   Dornik: Conrad von Hötzendorf and the "Smoking Gun":
A Biographical Examination of Responsibility and Traditions of Violence against Civilians in
the Habsburg Army

1918, this point of view remained unchallenged in the German-speaking historiography for a long time, which explains why the attacks on civilians were not subjected to critical evaluation in the public or in the research until the past twenty years or so.

For decades, the objections against these repressive anti-Ruthenian actions were swept under the carpet even though they had been raised at the time by the political leadership as well as the Ruthenian and Czech members of Parliament or the noble ruling elite. For decades, research had focused on the July Crisis and its origins (i.e. war guilt), the (botched) deployment (i.e. *B-Staffel* problem), the signs of decay within the military (i.e. the "treason" of certain national troop units), or the alleged "weakness" of the "Kakanian army" (i.e. *Kamerad Schnürschuh*, or "Comrade Lace-Up Shoe"). While these issues are important, these historiographical controversies, often infused with ideological fervor, have overshadowed more productive discussions.

To his credit, Hans Hautmann, the Marxist historian from Linz, was one of the first to consistently address the war crimes of the Austro-Hungarian army.[40] Manfried Rauchensteiner also referred to such war crimes in his *Tod des Doppeladlers* (1993).[41] After the turn of the millennium, further studies followed which were specifically devoted to the summary convictions and the Thalerhof internment camp. The question of responsibility has seldom been raised in this context. Hannes Leidinger was the first to clearly point to Conrad von Hötzendorf's responsibility for these acts of violence in the hinterland of the Habsburg Army in Galicia and Bucovina.[42] The internment camps for Serbs in Arad or the Italians in Katzenau—besides a couple of smaller ones throughout the Habsburg Empire—have yet to be the subject of more critical research in German-speaking research.[43]

Moritz/Hannes Leidinger/Gerald Jagschitz, *Im Zentrum der Macht: Die vielen Gesichter des Geheimdienstchefs Maximilian Ronge* (St. Pölten: Residenz Verlag, 2007).

40. Hans Hautmann, "Bemerkungen zu den Kriegs- und Ausnahmegesetzen in Österreich-Ungarn und deren Anwendung 1914-1918," *zeitgeschichte* 3, no. 2 (November 1975): 31-37; as well as numerous articles in various volumes, journals, and especially the *Mitteilungen der Alfred Klahr-Gesellschaft*.

41. Manfried Rauchensteiner, *Der Tod des Doppeladlers: Österreich-Ungarn und der Erster Weltkrieg* (Graz: Styria 1994), 177-181. Later also in his updated version of this book, see Rauchensteiner, *Der Erste Weltkrieg und das Ende der Habsburgermonarchie*, 271-279.

42. Anton Holzer, *Das Lächeln der Henker: Der unbekannte Krieg gegen die Zivilbevölkerung 1914-1918* (Darmstadt: Primus Verlag, 2008); Leidinger, "Der Einzug des Galgens und des Mordes"; Hoffmann/Goll/Lesiak, *Thalerhof 1914-1936*.

43. Matthew Stibbe, "Krieg und Brutalisierung: Die Internierung von Zivilisten bzw. 'politisch Unzuverlässigen' in Österreich-Ungarn während des Ersten Weltkrieges," in Alfred Eisfeld/Guido Hausmann/Dietmar Neutatz, eds., *Besetzt, interniert, deportiert: Der Erste Weltkrieg und die deutsche, jüdische, polnische und ukrainische Zivilbevölkerung im östlichen Europa* (Essen: Klartext Verlag, 2013): 87-106.

However, historical investigations into the responsibility of particular individuals have yet to discover a "smoking gun." So far, there is no evidence of Conrad von Hötzendorf actually committing a criminal act by directly ordering the execution of any Ruthenian peasant merely on suspicion.[44] In point of fact, there was a whole set of orders, regulations, and a certain culture of dealing with civilians within the army, which allowed them to take stern action against suspects. Rather, in this case, we have to assign responsibility to a wide range of people and a vast number of individual decisions. It is becoming more and more apparent that this case is not about presenting legal evidence but rather about investigating a *historical mentality*.[45]

International law on the treatment of civilians in the event of war is of little help here. Since crimes against ethnic minorities in the monarchy concern Austro-Hungarian subjects on imperial territory, Section III on the "Use of Military Force in an Enemy Occupied Country" of the Hague Convention respecting the Laws and Customs of War on Land of 1907 does not apply here.[46] Neither is the Geneva Convention the proper legal framework here. The 1906 version was valid at the outbreak of the war, but it only regulated the care of the wounded and sick as well as the work of medical and emergency services.[47]

Therefore, we have to draw on Austro-Hungarian laws. After the civil administrations in Galicia, Bucovina as well as in many other parts of the monarchy were dissolved on July 31, 1914, the highest commanding officer on site was responsible for "protecting the military interests" in these territories. This procedure was governed by the state of emergency regulations of 1912 (*"Dienstbuch J-25a"*). These regulations were one of the main milestones on the way to the totalization of war within the Habsburg

---

44. For this purpose, a search was done of the operational files of the Army High Command, as well of its *Evidenzbüro* (Office for Reconnaissance) from August to December 1914. An examination of the troop files might provide additional information.

45. On the definition of the term historical mentality, see that of Peter Dinzelbacher, "A historical mentality is the complex of the ways and contents of thinking and feeling that is characteristic of a particular collective at a particular time. The mentality is revealed through deeds," Peter Dinzelbacher, Eds., *Europäische Mentalitätsgeschichte: Hauptthemen in Einzeldarstellungen* (Stuttgart: Alfred Kröner Verlag, 2008), XXIV.

46. Completely different was the situation in occupied Serbian territory, see for this: Daniel Marc Segesser, "Kriegsverbrechen? Die österreichisch-ungarischen Operationen des August 1914 in Serbien in Wahrnehmung und Vergleich," in Wolfram Dornik/Julia Walleczek-Fritz/Stefan Wedrac, Eds., *Frontwechsel: Österreich-Ungarns "Großer Krieg" im Vergleich* (Vienna: Böhlau Verlag 2014), 213-234.

47. For the text of the Geneva Convention, see the official Swiss translation "Abkommen betreffend die Gesetze und Gebräuche des Landkriegs von 1907," in *Systematische Rechtssammlung*, 14 January 2014 <http://www.admin.ch/opc/de/classified-compilation/19070034/> (16 January 2014).

70   Dornik: Conrad von Hötzendorf and the "Smoking Gun":
A Biographical Examination of Responsibility and Traditions of Violence against Civilians in
the Habsburg Army

monarchy, long before the war broke out. Thus, according to the Military Code of Criminal Procedure of 1912, the army commanders could also fall back on the Military Criminal Code of 1855 for civilians. In accordance with the *Kriegsnotwehr*, short work was made of trials, and there were no provisions for detailed evidence or appeals.[48] More than a half-century old, this rule of law was characterized by the "excessive threat of the death penalty," which was implemented accordingly in autumn 1914.[49]

During the war, the main cornerstone of supervision within Cisleithania (Hungary was outside its sphere of activity) was the *Kriegsüberwachungsamt*, which was regulated within the *Dienstbuch J-25a*. It was established by an imperial decree and was beyond any parliamentary control. Its main task was to supervise and perform the regulations for the state of emergency. It started its work on July 25, 1914. The *Kriegsüberwachungsamt* supervised all censorship measures, political surveillance (which included the arrest and internment of suspicious persons), and control of the restricted wartime economy by the different civil and military departments of the Habsburg monarchy.[50] This included camps like the previously mentioned Thalerhof. On September 2, only five weeks after it was established, the *Kriegsüberwachungsamt* designated Thalerhof as an internment camp.[51] In this camp, at least 1,700 people died in the first months of its existence because of the life-threatening public health conditions and mismanagement.[52]

This was also recognized as a mistake at the time. Archduke Friedrich, the unknown and yet official Supreme Commander of the Austro-Hungarian troops between August 1914 and December 1916, had already given an order in November 1914 at the request of the Emperor after the intervention of the Hungarian Prime Minister Tisza. The order urged more differentiation in the treatment of the "Ruthenians," because otherwise there was the danger of alienating otherwise loyal groups. In January and June 1915, shortly after the reconquest of Galicia had begun, the Supreme Commander issued another order in which he explained the "political

---

48. Tamara Scheer, *Die Ringstraßenfront: Österreich-Ungarn, das Kriegsüberwachungsamt und der Ausnahmezustand während des Ersten Weltkrieges* (Vienna: Heeresgeschichtliches Museum, 2010), 137-140; Überegger, *Der andere Krieg*, 73-82. The regulations were set together within the top secret *Dienstbuch J-25a: Orientierungsbehelf über Ausnahmsverfügungen für den Kriegsfall für die im Reichsrate vertretenen Königreiche und Länder* (Vienna, 1912).
49. Hautmann, "*Todesurteile in der Endphase der Habsburgermonarchie,*" 15-38.
50. *Orientierungsbehelf über Ausnahmsverfügungen*, 3-13.
51. I would like to thank Mag. Nicole-Melanie Goll for her help in finding the following document: [no title], 2 September 1914, Nr. 2366, Österreichisches Staatsarchiv/Kriegsarchiv, Kriegsministerium/Kriegsüberwachungsamt. See for an overview on internment in Austria-Hungary: Stibbe, "*Krieg und Brutalisierung.*"
52. Hoffmann/Goll/Lesiak, *Thalerhof 1914-1936*, 95-124; Stibbe, "Krieg und Brutalisierung," 94-100.

orientation of the Ruthenian population" to the soldiers and called upon them to exercise moderation.[53]

After the war, the deposed Emperor Karl, who was living in exile, also criticized the actions of 1914 in his memoirs. The political crackdown on the suspected "pro-Serbian" or "pro-Russian" people at the beginning of the war and in the months that followed was attributed to the Army High Command and Conrad von Hötzendorf, who wanted to rule with a "mighty German hand." Many convictions and summary executions were conducted on the basis of false or very thin evidence. According to Karl, Franz Josef had also criticized this time and again.[54] During his term of office, the young Emperor reversed some of these measures. The Thalerhof camp was closed in May 1917 and turned into a prisoner of war camp. Moreover, he received both much praise as well as much contempt for an amnesty for political prisoners in spring 1917.[55]

"Crime and Punishment" – "Duty and Necessity"

Along the lines of Fyodor Dostoyevsky's famous title *Crime and Punishment*, the pair "duty and necessity" could be used to describe the discourse metaphors Conrad employed to reflect on his deeds. An important factor for understanding his approach is Conrad von Hötzendorf's personal biography. Where did he gain his military experience? He acquired it exclusively in "irregular" conflicts, in which the boundaries between regular military units and the civilian population blur: 1878/79 in Bosnia-Hercegovina, 1881/82 in Southern Dalmatia, and 1902 in Trieste. From the perspective of hindsight, he bluntly defended the attacks on civilians in Bosnia-Hercegovina. From his point of view, the population took advantage of how "kind-hearted our men were until they were driven to ruthlessness by the bestiality of the enemy."[56] In his eyes, only necessity could explain the ruthless crackdown of his men.

In addition, we need to consider a structural factor. In the late phase of the Habsburg monarchy, the Austro-Hungarian officer corps was defined by its role during the suppression of the Revolution of 1848. It was the army that ultimately saved the Habsburg Crown from the revolting workers, peasants,

---

53. Instruktionen zur politischen Orientierung über die Ruthenische Bevölkerung, Juni 1915, Nr. 5271, Kt. 903, Österreichisches Staatsarchiv/Haus-, Hof- und Staatsarchiv, Ministerium des Äußern/Politische Abteilung I/Krieg 8b/Ukraine August-Dezember 1918.
54. Erich Feigl, Eds., *Kaiser Karl: Persönliche Aufzeichnungen, Zeugnisse und Dokumente* (Vienna: Amalthea, 1984), 207.
55. Francis Roy Bridge, *The Habsburg Monarchy among the Great Powers 1815-1918* (New York: Berg, 1990), 359.
56. Conrad, *Mein Anfang*, 16.

72   Dornik: Conrad von Hötzendorf and the "Smoking Gun":
A Biographical Examination of Responsibility and Traditions of Violence against Civilians in
the Habsburg Army

and the rebellious bourgeoisie. Therefore, people like Conrad were skeptical or hostile of national, liberal, and democratic popular tendencies.[57] This was impressively demonstrated time and again in the *Danzer's Armeezeitung*, for instance, after the bloody days in Trieste in February 1902.[58]

This effect was further reinforced by the top leaders of the army being recruited from their own ranks. Since the 1880s, the aristocracy had been systematically replaced in high offices by an elite group of civil servants and officers, who served the Emperor over the course of several generations. Although most of them had roots extending throughout the monarchy, the big majority of them were German-speaking and Catholic, and over the course of generations had formed a homogeneous group whose social mobility was strictly regulated (marriage bond, limited pay, willingness to relocate, education etc.).[59] Given such blinkered views in the armed services, it is not surprising that during the fall of 1914, after the disastrous initial defeats became apparent, the search for guilty parties began. The Army was looking for scapegoats among "suspicious" minority nationalities, especially those, who were struggling for more rights and acceptance: Ruthenians/ Ukrainians, Serbs, Slovenians, Italians, or Romanians.

Of course, the laws were enacted by the Imperial Council or by imperial decree and expedited or approved by the relevant executive powers: the Chairman of the Council of Ministers, the Royal and Imperial War Ministry as well as the Emperor. While Conrad von Hötzendorf is not to be held accountable for each individual case, he still had upheld and fostered such a propensity for violence vis-à-vis the monarchy's citizens. In the case of crisis, his commanding officers saw no alternative other than the use of force. They had already gotten "practice" in shooting at their "fellow" citizens in the decades leading up to 1914.

Ultimately, however, Conrad von Hötzendorf clearly has to be held personally accountable. Since 1906—except for a short hiatus between November 1911 and December 1912, when he held the still influential post of army inspector—Conrad had served as the chief of the General Staff and had shaped the spirit and organization of the army. He was also involved in the legislative process as part of the consultation process on new laws. That the 1912 state of emergency regulations were adopted during the interregnum does not change the fact that Conrad had already made important provisions for the formulation of these in the years before. Moreover, he cannot claim ignorance because he had himself briefed on the

---

57. Gumz, *The Resurrection and Collapse of Empire in Habsburg Serbia*, 8-16.
58. *Danzer's Armee-Zeitung*, 20 February, 1902, 9.
59. Günter Kronenbitter, *"Krieg im Frieden": Die Führung der k.u.k. Armee und die Großmachtpolitik Österreich-Ungarns 1906-1914* (Munich: Oldenbourg, 2003), 17-28.

current situation by his staff shortly after his second appointment to chief of the General Staff in December 1912.[60]

In addition, he had already filled numerous key positions within the General Staff or within the *Kriegsüberwachungsamt* with trusted officers. These carried out their office in his spirit. As an instructor at the Military Academy between 1888 and 1892, he influenced two classes of future General Staff officers.[61] Throughout the course of his career, he always supported them and put them in appropriate posts to further their advancement in the military. The majority of posts within the *Kriegsüberwachungsamt* were to be filled by the chief of the general staff himself, or after consultation with him.

It comes as no surprise, then, that nearly a year after the riots in Galicia in August 1915 he stressed that the "Russophilism of the Ruthenians and Czechs [...] must be fought with all available means" and therefore the harsh measures had to be justified. Ronge also emphasized this in his autobiography using similar words: "Our harsh intervention and the many internments of suspicious Russophiles proved to be completely justified."[62] Although, since the beginning of the year, the throne and the army high command, Count Friedrich, had been trying to deescalate the situation and demanded more moderate behavior from their soldiers.

And yet how did Conrad von Hötzendorf attempt to defend these actions when, from a strictly strategic perspective, it was useless if not counterproductive to displace thousands as refugees, to execute them, or put them in internment camps without any legal basis? As the son of an officer who had been wounded in 1848, he found his basic purpose in life in upholding the duties of his office and those to the throne. This did not involve unquestioning obedience, which is what cost him his post twice. Conrad's combination of education, experience, and social environment— his social Darwinist, anti-liberal, and anti-democratic mindset—resulted in a dangerous propensity to violence against anyone or anything that seemed to undermine the order of the state. He mainly regarded the South Slavic, Italian, Romanian, Czech, and Polish nationalist movements as well as that of Georg Heinrich von Schönerer's radical German Nationalists as a threat to the multiethnic state. Conrad acted from the perspective of a clear racial hierarchy. While he considered the South and West Slavs as young, aspiring nationalities, which could be led to great heights under the

---

60. See the correspondence in Ausnahmsverfügungen für den Kriegsfall, Kt. 885, Österreichisches Staatsarchiv/Kriegsarchiv, Allerhöchste Oberbefehle/Generalstab/Etappenbüro.
61. Sondhaus, *Franz Conrad von Hötzendorf*, 39-58.
62. Quoted in Leidinger, "*Der Einzug des Galgens und des Mordes*," 253.

74   Dornik: Conrad von Hötzendorf and the "Smoking Gun":
A Biographical Examination of Responsibility and Traditions of Violence against Civilians in
the Habsburg Army

German-speaking ruling elite of the Habsburg monarchy, he saw the East Slavs or Asians only as "simpleminded" and "wild animals." For a soldier socialized in *Kakania* in this way, there was no contradiction between sophisticatedly speaking several languages of the monarchy and admiring its different cultures, while at the same time taking ruthless action against the various nationalist movements.[63]

He raised the notion of "doing his duty" to an ideology. This played a key role in his autobiographical defense strategy. Even without orders from above, he could thus argue that in the situation it was necessary to act in the way he did. So in the end, Conrad used this discursive strategy to suspend self-criticism and external critiques of his actions and to avoid giving a full explanation for them.

---

63. Peball, Eds., *Conrad von Hötzendorf*, 147. For a more detailed analysis of his anti-Slavism, racism and social Darwinism, see Dornik, *Des Kaisers Falke*, 188-192.

Count Leopold Berchtold in uniform, 203.808-D, Photo Atelier d'Ora,
Austrian National Library - Picture Archives and Graphics Department, Vienna

Amnesia and Remembrance – Count Berchtold on 1914

Günther Kronenbitter

The day of the anniversary of Archduke Franz Ferdinand's assassination didn't start badly. "Slept well" began the entry of 28 June 1919 in the diary of Count Leopold Berchtold von und zu Ungarschitz, Frättling und Püllütz. But in the evening, Austria-Hungary's former minister of foreign affairs got a phone call telling him that the peace treaty of Versailles had been signed on this very day. With indignation, Berchtold penned down: "At the fifth Anniversary of the bloody deed of Sarajevo!"[1] Article 231 of the Treaty of Versailles stipulated that the war had been "imposed upon" the Allied Powers "by the aggression of Germany and her allies." The Treaty of Saint-Germain-en-Laye of 10 September 1919 included the so-called War Guilt Clause in Article 177: "The Allied and Associated Governments affirm and Austria accepts the responsibility of Austria and her Allies for causing the loss and damage to which the Allied and Associated Governments and their nationals have been subjected as a consequence of the war imposed upon them by the aggression of Austria-Hungary and her Allies." As one of the key figures in the drama that had unfolded in July 1914, Berchtold would never waver in his conviction that neither Austria-Hungary nor Germany had to carry the wages of guilt for Armageddon—and therefore, reflecting on the outbreak of the Great War wouldn't cost him his sleep. Nevertheless, Berchtold, as a witness to the decision-making in July 1914, tried to analyze the developments that finally led to war and to give his account of what had happened on his watch.[2]

With regard to the "long debate"[3] about the origins of World War I, Berchtold's role as a public commentator on questions related to the

1. Berchtold, diary entry of 28 June 1919, diary no. 11, Berchtold Papers, box no. 11, ÖStA HHStA.
2. For Berchtold's role in 1914, see Samuel R. Williamson, Jr., "Leopold Count Berchtold: The Man Who Could Have Prevented the Great War," in *Contemporary Austrian Studies* 19 (2010): 24-51.
3. John W. Langdon, *July 1914: The Long Debate, 1918-1990* (Providence Oxford: Berg Publishers, 1991).

outbreak of war in 1914 was a rather negligible one. Every once in while he gave an interview, but he never contributed to the heated discussion of War Guilt with a substantial publication during his lifetime. While his successors Stephan Burián von Rajecz and Count Ottokar Czernin von und zu Chudenitz published their memoirs and Franz Conrad von Hötzendorf produced a hybrid between a major collection of sources and some memoir-like retrospection by the mid-1920s, Berchtold never got that far. This was not because of a lack of trying. From 1919 until his death in 1942, Berchtold worked on a book about his view of international relations and the Habsburg Monarchy's foreign policy on the eve of the Great War. The twists and turns of his efforts offer a glimpse on the difficult business of vindication by remembrance.

Among the first steps to claim Austria-Hungary's rightful stance in the July Crisis was the official publication of the diplomatic documents in 1915.[4] In the first months after his demission in January 1915, Berchtold was quite certainly more interested in clearing his name with regard to the ill-fated attempts to keep Italy out of the war than in defending his overall record in managing the July Crisis. The negotiations with Italy would be a sensitive topic for Berchtold until the late 1920s.[5] In early 1915, Janós Forgách de Ghymes et Gács, Second Section Chief at the *Ballhausplatz*, alerted his friend and former boss to the fact that Kajetán Mérey de Kapos-Mére, the former ambassador to Italy, might include documents concerning Article VII of the Triple Alliance treaty in the official publication that would make Berchtold's Italian policy look inconsistent.[6] Rather belatedly, Berchtold asked for and got access to the text of Austria-Hungary's *Rotbuch* or Redbook. On his request, Mérey sent him the proofs and Berchtold's objections were considered.[7]

In his new position as Lord Chamberlain to Emperor Charles in 1917 and 1918, Berchtold was still close to the epicenter of power in the Habsburg Monarchy but couldn't and wouldn't wield much influence. At least in one case, Berchtold nevertheless saw himself dragged into the politics of memory. In February 1918, foreign minister Czernin asked Berchtold to give his approval for a publication of his letter to István Tisza from July 1914, the Hungarian Prime Minister at the time. As Mérey told him, Czernin's request had to be understood against the backdrop of the

4. For the official Color Books, see: Sacha Zala, *Geschichte unter der Schere politischer Zensur. Amtliche Aktensammlungen im internationalen Vergleich* (Munich: Oldenbourg Verlag, 2001).
5. Hugo Hantsch, *Leopold Graf Berchtold: Grandseigneur und Staatsmann*, 2 vols. (Graz Vienna Cologne: Verlag Styria, 1963), vol. 2, 729.
6. Ibid., vol. 2, 746.
7. Berchtold, diary entry of 29 June 1915, diary no. 9, Berchtold Papers, box no. 11, ÖStA HHStA.

German debate about the relationship between Berlin and Vienna in the July Crisis. Prince Max Karl Lichnowsky, Germany's former ambassador to the court of St. James, had harshly criticized the German role in the outbreak of war since 1914 and in early 1918 his memoirs of his time as ambassador circulated in the political elites of Germany. Since Lichnowsky had accused the German leadership of having sacrificed vital interests by waging a Great Power war in order to prop up the sick man on the Danube, Czernin was obviously looking for documents to counter the narrative of Germany doing the Habsburg Monarchy's bidding in the July Crisis. Berchtold's letter to Tisza was meant to bring home the point that Berlin had pushed Vienna to act forcefully in the wake of Sarajevo.[8] Mérey was aghast at Czernin's request when Berchtold told him about it. According to Mérey, the German ambassador to Vienna had indicated that in his eyes, Austria-Hungary had actually dragged Germany into the war. It would be wise not to react to these insinuations by publishing anything on this issue. Austria-Hungary's prestige could only suffer, because, as Mérey said, using a slightly idiosyncratic metaphor, "we either look like bunnies [*Karnickel*] that have to bear the responsibility for the World War or like blind tools of German imperialism." Berchtold agreed and summed up his assessment of what had happened in 1914: "In line with our interests, we had considered the situation as leading to the destruction of the Monarchy unless we raised our shield. And Germany had supported us in this and assured us of her unconditional backing. That was how the roles were assigned."[9]

Whereas questions of War Guilt were of minor importance to Berchtold during the war, defeat in 1918 and finally the stipulations of the Paris peace treaties of 1919 gave them much more urgency and relevance. Among the most pressing problems Berchtold had to tackle as he began to pin down his version of the July Crisis was a lack of reliable information. In November 1918, Emperor Charles' Lord Chamberlain left Vienna for Switzerland, a safe distance from the tumultuous Habsburg Monarchy that had disintegrated almost overnight. It so happened that in particular Berne and its surroundings were also the refuge of other members of the late empire's elite. Berchtold would be able to get in touch with some of his former staff and build on a network of friends, relatives, and

---

8. Berchtold, diary entry of 20 February 1918, diary no. 14, Berchtold Papers, box no. 12, ÖStA HHStA. Probably, the document referred to in this paragraph, was published in 1930: Berchtold to Tisza, 8 July 1914, in *Österreich-Ungarns Außenpolitik von der Bosnischen Krise 1908 bis zum Kriegsausbruch 1914*, ed. Ludwig Bittner and Hans Uebersberger, 9 vols. (Vienna: Österreichischer Bundesverlag, 1930): vol. 8, no. 10.145.
9. Berchtold, diary entry of 21 February 1918, diary no. 14, Berchtold Papers, box no. 12, ÖStA HHStA.

acquaintances.[10] In his diaries of 1919 and 1920, social life in the circle of Austro-Hungarian and—to a lesser degree—German expats plays a prominent role.[11] Berchtold was a perfect example of aristocratic dominance in Austro-Hungarian diplomacy—wealthy, well-connected, certainly not dependant on a diplomatic career as a tool to climb the greasy pole of social status.[12] Berchtold's wife Ferdinandine (or Nandine) came from the highest echelons of Hungarian aristocracy. Her mother was an Erdödy; her father, Count Alois Karolyi, had been the Habsburg Monarchy's ambassador to Berlin and London.[13] Although the turmoil of revolution and the breakup of the Habsburg Monarchy cast a shadow over his privileged way of life, Berchtold would still be able to claim solidarity and respect among his peers and deference from his former staff. As he began to work on his own version of events in 1914, Berchtold became involved in a network of like-minded former diplomats and Ballhausplatz staff that provided him with valuable information on the past. In quite a few cases, Berchtold was also asked to give his permission for publishing accounts of his foreign policy.

Alexander Musulin von Gomirje, ambassador to Berne in 1918, but a relatively junior member of the foreign office's staff in 1914, was one of Berchtold's hosts in Switzerland and a major correspondent. Very soon after the Habsburg Monarchy's collapse, Musulin, who stayed in Switzerland until 1921, began to work on his memoirs that would finally be published in 1924.[14] In fall 1919, Musulin was already busy with his project and sent the text to his former boss, in order to make sure that it would capture Berchtold's view of the South Slav Question as a domestic problem and the foreign minister's motive for Musulin's mission to Zagreb in June 1913 correctly. He also wanted to get feedback on the background and scale of the deteriorating relations with Romania. It took some weeks and a few more letters to get all the information in question. A few months later, it was Musulin's turn to help and to send Leopold Mandl's publications on Serbia to Berchtold.[15]

Although Musulin was particularly close to Berchtold in early 1919, others would also collaborate with the former foreign minister over the

10. Hantsch, *Leopold Graf Berchtold*, vol. 2, 835-38.

11. Berchtold, diaries of 1919 and 1920, diaries no. 16 and 17, Berchtold Papers, box no. 12, ÖStA HHStA.

12. William D. Godsey, Jr., *Aristocratic Redoubt: The Austro-Hungarian Foreign Office on the Eve of the First World War* (West Lafayette, Indiana: Purdue University Press, 1999).

13. Memoirs of Ferdinandine Berchtold (manuscript) 1951, Berchtold Papers, box no. 13, ÖStA HHStA.

14. Alexander von Musulin, *Das Haus am Ballplatz: Erinnerungen eines österreichisch-ungarischen Diplomaten* (Munich: Verlag für Kulturpolitik, 1924).

15. According to Musulin to Berchtold, 3 September 1919, 21 September 1919, 7 October 1919, 4 November 1919, 12 February 1920, Berchtold Papers, box no. 15, ÖStA HHStA.

course of more than two decades. For his book on Franz Ferdinand, Leopold von Chlumecky, who used to be a member of the archduke's circle, assured Berchtold that he wouldn't publish anything on Berchtold's foreign policy without his approval.[16] Count Otto Czernin, the former envoy to Sofia, helped Berchtold to reconstruct his last pre-war visit to the Romanian king's residence at Sinaia.[17] Count Constantin Dumba hoped to get a chance to talk to Count Berchtold because he was afraid that his book on pre-war Alliance policy might have angered him.[18] He also stressed that he thought that Berchtold's memoirs should be published as they shed new light on the Serbian Question.[19] Karl Freiherr von Macchio, Balkan expert and First Section Chief at the *Ballhausplatz* in 1914, would supply his former boss with information on Habsburg foreign policy as late as 1941.[20] Just a couple of months before Berchtold passed away in 1942, Emanuel Urbas, another former *Ballhausplatz* staff member, provided Berchtold with a newspaper clip on his erstwhile predecessor Alois Lexa von Aehrenthal.[21] Urbas expected the almost octogenarian Berchtold to be interested in such matters and with good reason: the former minister had been working on his memoirs for many years and had always relied on his personal network to get access to information and to communicate his own assessment of historical events he had witnessed and shaped.

Probably his closest collaborator in summer 1914 also played a prominent role in Berchtold's early attempts to get a clear picture of the July Crisis. Just a few months after the Habsburg Monarchy's collapse, Berchtold resumed contact with Count Alexander (or Alek) Hoyos, his former chef de cabinet who had moved to Gut Enckendorff in Holstein after the war but had come to Switzerland in spring 1919. Hoyos had suffered from bouts of boasting and of feeling guilty because of his role in the July Crisis during the war. In spring 1919, Hoyos wrote Berchtold that "I'm living in the past very much and with memories of happier days, but I'm telling you that the disaster that has destroyed our poor Austria had been unavoidable and that

16. Chlumecky to Berchtold, 7 April 1929, 4 May 1929, Berchtold Papers, box no. 4, ÖStA HHStA.
17. Otto Czernin to Berchtold, 9 December 1931, Berchtold Papers, box no. 14, ÖStA HHStA.
18. Constantin Dumba, *Dreibund- und Ententepolitik in der Alten und Neuen Welt* (Leipzig: Amalthea Verlag, 1931).
19. Dumba to Nandine Berchtold, 23 June 1936, Berchtold Papers, box no. 14, ÖStA HHStA.
20. Macchio to Berchtold, 18 December 1941, Berchtold Papers, box no. 14.
21. Urbas to Berchtold, [ca. 17 December 1942], Berchtold Papers, box no. 14, ÖStA HHStA. Urbas would publish his own memoirs under a pseudonym after World War II: Ernest U. Cormons, *Schicksale und Schatten. Eine österreichische Biographie* (Salzburg: Otto Müller Verlag, 1951).

Count Alexander Hoyos, ca. 1914, NB 518.641-B, Foto Berliner Illustrationsgesellschaft,
Austrian National Library - Picture Archives and Graphics Department, Vienna

you can be sure at least that you have wanted and done the right thing."
Had it not been for the unwise policy of Charles, in particular the sacking
of Tisza, collapse even might have been avoided.[22] They met in Switzerland
briefly before Hoyos had to go back to Holstein. From there, Hoyos went
to his castle Schwertberg in Austria without a further visit to Berchtold in
Switzerland.

Obviously, both men were not just eager to talk and correspond about
the past. Both also seemed to have contemplated writing down their
views of 1914 by then. In a letter from Holstein in June 1919, Hoyos
told Berchtold how much of a consolation it had been to talk to him. He
added that Berchtold needn't worry about accusations in the vein of Count
Heinrich von Lützow zu Drey-Lützow und Seedorf who had been Mérey's

---

22. Hoyos to Berchtold, 29 April 1919, Berchtold Papers, box no. 15, ÖStA HHStA.

predecessor as ambassador to Italy and who had become an outspoken critic of Austro-Hungarian foreign policy. Lützow was wrong to assume that Austria-Hungary's relations with Serbia had been crucial: "Whether the war might have been avoided or not is an open question but our actions with regard to Serbia played a minor role in this."[23] Berchtold had already had a controversy with Lützow in 1917 about his Serbian policy.[24] Lützow had incurred not just Berchtold's wrath but was also unpopular with a number of his former colleagues.[25] In 1919, Berchtold felt provoked by Lützow's statements and wrote him a long letter in which he defended his stance in the July Crisis. "We were convinced that the clash could hardly be avoided but that it was absolutely clear to see it coming under the uttermost unfavorable circumstances if we had shown weakness vis-à-vis Serbia once more . . . ." Compared to Frederick the Great's approach in 1756, "our course of action against Serbia was quite considerate."[26]

Whereas Lützow was an intellectual sparring partner and inadvertently became the Berchtold's touchstone for his early reflections on the July Crisis, Hoyos was a trusted ally and help. In some way, both men not only shared a sense of allegiance to the Habsburg Monarchy, but in 1919 they found themselves in a similar situation as they tried to find a solid basis for their recollections. In the first place, both of them were deprived of access to official source material. Hoyos confided to Berchtold that "for me it is difficult to write anything, I don't have any documents here, I have never written notes."[27] Nevertheless, Berchtold tried to gain as much information as possible from Hoyos and sent him a questionnaire that Hoyos found quite difficult to answer.[28] Their exercise in Q & A offers a unique opportunity to gauge the blind spots in Berchtold's memory of the July Crisis.[29] Just five years after the events, he had to ask Hoyos, among other things: "For how long (from which day until according to my memory of July 6) had you been in Berlin? Whom did you talk to? B[ethmann] H[ollweg], J[agow] or Z[immermann]? Had you written a memorandum back then?" Hoyos, who hadn't started writing his account of the mission yet, answered that he didn't have "notes on my journey. The date was 5 and 6 July. On the first day I went

---

23. Hoyos to Berchtold, 20 June 1919, Berchtold Papers, box no. 15, ÖStA HHStA.
24. Hantsch, *Leopold Graf Berchtold*, vol. 2, 802.
25. See Musulin's remarks about Lützow, in Berchtold, diary entry of 26 January 1920, Berchtold diary no. 17, Berchtold papers, box no. 12, ÖStA HHStA.
26. Berchtold to Lützow (copy), 14 May 1919, Berchtold Papers, box no. 15. The differences didn't necessarily lead to personal estrangement. For a conversation about an article published by Lützow that took a conciliatory turn, see Berchtold, diary entry of 18 March 1920, diary no. 17, Berchtold Papers, box. no. 12.
27. Hoyos to Berchtold, 20 June 1919, Berchtold Papers, box no. 15, ÖStA HHStA.
28. Hoyos to Berchtold, 28 June 1919, Berchtold Papers, box no. 15, ÖStA HHStA.
29. Berchtold to Hoyos, 24 June 1919, Berchtold Papers, box no. 15, ÖStA HHStA.

with [Franz Freiherr von] Haymerle to Z. On the second day I was present when B.H. gave our ambassador the answer. J. and Z. were present also."

With regard to Berchtold's second question on "what was the misunderstanding that led to the break in our conversations with Petersburg back then (last days of July)," Hoyos wrote back that he "can't recall precisely. I think that [Count Friedrich] Szápáry [von Szápár, ambassador to St. Petersburg in 1914] had gone too far in his conversation with [Russian foreign minister Sergei Dmitrievich] Sazonov and was reined in but then he got order to talk to the Russians about the wording of our ultimatum, too. According to my knowledge, the conversation was stopped by the Russian mobilization." On Berchtold's third question about the differences "between the two British proposals (I think of 26 and 30 July)," Hoyos couldn't say much either. He advised Berchtold to get hold of a copy of the *Rotbuch*. Off the cuff, all he would be able to say was that "the British had proposed a conference of ambassadors first and then withdrew the proposal when they learned about our direct talks with Petersburg. But I think that I remember that we received a 2nd British proposal according to which we would occupy Belgrade and would stop then in order to negotiate. And here further deliberations were blocked by the Russian mobilization."

There is no reason to assume that this blatant lack of a clear memory, so striking in particular on Berchtold's side, was a deception or at least a delusion. Historians have scrutinized even the less important events of the July Crisis in detail but they have always enjoyed one advantage over the decision-makers of 1914: time. Neither Berchtold nor Hoyos had such luxury in July 1914 and they, just as all the key figures in the cabinets of the Great Powers, had to struggle with a deluge of information delivered by telegraph and digested by rather small ministerial bureaucracies. As long as they couldn't connect their faded memories of this or that detail in the unfolding crisis to existing narratives—or at least the unspoken agenda of selected archival sources—they had a hard time figuring out the exact chronology and relevance of their own crisis management in retrospect.

The search for sources became a fixture of Berchtold's work on his memoirs. To collect information from correspondents and to gather quotations and facts from published sources was an important part of the project. His old diaries provided him with a basic chronology and usually with some brief hints at this daily routine but offered little in terms of political topics. To make up for this lack of detail, Berchtold included the new information he had garnered in the diary entries. By the mid-1920s, Berchtold had at least finished a first chapter of his memoirs, but he was shying away from a publication because he didn't have all the relevant sources that were deemed necessary by him.[30] At his palace in Peresznye near Sopron (Ödenburg), Berchtold wrote an introduction to his opus, dated August 6, 1926. In answer to the rhetorical question of why he had waited for so long to come up with his own version of events, Berchtold pointed out that he had been too depressed in the wake of defeat to tell the true story. He also hadn't had any trust in a fair assessment of his arguments in the first post-war years, not to mention the lack of sources in his time in exile. Now, with a more reflective and calmer attitude, the time had come to join other Great Power statesmen of 1914 and tell the story of the July Crisis from the Austro-Hungarian perspective.[31]

At least, that's what Berchtold wrote in the manuscript. But when he was encouraged to take on his critics by publishing a book without waiting for ever more archival sources to become available, he couldn't bring himself to do it and changed tack. Victor Wallace Germains, a British writer on military and foreign affairs who would also author a book on Austria just a few years later, tried to persuade Berchtold to publish his own version of events on the Anglophone book market in fall 1926.[32] Germains implored Berchtold: "If you don't write your book *now* you will never write it because we shall all be in our graves before you ever have a chance of going through the archives in *propria persona*. After all, there is no one who can explain or defend your policy as you yourself, whilst the world is looking forward to hearing what you have to say. On the whole you may count on a certain sense of chivalry. In England at all events, nobody wants to kick you while you are down."[33] All this nudging of Berchtold to write a cohesive book based on his personal memories and his assessment of the events would be to no avail.

Nevertheless, Berchtold entered the public debate in Britain with an article for the *Contemporary Review* whose editor was no less a figure than George Peabody Gooch in 1928.[34] It was an extended review of Sazonov's assessment of Austro-Hungarian policy in the former Russian minister's

30. Berchtold, Memoires 23 March 1908-17 January 1913, Berchtold Papers, box no. 13, ÖStA HHStA.

31. Ibid.

32. Germains to Berchtold, 6 September 1926, 10 September 1926, 22 September 1926, ibid. For Germains' publication on Austria, see: Victor Wallace Germains, *Austria of to-day. With a Special Chapter on the Austrian Police* (London: Macmillan 1932). On Franz Ferdinand and Aehrenthal, Germains quoted from Berchtold's memoires without revealing his source: ibid., 13-14.

33. Germains to Berchtold, 6 September 1926, bid. Berchtold Papers, box no. 13, ÖStA HHStA.

34. For George P. Gooch, see: Annika Mombauer, *The Origins of the First World War: Controversies and Consensus* (Harlow: Longman, 2002), 63-64, 96-97.

memoirs, written as a contribution to a book on Sazonov in German.[35] The rather long-winded and circumspect rebuttal focused on Russia's ignorance or even outright rejection of Austria-Hungary's vital security interests in the Balkans. "Sazonoff [sic] pretends—consciously or unconsciously, not to have had the faintest idea of the tragic situation in which the Austro-Hungarian Monarchy found herself: a situation due very largely to the wanton duplicity of Russian diplomacy . . . . The murder of Serajevo [sic] was only one of the final manifestations of the work of destruction which was organised [sic] against us. The parts were well distributed and the time limit was nearly up. This last act was only one of the most obvious of a system to undermine and blow up our home. It was the knowledge of the terrible danger that threatened us which drove us to action, not hatred of Serbia."[36]

Berchtold wasn't just following the official line of War Guilt publications in Germany and Austria to the letter, his argument was also in keeping with his statements made in private.[37] He was consistent in his views and obviously convinced of the profoundly defensive posture of the Habsburg Monarchy in 1914. In 1934 the French newspaper *Le Temps* carried an article on "Les souvenirs du Comte Berchtold." Based on an interview with a Hungarian journal, Berchtold was quoted saying that he denied any particular responsibility for the outbreak of war. The article also mentioned that the former foreign minister was living in Rome with his son Sigmund and working on his memoirs. According to the article, he didn't know whether they were going to be published during his lifetime or whether he would rather leave them to his son and heir. In his memoirs, Berchtold wanted to show that the outbreak of war wasn't so much a result of actions taken by individual decision-makers as the result of long-term developments.[38]

As much as he was sure about the just cause of the Habsburg Monarchy in 1914, Berchtold was anxious to refute any allegations that he might have tricked the Emperor into declaring war on Serbia. In the draft version of the declaration of war that Berchtold had submitted to Franz Joseph, a Serbian attack on Austro-Hungarian soldiers near Temes Kubin (Kovin) had been mentioned. Due to concerns about the reliability of the Temes

---

35. Count Leopold Berchtold, "Russia, Austria and the World War," *Contemporary Review* 133 (1928): 422-432

36. Ibid., 429. For the German version, see *Rings um Sasonow. Neue dokumentarische Darlegungen zum Ausbruch des großen Krieges durch Kronzeugen*, ed. Eduard Ritter von Steinitz (Berlin: Verlag für Kulturpolitik, 1928), 39-55.

37. See Berchtold to Lützow (copy), 14 May 1919, Berchtold Papers, box. no. 15, ÖStA HHStA.

38. "Les souvenirs de comte Berchtold," *Le Temps*, 1 April 1934, 8.

Kubin report, Berchtold decided to omit the incident from the final version. Speculation about his motives hurt Berchtold, who had always been proud of his loyalty to the Habsburgs.[39] In 1936, Berchtold discussed the issue with Macchio, who in turn mentioned it to the Viennese archivist Ludwig Bittner. Macchio passed Bittner's response on to the former foreign minister and with a telling time lag Berchtold learned about a 1932 publication by Adolf Heyrowsky.[40] Heyrowsky was a former career officer and pilot of the Habsburg forces who had settled down in Germany and joined the German *Reichswehr*. As a retired Major, he published a book on the war guilt question. Based on a report by the Greek military attaché to Serbia about the Temes Kubin incident, Heyrowsky came to the conclusion that the Serbs had actually shot Austro-Hungarian soldiers and that Berchtold had acted with good faith when editing the text of the declaration of war and omitting the sentence on the Serbian attacks, because the news about Temes Kubin hadn't been confirmed yet by the military authorities.[41]

Both Heyrowsky and Bittner exemplified the close links between the War Guilt campaign in Vienna and Berlin in the 1930s, but the debate had engulfed Austrian publicists and historians just as German ones right from the beginning. Most who contributed to the avalanche of publications that the politically motivated discussion had triggered tried to shift the burden of responsibility onto the shoulders of the former Entente. Only very few dissenting voices made themselves heard in the young Austrian Republic. Journalist Heinrich Kanner's harsh critique of German and Austro-Hungarian policy before and during the July Crisis was an early and quite impressive example for the minority view on 1914.[42] Most historians sided with the opposite point of view, favored also by the republic's officials. Roderich Gooß made the first major effort to refute the theory of the Central Powers' War Guilt as early as 1919. Others would follow, with some using the government-sponsored periodical *Berliner Monatshefte* as a venue or taking part in the edition of official documents from the files of the foreign ministry on Austria-Hungary's foreign policy, ranging in date from 1908 until the outbreak of the war in 1914. Historian Hans Uebersberger

---

39. For an example of this interpretation of the Temes Kubin question, see Manfried Rauchensteiner, *Der Tod des Doppeladlers. Österreich-Ungarn und der Erste Weltkrieg* (Graz Vienna Cologne: Verlag Styria, 1993), 92-95.

40. Macchio to Berchtold, 19 March 1936, Berchtold Papers, box. no. 14, ÖStA HHStA.

41. Adolf Heyrowsky, *Neue Wege zur Klärung der Kriegsschuld mit einem Vorwort von Dr. Rudolf Günther* (Berlin: Verlag Buchkunst, 1932), 121-26. For Heyrowsky, who resumed his military career after 1933, see: *Ein österreichischer General gegen Hitler: Feldmarschalleutnant Alfred Jansa: Erinnerungen*, ed. Peter Broucek (Vienna Cologne Weimar: Böhlau Verlag, 2011), 535.

42. Heinrich Kanner, *Kaiserliche Katastrophen-Politik: Ein Stück zeitgenössischer Geschichte* (Leipzig Vienna Zurich: E. P. Tal & Co. Verlag, 1922).

and archivist Ludwig Bittner were among those involved and would further their careers and their role in the war guilt debate after 1938.[43]

In World War II, the two played a leading role in an attempt to unearth documents in Serbian archives that would help to prove the Belgrade government's responsibility for the assassination in Sarajevo and Russian authorities' complicity in the plot. Uebersberger, who had made a career in Nazi Germany after 1934, cooperated with Bittner, who had become head of the Viennese branch of the German *Reichsarchiv*, to publish an edition of documents seized in occupied Serbia on behalf of the *Reichsarchiv*.[44] The idea wasn't new—in World War I, a similar endeavor had been tried. What makes Uebersberger's and Bittner's efforts so remarkable was the fact that they worked relentlessly to get the project done even as the Third Reich's strategic situation deteriorated dramatically.[45] They managed to publish at least the first small installment of sources from Serbian archives in 38 pages in Vienna in March 1945—with the Soviet Army almost at the gates.[46] It is among the most telling episodes in the long struggle against the Versailles—and Saint-Germain-en-Laye for that matter—War Guilt Clause. For Bittner, it was probably one of his last accomplishments before he committed suicide on 2 April 1945, while Uebersberger would survive

---

43.   Ulfried Burz, "Die Kriegsschuldfrage in Österreich (1918–1938). Zwischen Selbstverleugnung und Identitätssuche," Brennpunkt Mitteleuropa: Festschrift für Helmut Rumpler zum 65. Geburtstag, ed. Ulfried Burz, Michael Derndarsky, and Werner Drobesch (Klagenfurt: Verlag Carinthia, 2000), 97-115. See also Ulfried Burz, "Austria and the Great War: Official Publications in the 1920s and 1930s," Forging the Collective Memory: Government and International Historians Through Two World Wars, ed. Keith Wilson (Providence Oxford: Berghahn Books, 1996), 178-91 and Ulrich Heinemann, *Die verdrängte Niederlage. Politische Öffentlichkeit und Kriegsschuldfrage in der Weimarer Republik* (Göttingen: Vandenhoeck & Ruprecht, 1983), 89-91. On Bittner's role in the war guilt debate, see Bittner Papers, box no. 10, ÖStA HHStA. Bittner's manuscripts in ibid.
44.   For Bittner's career, see Thomas Just, "Ludwig Bittner (1877–1945): Ein politischer Archivar," *Österreichische Historiker, 1900–1945: Lebensläufe und Karrieren in Österreich, Deutschland und der Tschechoslowakei*, ed. Karel Hruza (Vienna: Böhlau Verlag, 2008), 283-305.
45.   For an inside glimpse on the work of the German *Archivkommission* in charge of the seized archival files from all-over Europe, see Werner Frauendienst to Ludwig Bittner, 16 August 1943, Bittner Papers, box no. 3, ÖStA HHStA.
46.   *Veröffentlichungen des Reichsarchivs Wien. Reihe II: Serbiens Außenpolitik 1908-1918. Diplomatische Akten des serbischen Ministeriums des Äußern in deutscher Übersetzung. III. Band (26. Mai bis 6. August 1914): Erste Lieferung*, ed. Ludwig Bittner, Alois Hajek, and Hans Uebersberger (Vienna: Verlag Adolf Holzhausens Nachfolger, 1945). A copy and proofs in the files of the Würthle Papers, B/964:192, ÖStA KA.

the war's end in Upper Austria.[47] Their last-ditch attempt to prove Serbia and Russia guilty of bringing about the war of 1914 went unnoticed, not just because very few of the booklets survived the turmoil but rather because the sense of urgency that had inspired Bittner, Uebersberger, and many others to fight the War Guilt Clause was gone. The interwar system had become a rather distant memory in a Europe split between Soviet and American spheres of influence. When a French-West German commission of historians decided to defang the potentially poisonous hunt for the chief culprit of 1914, it seemed quite clear that new Cold War realities trumped traditional sensitivities.

To propagate Pan-German positions was no longer acceptable in post-1945 Austria. The urge to stress the specifics of Austrian nationhood, culture, and history didn't necessarily lead to a closer look at 1914. When the Viennese historian Hugo Hantsch gained access to Berchtold's diary and memoirs, the Catholic Conservative was more than willing to take the former foreign minister's assessment of his own record more or less for granted. Hantsch's biography of Berchtold refrained from any severe criticism of his hero's policy. It is remarkable that a historian of Hantsch's professional reputation would content himself with telling the story of the most fateful foreign policy decisions of the early 20th century as seen through the eyes of Berchtold—or rather, as narrated by the former foreign minister.[48] It escaped Hantsch's attention that the main source on which he had based his account of Berchtold's policy was the product of a careful, though arduous and drawn-out, project to vindicate political decisions that led to war in 1914.[49] Berchtold had struggled to reconstruct the chain of events that had culminated in the July Crisis. He used published material just as he used the memories of his former staff to fill the void in his own recollections of the past. Quite likely, Berchtold's poor memory was not a case of conscious denial. To him, his own actions probably were rather reactions to unfortunate circumstances. But amnesia could hardly be squared with an effort to clear one's name of unjustified accusations. To shape the remembrance of things past turned out to be hard work. When Berchtold passed away, it was still an unfinished project. In a way, Hantsch made sure

---

47. For Uebersberger's relentless work on the publication project, see Hans Uebersberger to Ludwig Bittner, 21 March and 26 March 1945, Bittner Papers, box no. 3, docs. no. 524 and 525, ÖStA HHStA. In his letter of 26 March 1945, written in Geinberg, Uebersberger wondered: "Will our work be published—the typesetters at Holzhausen carry on sabotage . . .—will Germany and will we live on or will we unable to last?"

48. Hugo Hantsch, *Leopold Graf Berchtold: Grandseigneur und Staatsmann*, 2 vols. (Graz Vienna Cologne: Verlag Styria, 1963).

49. Hugo Hantsch, "Die Tagebücher und Memoiren des Grafen Leopold Berchtold," *Südostforschungen* 14 (1955): 205-215.

that Berchtold's self-image would be transformed into historiography. The rather benign view of Austro-Hungarian foreign policy conveyed by Hantsch fitted in with a broader trend in some quarters of the Austrian public in the 1960s to focus on the positive aspects of the Habsburg Monarchy. The glory of Franz Joseph's empire thus seemed indispensable to Austrian national identity. But this view of Austria-Hungary wouldn't go unchallenged for long. New sources became available from the inner circle of decision-makers. It seems ironic that it would be Hoyos' account of his mission to Berlin, edited by Fritz Fellner in 1976, that would inaugurate a new wave of scholarly efforts to scrutinize the role of Austria-Hungary in the outbreak of war 1914. But neither Fellner nor any other Austrian historian would focus on Austria-Hungary's role in pre-1914 international relations and the outbreak of war.[50] It would be up to British and American scholars like Francis R. Bridge, John Leslie, Solomon Wank, and in particular Samuel R. Williamson to fill the void.[51]

---

50. For the debates in the 1960s in Austria, see Günther Kronenbitter, "Keeping a Low Profile – Austrian Historiography and the Fischer Controversy," *Journal of Contemporary History* 48, no. 2 (2013): 333-349.

51. For the historiography on Austria-Hungary's role in 1914, see Günther Kronenbitter, "Austria-Hungary's Decision for War in 1914," in a forthcoming volume on 1914, ed. by Andreas Gestrich and Hartmut Pogge von Strandmann. For the author's take on the July Crisis, see Günther Kronenbitter, *"Krieg im Frieden": Die Führung der k.u.k. Armee und die Großmachtpolitik Österreich-Ungarns 1906-1914* (Munich: Oldenbourg Verlag, 2003), 429-530.

Soldiers and Civilians
at War

"Officers of the k.u.k. 28th Infantry regiment during the Carpathian Winter War 1914-1915," Collection Kateřina Bečková

A Train Ride to Disaster:
The Austro-Hungarian Eastern Front in 1914

Richard Lein

For nearly a hundred years, Austrian historians and military experts have been debating whether the devastating defeat the army of the Habsburg Empire suffered in the initial battles in Galicia in summer 1914 should be ascribed to the concurrence of a series of mishaps during the early stages of the operation, or to insufficient planning and preparation by the Austro-Hungarian general staff. Very soon in the course of the debate, two factions began to form. Several former members of the k.u.k. army's general staff, backed by the *Wiener Kriegsarchiv* (whose personnel consisted largely of former k.u.k. officers) and the former chief of staff Franz Conrad von Hötzendorf, claimed that the Austro-Hungarian forces had been well prepared for the imminent conflict with Russia. The main causes of the military setbacks suffered especially on the eastern front during the first months of the war had been the enemy's numerical superiority, the absence of troop reinforcements promised by the German general staff before the war, and the partial unreliability of the k.u.k. army's Slavic soldiers as well as of the civilian population of East Galicia, they asserted.[1] These claims, which were spread by way of some books and officers' memoirs[2] as well as the *Kriegsarchiv*'s official publications,[3] were opposed by an increasing number of former k.u.k. officers, journalists, and historians. In their opinion, the military catastrophe Austria-Hungary had suffered on the Russian front in

---

1. On this matter see above all: Graydon A. Tunstall, "The Habsburg Command Conspiracy. The Austrian Falsification of Historiography on the Outbreak of World War One," *Austrian History Yearbook* 27 (1996), 181-198.
2. Carl Bardolff, *Soldat im alten Österreich. Erinnerungen aus meinem Leben* (Jena: Diederichs, 1938); Franz Conrad von Hötzendorf, *Aus meiner Dienstzeit*, 5 Vols. (Wien: Rikola, 1922–1925); Edmund Glaise-Horstenau, *Die Katastrophe. Die Zertrümmerung Österreich-Ungarns und das Werden der Nachfolgestaaten* (Zürich: Amalthea, 1929); Rudolf Kiszling, *Österreich-Ungarns Anteil am Ersten Weltkrieg* (Graz: Stiasny, 1958); Karl Friedrich Nowak, *Der Weg zur Katastrophe* (Berlin: Reiß, 1919).
3. Österreichisches Bundesministerium für Heerwesen – Kriegsarchiv Wien [=BMHW-KA] Eds., *Österreich-Ungarns letzter Krieg 1914–1918* [=ÖUlK], 7 Vols. (Wien: Verlag der Militärwissenschaftlichen Mitteilungen, 1930–1938).

summer/autumn 1914 had been self-inflicted, caused by inadequate training of the k.u.k. army and insufficient operation planning by the general staff.[4] The heated debate between the two groups continued throughout almost the entire interwar period and was only brought up short by the annexation of Austria by the German Reich in 1938 and the beginning of World War II the following year. After 1945, the topic wasn't revived since coming to terms with the events of World War II monopolized not only the public interest but also most of the resources available to the historical sciences in post-war Austria. Consequently, except for some notable examples,[5] the military history of the Habsburg Monarchy in World War I received only limited attention in Austrian historiography until the end of the twentieth century. Nowadays, in the light of the upcoming commemoration of the beginning of World War I one hundred years ago, public interest in Austria-Hungary's history in the era of the first global conflict has revived, bringing with it a renewal of the debate on the conduct of the k.u.k. army and its commanders, especially in the first months of the war. This paper aims to contribute to the ongoing debate by reevaluating the military operations of the k.u.k. armed forces on the Russian front in summer/autumn 1914, thereby attempting to answer the controversial question of who or what was to blame for the disastrous defeat the Habsburg Monarchy suffered in the East in the early stages of the conflict.

---

4. See for example: Moritz Auffenberg von Komarow, *Aus Österreichs Höhe und Niedergang. Eine Lebensschilderung* (München: Drei Masken, 1921); Alfred Krauss, *Die Ursachen unserer Niederlage. Erinnerungen und Urteile aus dem Ersten Weltkrieg* (München: Lehmann, 1920); Ernst Rabisch, *Streitfragen des Weltkrieges 1914-1918* (Stuttgart; Bergers literarisches Büro und Verlagsanstalt, 1924), 15-64, 88-106. On unpublished sources on this matter see above all: Tunstall, "Conspirancy," 192-196.
5. See for example: Richard Plaschka, *Cattaro – Prag. Revolte und Revolution. Kriegsmarine und Heer Österreich-Ungarns im Feuer der Aufstandsbewegungen vom 1. Februar und 28. Oktober 1918* (Graz/Köln: Böhlau 1963); Anton Wagner, *Der Erste Weltkrieg. Ein Blick zurück* (Wien: Ueberreuter, 1968); Rudolf Hecht, *Fragen zur Heeresergänzung der gesamten bewaffneten Macht Österreich-Ungarns während des Ersten Weltkriegs* (Wien: PhD thesis University of Vienna, 1969); Richard Plaschka, Horst Haselsteiner, Arnold Suppan, *Innere Front. Militärassistenz, Widerstand und Umsturz in der Donaumonarchie 1918*, 2 Vols. (Wien: Verlag für Geschichte und Politik, 1974); Gerhard Artl, *Die österreichisch-ungarische Südtiroloffensive 1916* (Wien: PhD thesis University of Vienna, 1982); Rudolf Jeřábek, *Die Brussilowoffensive 1916: ein Wendepunkt der Koalitionskriegführung der Mittelmächte* (Wien: PhD thesis University of Vienna, 1982); Manfried Rauchensteiner, *Der Tod des Doppeladlers. Österreich-Ungarn und der Erste Weltkrieg* (Graz: Styria, 1993). A revised version of Rauchensteiner's book was re-published in 2014 under the new title: *Der Erste Weltkrieg und das Ende der Habsburgermonarchie.*

Premises

Any attempt to assess the decisions made by Austria-Hungary's military commanders in the Russian theater in 1914 has to take the conditions under which the k.u.k. army had to operate into consideration. The first important factor in this context is the territory on which the battles were fought. At least on paper, the vast plains of Galicia,[6] which extended far beyond the Austrian border into Russian Poland (referred to as Priwislinskij Kraj by the Russian authorities),[7] seemed almost ideal for military operations. In the understanding of the strategists of the time, a landscape thus shaped would not only allow a large army to deploy without problems, but also to maneuver freely on the battlefield and possibly outflank the enemy in an engagement. At the same time, however, it was quite clear that defending the flat countryside against an attack by a numerically superior force would be an almost impossible task. The only lines of retreat provided by nature were the rivers San and Dnestr, which ran across a line between the towns of Sandomierz in the northwestern and Khotyn in the southeastern part of Galicia, effectively cutting its territory in half. If the Austro-Hungarian army failed to stop an advancing enemy at this line of almost 500 kilometers, its only remaining option was to fall back into the Carpathian Mountains along the Galician-Hungarian border.[8] Since such a large-scale retreat would have meant the occupation of almost the entire territory of Galicia, the Austro-Hungarian general staff was determined not to let the enemy advance beyond the San-Dnestr-Line. The first approach to the problem was a plan put together already in the late 1850s, which proposed the construction of large fortresses along the rivers Vistula, San, and Dnestr, to function as bases of operation as well as points of retreat for Austro-Hungarian troops deployed in Galicia.[9] Due to lack of funding, the plan

6. On the geography of Galicia see: Julius Jandaurek, *Das Königreich Galizien und Lodomerien und das Herzogtum Bukowina* (Wien: k.k. Hof- und Staatsdruckerei, 1884), 32-44.
7.   Rudolf Jaworski, Christian Lübke, Michael G. Müller, *Eine kleine Geschichte Polens* (Frankfurt am Main: Suhrkamp 2000), 269.
8.   BMHW-KA eds., ÖUlK, vol. 1, supplement 1; Paul Magocsi, *Historical Atlas of Central Europe* (London: Thames & Hudson, 2002), 36; Thomas E. Griess ed., *West Point Atlas for the Great War. Strategies & Tactics of the First World War* (Garden City Park: SquareOne, 2003), Map 24b.
9.   Eduard von Steinitz, Theodor Brosch von Aarenau eds., *Ergänzungsheft 10 zum Werk "Österreich-Ungarns letzter Krieg. Die Reichsbefestigungen Österreich-Ungarns zur Zeit Conrads von Hötzendorf"* (Wien: Verlag der Militärwissenschaftlichen Mitteilungen, 1937), 7-8; Franz Forstner, *Przemyśl. Österreich-Ungarns bedeutendste Festung* (Wien: Österreichischer Bundesverlag, 1987), 48-49; Walter Wagner, "Die k. (u.) k. Armee – Gliederung und Aufgabenstellung," in *Die Habsburgermonarchie, 1848 – 1918*, vol. 5: Die bewaffnete Macht, ed. Adam Wandruszka, Peter Urbanitsch (Wien: Verlag der Österreichischen Akademie der Wissenschaften, 1987), 142 – 633, here: 178-179.

"East Central Europe, 1914 borders," Copyright Richard Lein

was never implemented to its full extent and finally abandoned in 1906 by the new Austro-Hungarian chief of staff, Franz Conrad von Hötzendorf.[10] Conrad, who preferred offense over defensive operations, argued that large fortresses would be of little use in securing the flat countryside against an attack by a numerically superior enemy, and that the proposed budget should instead be spent on improving the equipment of the k.u.k. field army. Consequently, the fortresses of Cracow (on the Vistula) and Przemysl (on the San), which had been (re-)constructed during the 1880s,[11] were downgraded to fortified supply depots for the mobile armed forces operating in the area and received no further upgrading of their defensive capabilities.[12] By this, the Austro-Hungarian general staff basically gave up the idea of operating defensively in this theater and limited itself solely to offense operations.

The second factor to consider in the context of the k.u.k. army's operations on the Russian front is transportation. In order to stand a chance

10. On Conrad see: Lawrence Sondhaus, *Franz Conrad von Hötzendorf. Architekt der Apokalypse* (Wien: NWV, 2003); Wolfram Dornik, *Des Kaisers Falke. Wirken und Nach-Wirken Franz Conrad von Hötzendorfs* (Innsbruck: Studienverlag, 2013).

11. Steinitz, Brosch eds., *Reichsbefestigungen*, supplement 2; Forstner, *Przemyśl*, 50; Wagner, k.(u.)k. Armee, 180, 408-412.

12. Conrad, *Dienstzeit*, vol. 1 (Wien: Rikola, 1922), 126; Hew Strachan, *The First World War. Volume I: To Arms* (Oxford: Oxford University Press, 2001), 286; Steinitz, Brosch eds., *Reichsbefestigungen*, 8-9.

of successfully waging war against the numerically superior Tsarist army in the first place, Austria-Hungary needed to deploy large parts of its armed forces to the border of Galicia within a short time, so that the k.u.k. army would be able to open hostilities before the Russians had completed their own mobilization and prepared their troops for battle. Like in most European countries, the primary means of transportation for the Austro-Hungarian armed forces was the country's railway system. The construction of railroads on a large scale had started in the late 1850s in the Habsburg Monarchy, with the majority of projects financed and built by private investors.[13] Most of the lines completed in this time period, however, were only partly useful to the military, since they had been built to be profitable and not to handle the deployment of the k.u.k. army to potential theaters of war.[14] What's more, at first there was no connection between the railway networks of Cisleithania and Transleithania in the eastern part of the country, leaving the Vienna-Cracow-Przemysl-Lemberg line as the only one available for military transports to Galicia. This unfavorable situation improved somewhat in the 1870s with the completion of the Trans-Carpathian railroad line Budapest-Sanok-Przemysl[15] and the nationalization of the Austro-Hungarian railway network following the world economic crisis of 1873. However, due to lack of funding and dwindling political interest, the mistakes that had been made in the past were only partially corrected. Although the Austro-Hungarian authorities put much effort into increasing the transport capacities of the primary routes (Vienna-Lemberg, Budapest-Lemberg) by adding a second track,[16] there were almost no resources available to build new branches or optimize the routing of existing lines, especially around Przemysl, which had become the most important railway hub in Galicia.

---

13. Burkhard Köster, *Militär und Eisenbahn in der Habsburgermonarchie 1825 – 1859* (München: Oldenburg, 1999), 75 – 284; On the extension of the railway network see: Helmut Rumpler, Peter Urbanitsch eds., *Die Habsburgermonarchie 1848–1918, vol. 9/2: Soziale Strukturen. Die Gesellschaft der Habsburgermonarchie im Kartenbild. Verwaltungs-, Sozial- und Infrastrukturen. Nach dem Zensus von 1910* (Wien: Verlag der österreichischen Akademie der Wissenschaften, 2010), 248-249; On the building efforts in Galicia see: Bartosz Nabrdalik, *Galizische Eisenbahnen – ein rein strategisches oder auch ökonomisches Unternehmen?* (Wien: PhD Thesis University of Vienna, 2010).
14. Karl Bachinger, "Das Verkehrswesen" in *Die Habsburgermonarchie 1848 – 1918, Bd. 1: Die wirtschaftliche Entwicklung*, ed. Adam Wandruszka, Peter Urbanitsch (Wien: Verlag der Österreichischen Akademie der Wissenschaften, 1973), 278-287; Franz Saurau, *Unsere Eisenbahnen im Weltkrieg* (Wien: Steyremühl, 1924), 6-7. Köster, *Militär*, 238-239.
15. Peter Kupka, *Die Eisenbahnen Österreich-Ungarns 1822-1867* (Leipzig: Duncker & Humbolt, 1888), 276-282; Magocsi, *Atlas*, 91; Conrad, *Dienstzeit*, vol. 1, 442, BMHW-KA, eds., *ÖUIK*, vol. 1, supplement 1, 3 and 5.
16. Bachinger, *Verkehrswesen*, 289-295; Conrad, *Dienstzeit*, vol. 1, 442 – 443; BMHW-KA (eds.), *ÖUIK*, vol. 1, supplement 3; Conrad, *Dienstzeit*, vol. 4, (Wien: Rikola 1923), 284-285 and supplement 13.

In order to guarantee the speedy deployment of the k.u.k. army in case of war despite these shortcomings, the railway bureau of the Austro-Hungarian general staff was tasked with developing a schedule according to which the military transports were to run. This schedule, the so-called *Kriegsfahrordnung*, was a complicated logistics plan that determined exactly which train was supposed to run on which track at a specific time in the case of mobilization, guaranteeing optimal utilization of Austria-Hungary's railway capacities.[17] Although practically a masterpiece in theoretical logistics, the *Kriegsfahrordnung* was quite inflexible and therefore especially prone to trouble in cases of unforeseen events, which could, in the worst case, lead to a complete shutdown of railway traffic.[18] Trouble, however, had to be expected since Austria-Hungary had to prepare for at least three possible crisis scenarios: a war against Russia, a war against Serbia, or a war against both countries. Since each case required a different deployment of the k.u.k. army, three different mobilization plans had to be drawn up. As a consequence, the general staff divided the Austro-Hungarian forces into three groups: *Staffel A* (k.u.k. first, third and fourth armies, twenty-eight infantry divisions),[19] *Staffel B* (k.u.k. second army, twelve infantry divisions) and *Minimalgruppe Balkan* (k.u.k. fifth and sixth armies, eight infantry divisions). *Staffel A* was to be deployed to Galicia in the case of an imminent conflict with Russia, while *Minimalgruppe Balkan* was to be sent to the southeastern border in the run-up to a war with Serbia. *Staffel B*, on the other hand, was the key element in Austria-Hungary's military planning. If the Habsburg Monarchy went to war with Serbia, and Russia decided to stay out of the conflict, *Staffel B* was to be deployed to the Balkans in order to reinforce *Minimalgruppe* and enable it to launch an offensive in a southeastern direction. If, however, Russia chose to side with Serbia, *Staffel B* would be deployed in Galicia together with *Staffel A* to face the Tsarist army, while *Minimalgruppe* would take a defensive position on the Serbian border.[20] Considering the inflexibility of the deployment plans, the k.u.k. general staff had the difficult task of determining, in a situation of political crisis, which country the Habsburg monarchy would

---

17. Conrad, *Dienstzeit*, vol. 1, 365-367; Saurau, *Eisenbahnen*, 5-7; Rauchensteiner, *Tod*, 114-115.

18. Saurau, *Eisenbahnen*, 12-15; Rauchensteiner, *Tod*, 115-119; BMHW-KA (eds.), *ÖUIK*, vol. 1, 15-15.

19. An Austro-Hungarian Infantry Division consisted of about 20,000 Officers and Men. John Ellis, Michael Cox, eds., *The World War I Databook. The Essential Facts and Figures for All the Combatants* (London: Aurum Pree, 2001), 227. On details on the organization of the Austro-Hungarain Army in Summer 1914 see: Ibid, 172-173.

20. Strachan, *War*, 291; Rauchensteiner, *Tod*, 113-121; BMHW-KA (eds.), *ÖUIK*, vol. 1, 3-9; David Stevenson, *1914-1918. The History of the First World War* (London: Penguin, 2005), 64; Fiedler, *Taktik*, 270-271.

go to war with and, consequently, which version of the deployment plan had to be set in motion. This was especially crucial due to the fact that once mobilization had started, there was just a small time frame during which the transports could be stopped and redirected. Once that moment had passed, the trains could no longer be rerouted or turned around, but had to proceed to their original destinations, from where they would be redirected to the theater of war where they were actually needed.[21] Given the fact that the deployment areas in the Balkans and those in Galicia were only linked by a small number of railways with limited capacities,[22] it was obvious that troops accidentally sent to the wrong theater would arrive in their designated deployment areas with great delay. Such a mishap could have dramatic consequences, since the Austro-Hungarian forces could only hope to achieve military success over the numerically superior Russians if they managed to complete deployment and open hostilities before the Tsarist forces were fully operational. Given the fact that Russian mobilization had been greatly accelerated in the years before the war, thanks to improvements in the country's railway system,[23] it was clear that misdeployment of parts of the Austro-Hungarian fighting force designated for the northeastern theater could have severe consequences. The railway bureau, however, was confident that such a mishap would not happen. When asked by Conrad what could be done if the k.u.k. army's deployment had to be changed after mobilization had started, they claimed that it was possible to switch to a different deployment plan within fifteen days after the beginning of mobilization without causing any delays.[24] However, the possibility that a situation could occur in which two plans needed to be executed at the same time was considered neither by the chief of staff nor by the railway bureau.

The third factor that needs to be considered is how well prepared Austria-Hungary and its allies were for the impending conflict in the first place. Ever since the establishment of the Dual Alliance between the Habsburg Empire and the German Reich in 1879, the general staffs of both countries

---

21. Saurau, *Eisenbahnen*, 12-13; BMHW-KA (eds.), *ÖUIK*, vol. 1, 21-24; Strachan, *War*, 290-295.
22. Conrad, *Dienstzeit*, vol. 4, 284-285 and supplement 13; BMHW-KA (eds.), *ÖUIK*, vol. 1, supplement 3 and 5.
23. Stevenson, *History*, 62-64; William C. Fuller, *Strategy and Power in Russia 1600 – 1914* (New York: Free Press, 1992), 356-362; Magocsi, *Atlas*, 91; Conrad, *Dienstzeit*, vol. 4, 284-285 and supplement 13, BMHW-KA (eds.), *ÖUIK*, Vol. 1, supplement 5; Strachan, *War*, 291-293 and 297-298. On the military capacities of Russia in 1914 see: Norman Stone, *The Eastern Front 1914 – 1917* (London: Penguin, 1998), 17 – 36; Nik Cornish, *The Russian Army and the First World War* (Gloucestershire: Spellmount Publishing, 2006); BMHW-KA (eds.), *ÖUIK*, Vol. 1, 173-178.
24. Strachan, *War*, 292; Rauchensteiner, *Tod*, 115.

had been preparing plans for a joint military operation against Russia.[25] The main objective of these plans was that both Austria-Hungary and the German Reich should mobilize their military forces within a time frame of 30 days and then launch a simultaneous attack from Western Prussia and Galicia on the Russian forces gathering in Russian Poland, thus knocking out large parts of the Tsarist army before it was ready for battle.[26] However, these plans, which were actually never put in writing, were fundamentally changed after Alfred von Schlieffen became German chief of staff in 1891.[27] Contrary to his predecessor, Helmuth von Moltke, Schlieffen was highly skeptical that a decisive victory against the Russian army could be achieved in a short amount of time. Consequently, he became convinced that in case of an armed conflict against France and Russia, a threat that became imminent with the signing of the Franco-Russian Alliance in 1894,[28] the German Reich should try to achieve an early, decisive victory against France by deploying the bulk of its military forces in the west before engaging the Tsarist army. Austria-Hungary was supposed to fulfill the task of holding the line against the Russians, together with a small number of German troops stationed in Silesia and East Prussia, until victory had been achieved in the west and the bulk of the German army could be transported to the east.[29] The defeat of the Russian army in the war against Japan in 1904-05[30] fortified Schlieffen's belief that France posed a greater threat than Russia, and that he could therefore deploy the bulk of his forces in the west without

---

25. Hermann von Kuhl, *Der deutsche Generalstab in Vorbereitung und Durchführung des Weltkrieges*, (Berlin: Mittler und Sohn: 1920), 146-151; Marian Zagórniak, "Galizien in den Kriegsplänen Österreichs und Österreich-Ungarns," *Studia Austro-Polonica* 5, (1996), 295-307, here: 298-299; BMHW-KA eds., *ÖUIK*, Vol. 1, 12-13; Strachan, *War*, 285-286. On the Dual Alliance see: Helmut Rumpler ed., *Der "Zweibund" 1879. Das deutsch-österreichisch-ungarische Bündnis und die europäische Diplomatie* (Wien: Verlag der Österreichischen Akademie der Wissenschaften, 1996); Holger Afflerbach, *Der Dreibund. Europäische Großmacht- und Allianzpolitik vor dem Ersten Weltkrieg* (Wien: Böhlau, 2002); Rauchensteiner, *Tod*, 48-50.
26. Siegfried Fiedler, *Taktik und Strategie der Millionenheere 1871-1914* (Bonn: Bechtermünz, 1993), 81; Strachan, *War*, 286-288; Conrad, *Dienstzeit*, vol. 1, 368-372; Stone, *Front*, 37-38.
27. On Schliefen see: Wolfgang Petter, Schlieffen, Alfred Graf von, in *Neue Deutsche Biographie 23* (2007), 81-83.
28. On the Franco-Russian alliance see: George F. Kennan, *The fateful alliance: France, Russia, and the coming of the First World* (New York: Pantheon Books, 1984).
29. Terence Zuber, *Inventing the Schlieffen Plan: German War Planning 1871 – 1914* (Oxford: Oxford University Press, 2002), 35-39; Gerhard Groß, "Im Schatten des Westens. Die deutsche Kriegsführung an der Ostfront bis Ende 1915" in *Die vergessene Front. Der Osten 1914/15. Ereignis, Wirkung, Nachwirkung*, ed. Gerhard Groß (Paderborn: Schöningh, 2006), 49 – 64, here: 51-53; Strachan, *War*, 288; Fiedler, *Taktik*, 165-185, Kuhl, *Generalstab*, 142-179.
30. On the Russio-Japanese war see: Richard M. Connaughton, *Rising sun and tumbling bear: Russia's war with Japan* (London: Cassel, 2003).

having to fear any consequences. This decision caused sore feelings in the Habsburg Monarchy's armed forces and poisoned relations between Schlieffen and his Austro-Hungarian counterpart, Friedrich von Beck-Rzikowsky, who broke off all communication with the German general staff as a consequence.[31]

A working relationship between the military commands of the two allies was only reestablished in the light of the Bosnian annexation crisis of 1908,[32] when the new chiefs of staff of the German army and the Austro-Hungarian army, Helmuth von Moltke the Younger[33] and Franz Conrad von Hötzendorf, began to reevaluate their plans for war against Russia. Moltke was neither willing nor able to overthrow Schlieffen's plans of operation; however, he needed the Austro-Hungarian army to reliably hold the line in the east as long as the bulk of the German army was engaged in the west. Contrary to his predecessor, Moltke didn't make the mistake of underestimating Russia, which had, largely owing to French military and financial support, made good progress in strengthening its military forces ever since its defeat in 1905.[34] Given this unfavorable strategic situation, Moltke depended on Conrad to cover his back on the Russian front in case of war until France had been defeated.[35] Consequently, the German chief of staff made a number of informal concessions and promises to his Austro-Hungarian counterpart, who he corresponded with regularly, the extent of which is still a matter of debate even today.[36] Although there was never any kind of formal, signed agreement between Conrad and Moltke, it is a well-known fact that the Austro-Hungarian chief of staff agreed not only to hold the line in the east, but also to attack the Tsarist forces deployed in Russian Poland in order to prevent them from turning against Eastern Prussia with the bulk of their troops. It is also evident that Moltke, in turn, had assured Conrad that France would be forced to surrender no more than four weeks after the German army in the west had completed its mobilization, so the Austro-Hungarian forces would only have to face the Tsarist army on their own for a short span of time.[37] Given the expectation that the Russians

31. Fiedler, *Taktik*, 82-83; Zagórniak, *Galizien*, 300; Strachan, *War*, 288.
32. On the annexation crisis see: Horst Haselsteiner, *Bosnien-Hercegovina. Orientkrise und Südslavische Frage* (Wien: Böhlau, 1996); Jürgen Angelow, *Kalkül und Prestige. Der Zweibund am Vorabend des Ersten Weltkrieges* (Wien: Böhlau, 2000).
33. On Moltke see: Heinrich Walle, Moltke, Helmuth Graf von, in *Neue Deutsche Biographie 18* (1997), 17-18; Annika Mombauer, *Helmuth von Moltke and the origins of the First World War* (Cambridge: Cambridge University Press, 2001).
34. Stevenson, *History*, 61-63; Strachan, *War*, 300-307.
35. Strachan, *War*, 289; Stone, *Front*, 41-42.
36. Zagórniak, *Galizien*, 300-301; Fiedler, *Taktik*, 84-85; On the correspondence between Conrad and Moltke see: Conrad, *Dienstzeit*, vol. 1, 373-406.
37. Strachan, *War*, 288-290.

would need at least a month to deploy their forces to Poland,[38] this must have appeared to be a risk worth taking. After the war, Conrad claimed that Moltke and his associates had furthermore assured him that German forces stationed in East Prussia would launch an offensive in a southeastern direction in order to support the Austro-Hungarian forces advancing from the south, an alleged promise his German counterpart never kept.[39] German historians always denied that such a promise had been made to the Austro-Hungarian chief of staff and speculated that Conrad might have misinterpreted one of the general statements Moltke had made during their meetings.[40] Due to lack of written evidence, these assertions can neither be confirmed nor denied. It is, however, quite evident that a lack of communication between the German and Austro-Hungarian general staffs, as well as Conrad and Moltke's failure to sign a formal agreement on the planned military operations, led to differing expectations on both sides as to how the respective partner would act in the case of war against Russia. Nevertheless, even before the beginning of World War I, the Austro-Hungarian chief of staff decided to stick to the plan of opening hostilities against the Tsarist army with a large-scale invasion of Poland.[41] Given the growing strength of the Russian army and uncertainty if the German forces in East Prussia were going to provide any support, this was rather a risky strategy.

Just as important for military success as war plans and agreements, however, was how well prepared the k.u.k. army was for the impending conflict. Unfortunately for the Habsburg Monarchy, things in this context were not looking so good. Although the level of training and the quality of the military equipment of Austria-Hungary's peacetime army were comparable to most of its European counterparts, it was, compared to the size of the Habsburg Monarchy's civilian population, only half as large as the armed forces of France and the German Reich.[42] This unfavorable situation was the result of the ongoing quarrel between Cisleithania and

---

38. Zagórniak, *Galizien*, 302-303; Strachan, *War*, 286-288; Sondhaus, *Conrad*, 108.

39. BMHW-KA eds., *ÖUIK*, vol. 1, 13-14; Oskar Regele, *Feldmarschall Conrad. Auftrag und Erfüllung 1906-1918* (Wien: Herold, 1955), 319-323; Conrad, *Dienstzeit*, vol. 1, 373-406; Ibid., vol. 3 (Wien: Rikola, 1922) 85-89 as well as 669-673; Ibid., vol. 4, 279; Strachan, *War*, 290-291; Nowak, *Katastrophe*, 53-54.

40. Reichsarchiv ed., *Der Weltkrieg 1914-1918. Die militärischen Operationen zu Lande*, vol. 2 (Berlin: Mittler, 1925), 251; Theobald von Schäfer, "Deutsche Offensive aus Ostpreußen über den Narew auf Siedlec" in *Ergänzungsheft 1 zum Werke "Österreich-Ungarns letzter Krieg*, ed. Kriegsarchiv Wien (Wien: Verlag der Militärwissenschaftlichen Mitteilungen, 1930), 1-16, here: 1-2. Schäfer, Offensive, 11-16.

41. Stevenson, *History*, 64; Strachan, *War*, 291-292.

42. Strachan, *War*, 284; Sevenson, *History*, 63; BMHW-KA (eds.), *ÖUIK*, Vol. 1, 26-31; Wagner, *Armee*, 492; Rauchensteiner, *Tod*, 41-42, Fiedler, *Taktik*, 76-77.

Transleithania following the establishment of the Dual Monarchy in 1867, which caused the budget of the k.u.k. army (the so-called *Gemeinsame Armee*) as well as the number of recruits conscripted every year to remain at a low level for a considerable amount of time. At the same time, both parts of the country put much effort into building up their respective territorial forces, *k.k. Landwehr and k.u. Honvéd*, establishing structures like military academies, supply depots and administration offices identical to those of the k.u.k. armed forces. Despite the fact that *Landwehr* and *Honvéd* were to be placed under the command of the Austro-Hungarian general staff in case of war, the process of building up and maintaining three fully equipped armies at the same time took up a considerable amount of resources that could have been used for strengthening the k.u.k. armed forces.[43] The fact that the recruit contingents remained unchanged for years also prevented Austria-Hungary from enlarging its peacetime army, which would have been possible and necessary due to population growth. Consequently, every year almost two thirds of the draftees had to be sent home, since the military possessed neither the financial means nor the resources to provide them with at least minimal training.[44] While it didn't matter so much in peacetime, this state of affairs would have severe consequences in times of war, when men who had no military experience at all would be drafted en masse into the k.u.k. army. Given the fact that the Austro-Hungarian armed forces were supposed to be expanded from 415.000 to two million men in case of war, it is evident that three out of four soldiers going into battle in the k.u.k. army would be draftees with at best minimal military experience.[45] Only in 1912, the governments of Cisleithania and Transleithania agreed to increase the annual recruit contingent as well as the budget for the Austro-Hungarian armed forces, but the actions taken following this step came too late to have much of an effect before the beginning the war.[46] Further problems were expected to result from the lack of commissioned officers and NCOs. While

43. Johann C. Allmayer-Beck, "Die bewaffnete Macht in Staat und Gesellschaft," in: *Die Habsburgermonarchie, 1848 – 1918*, vol. 5: Die bewaffnete Macht, ed. Adam Wandruszka, Peter Urbanitsch (Wien: Verlag der Österreichischen Akademie der Wissenschaften, 1987), 1–141, here: 81–85; Wagner, *Armee*, 417–430, Fiedler, *Taktik*, 71-72.

44. Hugo Schmid-Boneti, *Heerwesen. Lehr- und Lernbehelf für Militär-Erziehungs- und Bildungsanstalten sowie Instruktionsbuch für Reserveoffizierschulen, dann für das Selbststudium*, 2 vols. (Wien: Seidl, 1915), 4; k.k. Statistische Central-Commission ed., *Österreichisches statistisches Handbuch für die im Reichsrathe vertretenen Königreiche und Länder. XIV. Jahrgang 1895* (Wien: k.k. Hof- und Staatsdruckerei, 1896), 304-305.

45. Strachan, *War*, 284; Rauchensteiner, *Tod*, 105.

46. BMHW/KA, *ÖUIK*, vol. 1, 28; Strachan, *War*, 283-284; k.k. Hof- und Staatsdruckerei (ed.) *Reichsgesetzblatt für die im Reichsrate vertretenen Königreiche und Länder. Jahrgang 1912* (Wien: k.k. Hof- und Staatsdruckerei, 1912), Nr. 128/1912; Leo Geller, Hermann Jolles, *Das neue Wehrgesetz und Landwehrgesetz nebst Durchführungsvorschriften* (Wien: Perles, 1913); Hecht, *Heeresergänzung*, 1-23.

the number of commanding personnel was sufficient for the peacetime army, it was clear that in a war, at least some tasks would have to be handed over to so-called reserve officers, former one-year volunteers who had received extensive training during their military service, but had in most cases left active service years before and were not fully qualified to lead troops into battle.[47]

But even those men who were actually conscripted were trained in a way that didn't prepare them properly for modern warfare. This circumstance was a result both of the fact that Austria-Hungary hadn't participated in a large-scale military operation since the occupation of Bosnia in 1878, and that its general staff had drawn the wrong conclusions from recent conflicts like the Franco-Prussian War of 1870-71,[48] the Russo-Japanese War of 1904-05, or the Balkan Wars of 1912-13.[49] Chief of staff Conrad von Hötzendorf, who favored attack over defense like most of his contemporaries serving in other European armies,[50] was convinced that although repeating rifles and machine guns had drastically increased the density of fire on the battlefield, an army needed to press on the attack at any cost.[51] In this context, Conrad's followers often cited the Russo-Japanese War as an example where the Japanese forces, who had charged the Russian entrenchments with bayonets, had been victorious despite fierce enemy resistance and the losses they had sustained. Many Austro-Hungarian officers began to believe that the k.u.k. army could prevail even against a numerically superior enemy if it managed to press on the attack while being willing to accept great human

---

47. Strachan, *War*, 284-285; István Deák, *Der k.(u.)k. Offizier 1848–1918* (Wien: OTR, 1995), 122-123 and 219-221; BMHW-KA eds., *ÖUIK*, vol. 1, 47-57; Hecht, *Heeresergänzung*, 155-162.

48. On the Franco-Prussian war see above all: Geoffrey Wawro, *The Franco-Prussian War. The German Conquest of France in 1870-1871* (Cambridge: Cambridge University Press, 2005); Jan Ganschow, Olaf Haselhorst, Maik Ohnezeit eds., *Der Deutsch-Französische Krieg 1870/71. Vorgeschichte, Verlauf, Folgen* (Graz: Ares, 2009), 83-120 and 229-242.

49. On the Balkan Wars see: Richard C. Hall, *The Balkan Wars 1912-1913: Prelude to the First World War* (London: Routledge, 2000); Katrin Boeck, *Von den Balkankriegen zum Ersten Weltkrieg. Kleinstaatenpolitik und ethnische Selbstbestimmung auf dem Balkan* (München: Oldenburg, 1996).

50. Conrad's ideas and actions were quite similar to those of some prominent commanders of the Entente armies. See for example: Denis Winter, *Haig's command. A reassessment* (Harmondsworth: Viking, 1991); Arthur Conte, *Joffre* (Paris: Orban, 1991); Gianni Rocca, *Cadorna* (Milano: Mondadori, 1985).

51. Wagner, *Armee*, 626-628; Franz Conrad von Hötzendorf, *Gefechtsausbildung der Infanterie* (Wien: Seidl, 1913), 24-36 and 52-61; Fiedler, *Taktik*, 79; Hans Linnenkohl, *Vom Einzelschuss zur Feuerwalze. Der Wettlauf zwischen Technik und Taktik im Ersten Weltkrieg* (Koblenz: Bernard & Graefe, 1990), 11-162; Ortenburg, *Waffen*, 47-119; Fiedler, *Taktik*, 85.

losses.[52] Consequently, the tactics and training of the Habsburg Monarchy's military forces were aligned solely with this idea. Infantry and cavalry thus became the key elements in Austria-Hungary's military planning; both were expected to move swiftly on the battlefield and to strike the enemy wherever they could. At the same time, however, only a little effort was put into training the troops for defense or even organized retreat. What's more, the option of different military branches like infantry and artillery conducting combined operations while benefiting from each other's capabilities was almost completely ignored by Austria-Hungary's military leaders.[53] Almost the same applied to progress in the field of military technology: modern equipment like machine guns and aircraft had been reluctantly introduced into the arsenals of the k.u.k. army since the beginning of the twentieth century, but played only a limited role in the minds of the Austro-Hungarian general staff despite the possibilities they offered for defense and reconnaissance. This omission was bound to have severe consequences, since the Habsburg Monarchy's potential enemies, Russia and Serbia, had gained much experience in modern-day warfare in their wars against Japan and the Balkan nations, respectively, and could be expected to make good use of that experience in the impending conflict.[54]

Mobilization

Although the Austro-Hungarian general staff had prepared plans for each possible scenario, the decision on which potential theater of war the majority of the k.u.k. armed forces were to be deployed to, and where hostilities were to be opened, was difficult to make. Conrad von Hötzendorf himself, who had long emphasized the necessity of a preemptive military operation in the Balkans,[55] preferred the option of crushing Serbia in a swift move and afterwards redeploying the bulk of the k.u.k. army to Galicia to face the Russians.[56] This plan had its merits, but it had been drawn up under the assumption that if St. Petersburg really decided to side with Serbia,

52. See: Hugo Schmid, *Taktisches Handbuch*, 12th edition, (Wien: Seidl, 1914), 199-217; Franz Conrad von Hötzendorf, *Die Gefechtsausbildung der Infanterie*, 5th edition (Wien: Seidl, 1913), 24-36, 52-61, 212-245; Ibid., *Zum Studium der Taktik*, 2 vols. (Wien: Seidl, 1891).

53. Strachan, *War*, 285; Georg Ortenburg, *Waffen der Millionenheere 1871 – 1914* (Bonn: Bechtermünz, 1992) 207-229; Conrad, *Dienstzeit*, vol. 1, 368-370; Ibid., vol. 4, 283; Fiedler, *Taktik*, 80-81.

54. Sondhaus, *Conrad*, 174; Fiedler, *Taktik*, 219-260.

55. Sondhaus, *Conrad*, 89-116; Strachan, *War*, 285-286; Dornik, *Falke*, 78-81 and 99-109.

56. Strachan, *War*, 294 and 335-337; Stevenson, *History*, 69-70; Rauchensteiner, *Tod*, 114-115; Zbyněk Zeman, *The Break-Up of the Habsburg Empire 1914-1918. A study in National and Social Revolution* (London: Oxford University Press, 1961), 39-40.

the Tsarist army would need at least a month to prepare for operations on the Galician border, and that the German forces stationed in East Prussia would launch at least a short offensive into Russian Poland, preventing the Tsarist army from turning with full force against the Habsburg Monarchy. In spring 1914, however, both assumptions no longer applied. Moltke had become even more cautious regarding the defense of East Prussia, which made a German military intervention in Russian Poland at the beginning of the war highly unlikely. At the same time, extensive investment had improved the Russian railway network in the west of the country to such a great extent that the time the Tsarist army would need for mobilization and deployment to the Austro-Hungarian border had effectively been cut by at least one third.[57]

Things were further complicated by the treachery of Colonel Alfred Redl, a high-ranking officer in the k.u.k. general staff, who had handed over at least parts of the Austro-Hungarian mobilization plans to the Russian secret service before his exposure in May 1913.[58] Unable to determine how much information had been given away—Redl committed suicide before he could be questioned—the Austro-Hungarian general staff was forced to change its operation plans for both anticipated theaters of war.[59] In Galicia, the k.u.k. armed forces were no longer scheduled to be deployed in the east of the country, but further to the west along the rivers San and Dnestr. From this position, the first, second, and fourth k.u.k. armies were to strike in a northeastern direction and attempt to crush the bulk of the Russian forces Conrad expected to be gathering on the other side of the border, while the k.u.k. third army was given the task of taking a defensive position east of Lemberg, thus protecting the Austro-Hungarian forces' right flank.[60] The relocation of the deployment areas further to the west was quite favorable to the war plans of the Habsburg Monarchy's military leaders, since the k.u.k. armies sent to this theater of war could now expect to complete their deployment much faster than before, given the shorter distances they had to cross by train. Against Serbia, the situation was more complicated, since Conrad, who had to take into account that Redl might also have given away

57. Stevenson, *Armaments*, 356; Strachan, *War*, 291-292 and 297-298; Tunstall, "*Conspiracy*", 196.

58. On the Redl affair see: Verena Moritz, *Oberst Redl. Der Spionagefall, der Skandal, die Fakten* (St. Pölten: Residenz, 2012); Peter Broucek, "Redl, Alfred, Offizier," *Österreichisches Biographisches Lexikon 1815-1950*, vol. 9 (1984), 7-8, Dornik, *Falke*, 109-112, Sondhaus, *Conrad*, 133-137.

59. On the exact deployment of the troops on both theatres of war see: BMHW-KA (eds.), *ÖUlK*, vol. 1, supplement 9; Griess, *Atlas*, Map 28 and 32a; Ellis, Cox eds., *Databook*, 26 and 38.

60. Strachan, *War*, 291-292; Stone, *Front*, 80-81; Nowak, *Katastrophe*, 53.

the deployment plans against Serbia, decided to completely overthrow all previous operation plans. The new scenario drawn up assigned the troops of *Staffel B*, the k.u.k. second army, the task of tying down the majority of the Serbian armed forces around Belgrade, while at the same time the forces of *Minimalgruppe*, the k.u.k. fifth and sixth armies, would cross the border from Bosnia into Serbia and attempt to attack the enemy defending the country's capital from the rear.[61] The new operation plans against Russia and Serbia were drawn up in spring 1914 and scheduled to be put to the test in staff maneuvers in autumn 1914 which, due to the course of events, never took place. What is more, due to lack of time, the railway bureau of the Austro-Hungarian general staff was not able to fully incorporate all the changes arising from the new deployment plans into the wartime train schedule. Apart from the fact that the train stations in central Galicia, contrary to those in the east, had not been constructed to receive a large number of transports unloading troops and military supplies within a short time, the necessity of rerouting many of the carefully scheduled trains made the entire *Kriegsfahrordnung* even more vulnerable to disturbances, especially if the attempt was made to implement further changes after deployment to one theater of war had begun.[62]

All these facts were fully known to the Austro-Hungarian general staff as well as to Conrad, who nevertheless decided, on July 25, 1914 when the July crisis was just reaching its climax, to mobilize the designated parts of the k.u.k. army, *Minimalgruppe* and *Staffel B*, for a war limited to the Balkans.[63] There has been much debate regarding the chief of staff's decision; some people later claimed that Conrad had been driven by a need to take revenge for the assassination of Franz Ferdinand, while others asserted that the chief of staff had perhaps hoped to secure Austria-Hungary the loyalty of the other Balkan states by defeating Serbia in one swift move. No matter what may have been the true reason, Conrad's decision had far-reaching consequences. Only when General Moltke, who surprisingly hadn't stayed in contact with the Austro-Hungarian general staff during the July crisis, clearly pointed out that Germany would not be able to assist its ally in the impending war against Russia, and that the k.u.k. army would therefore have to keep the Tsarist forces at bay on its own for the time being, did Conrad consider changing his plans.[64] On July 31, he gave the order to

61. Strachan, *War*, 294 and 338-340; BMHW-KA (eds.), *ÖUIK*, vol. 1, 91-110; Rauchensteiner, *Tod*, 128-129.
62. BMHW-KA eds., *ÖUIK*, vol. 1, 5-15; Stevenson, *History*, 64; Strachan, *War*, 292-293.
63. Strachan, *War*, 293-294; Stevenson, *History*, 69; BMHW-KA (eds.), *ÖUIK*, vol. 1, 17-18; Dornik, *Falke*, 130-131. On the July Crisis see above all: Christopher Clark, *Die Schlafwandler. Wie Europa in den Ersten Weltkrieg zog* (München: DVA, 2013), 475-708.
64. BMHW-KA (eds.), *ÖUIK*, vol. 1, 18-22; Strachan, *War*, 294; Stevenson, *History*, 69-70.

mobilize the troops of *Staffel A* against Russia while proceeding with the deployment of *Minimalgruppe* to the Serbian border. At the same time, the transports of *Staffel B*, which were already on their way to the Balkans, were to be stopped and rerouted to Galicia. The railroad bureau, however, informed the chief of staff that the latter maneuver could not be carried out, since the simultaneous deployment of the k.u.k. armed forces against Serbia and against Russia had already tested the limits of the capacities of the railway network, and the implementation of further changes could cause the entire system to crash, resulting in large-scale traffic disruptions and lengthy delays.[65] Consequently, it was decided to continue the transports of the troops belonging to *Staffel B* (the k.u.k. second army) to their deployment area near Belgrade and, following the guidelines of the wartime schedule, to reroute them from there to Galicia using the Trans-Carpathian railway lines in northeastern Hungary.[66] Besides the fact that this would cause a significant delay, the situation was even more unfortunate since the wartime schedule, as pointed out before, had been drawn up before the mobilization plans had been changed in spring 1914. As a consequence, the k.u.k. second army was now going to arrive in Galicia on the right flank of the Austro-Hungarian forces gathered in the area and not, as intended, on the left wing, where it was supposed to participate in the offensive into Russian Poland.[67] Consequently, it was obvious already at the beginning of August 1914 that the operation plans put together by the Austro-Hungarian staff could not be set in motion as intended, and that army command would have to improvise so as not to lose the initiative on the eastern front. Unfortunately, more unpleasant surprises and unforeseen circumstances lay yet ahead for the Habsburg Monarchy and its military leaders.

The Opening Round

Despite the war plans and the abilities of their troops, Conrad and Moltke lacked precise information on the deployment and the intentions of the Russian forces. They believed (or at least guessed) that the Russians, in an attempt to assist France, would turn large parts of their forces against East Prussia, while only a limited number of troops would confront Austria-Hungary.[68] If that was the case, the strategy of Conrad

---

65. Strachan, *War*, 295-296; Dornik, *Falke*, 134-135; Stevenson, *History*, 69; BMHW-KA (eds.), *ÖUIK*, vol. 1, 23-24. Latter text obviously aims at disguising Conrad's responsibility for the cause of events. See: Tunstall, "*Conspiracy*," 181-183.

66. BMHW-KA (eds.), *ÖUIK*, vol. 1, 24-25 and supplement 5; Stevenson, *History*, 69-70; Fiedler, *Taktik*, 271.

67. Strachan, *War*, 292 and 296; Stone, *Front*, 77-79.

68. Rauchensteiner, *Tod*, 135; Strachan, *War*, 291-297 and 350-351; Stevenson, *History*,

and Moltke made perfect sense: the German forces in East Prussia would dig in and try to fend of the Russian attack while the k.u.k. army started an invasion into Russian Poland, engaging the Tsarist forces gathering in the area and preventing them from sending further reinforcements to their armies fighting in East Prussia. Little did the two chiefs of staff know that Russian intelligence had correctly assumed prior to the war that the German Reich would send the bulk of its troops to the western front and leave the protection of East Prussia to a considerably smaller force. As a result, the Russian high command had decided that the Tsarist army would, as a first step, concentrate the bulk of its forces on the Galician border, engage the k.u.k. army and, after the Austro-Hungarian forces had been crushed, turn with full force against the Germans.[69] St. Petersburg's battle plan for the Galician theater was quite simple: two Russian armies were to cross the border from the west into East Galicia and engage the k.u.k. armed forces deployed in the area. Once the Austro-Hungarian army was embroiled in battle, the remaining two armies of the Russian striking force deployed further to the west in Poland were to strike in a southern direction, attack the k.u.k. forces' lines of communication and take the most important railway junctions (above all Przemysl), effectively cutting off the Austro-Hungarian forces' primary lines of retreat.[70] What the Russian general staff didn't know was that the deployment of the k.u.k. army, as pointed out before, had been relocated further to the west as a consequence of Colonel Redl's treason, a fact that would cause the first attack move of the Russian forces in East Galicia to come to nothing. At the same time, the Austro-Hungarian general staff was also almost completely oblivious to the enemy's intentions. It expected that the majority of the Russian troops would be concentrated well east of the Vistula and could therefore easily be engaged by k.u.k. forces advancing from their deployment area at the San in a northeastern direction. Conrad, however, was facing the problem that due to the belated decision to switch from mobilization in the Balkans to deployment against Russia, and the resulting misdirection of *Staffel B*, he would neither be able to finish mobilization within the foreseen time frame, nor would all parts of his striking force end up where they were supposed to be. Given the fact that *Staffel B* would in any case arrive too late for the initial operations, and that Russian forces had already opened hostilities

---

65.
69. Strachan, *War*, 316; Stone, *Front*, 82-85. On Russian war planning see: Cornish, *Army*, 12-14; Stone, *Front*, 33-36; Stevenson, *History*, 62-63; BMHW-KA (eds.), *ÖUIK*, vol. 1, 172-178.
70. Stone, *Front*, 84-85; Strachan, *War*, 351-352.

against East Prussia on 20 August,[71] the Austro-Hungarian chief of staff gave the order to begin the invasion of Russian Poland.[72] According to the plan, the first and fourth k.u.k. armies began to advance from their deployment areas east of the San river in a northeastern direction, while the k.u.k. third army assumed defensive positions east of Lemberg. At this time, the k.u.k. second army was still stuck on transports coming up from the Balkans, with the bulk of its forces not expected to arrive before the beginning of September.[73]

At first, everything seemed to work out according to plan. On 23 August, the k.u.k. first army engaged the Russian fourth army gathering in the area around Krasnik and managed to drive it from its position. Only three days later, on 26 August, the k.u.k. fourth army had attacked the Russian fifth army near Komarow and, after heavy fighting, ultimately forced it to retreat on 1 September.[74] These early victories were greatly praised by the Austro-Hungarian military leadership as well as the civilian population, but they came at a high price. Already during the first engagements, the k.u.k. forces suffered huge losses when they tried to press on the attack on Russian defensive positions without covering fire. The casualty rate was especially high among officers and NCOs since, following the Habsburg Monarchy's military doctrine at the time, they often commanded their troops from the front lines in order to set an example for their men.[75] Though hardly anyone really realized it at this point, the k.u.k. army had started to bleed out rapidly, a circumstance that would have severe consequences in the near future. The success of the Austro-Hungarian forces at Krasnik and Komarow was fuelled by the fact that they were engaging Russian troops that hadn't completed their deployment yet and had not anticipated meeting a large

---

71. On the initial campaign in East Prussia see: Reichsarchiv ed., *Weltkrieg*, vol. 2, 39-108; Stone, *Front*, 44-69; Strachan, *War*, 316-335.
72. Rauchensteiner, *Tod*, 135; Strachan, *War*, 350-353; Reichsarchiv (ed.), *Weltkrieg*, vol. 2, 247-258. For a map on the military operations in Eastern Europe in 1914 see: Magocsi, *Atlas*, 122. For a first-hand account of the Austro-Hungarian operations in the East see: Constantin Schneider, *Die Kriegserinnerungen 1914-1919* (Wien: Böhlau, 2003). For the soldiers' perception of the war in the East see: Bernhard Bachinger, Wolfram Dornik eds., *Jenseits des Schützengrabens. Der Erste Weltkrieg im Osten: Erfahrung-Wahrnehmung-Kontext* (Innsbruck: Studienverlag, 2013).
73. Strachan, *War*, 347, Stone, *Front*, 75-78.
74. Auffenberg, *Höhe*, 289-332; Rauchensteiner, *Tod*, 135-136; Strachan, *War*, 352-353; BMHW-KA eds., *ÖUIK*, vol. 1, 178-241; Ellis, Cox eds., *Databook*, 26; Griess, *Atlas*, map 28.
75. Sondhaus, *Conrad*, 168; Deák, *Offizier*, 234-235; Helmut Rumpler, Anatol Schmied-Kowarzik, *Die Habsburgermonarchie 1848-1918. Band XI/2: Weltkriegsstatistik Österreich-Ungarn 1914-1918. Bevölkerungsbewegung, Kriegstote, Kriegswirtschaft* (Wien: Verlag der Österreichischen Akademie der Wissenschaften, 2014), 161, 162, 164; Strachan, *War*, 356; Stevenson, *History*, 71.

k.u.k. force so far to the east at this time. The Habsburg Monarchy's high command was completely oblivious to this fact, since it believed that the main Russian striking force had been hit hard and that it was now vital to press on the attack in order to finish off the Tsarist army. What's more, with the Russian forces retreating in a northern direction and the k.u.k. first and fourth armies following them, a gap started to open between the Austro-Hungarian fourth and third armies, the latter still assuming defensive positions east of Lemberg.[76] This fact was even obvious to the high command, but since Conrad and his subordinates believed that the bulk of the Russian forces had successfully been engaged in Poland, they saw no imminent need to take action.

Unbeknownst to them, however, the primary striking force of the Tsarist army was already closing in from the east. The Russian third and eighth armies had crossed the Galician border on 23 August according to plan and were now advancing in the direction of Lemberg. Austro-Hungarian cavalry units, which had been sent out for reconnaissance, were hampered by the large distances they had to cross, as well as stiff enemy resistance, and failed to assess the strength of the approaching enemy troops,[77] a fact which was generally ignored by the overly optimistic Conrad. Unaware that he was facing superior forces, the chief of staff ordered the k.u.k. third army to advance eastwards in order to engage the approaching Russian troops. The commander of the third army complied, further enlarging the gap between his left wing and the k.u.k. fourth army marching north in pursuit of the Russian fifth army. At first the operation seemed to go as planned, but on 26 August the k.u.k. third army encountered superior Russian forces in an engagement near the town of Zloczow and, after being outflanked, had to withdraw on 30 August, leaving Lemberg to the enemy.[78] The realization that the bulk of the enemy's forces was not concentrated in Poland, but was approaching from the east, came as a shock to the Austro-Hungarian high command. Realizing that the k.u.k. third army was about to be overwhelmed on both its flanks, Conrad decided to recall the k.u.k. fourth army from its pursuit of the Russian forces and order it to strike in a southeastern direction, thus closing the gap and preventing the enemy from getting to the rear of the Austro-Hungarian forces holding the line around Lemberg. His hopes that the k.u.k. third army, together with elements of the k.u.k. second army arriving from the Balkans, would be able to stop the Russian onslaught were, however, crushed when the flanking maneuver of the k.u.k.

---

76. Rauchensteiner, *Tod*, 135-136; Strachan, *War*, 354; Stone, *Front*, 88-89.
77. Strachan, *War*, 348; Rauchensteiner, *Tod*, 125-127.
78. Stone, *Front*, 88-89; Strachan, *War*, 353-355; Sondhaus, *Conrad*, 166; Rauchensteiner, *Tod*, 160-161; BMHW-KA eds., *ÖUIK*, vol. 1, 204-218, 242-258.

fourth army came to halt as superior Russian forces were encountered in the battle of Rawa Ruska.[79] The fourth army soon came under even more pressure when the Russian fifth army, having recovered from the defeat suffered at Komarow, advanced toward its left flank, threatening to disrupt the k.u.k. forces' lines of communication and engaging them from the rear. At the same time, counterattacks by the k.u.k. second and third armies, aiming to recapture Lemberg, failed due to the numerical superiority of the enemy and the exhaustion of the k.u.k. forces. The decisive blow to the Austro-Hungarian front, however, was delivered further to the west when the k.u.k. first army, standing all alone due to the k.u.k. fourth army's redirection to Lemberg, came under attack from the Russian fourth and ninth armies, the latter having been redeployed to the south from its gathering area near Warsaw. Having already suffered considerable losses in the battle of Krasnik and facing the risk of being cut off, the k.u.k. first army was forced to retreat in a southern direction.[80] Realizing the imminent danger of a Russian breakthrough on multiple parts of the front and the threat of his troops being cut off by the enemy, Conrad ordered a general retreat of all Austro-Hungarian troops on 11 September. Given the fact that the numerically inferior k.u.k. forces stood little chance of making a stand in the plains of Galicia or on the banks of the rivers San and Dnestr, army command ordered them to fall back to the Carpathians and behind the Dunajec river.[81] Przemysl, the only Austro-Hungarian fortress in the area and the most important railway hub, was surrounded by the enemy on 21 September.[82]

As could be expected from the course of events, the Habsburg Monarchy's army had suffered horrific losses. In less than a month of fighting, the k.u.k. forces on the Russian front had lost about 350.000 men who had been killed, wounded, or captured.[83] Although, in a strictly numerical sense, these losses could quite easily be compensated by bringing in reserves already waiting in the hinterland, the Austro-Hungarian army had in fact received an almost crippling blow. Many of the officers, NCOs and soldiers who had been lost during the first month, had served in the peacetime army prior to the war and had therefore received extensive professional training.

---

79. Auffenberg, *Höhe*, 232-358; Stone, *Front*, 90, Strachan, *War*, 355; BMHW-KA eds., *ÖUIK*, vol. 1, 269-298.

80. Stone, *Front*, 90; Strachan, *War*, 355-356; Rauchensteiner, *Tod*, 161; BMHW-KA eds., *ÖUIK*, vol. 1, 294-298.

81. Auffenberg, *Höhe*, 358-377; Rauchensteiner, *Tod*, 161; Strachan, *War*, 356; Stevenson, *History*, 70-71, BMHW-KA eds., *ÖUIK*, vol. 1, 308-321; Ellis, Cox eds., *Databook*, 26; Griess, *Atlas*, map 28.

82. Rauchensteiner, *Tod*, 162; Strachan, *War*, 357; Stone, *Front*, 90, 95-96.

83. Strachan, *War*, 356; Rumpler, Schmied-Kowarzik, *Weltkriegsstatistik*, 162, 164.

"Grave of an Austro-Hungarian soldier in the Carpathians," Collection Kateřina Bečková

The reserves, which were now called up by the authorities, were mostly middle-aged men who had never seen any kind of military service and were now supposed to learn everything they needed to know as soldiers at the army's training camps in only six to eight weeks.[84] The losses of officers and NCOs were even worse, since the k.u.k. army had already suffered from a lack of professionals at the beginning of the war. Now, with so many young lieutenants and captains killed, wounded, or captured in the first month of the war, many units had to put reserve officers in charge of squads,

---

84. Deák, *Offizier*, 234; BMHW-KA eds., *ÖUIK*, vol. 1, 55-57; Hecht, *Heeresergänzung*, 29-35, 64-69, 128-129, 177.

companies, or even entire battalions.[85] Most of these men, who were called up from their civilian occupations as state officials, teachers, or doctors, had only limited knowledge of how to command troops in battle and often failed to rise to the tasks they were given. The fact that all able officers and NCOs were being called up for field duty was even more problematic, since as a consequence, the training of draftees in the hinterland had to be put into the hands of officers brought back from retirement, who lacked the knowledge and the energy to properly prepare the recruits for modern warfare, further reducing their fighting power.[86] Taking all this into consideration, it is evident that despite the fact that the k.u.k. army managed to replenish the losses it had suffered in the first battles relatively fast, the reserves that were now filling the ranks did not possess the same qualities as their fallen comrades. Given the critical military situation on the Russian front in autumn 1914, it was, however, clear that there would be almost no time for rest.

Counterattack

Given the inauspicious condition of his troops, Conrad, who had for a long time believed that the situation was manageable, had to swallow his pride and turn to the Germans for help. Although he openly claimed that the defeat Austria-Hungary had suffered had been caused by the fact that the Germans had, contrary to their pre-war promises, neglected to draw away Russian forces by launching an offensive from East Prussia, the Austro-Hungarian chief of staff had to accept that he was not in a position to make demands.[87] The military forces of both the Habsburg Monarchy and the German Reich had been confronted with numerically superior Russian forces in August 1914; the main difference, however, was that Paul von Hindenburg and Erich Ludendorff[88], who had resumed command of

---

85. Strachan, *War*, 284-285; Deák, *Offizier*, 232-235. The 28th Infantry Regiment, for example, reported at the beginning of September 1914 that the unit only had 19 professional officers left and that command over five companies had been taken over by reserve officers. See: IR 28 *Tagebuch ab 25. Juli 1914*, 26, *Vojenský ústřední archív Praha, Fond Vojsková tělesa – Pěší pluk 28*, Kt. 2.

86. Hecht, *Heeresergänzung*, 167, 190-191.

87. Strachan, *War*, 357-359; Rauchensteiner, *Tod*, 164-165; Stevenson, *History*, 71. Stone, *Front*, 90; Reichsarchiv ed., *Weltkrieg*, vol. 2, 259-264.

88. On Hindenburg and Ludendorff see: Wolfram Pyta, *Hindenburg. Herrschaft zwischen Hohenzollern und Hitler* (München: Pantheon, 2009); Anna von der Glotz, *Hindenburg. Power, myth, and the rise of the Nazis* (Oxford: Oxford University Press, 2011); Manfred Nebelin, *Ludendorff. Diktator im Ersten Weltkrieg* (München: Siedler, 2010); Robert B. Asprey, *German high command at war. Hindenburg and Ludendorff and the First World War* (London: Warner Books, 1994).

the German troops in East Prussia, had achieved military success, while Conrad had been defeated.[89] Consequently, the German high command took a dim view of the idea of sending reinforcements for the Habsburg Monarchy. In the end, however, logic prevailed. Since all German hopes of achieving a speedy victory over France had been crushed in the Battle of the Marne[90] at the beginning of September, the whole idea of "France first—Russia later" needed to be reconsidered. Before any further operations on the western front could be carried out, the eastern front had to be secured. The worries of the German high command revolved around the possible collapse of the Austro-Hungarian forces holding the line east of Cracow, since a Russian breakthrough at this point would have enabled the Tsarist army to advance into the German industrial heartland of Silesia, a scenario that had to be prevented at any cost. What's more, reconnaissance and intelligence reports suggested that further enemy forces were gathering in the center of Poland, from where they could easily advance into East Prussia or even in the direction of Berlin.[91] Fearing the consequences of being hit by the Russian steamroller, as the Tsarists army's offensives were called because of the Russian troops' numerical superiority,[92] the German high command decided that the eastern front needed to be dealt with once and for all. Under the circumstances, striking first seemed to offer the greatest chances of success.

The plan for the military operation, which was a counterattack for the Austro-Hungarian forces while it was an offense move for their German allies, was presented to Conrad shortly after the retreat of the k.u.k. forces in Galicia had been ordered. Needless to say, the Austro-Hungarian chief of staff was not too happy about it. His skepticism resulted largely from the fact that the German forces were not intending to come to the aid of the k.u.k. army, but instead, the already battered Austro-Hungarian forces were supposed to support them in their invasion of Russian Poland. In fact, Conrad was expected to redeploy the k.u.k. first army, which had taken a defensive position on the Dunajec river east of Cracow after completing its retreat, north of the Vistula. From this position, it was supposed to launch an attack in the direction of the border town Sandomierz, in

89. Stone, *Front*, 61-69; Strachan, *War*, 325-335; Reichsarchiv ed., *Weltkrieg*, vol. 2, 111-244.

90. On the Battle of the Marne see: Stevenson, *History*, 57-60; Strachan, *War*, 242-262; Reichsarchiv ed., *Weltkrieg*, vol. 4 (Berlin: Mittler, 1926).

91. Magocsi, *Atlas*, 122; Griess ed., *Atlas*, Map 28; BMHW-KA eds., *ÖUIK*, vol. 1, supplement 1.

92. Rauchensteiner, *Tod*, 166-167; BMHW-KA eds., *ÖUIK*, vol. 1, 351-356. The phrase was first used by the British newspaper *The Times* on 13. Aug. 1914. *The Times*, 14. Aug. 1914, 4.

this way supporting the troops of the newly established German ninth army advancing from the Silesian border in the direction of the Russian fortress Ivangorod. At the same time, the k.u.k. second, third, and fourth armies were supposed to break free from the defensive positions they had taken in the Carpathians and advance eastwards towards the rivers San and Dnestr.[93] Although the operation could bring relief to the besieged fortress of Przemysl, it was clear that such a move would stretch the lines of the Austro-Hungarian forces, already spread thin, to the limit. It was, in particular, the fact that the k.u.k. first army was not scheduled to fight on Austro-Hungarian soil, but to assist the German forces in the invasion of Poland that greatly enraged Conrad, who saw the possibility of these troops being put under German command as a personal affront. Since there was no real alternative to the plan, and the German high command was most enthusiastic about its prospects, the operation was set in motion in late September 1914 despite all doubts. However, since Conrad, who was the highest-ranking commander on the eastern front, refused to act on the orders of Hindenburg and Ludendorff, who commanded the German forces in the area, there was almost no communication between the two headquarters. Consequently, both sides conducted their own operations without worrying much about how their ally was holding up.[94]

When the offensive finally started on 28 September, the knowledge of both army commands regarding the deployment of the Russian troops was again limited. Conrad and his subordinates were well aware that the Tsarist forces had not yet advanced beyond the San River, but failed to figure out why. The Austro-Hungarian army command speculated that the Russian forces had sustained severe losses during the initial fighting in East Galicia and were therefore no longer able to advance any further or even to redeploy their troops. In reality, the Russians, who believed they had dealt a crippling blow to the Austro-Hungarian army, had stopped their advance at the San river to give their armies time to resupply before the offensive was continued. At the same time, the majority of the Russian forces were redeployed to a gathering area west and northwest of Warsaw, from where they were to launch a large-scale attack into the heartlands of Germany. As a consequence, both the German and the Austro-Hungarian troops were about to march right into the arms of a considerable Russian striking force.[95] Although enemy radio transmissions intercepted in late September gave the German and Austro-Hungarian army command a good impression of

93. Strachan, *War*, 360; Reichsarchiv ed., *Weltkrieg*, vol. 5 (Berlin: Mittler 1929), 402-500; Stone, *Front*, 96-97; Rauchensteiner, *Tod*, 165; BMHW-KA eds., *ÖUIK*, vol. 1, 341-345.
94. Strachan, *War*, 359; Stevenson, *History*, 77-78.
95. Stone, *Front*, 94-97; Rauchensteiner, *Tod*, 166; Strachan, *War*, 357.

what their troops might be up against, neither side chose to act on this information, and both proceeded with preparations for the attack, which began on 28 September.[96] While the German offensive was slowed down by bad weather, the advance of the Austro-Hungarian troops was progressing well, with the fortress of Przemysl being relieved on October 9. However, no matter where the k.u.k. armed forces tried to cross the San river, they met heavy resistance by Russian troops entrenched on the other side of the river. In some cases, the Austro-Hungarian forces managed to form bridgeheads on the east side of the river, but were ultimately repulsed after suffering considerable losses. At this point, it became painfully obvious that the Austro-Hungarian counteroffensive had become stuck.

At the same time, the German ninth army was facing similar, though self-inflicted difficulties. Making good progress in the eastward advance, the German military leaders became overconfident and drew up a plan to redirect the thrust of the ninth army northwards to threaten or even capture Warsaw.[97] However, to make such a redirection possible, someone had to take the position the German forces would have to abandon when they moved north. This task was supposed to be taken over by the Austro-Hungarian army, which had, at least in the eyes of the German high command, already achieved its primary objective with the relief of Przemysl and could therefore extend its lines further to the left. Consequently, the k.u.k. first army was ordered to stop its advance on Sandomierz and instead continue in a northeastern direction towards Ivangorod, while the k.u.k. second, third, and fourth armies attempted to keep the Russians under control at the San River.[98] As the entire operation was highly ambitious, and the lines of the Austro-Hungarian and German forces were spread far too thin, disaster was unavoidable. On 12 October, the ninth German army encountered a large number of Russian troops southeast of Warsaw. In danger of being overwhelmed by numerically superior forces on its left flank, it was finally forced to retreat on 20 October. Only a few days later, the advance of the k.u.k. first army on Ivangorod was halted by a counterattack of Russian troops, which forced the Austro-Hungarian forces to break off the fight and fall back along the Vistula River.[99] This withdrawal had severe consequences for the troops holding the line at the San river, since the retreat of the k.u.k. first army exposed their left flank, a fact that consequently forced them to

96. Strachan, *War*, 361; Reichsarchiv ed., *Weltkrieg*, vol. 5, 418-429; BMHW-KA eds., *ÖUIK*, vol. 1, 356-372; Griess ed., *Atlas*, map 29; Ellis Cox eds., *Databook*, 28.
97. Stone, *Front*, 97-98; Strachan, *War*, 361; Reichsarchiv ed., *Weltkrieg*, vol. 5, 435-462.
98. Rauchensteiner, *Tod*, 166-167; BMHW-KA eds., *ÖUIK*, vol. 1, 399-450.
99. Stone, *Front*, 99-100; Rauchensteiner, *Tod*, 167; Strachan, *War*, 165-167; Stevenson, *History*, 77-78; Reichsarchiv ed., *Weltkrieg*, vol.5, 435-491.

give up their position as well and to withdraw back to the Carpathians.[100] By mid-November, both the Austro-Hungarian and the German forces had resumed the defensive positions from where they had started the counteroffensive at the beginning of October. The fortress of Przemysl was once again surrounded by Russian troops; it would hold out until its surrender in March 1915.

But the newly established *Oberkommando Ost*,[101] which was headed by Hindenburg and Ludendorff, was not yet ready to accept defeat. In another daring plan, they proposed to move the German ninth army, which was holding the line at the Silesian border, up north and have it carry out a strike in the flank of the Russian troops gathered around Lodz. However, in order for this plan to work, the position the ninth army would leave when it was redeployed again had to be taken over by someone else. Since the Germans couldn't spare any further reserves, Conrad was approached, and agreed to withdraw large parts of the k.u.k. second army from the Carpathians and redeploy them to the border of Silesia.[102] This move, however, would leave a considerable gap in the Austro-Hungarian frontline just below Cracow, a fact that would certainly not go unnoticed by the Russians. Despite the risks, and the tensions between the two sides' commanders, the operation was set in motion in mid-November. Contrary to what could have been expected, given the boldness of the plan and the numerical superiority of the Russian forces, it was a resounding success. Even if the Germans ultimately failed to capture Lodz, the Russian forces decided to stop their counterattacks in the end and began to withdraw further into the east of Poland to take a defensive position.[103] In a last attempt to achieve a breakthrough before the beginning of winter, the Tsarist army launched a large-scale attack shortly afterwards on the positions of the Austro-Hungarian forces south of Cracow, where the withdrawal of the k.u.k. second army had left a hole in the frontline. However, since the Austro-Hungarian army command managed to figure out the enemy's intentions in advance, the k.u.k. forces were regrouped in order to successfully meet the enemy. In an intense battle that raged southeast of Cracow between 1 and 12 December, and inflicted huge casualties on both sides, the Austro-Hungarian army ultimately managed to stop the Russian attack and to

100. Stevenson, *History*, 78; Stone, *Front*, 99-100; BMHW-KA eds., *ÖUIK*, vol. 1, 489-521; Griess ed., *Atlas*, map 29; Ellis, Cox eds., *Databook*, 28.

101. Strachen, *War*, 368; Rauchensteiner, *Tod*, 168; Reichsarchiv ed., *Weltkrieg*, vol. 6 (Berlin: Mittler, 1929), 34-57; BMHW-KA eds., *ÖUIK*, vol. 1, 501.

102. Rauchensteiner, *Tod*, 181-182; Strachan, *War*, 368; Stone, *Front*, 101; BMHW-KA eds., *ÖUIK*, vol. 1, 506-513.

103. Strachan, *War*, 369-371; Stone, *Front*, 104-107; Reichsarchiv ed., *Weltkrieg*, vol. 6, 98-226.

drive the Tsarist army back behind the Dunajec River.[104] The Battle of Limanowa-Lapanow, as the engagement was later called, effectively ended large-scale military operations on the eastern front in 1914, with both sides now concentrating on fortifying their positions and preparing their troops for the approaching winter.[105] The Central Powers had definitely succeeded in crushing the offensive power of the Tsarist army, derailing the Russian steamroller for the time being. For Austria-Hungary, however, this victory had come at a high price.

Conclusion

The question who or what exactly was to blame for the military catastrophe Austria-Hungary suffered on the Russian front in summer/autumn 1914 is difficult to answer, since throughout the entire campaign several factors contributed to the course of events. There was not so much the Austro-Hungarian army could do about the enemy's numerical superiority, the bottlenecks in the country's railway network, or the vast terrain of the Galician plains that was difficult to defend. However, even in 1914, it was obvious that the Habsburg Monarchy's military leaders had made a series of grave mistakes. Consequently, by December 1914, four Austro-Hungarian army commanders had been removed from their posts and forced to retire.[106] The only person who denied any responsibility for the tragic events and was left in his position was chief of staff Conrad von Hötzendorf. In his opinion, the k.u.k. army's defeat in the first battles in August had, for the most part, been caused by the fact that, contrary to the promises given before the war, the German Reich had failed to support its ally by launching an offensive from East Prussia into Russian Poland.[107] Given the fact that the German eighth army concentrated in East Prussia was facing numerically superior Russian forces as well, and was already engaged in heavy fighting when the Austro-Hungarian army started its operation on the eastern front, this accusation is quite inaccurate. Conrad's further claim that his subordinates and his troops had failed him and thus also contributed to the adverse course of events is even more unfair since the soldiers, regardless of their nationality, had performed well during the initial battles, and most of the

104. Rauchensteiner, Tod, 182; Stone, Front, 108; Stevenson, History, 78-79, BMHW-KA eds., ÖUIK, vol. 1, 765-812; Griess ed., Atlas, map 29; Ellis, Cox eds., Databook, 30; Reichsarchiv ed., Weltkrieg, vol. 6, 227-323.
105. Strachan, War, 372-373. On the winter war in the Carpathians see above all: Graydon Tunstall, Blood on the snow. The Carpathian Winter War of 1915 (Lawrence: Kansas University Press, 2010).
106. Rauchensteiner, Tod, 163.
107. Conrad, Dienstzeit, vol. 1, 373-406.

operations of the Austro-Hungarian forces that had ultimately ended in disaster (above all the advance of the k.u.k. third army east of Lemberg) had been ordered by the chief of staff himself. His claims, however, were grist for the mills of those military commanders who later tried to blame their misfortune on the battlefield on the passive attitude of their non-German or, conversely, non-Hungarian soldiers, further fuelling the national conflict within the Habsburg Monarchy.[108] Military historians today also attribute some of the military mishaps in autumn 1914 to the fact that Conrad had failed to understand that the losses sustained by his troops during the initial battles had reduced the fighting strength of many units to such an extent that they were no longer able to perform the way they had in peacetime military maneuvers.

Conrad is furthermore faulted for not intervening in the railway transports after it had become obvious that Russia would enter the war, a decision that, as pointed out, led to the misdeployment of the k.u.k. second army in the Balkans.[109] The former chief of staff later stated that St. Petersburg's decision to side with Serbia could not have been foreseen from the beginning, and that the misdeployment of the troops of *Staffel B* had been caused by the overly complex schedule put together by the railway bureau which, contrary to what had been promised to him, had allowed no major changes once mobilization had begun. Even if part of the blame can actually be put on the railway bureau for putting together such an inflexible mobilization plan, it is obvious that it was Conrad who had eliminated all scope of action with his overly hasty decision, on 25 July, to mobilize for a conflict limited to the Balkans instead of just calling up *Minimalgruppe* and waiting with the deployment of *Staffel B* until the Russian position in the conflict had become evident. Nevertheless, even if the k.u.k. second army had not been redirected to the Balkans but had proceeded to Galicia as planned, it would most likely not have prevented the course of events, since it would have operated on the left wing of the Austro-Hungarian forces and therefore have been unable to come to the aid of the k.u.k. third army when it came under attack east of Lemberg. This fact also shows the major flaw in the new Austro-Hungarian battle plan put together in spring 1914 quite well. The assumption that the Tsarist army would concentrate the bulk of its forces alongside the northern border of Galicia, where they could be engaged by the Austro-Hungarian forces in an attack launched in a northeastern direction, was somewhat unrealistic, especially given the fact that the original operation plans leaked to the Russian secret service by

108. Bardolff, *Soldat*, 236; Stone, *Front*, 126-127.
109. Stevenson, *History*, 69; Strachan, *War*, 294-296.

Colonel Redl had included a similar move just a few hundred kilometers further to the east. Combined with the almost complete failure of reconnaissance—the k.u.k. army was forced to begin operations without any detailed information on where the bulk of the enemy forces were located—this fact contributed greatly to the defeat suffered by the Austro-Hungarian armed forces in Galicia in August 1914.

Despite these facts, the blame for the military mishaps suffered by the armies of the German Reich and the Habsburg Monarchy in the eastern theater in summer/autumn 1914 cannot be placed on Conrad alone. In fact, it had been Hindenburg and Ludendorff who had drawn up the highly ambitious plan for the counteroffensive in Poland in September/October. What is most striking about the operation, besides the fact that it had to be started almost without any reconnaissance information, is that there was almost no communication between the Austro-Hungarian and German headquarters when it was carried out.[110] For the most part, this was because the two sides' army commanders neither respected nor trusted each other. While Conrad had sore feelings because he was convinced that the Germans had broken their promise to support him in the opening battles, and was furthermore unwilling to accept orders from Hindenburg and Ludendorff, who had a lower military rank than he did, the two German generals saw the Austro-Hungarian chief of staff as just an elderly k.u.k. general who had failed to lead his troops properly on the battlefield. Ludendorff can furthermore be accused of having become overconfident in the course of the attack; his decision to redirect the German ninth army in a northeastern direction finally overstretched the lines of the allied troops and ultimately doomed the entire operation to failure. His claim that the counteroffensive had broken down due to the failure of the Austro-Hungarian troops is highly unjustified, since the k.u.k. armies had performed well despite the previously sustained losses and were only forced to retreat when numerically superior Russian troops penetrated the overstretched lines of the k.u.k. first army west of Ivangorod. The fact that the second counteroffensive aimed at Lodz, which was as overly ambitious as the previous one, was carried out successfully was largely owed to luck and the incompetence of local Russian commanders.[111] However, in the end, the victory cemented the status of Hindenburg and Ludendorff as the military masterminds of the Central Powers in the east.[112] Conrad, who could only claim the battle of Limanowa-Lapanow as an undisputed military success, managed to keep his position, but reluctantly had to accept the supremacy of the German military leaders

110. Strachan, *War*, 359-360.
111. Stone, *Front*, 101-108; Strachan, *War*, 371.
112. Strachan, *War*, 368.

after the establishment of *Oberkommando Ost*. This, however, didn't mean that relations between the two allies would improve; in fact, there were more quarrels to come in the next years of the war.

Regardless of who was actually to blame for the military setbacks on the eastern front in 1914, it must be pointed out that it was the k.u.k. army that had paid an exceptionally high price for the mistakes made. Between August and December 1914, the k.u.k. armed forces lost more than 700.000 officers and men, about 126.000 of them killed, 597.000 wounded, and 271.000 captured or missing.[113] The loss of 14.000 officers (of whom 3.000 had been killed and 2.800 had been captured) was especially painful, since these men could not easily be replaced.[114] These extreme casualty rates were above all the outcome of the flawed Austro-Hungarian military doctrine that forced every k.u.k. officer, NCO, and soldier to press on the attack on the battlefield regardless of the lives and resources it would cost. While such a strategy was foolish even in a local engagement of limited duration, it came close to suicide in a large-scale, lengthy armed conflict. The Austro-Hungarian armed forces learned their lesson rather quickly, reorganizing the training of the troops as well as their tactics on the battlefield. Terms like entrenchments, barbed wire defenses, covering fire and caution, which had been almost unknown to the k.u.k. officers and men, suddenly filled the tactical handbooks from spring 1915 onwards.[115] These steps achieved the desired effect: the casualty rates of the Austro-Hungarian army never again rose to the level of summer/autumn 1914.[116] By that time, however, most of the damage had already been done. By January 1915, the Austro-Hungarian army had lost two thirds of the officers and about one half of the soldiers that had served in the armed forces during peacetime.[117] The men who were brought in to replace them—reserve officers and draftees without any military experience—managed to fill the ranks, but ultimately lacked the operational capabilities the army had possessed prior to 1914. Even though the battles of 1914 had not broken its back, the k.u.k. army was limping from then on and would never fully recover. The fact that warfare now had to be put into the hands of "civilians in uniform," as István Deák

---

113. Rumpler, Schmied-Kowarzik, *Weltkriegsstatistik*, 161.
114.   Deák, *Offizier*, 232-235; Rumpler, Schmied-Kowarzik, *Weltkriegsstatistik*, 161; BMHW-KA eds., *ÖUIK*, vol. 2 (Wien: Verlag der Militärwissenschaftlichen Mitteilungen, 1931), 10.
115.   Hugo Schmid, *Taktisches Handbuch*, 15th edition (Wien: Seidl, 1916). Conrad's book on the battle training of infantry, which was reprinted in 1917, was on the contrary never brought up to date. See: Franz Conrad von Hötzendorf, *Die Gefechtsausbildung der Infanterie*, 5th edition (Wien: Seidl, 1913); Ibid., 6th edition (Wien: Seidl, 1917).
116.   Rumpler, Schmied-Kowarzik, *Weltkriegsstatistik*, 164-165.
117.   Rauchensteiner, *Tod*, 188; Deák, *Offizier*, 234.

once put it,[118] not only diminished the reputation of the k.u.k. army in the eyes of the German high command, but to some degree also hampered future military operations. Even Conrad once complained that a certain operation could easily have been carried out if he had had the army of 1914 at his disposal. Given the fact that he was one of the people directly responsible for the huge losses the k.u.k. army had suffered during the first months of the war, this statement seems downright cynical.

118. Deák, *Offizier*, 233.

The Habsburg Empire, Serbia, and 1914: The Significance of a Sideshow

Jonathan Gumz

One can easily construct a narrative around the Habsburg Empire's encounter with Serbia in World War I that reduces it to a sideshow. If anything surprises us, it is Serbia's residual military capacity after the Balkan Wars and its infliction of not just one, but two stunning defeats on the Habsburg Army in the short period of the final five months of 1914. At one level, the long-term outcome never really was in doubt. Yet the surprises that created such detours in the road to that outcome do have significance, in particular for the Habsburg Empire. Moreover, the Empire's war against Serbia in 1914 needs to be viewed as something that encapsulated a much larger set of pressures placed on war as a whole within Europe at the beginning of the 20th century. Studying this war, it is possible to see how international legal structures intended to govern the divide between civilian and soldier came under pressure. Finally, the Habsburg Army's war with Serbia reflected the difficulty the Army had containing its own war at home against those it believed were at the heart of the nationalization and subversion of the Empire. This internal war, hastily and carelessly prosecuted by the Army, flowed almost seamlessly into the war with Serbia and led the Army to place pressure on the very international norms that it believed it represented.[1]

Though not yet extensively researched, a picture of the military technical elements of the Habsburg invasion of Serbia is beginning to emerge. This invasion was marked by a contradictory blend of expectations, shaped in part by hope and in part by a determination to thoroughly punish Serbia for its role in the assassination in Sarajevo. Moreover, a kind of great power arrogance marked the Habsburg planning for the invasion of Serbia.

---

1. The standard work on the Army's internal war remains: Christoph Führ, *Das k.u.k. Armeeoberkommando und die Innenpolitik in Österreich, 1914-1917*, vol. 7, Studien zur Geschichte der Österreichisch-Ungarischen Monarchie (Graz: H. Böhlau, 1968). The ideological basis for this war can be explored in: Günther Kronenbitter, *"Krieg Im Frieden": Die Führung der k.u.k. Armee und die Grossmachtpolitik Österreich-Ungarns 1906-1914*, vol. 13, Studien zur internationalen Geschichte (München: Oldenbourg, 2003).

Strictly speaking, the Army's military goals were extensive and required no less than the destruction of the Serbian Army. This was not an attempt to quickly stun or paralyze the Serb state and Army. Taking Belgrade would have sufficed for that. The Habsburg invasion plan aimed at the complete defeat of Serbia.

That grand vision of Serb defeat ran into a host of stumbling blocks, some unique to the Habsburg Army. First, it must be said that the Serb Army was a formidable force, though we should be careful not to overexaggerate here. The Serb Army had extensive combat experience from the Balkan Wars, but the obverse of such experience can be a degree of exhaustion. In any terms, Serbia was already more deeply mobilized in 1914 than any of the other Great Power combatants that year. In terms of armaments, the Serb Army possessed good numbers of modern artillery pieces and, at least for the initial round of fighting, sufficient, though not plentiful, amounts of shell. Yet, Serbia was by and large heavily dependent on imports for armaments. The long-term prospects for such imports in an extended conflict in which all belligerents would eventually find themselves short of shell was problematic.[2] At the same time, the recent fighting from the Balkan Wars meant that some of the Serb Army's equipment and armaments were damaged and in need of replacement. Again, caution is in order before we overexaggerate Serb strengths, but the Habsburg Army did have weaknesses when it came to artillery. The Habsburg side lacked sufficient numbers of quick firing artillery effectively distributed and integrated across the force.[3]

The prospect of fighting a great power coupled with the years of prior war led Serbia to overmobilize. This overmobilization points to how far Serbia was willing to push the limits of fighting. In addition to its first 3 levies, Serbia had a fourth levy planned that included the call up of men between the ages of 18 and 20 and those over 50. Appropriately, this levy was called "last defense." The call up for this levy had already begun on 5 September, 1914. Serbia went further and faster when it came to mobilizing portions of its population than any other combatant at this point in the war. Just by way of comparison, it would take Germany over two years of fighting to get to the point that Serbia was at in terms of the depth of mobilization during the first month of the conflict.[4] This led to shortages

---

2. Hew Strachan, *The First World War: To Arms* (New York: Oxford University Press, 2001), Vol. 1, 345-347.

3. David G. Hermann, *The Arming of Europe and the Making of the First World War* (Princeton: Princeton University Press, 1996), 202.

4. Roger Chickering, *Imperial Germany and the Great War, 1914-1918* (New York: Cambridge University Press, 2004), 82.

throughout the Serbian force in terms of basic equipment and armaments. While Serbia attempted to outfit the soldiers of the first levy, the soldiers of the second and third levies were only partially outfitted at best. Soldiers could not be outfitted with proper footwear, only receiving makeshift *opanci*, a cheap substitute. According to James Lyon, one division's *opanci* were so poorly made that portions of that division went barefoot early on in the fighting. Shortages rippled out through the force in other areas. Rifles, horses, coats, entrenching tools—all were in short supply. Most critically, the soldiers of the third levy, men between the ages of 38 and 45, lacked any uniforms whatsoever and were armed only with black powder rifles. Soldiers of the second levy were issued caps and coats, but the coats were hardly needed in the searing August heat.[5]

Thus, neither side was in a position of overwhelming superiority at the beginning of the war. Yes, Serbia would be in a precarious position in a long drawn out conflict with the Habsburg Empire as well as Germany and any other allies the Central Powers could draw to their side. Yet, seen from the perspective of August 1914, few were anticipating a long war. What quickly becomes apparent to anyone who examines these campaigns are the problematic elements of the Habsburg military leadership. The experience of fighting in August 1914 would quickly unearth the disunity and jealousies rife throughout the Habsburg Army leadership.[6] In addition, the invasion plans for Serbia were overly ambitious given the strategic situation that the Empire faced in 1914.

From a strictly military perspective, Serbia presented several challenges for both the defenders and the attackers. Serbia shared long borders with the Habsburg Empire, bordered by Bosnia to the west and Syrmia to the north. Belgrade, though at one point a formidable military strong point, was more of a vulnerability than anything else in 1914. The impressive Kalimegdan fortress was not the defense bulwark that it had been in the 18th century. The Serb military leadership had to make choices about organizing the defense of the country. An all-out perimeter defense was impossible. Even though the Empire was Serbia's only opponent in the

5. On the state of the Serbian Army in 1914, see James B. Lyon, "Serbia and the Balkan Front, 1914," (Diss., University of California-Los Angeles, 1995). See also, James B. Lyon, "'A Peasant Mob': The Serbian Army on the Eve of the Great War," *The Journal of Military History* 61, no. 3 (July 1997): 481–502; Gunther E. Rothenberg, "The Austro-Hungarian Campaign Against Serbia in 1914," *The Journal of Military History* 53, no. 2 (April 1989): 127–146; John R. Schindler, "Disaster on the Drina: The Austro-Hungarian Army in Serbia, 1914," *War in History* 9, no. 2 (April 2002): 159–195.

6. On this rivalry, see, Rudolf Jeřábek, *Potiorek: General im Schatten von Sarajevo* (Graz: Styria Verlag, 1991); Lawrence Sondhaus, *Franz Conrad von Hötzendorf: Architect of the Apocalypse* (Boston: Humanities Press, 2000); Wolfram Dornik, *Des Kaisers Falke: Wirken und Nach-Wirken von Franz Conrad von Hötzendorf* (Innsbruck: Studien Verlag, 2013).

initial stage of the conflict, it also could not denude its southern and eastern borders of units because these areas bordered Greek and Bulgarian rivals. Despite the relative challenges that the Save (Sava) River presented to northern invaders, Serbia was still most vulnerable to these attacks since they would offer the invader access to a north-south invasion route that cut through to strategic cities such as Kragujevac. In the west, however, Serbia not only had the advantages of the Drina River border with the Empire, but also the terrain in this area was quite mountainous. For a conscript army with limited specialized mountain units, attacking over the mountains would present an array of problems. In addition, rail transport within the Empire itself flowed toward the northern border of Serbia, not its western border. The rail network in Bosnia was underdeveloped and east-west lines running to the Serbian border were nonexistent.[7]

The Serbian Army's plans for the defense of the country centered on drawing the Habsburg Army into Serbia, where it could concentrate its forces more effectively. As the Habsburg armies moved into the country, the Serb Army would attack their flanks and undermine stretched Habsburg supply lines. Thus, the highest quality Serb units would be husbanded away from the borders of the country in order to avoid attrition at the hands of the Habsburg Army. The plan was not without risk. Once the invading Habsburg units were in the interior of the country, a Serbian loss could be potentially catastrophic. From the Habsburg side, the invasion plan in August 1914 was concentrated away from Belgrade and on the west and northwest corners of the country. The thought from the commander of the Habsburg invasion forces and the Governor of Bosnia-Herzegovina, Oskar Potiorek, was that the 5th and 6th Armies in the west combined with elements of the 2nd Army attacking from the north would steadily concentrate and lock down the Serb forces. The result would be a quick, decisive fight in which the Serb forces would find themselves cornered and driven eastwards in the direction of Kragujevac.[8]

This ideal plan quickly fell apart in practice. The invading Habsburg forces did not enjoy numerical superiority to begin with.[9] Moreover, the growing crisis in Galicia, strategically the more important front, meant that the 2nd Army, with the exception of the 8th Corps, was to be routed northwards by 18 August. This was not without its problems, however, and

---

7. On Habsburg rule in Bosnia, see, Robin Okey, *Taming Balkan Nationalism: The Habsburg Civilizing Mission in Bosnia, 1878-1914* (New York: Oxford University Press, 2007).
8. Edmund Glaise von Horstenau, ed., *Österreich-Ungarns letzter Krieg, 1914-1918, vol. 1: Das Kriegsjahr 1914. Vom Kriegsausbruch bis zum Ausgang der Schlacht bei Limanowa-Łapanów* (Vienna: Bundesministerium für Landesverteidigung and the Kriegsarchiv, 1930).
9. Schindler, "Disaster on the Drina," 163.

the lack of unity in the Habsburg command—Potiorek was not technically under the command of the Conrad's *Armeeoberkommando* at the beginning of the war—led to critical delays. Moreover, the portion of Liborius Frank's 5th Army tasked with attacking across the Drina River in the West was poorly prepared for task in front of it. The 5th Army had trouble bridging the Drina River, was not at all equipped for mountain warfare, and could not keep in contact with the 6th Army to the south. In general, the Habsburg command was hampered by a combination of overambitious goals and confusion as to the overall importance of Serbia to the war. These circumstances led to redeployment of most of the 2nd Army to Galicia to shore up the defenses against the Russian Army. By contrast, the Serb Army leadership had a much more coherent sense of the challenges ahead of it, especially in the short term, and a clear operational concept for dealing with the challenges posed by the Habsburg invasion in August 1914. Putnik skillfully drew the Habsburg invasion into Serbia, dealt with the invasion armies individually from a position of strength—most notably with the 5th Army at the Battle of Mt. Cer on 20 August—and threw back the Habsburg invasion before August had even ended.[10]

Potiorek would attempt to invade Serbia twice more over the course of 1914. The final invasion attempt in November 1914 met with initial success, leading to the capture of Belgrade in early December 1914, but collapsed spectacularly under a Serb Army counteroffensive from the east that led to the retaking of Belgrade on 16 December, 1914. Potiorek was dismissed, his connections to court notwithstanding, and the Empire's attempt to "punish" Serbia had come to a humiliating end, at least for the moment.

The Other Part of the War

While the imperial leadership in December 1914 was concerned about the implications of defeat in Serbia for its image abroad, the widespread Habsburg violence against civilians during the August invasion was representative of the broader problems of war in 1914. As they did elsewhere in Europe, the international norms that governed war and attempted to legally codify the concept of the civilian and legitimate belligerent came under severe pressure in Serbia. For the Habsburg Army, the fighting in the first month in Serbia cut directly against its vision of how war should be conducted. This fighting helped solidify the image of Serbia as a near-criminal regime, at least one that consistently violated international law. The

---

10. Andrej Mitrović, *Serbia's Great War, 1914-1918* (London: Hurst, 2007).

first month of the war also helped situate the Habsburg Empire, at least when it came to military practice, on the edge of international norms. In Serbia, the European vision of contained conflict, itself increasingly intertwined with the international legal project to shape the conduct of war, came under severe pressure. The pressure on contained conflict outside the Empire also linked closely with the broader legal transformation of portions of the Habsburg Empire in the early months of the conflict.

Perhaps the most important place to begin is with a clear understanding of the international norms that governed conflict in 1914. In this, it will do no good to simply consider these norms as attempts to create a peaceful Europe. It will also do no good to view these norms in a straightforward genealogy that ends with the human rights norms established in the aftermath of the World War II or those norms that developed during the 1970's.[11] It is best to recall the specific context of the creation of those legal norms in the late 19th century. Especially with regard to land warfare, those norms, aside from those embodied in the Geneva Convention of 1864 and St. Petersburg Declaration of 1868, arose in the aftermath of the Franco-Prussian War.[12] The problem in the Franco-Prussian War was essentially one of war termination above all. For both France and the North German Confederation, the future Germany, the trauma of the war emanated out of events after the Battle of Sedan. For France, the problem was one of a fracturing state and army after Sedan, culminating in the Paris Commune. For Prussian Army and Bismarck, the post-Sedan atmosphere made it difficult to bring the war to a close. For Bismarck, the threatening and precarious international situation demanded a quick cessation of hostilities. For the Prussian Army, its strategic victory over the French at Sedan did not make its position in France any easier. Dispersed French forces were difficult to subdue, supply lines were stretched, and the phenomenon of the *franc-tireur*, both perceived and real, combined to create a combustible atmosphere for the Prussian Army. The essential problem was one of a power that fought past the point of defeat. The reaction of the Prussian Army, marked by hostage taking, reprisals and the shelling of Paris, only enflamed it. In short, the war threatened to become dangerously uncontained.[13]

---

11. Samuel Moyn, *The Last Utopia: Human Rights in History* (Cambridge: Belknap Harvard University Press, 2010).

12. On the centrality of the Franco-Prussian War, see, Daniela L. Caglioti, "Waging War on Civilians: The Expulsion of Aliens in the Franco-Prussian War," *Past & Present* 221, no. 1 (November 2013): 189-190; Isabel V. Hull, *Absolute Destruction: Military Culture and the Practices of War in Imperial Germany* (Ithaca: Cornell University Press, 2005).

13. Michael Howard, *The Franco-Prussian War; the German Invasion of France, 1870-1871* (New York: Macmillan, 1961); Geoffrey Wawro, *The Franco-Prussian War the German Conquest of France in 1870-1871* (New York: Cambridge University Press, 2003).

It is this context that gave birth to the international norms governing land warfare in the late 19th century. The issue was so fractious that the first attempt to regulate land warfare in Brussels in 1874 failed to produce a treaty. Instead, a declaration was issued. Reflecting the experience of the Franco-Prussian War, the conference concentrated only on regulating land warfare. The Brussels Declaration of 1874 created the concept of belligerent occupation and attempted to expressly demarcate the line between civilians and belligerents. The occupying state became a trustee for the defeated sovereign state, giving that state an incentive to accept defeat. The occupier was referred to as a "usufructuary." In belligerent occupation, sovereignty did not pass into the hands of the occupier. At Brussels, four qualifications for belligerent status were laid out as well. To qualify as belligerents, people had to "be commanded by a person responsible for his subordinates," "have a fixed distinctive emblem recognizable at a distance," "carry their arms openly," and "conduct their operations in accordance with the laws and customs of war."[14] At the same time, Article 10 declared "the population of a territory which has not been occupied, who, on the approach of the enemy, spontaneously take up arms to resist the invading troops without having had time to organize themselves in accordance with Article 9, shall be regarded as belligerents if they respect the laws and customs of war." Of course, this article raised and left unanswered the question of what precisely the "laws and customs of war" were. This clause also seemed to imply that once occupation had commenced, resistance to occupation no longer received international legal sanction.

All of this was later codified in the Hague Convention of 1900 despite various attempts to change elements of it. At The Hague, one of the Belgian delegates, Auguste Beernaert, maintained that occupation actually instituted a "regime of defeat." There were also efforts to loosen restrictions around belligerent status and officially sanction resistance into the period of occupation. The German representative in particular vigorously fought back against any suggestion of extending resistance into the period of occupation. Ironically enough, the Belgian delegate argued that international law set limits to patriotism in this instance. Later historians, such as Geoffrey Best, argued that this was a clash of interests between great powers and small states with the great powers wanting to restrict resistance as much as possible and small states wanting to open up as much room for resistance as possible.[15] While this is in some sense true, perhaps it is better to remove

14. Article 9, Project of an International Declaration Concerning the Laws and Customs of War on Land, Brussels, 27 August 1874, at http://www.icrc.org/applic/ihl/ihl.nsf/ART/135-70009?OpenDocument, (13. January 2014)
15. Geoffrey Best, *Humanity in Warfare* (New York: Columbia University Press, 1980).

this from the realm of interest to a certain extent and merely note what appeared as a norm out of The Hague Conventions. Increasingly, the word "civilian" was sharply defined in terms of who was and was not a belligerent. The Conventions still embodied the clean categories of the 19th century approach to war as Michael Geyer called it, but those categories became hazy during the period of invasion.[16]

The problems of civilians in war began for the Habsburg Army before the army even crossed the border into Serbia. The beginning of the war heralded a massive military intervention into civil society across the Empire, in particular in Cisleithania and those areas considered unstable along the border. Of course, Bosnia-Herzegovina provided a prime target for the Army's crackdown. The flourishing of political and associational life in Bosnia-Herzegovina drew the wrath of Army leaders. Potiorek directly connected politics in Bosnia with subversion from Serbia. Political parties influenced schools and associations. They "made it possible for the enemies of the Monarchy to pour the poison of high treason systematically and drop by drop into the population," according to Potiorek.[17] This political and associational activity concealed a Serb "military shadow government" which coordinated "acts of high treason" throughout Bosnia-Herzegovina. Reflecting the uncertainty of the border and the feeling that Serbia was constantly exercising influence in Bosnia, Potiorek tied Serbian state and Army circles with Serbian nationalist organizations in the Monarchy. In Vienna, Conrad, despite a long history of personal animosity with Potiorek, found all these claims convincing. Potiorek's flow of reports revealed a "widely branched out, deeply rooted, and well-organized conspiracy" in Bosnia. "For me there never existed a doubt," explained Conrad, "that revolutionary actions directed against the Monarchy took place with the knowledge and patronage of the Serbian government."[18]

Politics and treason crossed the line into war, drawing Serb civilians from within the Empire into the ranks of guerrillas or *Komitadjis*. *Komitadjis* recruited from within the Empire as well as some from Serbia itself would move among the Serb population and encourage a broader Serb revolt. Colonel Oskar Hranilović, the chief of Army intelligence, predicted the *Komitadjis* would "drive into the areas inhabited by Serbs and try to

16. Michael Geyer, "The Militarization of Europe, 1914-1945," in John R. Gillis, ed., *The Militarization of the Western World* (New Brunswick: Rutgers University Press, 1989), 72-79.

17. Kriegsarchiv Wien (herafter KAW), Nachläße, Nachlaß Potiorek, B/1503: 5, Persönliche Vormerkungen XIV, "Entwicklung der innerpolitischen Lage in der Zeit vom 1. bis 10. Juli 1914," p. 3, 14-15.

18. KAW, Nachläße, Nachlaß Potiorek, B/1503:5, Nr. 74, Conrad to Potiorek, Res. Gstbs Nr. 2702, July 21, 1914.

organize an insurgency." Thus, according to his prediction, the Habsburg Army would face civilian fighters on its home soil before it ever encountered them in Serbia. The "main task of the bands," contended Hranilović, "is to transform the population of Bosnia and Herzegovina into insurgents."[19]

Such predictions were reinforced as reports of *Komitadjis*, sabotage, and subversion by Serb communities in Bosnia-Herzegovina and other territories surfaced within the Army. Reports such as these had a perverse way of confirming predictions of *Komitadjis* and sabotage in Bosnia even for those soldiers who never saw this themselves. The *Militärstationskommandant* in Banja Luka believed that Serb nationalists had already turned most of the rural Serb population. They were prepared to "reach the great goal and prepare for the decisive hour."[20] The 9th Corps thought Serb villages in the Fruska Gora region were "signaling" the enemy. In the course of their searches of these villages "reports of numerous weapons, hand grenades, and bombs" had been received.[21] The 9th Corps forbade the ringing of church bells near the border because they believed these were part of a system to signal the Army's positions.[22] Further enraging the Army was the conviction that Serb women were involved in subversion and insurgency. Soldiers near one town, for example, complained they were "fired upon from behind by women."[23] The involvement of women from a peaceful territory in the prosecution of war and high treason underlined the way in which the war was spilling out of its 19th century boundaries already in the early days of the conflict. "Words do not suffice to describe the perfidious conduct of the population here," said the commander of the Second Army.[24] General Lukas Snjarić, the commander of the gendarmerie in Bosnia, claimed that Habsburg Serb citizens "have shot at our troops, trains, even hospital units

---

19. KAW, NFA, 2. Armee, AOK, Kriegsfall B 1914/15, Subbeilage c) der Beilage 21, Colonel Hranilović, "Über Wesen, Ausrüstung und Kampfesart der Komitadschis," Juli 1914, Karton 2.
20. KAW, NFA, 6.Armee, *k.u.k. Militärstationskommando Banja Luka to the k.u.k. 6. Armeeoberkommando*, "Militärischer- und politischer Situationsbericht," Res. Nr. 99/Mob., 8 August 1914, Karton 12.
21. KAW, NFA, 6.Armee, *9 Korps to the k.u.k. 29.Infanteriedivision*, Op. Nr. 70, 6 August 1914, Karton 2. See also KAW, NFA, 6.Armee, *9.Korps to the k.u.k. 29.Infanteriedivision*, zu Op. Nr. 70, 7 August 1914, Karton 2; KAW, NFA, 5.Armeekommando, *Petrowardin to 5.Armeekommanndo*, Nr. 183, 19 September 1914, Karton 892. The efforts to spot signals were notoriously prone to error. See, KAW, NFA, Unknown Gendarmerie Officer to the *5.Armeekommando-Etappen-Kommando*, "Hinanhaltung unbegründeten Verdächtigen," Nr. 161, 28 September 1914, Karton 924.
22. KAW, NFA, 2. Armee, *9.Korps*, Res. Nr. 2 (Op. 287), 8 August 1914, Karton 2.
23. KAW, NFA, 5.Armeekommando, Unknown K-Stelle Report to *5.Armeekommando*, 6-7/26-24, 9 August 1914, Karton 892.
24. KAW, NFA, *Oberkommando der Balkanstreitkräfte, k.u.k. 2. Armeeoberkommando* (General Böhm) to Potiorek, K. Nr. 40., 17 August 1914, Karton 86.

while in transit and in villages, have fought with the enemy against us, have led reconnaissance and served as scouts in different ways, [and] then attempted to attack trains, telegraph and telephone lines…"[25] The "entire population in the areas of deployment," General Aurel Le Beau wrote in his diary, "was unreliable because they were Serb." "We were entirely surrounded by enemies in our own country and knew they had connections to the Serbs on the other side of the Drina," explained Le Beau.[26]

In countering what it viewed as Serb subversion, the Army availed itself of a fearsome legal arsenal. Civilians were made subject to military courts in large portions of the Empire, in particular in Cisleithania and in operational zones near the front. The whole of Bosnia-Herzegovina and Syrmia, in northeastern Croatia, were subjected to this massive intervention of military courts. Summary justice or *Standrecht* was declared for particular crimes such as the notoriously open §327, "crimes against the war making power of the state." Local politicians were arrested for security reasons. Some Army units invoked *Kriegsnotwehrrecht* (the martial law of self-defense), a shadowy concept that essentially allowed for summary executions of people deemed threats to soldiers. Coupled with this was a massive, extralegal program of hostage taking from among communities, primarily Serb, considered dangerous to the Army. Army regulations, the so-called *Dienstreglement*, did authorize the taking of hostages in such situations, but how this worked within the context of Habsburg *Rechtsstaat* was never really worked out.[27] In order to contain threats to transportation lines, the *Dienstreglement* dictated that "an enemy or unreliable population is to be placed under the constraint of severe reprisals (taking of hostages, *Standrecht* (summary justice), punishments, and the like)." The Army was

---

25. KAW, NFA, 6.Armee, *k.u.k. Gendarmeriekommando für Bosnien und die Hercegovina to the k.u.k. 6.Armeeoberkommando*, "Landesbewohner, Warnung vor Unternehmungen gegen k.u.k. Truppen," Res. Nr. 271/II mob., 22 August 1914, Karton 12. For further references, see, KAW, NFA, *Oberkommando der Balkanstreitkräfte, k.u.k. Militärkommando in Temesvár*, "Kundmachung," Präs. Nr. 886, in Op. Nr. 214., 17 August 1914, Karton 86; KAW, NFA, 15.Korps, Op. Akten, *7.Gebirgsbrigade to 1.Infanterietruppendivision*, Op. Nr. 31, 6 August 1914, Karton 1876; KAW, NFA, 15.Korps, Op. Akten, *Telefondepesche des 1.Infanterietruppendivision to 15.Korps*, Op. Nr. 45, 8 August 1914, Karton 1876; KAW, NFA, 15.Korps, Op. Akten, *Telefondepesche des 1.Infanterietruppendivision to 15.Korps*, Op. Nr. 62, 10 August 1914, Karton 1876; KAW, NFA, *Oberkommando der Balkanstreitkräfte*, Potiorek to AOK, Op. Nr. 123/OK., 21 August 1914, Karton 86; KAW, NFA, 6.Armee, Telegram from the *Militärkommando Mostar* to the *k.u.k. 6.Armeeoberkommando*, Res. Nr. 752, 31 August 1914, Karton 13.
26. KAW, Nachläße, Nachlaß le Beau, B/558, Tagebuch Nr. 1, pp. 12.
27. *Dienstreglement für das kaiserliche und königliche Heer*, Part I, §71: „Verhalten vor und bei einem Aufstande oder Aufruhe", (Vienna, 1912), p. 235.

"to move…with the greatest severity" against such a population.[28] Almost as soon the war began, the 15th Corps directed its officers to "take as hostages Serbian Orthodox residents who are suspected of Serbophile propaganda and stand in position of respect among fellow residents."[29] Hostages were threatened with execution should sabotage befall Habsburg Army units. Quickly, hostage taking got completely out of hand and the 6th Army had to assign a hostage "expert" in order to keep track of the high number of hostages. The vast majority of the hostages were Serbs.[30] The important point here is that the Army was already getting used to operating on the margins of domestic legality before it ever crossed the border into Serbia. Moreover, this was by no means limited to Bosnia-Herzegovina or Syrmia. Rather, this move to the margins of domestic legality also typified Army behavior in areas such as Bukovina and Galicia.[31]

In Serbia, the Habsburg Army intended to adhere to the Hague Convention of 1907, although Serbia was not a signatory. The Army would not entirely stray from the fold of international law. The order regarding the Hague Conventions acknowledged the possibility of reprisals for Serb violations of the convention, but reserving the right to reprisals was all in line with standard international legal practice.[32] The Balkan Wars had primed the Habsburg Empire's readiness for potential Serb atrocities and violations of the laws of war. As with all participants in this war, Serbia hardly conducted its portion of the conflict in accordance with the Hague Convention. In this, one should recall that the Empire adopted a sympathetic attitude towards the creation of an independent Albania in an effort to block Serbian access to the Adriatic Sea. The Serb treatment of the Albanian population in regions it had annexed after the Second Balkan War was particularly harsh. Once the war began, the forms assumed by Serbian resistance reinforced the Army's conviction that Serbs were irrational fanatics, legitimizing increasing levels of force against the civilian

---

28.   *Dienstreglement für das kaiserliche und königliche Heer*, Part II, §12, Pkt. 62: "Unbrauchbarmachen von Verkehrswegen und Verbindungen; Maßregeln zu ihrem Schutze", (Vienna, 1912), p. 26.
29.   KAW, NFA, 6.Armee–Zivilkommisariat, *k.u.k. 15.Korpskommando*, "Aushebung von Geiseln," Präs. Nr. 2796, 27 July 1914, Karton 55.
30.   KAW, NFA, 6.Armee, *6. k.u.k. Etappen-Armee-Kommando to Präsidium der Landesregierung für Bosnien und die Hercegovinen*, "Geiselaufhebung," Civ.Kom. Nr. 119a, 20 October 1914, Folder 119a, Karton 55.
31.   Oswald Überegger, "Verbrannte Erde' und 'baumelnde Gehenkte': Zur europäischen Dimension militärischer Normübertretungen im Ersten Weltkrieg," in: Sönke Neitzel and Daniel Hohrath, eds., *Kriegsgreuel. Die Entgrenzung der Gewalt in kriegerischen Konflikten vom Mittelalter bis ins 20. Jahrhundert* (Paderborn: Schöningh, 2008), 241–278.
32.   KAW, NFA, 6.Armee, AOK to the *k.u.k. 6.Armeeoberkommando*, 29 July 1914, Res. Nr. 7, Karton 12.

population, however draconian. Moreover, these reactions quickly escalated from legalized reprisals as understood in international law to erratic, fear-driven violent practice by the Habsburg Army in Serbia.

When the Army entered Serbia proper, it quickly felt beset on all sides by an armed population and a Serb Army that tended towards atrocity. This was a fundamentally new war in which the old rules for fighting no longer seemed to apply according to the Army. Part of this was a problem with encountering non-uniformed elements of the Serb 2nd and 3rd levies. In Serbia, as one officer main-tained, "every peasant...carries a rifle or the soldiers dress in peasant clothes."[33] Similarly, in his contemporary report on Austrian atrocities in Serbia, R. A. Reiss noted it was possible "that the Austro-Hungarian troops occasionally looked upon the non-uniformed soldiers of the 2nd and 3rd levy as peasant *franc-tireurs*."[34] From the Habsburg side, one unit also noted that "a part of the [Serb] second levy is without uniforms."[35] The absence of uniforms allowed the Army to situate itself on the side of international law since being in a military organization and fighting without markings constituted a violation of the Hague Convention. While shortage of uniforms due to the massive size of the Serbian mobilization might have been the actual reason for non-uniformed Serbs who appeared in the field, the Army viewed this as a deliberate effort to subvert the rules of war.

Accounts of Serb atrocities and duplicitous methods of fighting quickly gripped the entire Army.[36] The 5th Army *Etappenkommando* asserted that "atrocious actions" by Serb opponents, including civilians, "violated international law."[37] Several soldiers from the 13th Corps reported overhearing captured Serbs declare "captured Švabas (derogatory term for Austrians) are not to be killed, one must torture them."[38] According to

---

33. Joseph Schön, *Šabac! Der Kampf der Deutschböhmischen 29. Inf.-Div., des Prager VIII. und des Budapester IV. Korps im August 1914 in Nordwest Serbien* (Reichenberg, 1928), 36.

34. R.A. Reiss, *Report on the Atrocities Committed by the Austro-Hungarian Army*, p. 145.

35. KAW, NFA, 13.Korps, Op. Akten, *7.Feldkompagnie* to the *k.u.k.16.Infanterieregiment*, Op. Nr. 180, 22 August 1914, Karton 1668.

36. See, for example, KAW, Nachläße, Nachlaß Zanantoni, B/6, Nr. 1, Manuscript, "Erinnerungen aus meinem Leben," p. 256.

37. KAW, NFA, 6.Armee, Telegram from *k.u.k. 5.Armee-Etappenkommando* to *5 Armeekommando*, "Serbische Grausamkeiten und Völkerrechtswidrigkeiten," 28 August 1914, Karton 13.

38. KAW, NFA, 6.Armee, *13.Korps* to *5.Armeekommando*, Op. Nr. 193/58, 25 August 1914, Karton 13. For other examples of atrocity reports, see, KAW, NFA, 6. Armee, *5 Armee-Etappenkommando* to *5 Armeekommando*, "Serbische Grausamkeiten und Völkerrechtswidrigkeiten," Res. Nr. 137, 28 August 1914, Karton 13; KAW, NFA, 6.Armee, Telegram from *8.Korps* to *5.Armeekommando*, Zu Op. Nr. 159., 25 August 1914, Karton 13; KAW, NFA, 6.Armee, Report by the *k.u.k. Infanterieregiment* Nr. 91, (*k.u.k. 8.Korps* - Res. Nr 8), 10 August 1914, Karton 13.

Josef Schön, even women and children took part in such atrocities. He had heard about "atrocious acts against [Habsburg] wounded perpetrated by women and children." The "mental burden" created by this was "harder to bear than hunger and thirst."[39] Reports of mutilations only reinforced the Army's image of the Serbs as a nation of brutal extremists and easily enabled the Austrians to argue that the Serbs had placed themselves outside international law. Of course, the actual veracity of such reports was often uncertain, but they quickly became accepted fact within the Army.

Already primed to use force against the Empire's own civilians, Army units wasted little time in immediately escalating the level of force in Serbia, leading to widespread violence against civilians. The *Dienstreglement* continued to provide cover for such escalations. Thus, the Army continued hostage taking, imposed martial law, and burned down villages in punitive raids, all measures allowed by section 61 of the *Dienstreglement*.[40] The Army also treated the civilians from whom they encountered resistance as combatants without uniforms and summarily executed them. There was no internal Army discussion about Article 2 of the Hague Conventions which did allow for a population to spontaneously defend itself during an invasion as long as it fought within the "laws and customs of war."[41] The Army invoked the martial law of self-defense (*Kriegsnotwehrrecht*) in these cases, though because it executed civilians after taking them prisoner, the self-defense aspect of this was extremely questionable.

The Army's tendency towards quick executions of civilian fighters was inseparable from the constant exhortations that units employ "the sharpest measures" against perceived civilian combatants. This created the possibility for extreme violence on the ground in Serbia since local commanders were left to determine just how "ruthless" or "harsh" they would be and where such measures would be applied. Units resorted to violence when they thought they faced civilians fighting against Habsburg soldiers. The 9th Infantry Division shot hostages in the villages of Guzič and Radlovac and "burned down [the villages] for the most part." In these villages, the "guilty inhabitants," including women, were accused of having taken part in the fighting. In another instance, the soldiers from the division hung a 60-year old woman for possession of an old pistol.[42] Egon Kisch, who would later

39. Joseph Schön, *Šabac! Der Kampf der Deutschböhmischen 29. Inf.-Div., des Prager VIII. und des Budapester IV. Korps im August 1914 in Nordwest Serbien* (Reichenberg, 1928), p. 346.

40.   KAW, NFA, 6.Armee, *k.u.k. 6.Armeeoberkommando*, "Repressalien gegen die Bevölkerung," Res. Nr. 431, 19 August 1914, Karton 12.

41.   Article 2, Annex to the Hague Convention of 1907, Regulations Respecting the Laws and Customs of War on Land, Section I: On Belligerents, at http://avalon.law.yale.edu/20th_century/hague04.asp#art1, (19. Jan. 2014).

42.   Testimony of Stana Maritch, in R.A. Reiss, *Report on the Atrocities Committed by the*

gain fame as a journalist after the war, fought in the 8th Corps and related
a story of the execution of five Serb civilians. After the civilians were led
past Kisch, a colonel's adjutant went up to another officer and asked him if
he saw these men shooting. When this officer answered affirmatively, the
adjutant had the Serbs executed. Kisch estimated that the youngest of the
Serbs was only fifteen years of age.[43]

In the face of what they considered deeply transgressive Serb violence,
not only did the Army units find ways to escalate violence on the ground,
even high-ranking Army commanders began to consider waging a war of
devastation in Serbia. Talk about setting aside the Geneva Convention when
dealing with the Serbs began to float around, for example, but it was quickly
shut down. This was hardly driven by any concern for the Serb civilian
population itself, which was held in utter contempt by most Habsburg
officers. Rather, it was the fear that conducting a war of devastation in Serbia
and setting aside international law entirely would undermine the Empire's
own position in the "civilized world." As always, such considerations were
simultaneously laced with contempt for the Serbs. The commander of the
5th Army, General Liborius Frank, declared that the vicious behavior he
had witnessed in Serbia could come "only from the side of a culturally low-
lying *Volk*." When in the same report he considered the possibility of laying
waste to Serbia, he rejected that as inconsistent with his sense that the
Austrians were a "civilized people." If the Army destroyed Serbia, it would
fall from the circle of "European culture." According to Frank, "one cannot
deport the population of an entire country to the interior of the Monarchy,
nor drive them out, nor exterminate them."[44] Insofar as "the atrocities of
the Serbs and Montenegrins," Frank later wrote "…a competition with our
opponent in this area is out of the question." Such comments revealed the
extent to which Frank recognized the potential dangers involved in a series
of escalations and counter-escalations.[45] During a second invasion attempt
later in 1914, Potiorek acknowledged the "bitterness against the enemy,
who many times had violated the provisions of international law." Yet, he
warned against tactics like "burning villages, devastated farms, and

---

Austro-Hungarian Army, p. 54.
43. Egon Kisch, *Soldat im Prager Korps* (Prague, 1927). See also, KAW, NFA, 6.Armee,
k.u.k. 11. Gebirgsbrigadekommando to *k.u.k. 48.Infanterietruppendivisionkommando*, Nr. 3/26,
26 August 1914, Karton 13. See also the list of reprisals by the 18th Infantry Brigade
in this regard, in, KAW, NFA, 8.Korps, *k.u.k. 18. Infanterie-Brigade-Commando* to *k.u.k.
9.Infanterietruppendivision*, "Repressalien," 24 August 1914, Res. No. 16, Karton 923.
44. KAW, NFA, 6.Armee, *k.u.k. 5.Armeekommando* to *k.u.k. 6.Armeeoberkommando*, Op. Nr.
403/20 zu I., 25 August 1914, Karton 13.
45.   KAW,   NFA,   5.Armeekommando,   *5.Armee-Etappen-Kommandos*,
"Etappenkommandobefehl Nr. 3," Nr. 446, 9 September 1914, Karton 953.

exterminated inhabitants." "Such an advance," argued Potiorek, "is unworthy of an Army of a great power."[46] It was this consideration that eventually helped limit the violence of the Habsburg Army against Serb civilians, reining in the atrocities that dominated the war with Serbia in August 1914.

Conclusion

Militarily, the Habsburg Empire's attempt to conquer Serbia in 1914 came to naught. For Oskar Potiorek, temporary success in December 1914 with the occupation of Belgrade only provided a glimpse of success that would be crushed weeks later, leading to his dismissal. The severity of the Habsburg defeats was also part of a growing story of Habsburg weakness, one that has its origins in arguments circulating about long-term Habsburg decline. In a sense, the military defeats became one piece of concrete proof of Habsburg feebleness that was now played out on the stage of international politics and war. The challenge for historians is to integrate the history of the Habsburg-Serb conflict into the broader history of the war. To the extent that we view the war's start as something dominated by violence against civilians on the part of all armies on enemy territory, the first months of the Habsburg Empire's war against Serbia becomes part of a much wider story. To be sure, there is a particular context to this story insofar as the Serbian overmobilization of 1914, played out against a backdrop of a war that quickly became existential beyond all expectations, provided something of a final confirmation of the Habsburg Army's beliefs that Serbia had transgressed the rules of war. The result was widespread violence against civilians that quickly rivaled German atrocities in Belgium in intensity. Yet at the same time, this tendency toward atrocity in the early part of the war marked virtually every army on enemy soil, from the Russians in East Prussia and Galicia to the Germans in Belgium and Poland.[47] What was interesting about the resulting uproar from this was how all sides quickly focused on violations of *jus in bello* provisions of the Hague Conventions. For all the talk of the justice of the war's cause, the

---

46. KAW, NFA, 15.Korps, Befehle 1914/1916, Oberkommando der Balkanstreitkräfte, Res. Nr. 739 (in 15.Korpskommandobefehl Nr. 31), 5 November 1914, Karton 1892. See also, KAW, NFA, 8.Korps, *8.Korps*, "Kundmachung," 28 November 1914, Karton 923.

47. John Horne and Alan Kramer, *German Atrocities, 1914: A History of Denial* (New Haven: Yale University Press, 2001); Peter Holquist, "Les Violences de L'armée Russe À L'encontre des Juifs en 1915: Causes et Limites," in *Vers La Guerre Totale: Le Tournant de 1914-1915* (Paris: Tallandier, 2010), 191–219; Laura Engelstein, "'A Belgium of Our Own': The Sack of Russian Kalisz, August 1914," *Kritika: Explorations in Russian and Eurasian History* 10, no. 3 (2009): 441–473.

jus ad bellum aspects of the war did not serve as explanations for violence against civilians. A 19th century European mindset prevailed in which war was still an accepted practice for a great power, but it was *how* it was fought that mattered. Every side in the war quickly positioned itself on the side of international law in 1914 in this regard. In response to a protest from the Serb government regarding atrocities against civilians, the Habsburg Minister of War, General Alexander Krobatin, quite openly admitted that "against civilians of either sex who take part in hostilities, we will continue to relentlessly proceed according to the laws of war."[48] A cynical view of this legal positioning might be that it proved the powerlessness of international law and the degree to which it could be manipulated to serve any argument. Yet, another view is that this legal framework proved important to belligerents of all sides, as least as a screen through which they understood and framed their actions. Even when operating on the very edge of international norms, the Empire insisted upon framing its actions within those parameters.

---

48. Haus-, Hof-, und Staatsarchiv, Ministerium des Äußern, Administrative Registratur, F 36, Krieg 1914-1918, Dep. 7, Völkerrechtliche Fragen, "Protest der serbischen Regierung," Verbal Note to the Spanish Ambassador (representing Serbia), January 30, 1915, Karton 378.

Carinthian Front 1916/17, Patrolling soldiers in the Rattendorf Alps, ca. 1916
61.074-B, Foto K.u.k. Kriegspressequartier, Lichtbildstelle Vienna,
Austrian National Library – Picture Archives and Graphics Department, Vienna

"This monstrous front will devour us all"[1]
The Austro-Hungarian Soldier Experience, 1914-15

Jason C. Engle

While military historians have extensively detailed life in the troglodyte world of the Western Front, the experience of soldiers fighting on the many other fronts of the First World War remains relatively obscure.[2] Glimpses into the Austro-Hungarian soldier's war have typically been anecdotal, as texture for campaign studies or in institutional evaluations of the Royal and Imperial (*Kaiserlich und Königlich* or *k.u.k*) Army, especially in the English language historiography.[3] Sadly, there is a negligible number of studies that flesh out the daily lives of Habsburg soldiers.[4] This article seeks to redirect the historiographical lens away from the map tables of general headquarters

1. I would, first, like to thank Günter Bischof for the opportunity to contribute this essay. I would also like to thank Professor Bischof, Andrew Wiest and Jeff Bowersox for their helpful comments and feedback, which has greatly improved this essay. Title quote taken from Rolf Rungen, *Brennende Südfront: ein österreichischer Kriegsroman* (Berlin: Paul Aretz Verlag, 1993), 329 and cited in Tait Keller, "The Mountains Roar: The Alps during the Great War," *Environmental History* 14 (April 2009), 265.
2. See, amongst many others, John Ellis, *Eye Deep in Hell: Trench Warfare in World War I* (Baltimore: Johns Hopkins University Press, 1977); Dennis Winter, *Death's Men: Soldiers of the Great War* (London: Allen Lane, 1978); Tony Ashworth, *Trench Warfare 1914-1918: The Live and Let Live System* (Boulder: Holmes & Meier, 1980); Alexander Watson, *Enduring the Great War: Combat, Morale and Collapse in the German and British Armies, 1914-1918* (New York: Cambridge University Press, 2009); Leonard V. Smith, *The Embattled Self: French Soldiers' Testimony of the Great War* (Ithaca: Cornell University Press, 2007); Robert L. Nelson, *German Soldier Newspapers of the First World War* (New York: Cambridge University Press, 2011).
3. See, for instance, Gunther E. Rothenberg, *The Army of Francis Joseph* (West Lafayette: Purdue University Press, 1976); István Deák, *Beyond Nationalism: A Social and Political History of the Habsburg Officer Corps, 1848-1918* (New York: Oxford University Press, 1991); Scott W. Lackey, *The Rebirth of the Habsburg Army: Friedrich Beck and the Rise of the General Staff* (Westport: Praeger, 1995); Holger Herwig, *The First World War: Germany and Austria-Hungary, 1914-1918* (New York: Arnold, 1997); Timothy C. Dowling, *The Brusilov Offensive* (Bloomington: Indiana University Press, 2008); Graydon A. Tunstall, *Blood on the Snow: The Carpathian Winter War of 1915* (Lawrence: Kansas University Press, 2010); Richard L. DiNardo, *Breakthrough: The Gorlice-Tarnow Campaign, 1915* (Santa Barbara, CA: Praeger, 2010).
4. One notable exception is Isabelle Brandauer, *Menschenmaterial Soldat: Alltagsleben an der Dolomitenfront im Ersten Weltkrieg 1915-1917* (Innsbruck: Golf Verlag, 2007).

and the halls of the War Ministry and onto the Austro-Hungarian soldier in the field.

According to the conceptual model based on the findings of the inter-disciplinary, Special Research Project 437, conducted at the University of Tübingen, an individual's experience is a result of his or her interpretation, actions, and perception (internalization) of events, which are influenced by objective factors such as time, as well as subjective factors such as their environment. As individuals internalize their experiences and attitudes, values, and behaviors become entrenched, they find expression in society through institutions, symbols, images, rituals, and in oral and written language.[5]

With this model supplying as a conceptual framework, this essay will seek to construct something of a composite experience of Austro-Hungarian soldiers based on careful reading of published diaries, memoirs, and secondary scholarship. Three fundamental points of analysis underpin the experience of Habsburg soldiers: Language, Landscape, and Violence. With the outbreak of war, reservists and draftees flooded into the Austro-Hungarian Army, bringing civilian politics in tow. The issue of language—the crux of national political tensions in both halves of the Dual Monarchy—prompted ill-advised changes to the army's system for the deployment of replacement formations, which exacerbated the difficulties inherent to a multi-lingual army. While military historians long argued political nationalism compromised the Austro-Hungarian Army, they frequently overlooked the essential role of language and communication barriers in the daily lives of Habsburg soldiers and the ways in which it crippled the Habsburg Army in very fundamental ways beyond drawing the lines between nationalities.

On 28 July 1915, one year after Austria-Hungary declared war on Serbia and initiated what would become a global conflict, Serbia, Galicia, and Alps represented the principle theaters of operation for Austro-Hungarian armies. These theaters should not be perceived as mere backdrops for combat operations, but must be understood as an active force in the war, a third belligerent if you will, unleashing its wrath both sides. As has long been the case for the infantry soldier, the landscape of the theater of operations was the chief external factor underpinning their wartime experiences; life in the field, though cathartic at times, challenged the soldiers mentally and physically. Weather, climate, and terrain often made trivial duties difficult

---

5. "Sonderforschungsbereich 437 Kriegserfahrungen. Krieg und Gesellschaft in der Neuezeit," (11. Jan. 2010). http://www.uni-tuebingen.de/SFB437/index.htm; Igor V. Narskii, "The Frontline Experience of Russian Soldiers in 1914-16," *Russian Studies in History* 51 (Spring, 2013): 31-49.

and combat all the more terrifying.

The landscape of the fighting front provided the stage on which organized, industrial violence was acted out, creating, in Clausewitzian terms, an environment of danger.[6] This environment of danger, manifested in the violence, dread, fear, exhilaration, and destructive force of combat, was naturally formative in molding the soldier experience. Violence—the principle attribute of war—left deep psychological impressions on Habsburg soldiers, effecting their attitudes and responses to fighting and frequently prompted desperate measures to avoid the firing lines. Simultaneously, violence helped Habsburg troops to demonize the enemy, particularly Serbs, precipitating and justifying violent excesses on war prisoners and non-combatants.

"A Babel of Sound": The Problem of Language

Language perhaps best exemplified the complexity and challenges facing the Austro-Hungarian Dual Monarchy. As the fundamental feature delimiting nationality, it was consistently a point of contention in the mass politics of Habsburg society. Austria-Hungary's declaration of war on Serbia set in motion the mass mobilization of civilian reservists, reproducing the same complications and tensions in the army, an "anational" bedrock of dynastic loyalty.[7] In the setting of war, the consequences were more dramatic. Language barriers became a fundamental source of frustration and operational inefficiency that diminished morale, prompted discrimination, and fostered hatred between enlisted men and their officers. The memoirs and diaries of enlisted men and officers, alike, often record the inability of Habsburg soldiers and officers to understand one another, which complicated day-to-day duties, and made coordinating assaults and defensive operations particularly difficult. These communication barriers only exacerbated the pressure placed on officers to manage their units, creating frustration that too often led to physical abuse and ethnic slurs.

Overall, the composition of the Habsburg Army paralleled the ethno-linguistic makeup of the Empire. That is, for every 1.000 soldiers, 267 were German speakers, 223 spoke Magyar, 135 Czech, eighty-five were Polish speakers, eighty-one spoke Ukrainian, sixty-seven spoke Serbo-Croat, sixty-four spoke Romanian, thirty-eight were Slovak speakers, twenty-six

---

6. Carl von Clausewitz, *Vom Kriege* (1832), 44-5; Antulio J. Echevarria II, *Globalization and the Nature of War* (Carlisle: U.S. Army War College, Strategic Studies Insitute, 2003), 8.
7. Jonathan E. Gumz, *The Resurrection and Collapse of Empire in Habsburg Serbia, 1914-1918* (New York: Cambridge University Press, 2009), 12.

spoke Slovene, while fourteen spoke Italian.[8] The composition of the individual Habsburg regiments mobilized in 1914, however, corresponded more closely to the ethno-linguistic distribution of the districts from which they were mustered. For example, in the k. u. k., Pozsonyer Landwehr (*Honvéd*) Infantry Regiment Nr.13 (mustered in Preßburg/Bratislava), fifty-one percent were Slovak speakers, twenty-eight percent spoke Magyar, twenty percent were German speakers, while the remaining one percent spoke various other languages.[9] At the war's outset, 142 units in the Habsburg Army were monolingual, 162 were bilingual, with twenty-four being trilingual, and only a handful of units where four or more languages spoken by its members.[10]

The relative linguistic uniformity was not to last. The Habsburg *Armeeoberkommando* (or *AOK*) sought to dilute regiments with high concentrations of ethno-linguistic minorities that they feared to be disloyal. For instance, the *AOK* might have replaced casualties in a Bohemian Czech regiment with Hungarian or Croat replacements, rather than Bohemian Czechs. Instead of allaying the potentially corrosive effects of political nationalism, the strategy created regiments that struggled to communicate with one another, and, as a result, reduced the offensive capability of those regiments. As the commander of the 7th Company of the II/II Tiroler Kaiserjäger admitted, it was very reassuring to be in an exposed position with someone you could have a conversation with in periods of rest.[11] By late 1917, however, the *AOK* finally realized that "new recruits were unsettled by serving next to troops speaking a different language," and abandoned the strategy of intermingling ethno-linguistic replacements.[12]

8. Gunther Rothenberg, "The Habsburg Army in the First World War," in Robert A. Kann, Bela K. Király, Paula S. Fichtner, eds., *The Habsburg Empire in World War I* (Boulder: East European Quarterly, 1977), 74-75.

9. The 1881 reforms proposed by Habsburg General Staff Chief, Friedrich Beck, divided the empire into sixteen military districts which were responsible for mobilizing specific corps and the *marsch* formations to replenish its numbers during wartime; See Scott W. Lackey, *The Rebirth of the Habsburg Army: General Friedrich Beck and the Rise of the General Staff* (Westport: Greenwood Press, 1995), 108. The official General Staff history, Edmund Glaise-Horstenau, et al., *Österreich-Ungarns letzter Krieg* (Verlag der Militärwissenschaftlichen Mitteilungen: Wien, 1931-38) contains the ethno-linguistic breakouts of *K.u.k Army.*, *k.k. Landwehr*, and *k.u. Honvéd* regiments in 1914. The figures were based on the mother tongue of enlisted ranks and NCOs.

10. István Deák, *Der k.(u.)k. Offizier 1848-1918* (Wien, 1995), 122, cited in Richard Lein, *Pflichtfüllung oder Hochverrat? Die Tschechischen Soldaten Österreich-Ungarns im Ersten Weltkrieg* (Wien: Lit Verlag, 2011), 44.

11. KA, Nachlass Robert Nowak, B/726, Nr. 1/I, II, III: "Die Klammer des Reichs: Das Verhalten der elf Nationalitäten in der k.u.k. Wehrmacht 1914-1918," 694, cited in Brandauer, *Menschenmaterial Soldat*, 20.

12. Perhaps more importantly, as General Staff Chief, Conrad von Hötzendorf, declared, the practice should be avoided, especially for "unreliable elements" – Serb, Czech, Romanian

To be sure, the language issues of the Habsburg Army were only worsened by the infusion of "reliable" replacements (Austrians, Hungarians, Croats, Bosnians, Poles) into units with heavy concentrations of nationalities deemed "suspect" by the *AOK* (generally speaking, Serbs, Ruthenians/ Ukrainians, Romanians, and Czechs). As John Schindler has argued, the issue of 'reliability' based on nationality was a problem created by the *AOK* and its reactions to any event it might construe as being undermined by political nationalism.[13] Nationalist tensions within the army, irritated by the *AOK*, eventually became a focal point for the Italian Army, who waged a propaganda campaign in the last year of the war, aimed at exploiting this festering issue within the Habsburg ranks.[14] It proved a very real problem that many Habsburg soldiers could better understand their enemy than their own comrades and superiors.

Ethno-linguistic diversity had long presented tactical issues that Habsburg army commanders had to consider. During the Austro-Prussian War of 1866, this "linguistic gap," was an important factor underpinning the Austrian Army's reliance on shock tactics, as opposed to a more sophisticated tactical approach that would require clear communication and well-choreographed maneuvers.[15] That is, the limited degree to which officers could communicate instructions to their men restricted the sophistication of Habsburg army maneuvers on the battlefield. In the Austro-Prussian War, Austrian frontal assaults allowed the Prussian Army, using faster, breech loading needle guns, to cut them to pieces, as was the case at Königgrätz.

The challenges of a multi-lingual army persisted as Austro-Hungarian Armies marched out in the summer of 1914. Though German was the language of command and administration in the K.u.k. Army, officers were required to be able to communicate proficiently in the languages of their direct subordinates. Enlisted men, on the other hand, were required to at

and Ruthene replacements – for fear of further diluting remaining "reliable" units. See Mark Cornwall, *The Undermining of Austria-Hungary: The Battle for Hearts and Minds* (London: Macmillan Press, 2000), 34.

13. John R. Schindler, "Disaster on the Drina: The Austro-Hungarian Army in Serbia, 1914," *War in History 9* (2002): 159-60.

14. See Mark Cornwall, *The Undermining of Austria-Hungary: The Battle for Hearts and Minds* (New York: St. Martin's Press, 2000) for an in-depth study of the propaganda war waged by Austria-Hungary and the Entente Powers during World War I.

15. Geoffrey Wawro, "'An Army of Pigs': The Technical, Social, and Political Bases of Austrian Shock Tactics, 1859-1866," *Journal of Military History 59* (July, 1995): 407-433. While this might have indeed been a factor, shock tactics were part and parcel of the "cult of the offensive" that prevailed among commanders throughout Europe, the Prussians themselves suffering horrendous casualties taking St. Privat in 1870. See Eric Dorn Brose, *The Kaiser's Army: The Politics of Military Technology in Germany during the Machine Age, 1870-1918* (New York: Oxford University Press, 2001).

least learn a set of 80 German instructions. After the Habsburg Army's initial bloodlettings in 1914, these requirements became untenable, as linguistically unqualified reserve officers replaced the professionals. One young officer, Otto Gallian, described an incident where a Hungarian and Croatian officer from neighboring units came to him, with what one would presume to be important information, when he admits that he could not understand a word of either of their messages. The sum of the instance found the comrades sharing cigarettes and staring "blankly" at one another.[16] In some instances, Romanian, Croat, or Serb reservists mobilized into k. u. k. Landsturm formations in 1914, had performed their active duty in the Joint/Common Army where German was the language of command. However, in Hungarian Landsturm formations, Magyar was the language of command, forcing them to learn the Magyar equivalent to the German phrases they already knew. What resulted was, as diarist Octavian Tăslăuanu described, a "strange compound of two tongues…a babel of sound."[17] One German army observer noted, "it often happens that the officers neither speak nor understand the languages of their men, and think themselves too civilized to bother learning them."[18] While this attitude was surely not uncommon, reserve officers had little chance to learn the languages of their men even if they wanted, especially given the *AOK*'s policy of intermixing nationalities. Moreover, with the inordinately high ratio of officers deaths in Austro-Hungarian Army during the opening months of World War I made the commands of field-grade officers a veritable revolving door.[19]

In effort to assuage the issue of language, commanding officers often utilized bilingual soldiers and NCOs to serve as translators, relaying the commander's instructions to his subordinates; of course, the officer could not be sure the translator interpreted his orders accurately or at all. In his memoir, Karl Freiherr von Bardolff—commander of the 29th Infantry

16. Otto Gallian, *Der Österreichische Soldat im Weltkrieg: Die Legende vom "Bruder Schnürschuh"* (Graz: Leykam Verlag, 1934), 51-52.
17. For those unfamiliar with the organization of the "Austro-Hungarian Army," it was not a single, monolithic institution. In fact, there were three armies: the 'Common Army' or *K.u.k. Armee* (*Kaiserlich und Königlich* or Imperial and Royal), the *k.k. Landwehr* (the army of the Cisleithanian (Austrian) half of the Dual Monarchy, and the *k.u. Honvéd*, the army of the Transleithanian (Hungarian) half of the Dual Monarchy. Men aged 32-42 in both halves, were called up and assigned to reserve, *Landsturm* regiments. Octavian C. Tăslăuanu, *With the Austrian Army in Galicia* (London: Skeffington & Son, 1918), 21.
18. Stone, *"Army and Society,"* 100.
19. Habsburg officers were mandated to become proficient in the language of their subordinates; in some cases this could entail up to three or four different languages. Likewise, soldiers were expected to understand a limited set of German instructions. As opposed to the 15 percent suffered by the German army and the 25 percent estimated for the Russian army, the Habsburg army lost 50 percent of its officer corps by the end of 1914. See Herwig, *The First World War*, 110, 139; Dowling, *The Brusilov Offensive*, 24.

Brigade in 1914—wrote of an instance where an Austrian major, who understood neither Magyar nor Slovakian, used English to communicate with his men, many of whom had left the Habsburg Empire for the United States and since returned. "Yes, there were quite peculiar realities in this old Austria-Hungary," Bardolff acknowledged matter-of-factly.[20]

In Serbia, the polyglot character of the Habsburg army repeatedly caused it problems. Units of the Czech 21st Division repeatedly fired upon the largely Serbo-Croat speaking 42nd Division, mistaking them for Serbian troops.[21] The same issue proved critical in the Battle of Čer Mountain. In a night attack, Serbian troops were able to fool Czech sentries by identifying themselves as a patrol from the neighboring 42nd Division. For those encamped Austro-Hungarian formations, the close proximity of the enemy meant that by the time they realized what was happening, it was too late.[22] What resulted was "murderous," firefight at point-blank range and frantic hand-to-hand combat. The severe losses of the 21st Division forced it to withdraw from Čer Mountain, which "caused the immediate failure of the 5th Army's offensive and precipitated a general Habsburg retreat."[23]

Camaraderie and, thus, unit cohesion, was another area in which language barriers hurt Austro-Hungarian regiments. "Linguistic and national differences would have made comradeship in the Habsburg army even more difficult than in other armies," Marsha Rozenblit concludes in her examination of Austro-Hungarian Jews in the First World War.[24] With multiple language speakers within single regiments, linguistically homogenous groups formed, making overall unit cohesion a challenge. As Rozenblit points out, most of the Jews in the Habsburg army were in regiments mustered in Galicia, Bukovina, or Hungary and were Yiddish speakers; given this concentration, it was easy for Jews to establish close relationships with one another, without having to socialize with Polish or Ruthenian Gentiles.[25] As Otto Gallian noted, a German-speaking soldier could find himself leading a hermit-like existence in the trenches with a Slavic regiment, intercepting only small fragments, or having to rely on sign language to communicate.[26] The language barrier also prevented soldiers, in

20. Carl von Bardolff, *Soldat im Alten Österreich* (Jena: Eugen Diederichs Verlag, 1938), 190, cited in Norman Stone, "Army and Society in the Habsburg Monarchy, 1900-1914" *Past and Present* 33 (April, 1966): 100.

21. Schindler, *"Disaster,"* 169, 171-2. The Habsburg regiments enduring the brunt of this attack was the 6th, 8th, and 28th.

22. Ibid., 172.

23. Ibid., 174.

24. Marsha E. Rozenblit, *Reconstructing a National Identity: The Jews of Habsburg Austria during World War I* (New York: Oxford University Press, 2001), 91.

25. Rozenblit, *Reconstructing*, 91.

26. Otto Gallian, *Der Österreichische Soldat*, 50; Rozenblit, *Reconstructing*, 92 provides a

various cases, from being able to understand religious services and masses. In such instances, field chaplains might hear a soldier's confession in a tongue he could not understand and, in turn, absolve him of his unknown sins.[27]

Language barriers inside Habsburg units also prompted frustration for officers and enlisted men, alike, and was a principle catalyst triggering national antagonisms. Over time, this antagonism became increasingly shrill, decaying morale, unit cohesion, and the army's offensive capacity. Romanian reserve officer, Octavian Tăslăuanu, detailed several occasions on which language barriers provoked abuse; in one instance, a Hungarian officer, who, after failing to be understood, "became irritable, and finally lost his temper and treated the poor [Romanian] wretches to blows, kicks, and Hungarian curses: 'dinzo olah, budos olah' (Wallachian swine, Wallachian dung), the usual Magyar amenities toward us."[28] As a captured Austrian officer informed his Italian jailers, "It was rare to encounter [a German] who had *any* affection for his Slavic, Italian or Rumanian comrades. Germans, from the lowliest corporal all the way up to the battalion commandant, attributed every error or oversight [on the part of the non-German] to 'ill-will' or, worse, 'treachery.'[29] When not administering beatings with their swagger canes, their favorite epithets were: *'dalmatinische Bagage,' 'italienische Schweine,' 'croatische Schufte,' 'Hunde,'* and *'feige Kerle.'*" Austrian officers also frequently used the slang and disparaging term *'cus'* – which might roughly equate to the term 'nigger' or 'wog' – to summon Serb and Croat soldiers.[30] Other epithets such as "tirolisches Schwein," and "Saubohm," punctuate recurring complaints of "cruel" treatment and "reckless" practices found in Austrian soldiers' diaries.[31] What resulted was that "many soldiers came to hate their officers, the Imperial General Staff, and, in time, the Monarchy

---

similar example for German-speaking, Viennese Jews who were required to serve in regiments mustered in the region from which they emigrated.

27. Patrick J. Houlihan, "Clergy in the Trenches: Catholic Military Chaplains of Germany and Austria-Hungary during the First World War" (PhD Diss., University of Chicago, 2011), 173, 180.

28. Tăslăuanu, *With the Austrian Army in Galicia*, 13.

29. "German," in this context, refers to German-speaking Austrians, not Reich Germans.

30. The German phrases translate to English as follows: "Dalmatian baggage," "Italian swine," "Croatian scoundrels," "dogs," and "cowardly buggers," Vincennes, Archive de l'Armee de Terre (AAT), Etat-Major de l'Armee (EMA), 7N846, Rome, 13 April 1916, Col. Francios to Minister of War, 'Obeservations of "Lt. X," a captured Austro-Hungarian officer," cited in, Geoffrey Wawro, "Morale in the Austro-Hungarian Army: The Evidence of Habsburg Army Campaign Reports and Allied Intelligence Officers," in *Facing Armageddon* (London: Leo Cooper, 1996), 399-412.

31. Brandauer, *Soldat*, 109. Those terms translate as "Tyrolean swine/pig," and "Bohemian sow."

itself."[32]

Landscapes of War

Just as language was a formative element impacting the daily lives of Habsburg soldiers, so too were the various landscapes in which they lived, fought, and died. Features of the terrain, climate, and weather determined modes of living in the field, and, thus, helped to forge the experiences of Austro-Hungarian soldiers. The landscape of the front affected Habsburg troops in various ways; while soothing their angst and inspiring awe on one hand, nature presented them with a myriad of challenges and miseries on the other.

Upon arriving in the theater of operations and detraining, long exhausting marches—part and parcel of soldiering—provided a rather brutal introduction to life in the field; wading through knee-deep streams, muddy roads, and marshlands often highlighting marches. In August 1914—the height of summer with temperatures exceeding 95°F—Habsburg soldiers in Serbia and Galicia, alike, sweltered under the blistering heat while having insufficient water supplies. The soldiers cursed prolifically, a reserve officer in Galicia recalled, as it was "the only relief open to them" while they lumbered down a dirt road, half-choking on the dust and dirt they stirred.[33] Soldiers of the Austro-Hungarian 5th Army, deployed to Serbia, were saddled with full packs weighing in excess of 50lbs and faced an uphill march to the Čer Mountain plateau, as Serbian guerilla fighters, known as *"Komitatschi,"* sniped at Habsburg troops from the surrounding forests.[34] In the harsh winter weather of the Carpathian and Alpine sectors, avalanches and snowstorms covered roads, walking paths, and ice, making marches in the mountainous terrain even more dangerous, often causing soldiers to slip on rocks and fall to their deaths.[35]

Habsburg soldiers in the field faced not just the enemy and the elements, but also vermin and infectious disease. Extended periods in the field often meant extended periods without bathing or changing clothes, which lent

---

32. Spence, *"Yugoslavs,"* 40-41.
33. Tăslăuanu, *With the Austrian Army*, 46.
34. Schindler, "Disaster on the Drina," 171; *ÖUlK, Das Kriegsjahr 1914*, 114. Schindler draws from Fritz Kreisler's memoir as to the contents of infantry packs: rifle, bayonet, ammunition, spade, knapsack full of emergency provisions such as tinned meats, coffee, sugar, salt, rice, biscuits and cooking and eating utensils, an additional pair of shoes, shirt, underwear, as well as an overcoat, and tent equipment. Fritz Kreisler, *Four Weeks in the Trenches: The War Story of a Violinist* (Cambridge: Riverside Press, 1915), 13.
35. Tunstall, Blood on the Snow, 3; Brandauer, *Menschenmaterial Soldat*, 38-40; Keller, "Mountains Roar," 260.

itself to dysentery. As winter neared, soldiers were compelled to plunder heavier coats and hats from the dead; coupled with the typically close quarters in which soldiers lived, lice and typhus spread quickly. To make matters worse, starving Austro-Hungarian armies traversed from one poorly sanitized rural village to another, drinking water from polluted waterways and eating uncooked fruits and vegetables and, in the process, transmitting cholera.[36]

While life in the field was often grueling, soldiers' diaries and memoirs nevertheless speak of the appeal of their new austere existence in nature. "I confess I began to have a liking for our nomadic…primitive existence," wrote Tăslăuanu by 3 September 1914, having complained about sleeping in the open-air only days before.[37] The majesty that only nature possesses, helped calm and sooth the angst of war. As one Hungarian officer on the Isonzo front described, "to feel the soft summer night all around me… [p]ictures of home drift across my consciousness, my family, my dog, my horses." [38] Fritz Kreisler described what many soldiers likely felt in their new circumstances:

> In the field all neurotic symptoms seem to disappear as by magic, and one's whole system is charged with energy and vitality. Perhaps this is due to the open-air life with its simplified standards, freed from all the complex exigencies of society's laws, and unhampered by conventionalities, as well as to the constant throb of excitement, caused by the activity, the adventure, and the uncertainty of fate.[39]

It is clear that life in the field and in nature possessed a primeval, soothing quality for many soldiers. As Tait Keller explains, for many Habsburg soldiers in the Dolomites, "the towering white peaks and the vast blue sky made them forget for a moment that they were in the middle of a war…the mountains helped reverse the despair of war."[40] Patrick Houlihan has noted that religious services held in Alpine peaks placed soldiers in "unsurpassed

36. Tăslăuanu, *With the Austrian Army*, 90-96, 222; Brandauer, *Menschenmaterial Soldat*, 245-54; *ÖUIK: Das Kriegsjahr 1914*, 435, 599, 760; Herwig, *The First World War*, 89, 94, 110.
37. Tăslăuanu, *With the Austrian Army*, 59.
38. Michael Maximilian Reiter, *Balkan Assault: The Diary of an Officer 1914-1918* (London: The Historical Press Ltd, 1994), 14.
39. Kreisler, *Four Weeks*, 15.
40. Tait Keller, "The Mountains Roar: The Alps during the Great War," *Environmental History* 14 (April 2009): 267.

symbolic proximity to the heavens," while services held in chapels carved out of the glaciers at Marmolada, for instance, exuded a sense of otherworldliness.[41]

As cathartic as nature might have been, it presented just as many challenges. Before Austro-Hungarian units advancing into Serbia even engaged the enemy, the underbrush, stinging nettles, and cornfields tore at their clothes and skin. Cornfields also concealed landmines and the enemy.[42] During the Battle of the Drina, the river itself presented a formidable obstacle that incited panic for the regiments of the Habsburg V Army as Serbian artillery and rifle fire pressed their advance. First-hand accounts, such as that of Egon Erwin Kisch, testify to the terrifying chaos that awaited the Bohemian regiments crossing over to the Serbian shore. "I had only one thought: now you are going to paddle over there in a few minutes and, likewise, be standing in the same place, like the others, demoralized, crippled, and pleading," Kisch recounted in his diary.[43]

The Habsburg V Army's retreat back across the Drina, under harassment from *Komitatschi* fighters and pursuit by enemy cavalry units, was more frenzied. Many of the troops of the 11th Prague Regiment, for instance, discarded their rifles, packs, and other equipment to avoid being weighed down in the water. "Everywhere the same image: some thirty men drowning, screaming, gasping, emerging from the water, trying to cling to the air... non-swimmers clung to swimmers who wanted to shake off the burden, beat at them, soon they sank together into the depths," wrote Kisch.[44] As full pontoons struggled to depart the Serbian shore, anxious soldiers still on the bank, jumped into the water, attempting to climb aboard. Those on the pontoon smashed down on the fingers of the interlopers with rifle butts and fists or pried their fingers open until they lost their grip, often sinking beneath the surface. All the while, Serbian bullets whistled, picking off Habsburg soldiers on the pontoons and in the water.[45] Those who were fortunate enough to make it back to the Austro-Hungarian bank, shortly found themselves "sad and disconsolate," contemplating their harrowing experiences, the many friends they lost. Kisch, in his diary, unflinchingly reveals the mental and emotional strain, writing that "Throughout the morning I cry suddenly for no reason, in the afternoon I laugh and am

---

41. Houlihan, "Clergy in the Trenches," 213-4.
42. Egon Erwin Kisch, "*Schreib das auf, Kisch!*" *Das Kriegstagbuch von Egon Erwin Kisch* (Berlin: Erich Reiss Verlag, 1930), 40. Kisch served in the 15th Co. of the 11th Infantry Regiment (Prague), part of the 9th Division, assigned to the VIII Corps, V Army.
43. Ibid., 98.
44. Ibid., 109.
45. Kisch, *Schreib das auf*, 110-111.

childish… All are in a similar mood."[46]

The open plains of the Galician theater—roughly four times larger than the Western Front—permitted large, traditional set-piece battles.[47] Quite unlike the static, entrenched firing lines of the Western Front, Austro-Hungarian divisions fought to outflank and encircle the Russian enemy in quick, sweeping maneuvers. Like Austro-Hungarian fortunes in Serbia, however, operations in Galicia proved equally calamitous; by the end of September 1914, virtually all of Galicia was in Russian hands.[48] For Habsburg soldiers in the field, the opening months consisted of a series of repelled advances and chaotic retreats. As violinist and reserve officer, Fritz Kreisler, recounted, "with conditions utterly unsteady and positions shifting daily and hourly, only the most superficial trenches were used."[49] The fluidity of the front lines and the haphazard nature in which Austro-Hungarian formations fled, lent itself to large numbers of soldiers taken prisoner in early months.

Early studies of the Habsburg Army in Galicia attributed the inordinately high number of Austro-Hungarian war prisoners taken on the Eastern Front to anti-Habsburg sentiments, compelling entire units, or large portions of them, to surrender with little resistance. Alon Rachamimov skillfully demonstrates, however, in most cases, soldiers became prisoners in "large catches," having very little "control over the situation or any real possibility of agency."[50] In captivity Austro-Hungarian soldiers typically reported to have been treated decently by their Russian captors, aside from regular complaints of being robbed of their belongings. Hungry, tired, and bewildered Habsburg prisoners marched on average 15.6 miles a day to Russian train stations. On Russian POW trains, Austro-Hungarian prisoners found cramped, unsanitary conditions made the transmission of typhus a particular problem made worse by the lengthy journey to assembly camps in Kiev and Moscow. Captivity was strikingly different for officers

---

46. Ibid., 115.
47. Narskii, "The Frontline Experience of Russian Soldiers," 34.
48. See Herwig, *The First World War*, 87-96, 107-113 for a concise operational account of the first months of fighting in Galicia.
49. Kreisler, *Four Weeks in the Trenches*, 25.
50. Alon Rachamimov, *POWs and the Great War: Captivity on the Eastern Front* (New York: Berg, 2002), 33, 43. See also the recent study, Richard Lein, *Pflichterfüllung oder Hochverrat? Die tschechischen Soldaten Österreich-Ungarns im Ersten Weltkrieg* (Wien: LIT Verlag, 2011). Lein debunks infamous myths of mass desertion in the largely Czech 28th, 35th, and 75th Infantry Regiments. Drawing on archival materials he concludes that poorly trained replacements and communication issues doomed the 28th, while poor assessments by the *AOK* of the situation on the Russian Front placed the 35th and 75th regiments in untenable situations. Post-war Czechoslovak propaganda fabricated the notion of "mass desertion," based on the large numbers from those regiments taken prisoner.

and enlisted men; as future historian Hans Kohn explained in his memoirs, his five years of captivity were spent reading, mastering languages and observing local populations as opposed to the backbreaking labor that awaited the enlisted man.[51]

If the environment was an influential factor in shaping the experience of Habsburg soldiers in Serbia and Galicia, it was unquestionably *the* fundamental factor that defined the war in the Carpathians and the Alps. Mountain warfare in the Carpathians and the Alps was tactically unconceivable to military strategists prior to the outbreak of war. However, desperate Habsburg retreats from Galicia and the Italian entry into the war turned what was previously improbable into reality. Though providing the Austro-Hungarian Empire with natural defensive barriers, the Carpathian and Alpine mountain ranges exerted terrible hardships on the crown's soldiers, in every conceivable way.

Fighting in its foothills and narrow passes of the Carpathian Mountains was extraordinarily brutal, requiring "the utmost physical and mental fortitude," Graydon Tunstall explains. In the depths of winter, temperatures plunged to -13°F (-25°C) as snowstorms often swallowed patrols whose compasses froze; these victims fell prey to "*der weiße Tod,*" hungry wolves, or in some cases, both, in that order.[52] Worse, Austro-Hungarian soldiers lacked adequate rations and winter clothing. "Hundreds freeze to death daily; every wounded soldier who cannot get himself back to the lines is irrevocably sentenced to death…Entire lines of riflemen surrender in tears to escape the pain," Colonel Georg Veith recorded. After stopping to rest, one regiment of the Austro-Hungarian Third Army discovered that twenty-eight officers, and 1.800 enlisted men had frozen to death in their sleep.[53] Winter snowstorms and avalanches forced Austro-Hungarian soldiers who had escaped hypothermia to spend significant amounts of their time and energy digging out from under the snow, rescuing buried patrols, and repairing damaged barracks and forward positions.[54] As temperatures fluctuated, rain and snow mixed, creating icy conditions that made transporting food and supplies to the firing lines extremely difficult. The little food that did make it to the front lines had often frozen solid in the process. Shortages of reinforcements only aggravated the soldiers' plight, requiring them to remain on the firing lines for months on end,

51. Rachamimov, *POWs and the Great War*, 47-60.
52. Tunstall, *Blood on the Snow*, 3; Manfried *Rauchensteiner,* Der Tod des der Doppeladlers: Österreich-Ungarn und der Erste Weltkrieg (Graz: Verlag Styria, 1993), 203.
53. W. Bruce Lincoln, *Passage through Armageddon* (New York: Simon and Schuster, 1986), 121; Herwig, *First World War*, 136; Dowling, *Brusilov Offensive*, 22-3.
54. Brandauer, *Menschenmaterial Soldat,* 44; Keller, "Mountains Roar," 266.

without relief.[55] Such extreme conditions drove many Habsburg soldiers to madness, causing hallucinations of having food, and driving men to suicide.[56] "Those who have not taken part in it can have no idea of what a human being is capable,"Tăslăuanu concluded.[57]

The assumption of positions in the high Alpine peaks bred a different kind of war than what Austro-Hungarian soldiers had experienced in Serbia, Galicia, or even in the Carpathians. The steep, rocky terrain of the Alps prohibited the larger offensives taking place in the Isonzo River Valley. Instead, fighting entailed artillery bombardment and small unit assaults on carved out mountainside positions. While rifles and machine guns remained the chief tools of the infantryman, Austro-Hungarian troops also hurled grenades, released "roll bombs," and heaved large rocks down the steep slopes at the Italian attackers.[58] In one instance, Habsburg defenders reportedly pelted Italian troops with tins filled with feces.[59] By the end of 1915, the futility of Italian efforts to take the well-fortified Austro-Hungarian positions spurred the development of *Minenkriege* or "mine wars" in which Italian and Habsburg units tunneled beneath the other's positions, filled the tunnels with munitions, and exploded the mines, blowing up the positions.[60] To be sure, the unique landscape of the Alpine Front helped mitigate the soldiers' sense of futility relative to the Eastern plains and rugged hills of Serbia; unlike the other principle warfronts, the natural barrier of the Alpine Front's snow-capped peaks symbolized the purity of soldiers' selfless perseverance in the defense of the fatherland.

Violence and Danger in the Landscape of War

"[T]o neglect the violence of war is to neglect all those men who... endured that immense ordeal," Stéphane Audoin-Rouzeau and Annette Becker emphasized in their critique of Great War historiography.[61] Indeed, neglecting the violence of war precludes any understanding of the soldiers' experience and, in turn, a comprehensive understanding of the war itself. Violence and the landscape of the theater of operations are inseparable in

---

55. Tunstall, *Blood on the Snow*, 4-6.
56. Ibid., 5.
57. Tăslăuanu, *With the Austrian Army*, 218.
58. Langes, *Die Front in Fels und Eis*, 26; Keller, "Mountains Roar," 261.
59. Mark Thompson, *The White War: Life and Death on the Italian Front, 1915-1919* (New York: Basic Books, 2008), 134.
60. Langes, *Die Front in Fels und Eis*, 138-48.
61. Stéphane Audoin-Rouzeau and Annette Becker, 14-18: *Understanding the Great War,* (New York: Hill and Wang, 2002), 16. See also Bourke, *An Intimate History of Killing*, for an examination of violence in the First World War.

that it is the setting in which combat takes place. Thus the theater of operations is, at once, an environment of danger, fear, destruction, and death, naturally exercising tremendous influence in forging the soldier experience.

For those Austro-Hungarian troops participating in the initial clashes on the Eastern Front, an ominous pattern emerged:

> The Russians usually entrenched at the edge of a wood, let us approach within three or four hundred paces and, just as we yelled our "Hourra!" for the "final assault" with the bayonet, opened rapid fire with rifles and machine guns which decimated our ranks in a few seconds. The few who survived wandered panic-stricken all over Galicia and soon lost any military identity they ever had...this was the kind of fate that befel (*sic*) most of the Austro-Hungarian front-line units.[62]

Habsburg soldiers died needlessly in those early engagements in "suicidal" frontal assaults. The 76th Infantry Regiment (Ödenburg) lost nearly fifty percent of its infantrymen during the course of three such attacks, while the 2nd Regiment, Tiroler Kaiserjäger, senselessly charged an entire Russian infantry division at Hujcze, losing nearly 2.000 men in the process. The "ill-timed bravado" of Habsburg units who commenced attacks without artillery support, did irrevocable damage to the Austro-Hungarian Army. So much so that the *AOK* had to pass down orders to its regimental commanders to utilize flanking movements, and not charge headlong into the teeth of the enemy.[63]

Those front-line soldiers who escaped physical injury often endured mental and emotional wounds. Survivors could not escape the images of friends and comrades dying before them in their mind. Fritz Kreisler recounted the first of his men to be killed in battle, "I saw a great many men die afterwards, some suffering horribly, but I do not recall any death that affected me quite as much as that of this first victim in my platoon."[64] The dead soldiers that littered the contested landscapes haunted the living, forcing them to consider their own mortality and contemplate the idea of 'civilization,' and the true nature humankind. One diarist provided what would have been a common scene for Austro-Hungarian soldiers traversing

---

62. Tăslăuanu, *With the Austrian Army in Galicia*, 59.
63. BA-MA, PH 3/328 Oberste Heeresleitung. Berichte Freiherr v. Freytag-Loringhoven 1912-1915, cited in Herwig, *First World War*, 91-2, 107; Anton Graf Bossi-Fedrigotti, *Die Kaiserjäger im Ersten Weltkrieg* (Graz: Ares Verlag, 2009), 11-20; *Österreich-Ungarns letzter Krieg: Das Kriegsjahr 1914*, 345-348.
64. Kreisler, *Four Weeks*, 30.

the Galician Front:

> Just off the road a dead Russian was lying on his back, his face
> contorted, his lips flecked with foam, and his arms crossed. His
> large, glassy eyes stared vacantly at the sky. He was a fine man of
> twenty-five or so, whom Fate had destined to this horrible end:
> a rotting corpse in a field, victim of human savagery. His torn
> tunic disclosed a pool of blood in which the worms were already
> beginning their loathsome work. Someone had turned is pockets
> inside out, and they flapped heavily in the wind. Death had left a
> sarcastic smile on his lips. He seemed to be railing at Humanity,
> with its so-called culture and morality.[65]

The cries of the wounded also made deep psychological impressions.
Hungarian reserve lieutenant, Maximilian Reiter, stationed on the Vodil
vrh, in the Isonzo sector, documented the haunting screams and shouts of
wounded and dying comrades laying for days in front of their trenches as
Italian rifle fire raked the ground, preventing the retrieval of the wounded.
Not until the stench of rotting corpses became unbearable did Austro-
Hungarian and Italian burial parties cease hostilities long enough to bury
their dead.[66] The darkness of night, typically a period of eerie quiet, "was
interrupted only by the low moaning of the wounded that came regularly to
us. It was hideous in its terrible monotony," another officer recounted from
his time in Galicia.[67]

Combat was not the only mentally exhausting experience for the
front-line Habsburg soldier. Veterans who chronicled their experience
consistently acknowledged the anxiety and trepidation of night watch duty.
While night provided the ideal setting for resupplying formations on the
front lines, the darkness concealed the enemy. "[T]he slightest roll of a
pebble or scuffle of some nocturnal creature, a soldier's head will jerk up. Is
it the beginning of a night attack? Enemy scouts probing the wire? The
tension keeps up all night and every night," one diarist recorded.[68] Likewise,
night patrols and marches were commonplace and no less mentally taxing.
"The nightly breath of nature, falling rocks and rushing water bore into
mind and heart," wrote one soldier who patrolled the Alpine Front.[69]

65. Tăslăuanu, With the Austrian Army in Galicia, 74.
66. Reiter, Balkan Assault, 17.
67. Kreisler, Four Weeks, 54.
68. Reiter, Balkan Assault, 17-18.
69. Walter Schmidkunz, Der Kampf über den Gletschern: ein Buch von der Alpenfront (Erfurt:
Gebr. Richters Verlaganstalt, 1934), 15 cited in Keller, "Mountains Roar," 260.

Austro-Hungarian soldiers no longer able to cope in the environment of danger on the fighting front utilized a variety of ways to escape the firing lines. As the war dragged on, the efforts to avoid the front lines became increasingly commonplace. As one soldier apathetically noted in his diary, returning to the front after recovering from wounds, "naturally I reported sick."[70] Beyond merely feigning illness, troops utilized illness-invoking products such as oleander leaf, temporarily poisoning themselves to avoid the dangers of the firing line.[71] Concoctions such as chewing tobacco, rum, and dynamite caused tremors, dizziness, heart palpitations, and delirium, was just one of many.[72] Habsburg soldiers resorted to even more desperate measures, as army doctor, Käte Frankenthal, recalled:

> Gonorrhea-pus had driven a flourishing trade. Once an entire hall was punished because several people had procured this precious material and infected themselves. Even tubercular discharge was bought and sold. People swallowed the disgusting and deadly substance. They would rather get tuberculosis than go back into the trenches.[73]

Austro-Hungarian soldiers, like their counterparts in the Great War's many fronts, resorted to self-inflicted gunshot wounds to escape front line duty, and in extreme cases, suicide. It is worth noting that the Austro-Hungarian Common Army had long maintained the highest suicide rate of any army in Europe, due, largely, to the harsh discipline, which frequently bordered on mistreatment.[74]

Violence was not confined to combatants, as the Austro-Hungarian invasion of Serbia demonstrates. Serbia's purported role in the assassination

---

70. Rozenblit, *Reconstructing a National Identity*, 88. As Rozenblit notes, religious and cultural backgrounds were also influential factors amongst individual soldiers and their attitudes toward particular enemies. Looking at Jewish soldiers in the Austro-Hungarian Army, she notes that they were particularly ardent fighters on the Galician Front against an infamously anti-Semitic Russian enemy, while harboring less disdain toward the Italians on the Alpine Front.

71. Brandauer, *Menschenmaterial Soldat*, 114.

72. Brandauer, *Menschenmaterial Soldat*, 115; Herwig, *The First World War*, 130 details how similar practices were utilized by those wishing to evade being drafted into the war.

73. This excerpt is taken from the memoirs of Dr. Käte Frankenthal, a German doctor who treated Austro-Hungarian soldiers during the First World War, cited in Elisabeth Malleier, "Formen männlicher Hysterie: Die Kriegsneurosen im Ersten Weltkrieg," in Elisabeth Mixa et. al., *Körper-Geschlecht-Geschichte: Historische und Aktuelle Debatten in der Medizin* (Innsbruck, 1996), 147-163; Brandauer, *Menschenmaterial Soldat*, 114.

74. Herwig, *The First World War*, 130; Kisch, *"Schreib das auf, Kisch!,"* 123; Deák, *Beyond Nationalism*, 107.

of the heir-to-the-throne, Archduke Franz Ferdinand supplied the basis for officers and chaplains to emphasize the "moral righteousness of the Empire and the ethical depravity of Serbia."[75] The Austro-Hungarian Army's initial contact with Serbian military resistance seemingly validated this characterization. The Serbian high command assigned units comprised of second and third levee draftees—who lacked uniforms almost entirely— to the Sava and Drina River borders, thus appearing to Habsburg soldiers as Serbian *francs-tireurs*.[76] Official Austro-Hungarian records also document widespread incidents of Serbian women and children firing on Habsburg troops. Furthermore, Serbian *Komitatschi* were trained to attack and blend into civilian populations, eroding "the barrier between civilians and war" and intensifying the indignation of the Austro-Hungarian high command.[77] Such blurring of the lines between civilian and combatant justified harsh retribution on civilians when Habsburg units encountered guerrilla resistance.[78]

Retribution for these "deceitful" practices took multiple forms. As R.A. Reiss reported, "punitive" incendiary bombardments of Serbian cities and towns destroyed civilian residences, businesses, museums, university buildings, cathedrals, and hospitals.[79] Reiss also cites numerous depositions where Austro-Hungarian prisoners admitted to having witnessed Serbian POWs executed—Austrian, Hungarian, and Croatian officers and enlisted men overwhelmingly cited as the perpetrators. Wounded Serbians seemed to have been the principle victims. Rather than dressing their wounds or sending them to the rear for medical attention, Habsburg soldiers were ordered to "finish off" enemy combatants.[80] Serbian civilians also suffered atrocities such as rape, pillaging, and poisoned wells, mass executions, and bayoneting and dismembering men, women, and children, killing, in sum, over 3.000 civilians.[81]

Conclusions

According to Jay Luuvas, "Kamerad Schnürschuh," the rather pejorative moniker German soldiers coined for their lace-booted Austro-

75. Gumz, *The Resurrection and Collapse*, 46.
76. Crawfurd Price, *Serbia's Part in the War, Vol. I: The Rampart Against Pan-Germanism* (London, 1918), 84-85; R.A. Reiss, *Report on the Atrocities Committed by the Austro-Hungarian Army* (London, 1916), 145; Schindler, "Disaster," 170.
77. Gumz, *Resurrection and Collapse*, 48-9; Kisch, "*Schreib das auf, Kisch!*," 32.
78. Gumz, *Resurrection and Collapse*, 45.
79. Reiss, *Report on the Atrocities*, 17-23; Kisch, "*Schreib das auf, Kisch!*," 105.
80. Reiss, *Report on the Atrocities*, 24-26.
81. Gumz, *Resurrection and Collapse*, 45.

Hungarian brothers in arms, "may have served in a unique army, but his was the common experience." While they were indeed members of "a community of sufferers," just like every other front-line soldier in the war, they faced an even greater burden than their counterparts.[82] The issue of language placed Habsburg soldiers—already materially lacking—at an even greater disadvantage. As this essay has demonstrated, the linguistic diversity of the Habsburg Army was aggravated by reactionary policies of the *AOK*. Its policy of 'mixing' troops of loyal nationalities with those deemed "unreliable," greatly reduced the camaraderie and unit cohesion of many Habsburg formations and engendered the tendency to form linguistically homogenous groupings inside units, thus, creating a markedly different group dynamic than what would have been found in linguistically homogenous character of other armies. This is not to say that other belligerents involved did not have their own internal divisions; the newly formed German Reich had its own sectional and religious tensions, as did Great Britain in the turmoil over Irish home rule.[83] These strains, however, did not translate into significant impediments on the battlefield, as in the Austro-Hungarian case. Adherence to territorial systems of conscription by Russia, Great Britain, and in Germany, helped foster local patriotism, and strengthened national identities, while the *AOK*'s reactionary and dismissive policies destroyed any potentially galvanizing sentiments.[84] To be sure, the challenges presented by the issue of language created difficulties not experienced by troops in other armies and, thus, represents a unique feature of the Austro-Hungarian soldier experience.

The landscape, climate, and weather of the front environment was as much more than a setting for war, it was a living force whose indiscriminate wrath only compounded on the burdens of frontline soldiers. Habsburg soldiers were deployed in significant numbers on three major theaters of operation in the first twelve months of the war—more than any other their Great Power counterparts—spreading their ranks thin and placing even greater strain on its troops. In Serbia, unlike any other theater of operations,

---

82. Jay Luuvas, "A Unique Army: The Common Experience," in *The Habsburg Empire in World War I: Essays on the Intellectual, Military, Political, and Economic Aspects of the Habsburg War Effort*, Robert A. Kann, Béla K. Király, Paula S. Fichtner, eds. (Boulder: East European Quarterly, 1977), 89.

83. See Roger Chickering, *Imperial Germany and the Great War, 1914-1918* (New York: Cambridge University Press, 1998) for treatment of the divisions within the German Reich. See also Timothy Bowman, Irish Regiments in the Great War: Discipline and Morale (Manchester: Manchester University Press, 2003).

84. Narskii, "The Frontline Experience," 41. For an extensive examination of the development of Russian patriotism and nationalism, see Joshua A. Sanborn, *Drafting the Russian Nation: Military Conscription, Total War, and Mass Politics, 1905-1925* (DeKalb: Northern Illinois University Press, 2003).

Habsburg soldiers faced significant resistance from guerilla (*Komitatschi*) formations that were largely indistinguishable from the civilian population. Natural features such as woods and cornfields concealed *Komitatschi* ambushes and landmines, while the Drina and Save Rivers presented problematic obstacles. Habsburg troops responded to the guerrilla attacks with brutal reprisals on Serbian civilians, POWs, and captured guerrillas. The much larger front in Galicia allowed for larger combat operations, creating a fluid and volatile war of movement. Long, arduous marches to the firing lines and hasty retreats bookended frivolous assaults and needless Austro-Hungarian bloodletting of the opening months of fighting. This recurring pattern contributed significantly to Austria-Hungary losing the greatest number of troops to captivity than any army of the war and the subsequent loss of Galicia, forcing the army's withdrawal to the Carpathians where they faced brutal fighting in the subzero depths of winter. Already spread thin, Habsburg Army assumed a defensive posture on the Italian border in May 1915. The natural barrier the Alps provided enabled Habsburg troops to carve out strong defensive positions, allowing them to repulse repeated Italian assaults. Mountain warfare limited offensive capacity of both armies to supporting mountain artillery fire and small unit combat, which favored the well-constructed Austro-Hungarian positions.

As distinctive as the Austro-Hungarian soldiers' experience may have been, the fear, violence, and trauma of combat was universal. By the end of 1915, the Habsburg Army had suffered 2.1 million casualties, the most of any belligerent involved in the war.[85] Much of this is attributable to the reckless frontal assaults prevalent in the opening battles in the East. Soldiers' desperate efforts to evade the front lines reflected the reality of these figures. While each soldiers' experience was unique, their writings consistently revealed: the exhilaration of combat, a morose acceptance, but disdain for the death and destruction of war, post-traumatic stress, insufficient food, water, and supplies, and mental and physical exhaustion.

Since Austro-Hungarian soldiers were never engaged on the Western Front in significant numbers, their experience has largely stood outside the popular imagination of the Great War and accounts for much of the scholarly neglect. This article has sought to contribute toward filling this gap by highlighting the three principle elements that, together, frame the Habsburg soldier experience. In emphasizing these features, this essay, in the space available, has attempted to create something of a representative framework, which might hopefully serve as a basis for further investigation.

---

85. Herwig, *The First World War*, 172.

Exiles of Eden: Vienna and the Viennese during and after World War I

Peter Berger

Memories

My earliest childhood recollections of Vienna go back to the mid-1950s when my father's business projects compelled our family to lead a life divided between the Netherlands, the place of my birth, and a Republic of Austria just recently restored to independence. Little more than a decade after the end of World War II, Vienna still displayed the wounds inflicted upon the city first by Anglo-American air raids and later by Soviet as well as German artillery shelling. I vividly remember the blackened, windowless façade of what once used to be Vienna's most famous public bath, the Dianabad, on the banks of the Danube canal. A few hundred yards away on Rotenturmstrasse, a street connecting the canal front with Saint Stephen's square in the middle of town, impressive ruins of a semi-rotund building bore witness to the final stages of the battle of Vienna in April 1945. It took until the early 1960s to have the structure, slightly reminiscent of Rome's Colosseum, replaced by a new and equally unorthodox apartment and office block.

Although it was more of a vague feeling than something I could have expressed in convincing terms, Vienna to me seemed—way into the 1960s—a grey and dull place, the more so if held against my native city Amsterdam, which had been spared the horrors of aerial bombing and large-scale fighting on the ground. For a child under ten, Amsterdam's speedy postwar economic recovery was evidenced by the many US or French-made motorcars parked alongside the canal houses of the historic city center, and by the sophistication of the kitchen and bathroom hardware those houses would boast of. Vienna, by way of comparison, seemed sullen and poor.

Of the people one met in the streets of Vienna in the 1950s, many (probably a majority) had been there in 1918 to witness Austria-Hungary's defeat in World War I and the ensuing dismemberment of the Habsburg Empire. For them, 1945 must have brought a sense of Déja-vu, albeit that the Nazis' war caused, in the words of Viennese-born writer Ilsa Barea, much worse destruction and was followed by worse moral degradation than the events of 1914-18.[1] Indeed Vienna never became the scene of a battle during World War I. Her single contact with enemy aircraft occurred when, in the summer of 1918, a small band of Italian amateur pilots led by the poet, Gabriele d'Annunzio, triumphantly circled above Saint Stephen's cathedral in their planes. Instead of bombs, they dropped leaflets urging the Viennese to oppose war and appreciate "Italian freedom."[2] When surrender came in October 1918, the consequences seemed to establish the truth of Karl Kraus', the satirist's, famous pun of Austria being a "laboratory of world destruction."[3] In 1918, moral degradation in the sense of a general corruption of ethical standards may not have occurred on a scale comparable to the Nazi era, but the Austrians, and the Viennese bourgeoisie in particular, literally lost the ground under their feet. Stefan Zweig, the novelist, may serve as the embodiment of the Austrian *Déraciné*, especially after his emigration in 1936 to Brazil: "Cut off from all roots, and even from the earth that used to nourish these roots—this is how I truly feel. . . . I was born into a great and powerful Empire, the monarchy of the Habsburgs, but you'd better not search for it on the map: it got washed away without a trace."[4]

This paper is about the gradual transformation between 1914 and 1918 of Vienna, the once illustrious metropolis of the Austro-Hungarian Empire-Kingdom, into an "urban has-been" (The expression is borrowed from Paul Hofmann, a native Viennese and long-time Austrian correspondent of *The New York Times*[5]). My account is published at a moment when the world commemorates the one-hundredth anniversary of the beginning of the "Great War," an avoidable disaster of mankind, as German essayist Cora Stephan rightly stated in an article printed in December 2013 by *Neue Zürcher Zeitung*.[6] Historians and political scientists, in an avalanche of weighty studies dedicated to World War I, largely side with Mrs. Stephan's

---

1. Ilsa Barea, *Vienna* (New York: Knopf, 1967), 366.
2. One paragraph of D'Annunzio's message referred to "the intelligence of the Viennese people," which immediately prompted cynical reactions of those who read it on the ground. A typical comment, reported in the memoirs of Austrian composer Ernst Krenek, was: "This foreigner certainly does not know us!" Ernst Krenek, Im Atem der Zeit. Erinnerungen an die Moderne (Hamburg: Hoffmann und Campe, 1998), 152-3.
3. Franz Ferdinand und die Talente, *Fackel* 400-403, XVI. Jahr, 10 July 1914, 2.
4. Stefan Zweig, *Die Welt von Gestern* (Berlin, Frankfurt: G. B. Fischer, 1962), 7. See also: Alberto Dines, *Tod im Paradies. Die Tragödie des Stefan Zweig* (Frankfurt, Wien, Zürich: Büchergilde Gutenberg, 2006).
5. Paul Hofmann, *The Viennese. Splendor, Twilight, and Exile* (New York, London: Doubleday, 1988), 163.
6. Hundert Jahre Traurigkeit, *Neue Zürcher Zeitung* 302, 30. Dezember 2013, 17.

argument: neither was the carnage inevitable, nor were the Germans and Austrians the sole villains in the piece. Christopher Clark's opus magnum on the origins of the war, with its telling title *The Sleepwalkers*, was acclaimed by a Swiss reviewer, Andreas Ernst, as an "Anti-Fischer" (Fritz Fischer being, in the early 1960s, the spiritual father of a school of historians insisting on Germany's unshared war guilt).[7] In Clark's book, like in others by Herfried Münkler[8], Peter Hart[9], Oliver Janz[10], and Ernst Piper[11] that deal with the war itself rather than with its genesis, the acting personnel are politicians, generals, admirals, planners of the wartime economy, and sometimes unruly crowds (of workers, of housewives, etc.). Military strategies and tactics are discussed in great detail, along with the impact on belligerent societies of "great movements," political and social: workers against capitalism, female emancipation, the idolization of (male) bravery, sacrifice, and violence—one of the sources of interwar fascism. But, interestingly enough, most recent monographs on the Great War do not care much about the *places* where "great individuals" made their decisions, where crowds hailed or opposed them, and where strategies and ideologies were carved out and discussed with fervor. Those places were the mega-cities of Europe, Vienna among them. Leif Jerram of Manchester University calls the urban history of Europe's twentieth century "a history untold."[12] Taking up Jerram's line of reasoning, one could also speak of an untold history of World War I, meaning the story of how the Great War was devised, administered, and suffered in cities like London, Paris, Petersburg, Berlin or Vienna, and what those cities looked like when the weapons were silent again.

For most of the insights presented in this paper I am indebted to the work of pioneering urban historians, sociologists, and economists who have devoted their energies and talent to the study of both late imperial Vienna, and Vienna, the capital of a tiny republic reduced to political near-insignificance. Many of them have contributed to a recently published volume on Vienna in wartime, to my knowledge the first of its kind, edited by Alfred Pfoser and Andreas Weigl. The book is a practical guide for anyone interested in this long-neglected field: the history of large cities

7. Andreas Ernst. "Dunkler Fleck? Christopher Clarks serbischer Sonderfall," *Neue Zürcher Zeitung* 297, 21 December 2013, 27. Christopher Clark, *The Sleepwalkers. How Europe went to War in 1914* (London: Allen Lane, 2013); Fritz Fischer, *Griff nach der Weltmacht. Die Kriegszielpolitik des kaiserlichen Deutschland* (Düsseldorf: Droste, 1961).

8. Herfried Münkler, *Der Grosse Krieg. Die Welt 1914-1918* (Berlin: Rowohlt, 2013).

9. Peter Hart, *The Great War* (London: Profile Books, 2013).

10. Oliver Janz, *14 – Der Grosse Krieg* (Frankfurt: Campus, 2013).

11. Ernst Piper, *Nacht über Europa. Kulturgeschichte des Ersten Weltkriegs* (München: Propyläen-Verlag, 2013).

12. Leif Jerram, *Streetlife. The Untold History of Europe's Twentieth Century* (Oxford: Oxford University Press, 2011).

under conditions of war.[13]

Promises

In 1890, Austrian authorities published the results of a nationwide census which New York's Deputy Commissioner of Labor Statistics, Adna Ferrin Weber, would later praise as "a model work."[14] The census revealed the impressive growth of Vienna and her suburbs from a population of 511.147 in 1850 to 1.341.897 forty years later.[15] On the eve of the outbreak of war in August 1914, 2.149.834 persons were registered as residing in Vienna, meaning that the city's population had once more grown by almost fifty percent.[16] In Europe around 1900, no more than five capitals exceeded the one million mark. Besides Vienna, these were London, Paris, Berlin, and St. Petersburg.[17]

Discounting the effect of repeated incorporations of nearby settlements into Vienna, the city owed its nineteenth-century growth largely to a pair of interrelated events. One was the building and extension of the Austrian railroad network, a process that unfolded from the 1840s onward. The other was the bold decision in 1857 of Emperor Francis Joseph and his counselors to authorize demolition of Vienna's city fortifications, and to have walls and bastions replaced with a boulevard worthy of Georges-Eugène Haussmann, flanked by stately apartment buildings, seats of municipal and government agencies, and temples of culture and learning like the Opera, *Burgtheater*, and University. The "pull factor" of a metropolitan labor market created by both (railroad-centered) industrialization and the building boom coincided with widespread rural misery in regions near enough to Vienna to make people consider moving for a job.[18] Rural workers and young women without formal education who looked for employment in Vienna's upper-class households were, however, but two groups of would-be labor migrants attracted to the Austrian capital. Villagers and townspeople from all corners of the realm were attracted by the promise of upward social mobility held

13. Alfred Pfoser, Andreas Weigl eds., *Im Epizentrum des Zusammenbruchs. Wien im Ersten Weltkrieg* (Wien: Metroverlag, 2013).

14. Adna Ferrin Weber, *The Growth of Cities in the Nineteenth Century. A Study in Statistics* (Ithaca, New York: Cornell University Press, 1899), 94.

15. Weber, 95. In 1890, sixteen suburbs were formally united with Vienna proper to form the area of "Greater Vienna". Without these suburbs, the city in 1890 numbered 798.719 souls.

16. Weigl in Pfoser and Weigl, 64.

17. Peter Clark, *European Cities and Towns 400-2000* (Oxford: Oxford University Press, 2009), 231.

18. Michael John, Albert Lichtblau, *Schmelztiegel Wien – einst und jetzt. Zur Geschichte und Gegenwart von Zuwanderung und Minderheiten* (Wien: Böhlau, 1990), especially 89-126.

by Vienna's trade and services economy, and the steady expansion of state and municipal bureaucracies connected with Austria-Hungary's status as a European power.

Already during the first of two large waves of labor-migration into imperial Vienna (1859-1873 and 1890-1900[19]), the city suffered, like other nineteenth century metropolises, from what the British historian Tony Judt described as opening scissors between "the scale of urban increase and the scale of state action."[20] In the Viennese case, state, or rather communal government action to mitigate the effects of explosive urban growth is usually associated with the name of the city's notorious mayor of 1897-1910, Karl Lueger. To the extent that Lueger can be called a social reformer, he was most of all interested in the fate of his recently enfranchised constituency of lower middle class homeowners, shopkeepers, artisans, and public servants. This was the catholic petty bourgeoisie of Vienna's girdle of fast-expanding, overcrowded, industrial suburbs with its suspicion of everything that smacked "foreign" (Jewish in the first place, but also Czech), or proletarian, or simply held a perspective that could uproot the traditional social fabric. Lueger's historical greatness rests, somewhat paradoxically, on his achievement as an urban modernizer for his clientele of "Christian" anti-modernists. It owes nothing to either his very marginal concern for the "indigenous, impoverished, disadvantaged, permanently poor people who had moved to industrial cities and without whose labor the flourishing capitalism of the age would have been inconceivable"[21] or his qualities as a politician per se. A lifelong reckless demagogue and opportunist, Lueger may be hard or even impossible to acquit before the tribunal of history, says his most recent biographer, John Boyer of the University of Chicago.[22] But Boyer, justifiably, goes into great detail when describing Lueger's truly revolutionary approach to matters of urban governance, including the creation of a financially self-sustained communal public services sector (transportation, water, electricity, gas, hospitals, schools) meant to avoid excessive burdens for the resident taxpayer, and the conscious preservation of Vienna's natural oxygen reservoir, the forest areas bordering on the city in the North and Northwest.

When Lueger died of diabetes in 1910, Vienna could boast of an excellent urban technical infrastructure fit for a population of four million,

---

19. John and Lichtblau, 91.
20. Tony Judt with Timothy Snyder, *Thinking the Twentieth Century* (London: Penguin Books, 2012), 334.
21. Ibid.
22. See my review of Boyer's book on Lueger in *Contemporary Austrian Studies*, Volume 20 (2011), 309-317.

forecasted by experts for a not-so-remote future but never attained due to
the interference of World War I. The imperial capital in the period between
1895 and 1913 passed through its final stage of physical expansion. The
added space of streets and squares amounted to fifty percent. Sewage canals
were extended by two thirds of their original length.[23] With the almshouse
of *Lainz*, Vienna possessed one of Europe's most impressive charitable
institutions for the elderly poor. In sharp contrast to these achievements,
Lueger's administration completely neglected to deal with the dramatic
shortage of affordable housing for the masses. According to a widely
quoted contemporary report on the living conditions of the working poor
by the social statistician, Eugen von Philippovich, an average worker's
accommodation in 1894 failed to comply even with the minimum space-
per-person standard applied in barracks of the Austro-Hungarian army.[24]
Of course, failure to tackle the housing problem was in full accordance with
Lueger's and his Christian Social party's adherence to the rule of market
forces in the real estate business. Despite an extension of the franchise in
1882 to admit into the ranks of voters everybody with a tax contribution of
more than five guilders a year, Lueger's political success remained heavily
dependent on the support of private providers of mass housing. When
three years upon Lueger's death Richard von Weiskirchner, formerly head
of the Vienna magistrate ("*Magistratsdirektor*"), became mayor of Vienna,
he broadened the Christian Socials' political base to include bosses of
industry, top-level bureaucrats, and influential professionals—but not the
workers who were left for the ascendant Social Democracy to organize
them. Blocking the road to political participation for the proletariat
remained a major Christian Social concern during Weiskirchner's tenure.
To achieve this end, the instrument of discriminatory communal franchise
was employed in a most skillful fashion, thereby preserving the thoroughly
middle-class character of "official" Vienna until 1914 and beyond.

On the eve of the murders of Sarajevo, Vienna was a place of blatant
contradictions. Within its boundaries, one would meet striking poverty in the
heavily industrialized peripheral districts, the "no man's land of social life" (to
quote the American sociologist and architecture critic Lewis Mumford).[25]
Violent manifestations of working class discontent were not the norm, but
one particular instance of revolt, the "price-hike riots" of September 1911,
had left a lasting impression on the rulers in Vienna's *Rathaus*. Coexisting
with widespread urban poverty, but mostly ignorant of it, was Vienna's

23. Wolfgang Maderthaner in Peter Csendes, Ferdinand Oppl, Wien. *Geschichte einer Stadt*,
Band 3: Von 1790 bis zur Gegenwart (Wien, Köln, Weimar: Böhlau, 2006), 228.
24. Ibid., 190.
25. Ibid., 190.

affluent and numerically small business and professional elite. This included a few upper and upper-middle class Jewish families like the Ephrussi's or the Gallia's[26] who commissioned or collected works of contemporary artists like Klimt, Schiele, and Gerstl, had their houses built and furnished by Adolf Loos and Josef Hoffmann, and sometimes donated generously to prestigious cultural institutions such as *Musikverein* or *Künstlerhaus*. Vienna possessed a prolific scene of literary and journalistic talent. Some of Central Europe's best daily papers resided there. One of them, the *Neue Freie Presse*, drew venomous attacks from Karl Kraus, himself a journalist, satirist, and self-appointed guardian of the purity of the German tongue. So great was Kraus' influence on matters of language and style that the authors of Austria-Hungary's declaration of war on Serbia in the cabinet of foreign minister Leopold Count Berchtold wondered if their product would meet the approval of the merciless gatekeeper of the written word. Normally, the spheres of an aristocratic courtier and minister like Berchtold and that of Kraus (Jewish bourgeoisie obsessed with language, philosophy, and art) would not have much in common. One can even argue, as Carl E. Schorske did in his famous study of Fin-de-siècle Vienna, that it was the refusal of Austria's "first" society to grant attention, let alone equal opportunities, to the "second" which caused Jewish preoccupation with matters remote from politics and the running of the state in a broader sense.[27] But there are equally influential voices like that of the art historian, Ernst Gombrich, who decidedly refused discussing Vienna's contribution to scientific, artistic, or intellectual developments around 1900 from a Jewish standpoint. Most of the names generally associated with the Viennese cultural boom of the Fin-de-siècle were not Jewish in the first place, says Gombrich. And if there was a Jewish connection, why mention it at all? Only Nazis should have an interest in emphasizing the Jewishness of people like Freud, Mahler, or Schnitzler who wanted to be (and were) Austrians, first and foremost.[28]

Eyewitnesses' accounts of the condition of Vienna and the Habsburg Empire shortly before the outbreak of the Great War were widely at variance from each other and in fact no less contradictory than Viennese reality. Reading the 1914 diaries of one of the very few influential politicians of Jewish extraction of the time, Josef Redlich, a law professor and member of

---

26. For the history of the Viennese branch of the Ephrussi-family see Edmund de Waal, *The Hare with Amber Eyes. A Hidden Inheritance* (London: Random House, 2010); the Gallia's story can be found in Tim Bonyhady, *Good Living Street. The Fortunes of my Viennese Family* (Sydney: Allen & Unwin, 2011).

27. Carl E. Schorske, *Fin-de-Siècle Vienna – Politics and Culture* (New York: Alfred Knopf, 1980).

28. Ernst H. Gombrich, *Jüdische Identität und jüdisches Schicksal. Eine Diskussionsbemerkung* (Wien: Passagen Verlag, 1997).

the Vienna Reichstag, one gets the impression of "an overripe civilization doomed beyond any possibility of retrieve."[29] The polycratic nature of Austro-Hungarian power politics[30], with Francis Joseph's government and the shadow-cabinet of the heir to the throne, Francis Ferdinand, undermining each other's efforts, may have contributed to Redlich's bleak view. At the same time, Henry Wickham Steed, local correspondent in Vienna for the London *Times*, expressed confidence in Austria's capability to maintain her current position within the community of European nations. There exists a telling remark by Steed connecting Austria's problems to her rapid economic growth rather than her decline.[31] In the 1970s and 1980s, "revisionist" economic historians sided with Steed's optimism. They challenged their mainstream opponents with the notion that, economically, the Habsburg Empire of 1896-1913 had performed much better than was generally assumed. For the revisionist school, underdevelopment of some remote parts of Austria-Hungary, but not a lack of potential for growth in general, jeopardized an otherwise remarkable catching-up process.[32]

Behind the imposing façades of Vienna's bank palaces, corporate headquarters, and government buildings, one may thus have detected enough promises for a bright and prosperous Austrian future. Instead, paucity of thought[33], widespread among the country's political and military leadership, helped trigger the seminal catastrophe of the twentieth century. When war came, it was enthusiastically welcomed by a former resident of Vienna: Adolf Hitler, whose home for several years had been a men's dormitory for the destitute in the city's twentieth district. In May 1913, Hitler and a friend left Vienna for Munich.[34] There, Hitler joined the crowd assembling on Odeon Square to hail German (and Austro-Hungarian) mobilization.

People on the move

August 1914 was a hectic month for press photographers. Wherever

---

29. Barea, 366.

30. Usually, the term "polycracy" (used, among others, by the German historian, Karl-Dietrich Bracher, and meaning government by a multitude of competing centers of power) is reserved for the Third Reich. Christopher Clark applies it to the Habsburg Empire, Clark, 146.

31. See Clark, 115. Twenty years later, Steed would insist upon his early conviction that the Habsburg Empire was bound to fail.

32. See, among others, David Good, *The Economic Rise of the Habsburg Empire 1750-1914* (London: University of California Press, 1984).

33. Barea, 356.

34. Brigitte Hamann, *Hitlers Wien. Lehrjahre eines Diktators* (München, Zürich: Piper, 1996), 568.

soldiers were dispatched to the fronts, an "official" camera must have been on the scene. One of probably thousands of similar pictures shows the departure of a band of Austrian recruits from one of Vienna's metro ("*Stadtbahn*") stations designed by the star architect, Otto Wagner. On the platform, the young men stand in three rows, one additional row sitting in front. Except for the long rifle held by one of the sitting men, nothing in the picture suggests a martial spirit. Quite to the contrary: the faces look solemn, pensive, and even sad.[35]

While Vienna was slowly drained of its young male population deemed fit to fight[36], an influx of newcomers almost immediately made up for the loss. The first transport of wounded combatants arrived in the Austrian capital as early as 24 August 1914. In the initial seven months of the conflict alone, an estimated 260.000 war casualties were treated in Vienna's medical facilities, hospitals in the first place, but also buildings which originally had served other purposes like the university, parliament, etc., and now got subsequently converted into makeshift infirmaries.[37]

Vienna being the largest garrison town of the Austrian half of the Empire, it became the transitory home of tens of thousands of fresh troops who were prepared for deployment on the Eastern and Southern war fronts. Czechs, Magyars, Bosnians, and Slovaks—not to speak of conscripts from neighboring Lower Austria and the Alpine provinces—flowed in and out of Vienna's barracks. In addition, the city had to provide accommodations for officers and generals attached to the planning staff of the Austro-Hungarian army, and later to Emperor Charles's military high command stationed, as of 1917, in the idyllic wine-growing village of Baden a few miles south of the capital. As the Austrian economy gradually adapted to the requirements of centralized war planning, forced cartels ("*Zentralen*") were formed under state aegis. They were manned with bureaucrats, many of whom came from outside Vienna and hence caused the ranks of "resident aliens" to swell.[38]

The most conspicuous group of newcomers consisted of Jewish refugees from the poverty-stricken Northeast of the Habsburg realm, the "Galicians." Very early in the war, Russian troops had temporarily crossed the borders into their province. The atrocities committed by this enemy (and, to a lesser extent, by retreating Austrians) had caused a mass flight of an estimated 400.000, of which 100.000 at least made their way to Vienna.[39]

---

35. Peter Berger, *Kurze Geschichte Österreichs im 20. Jahrhundert* (Wien: Facultas, 2008), 6, 7.

36. An estimated 240.000 Viennese were drafted until 1918. Weigl in Pfoser and Weigl, 69.

37. Pfoser and Weigl, 17.

38. Ibid., 16.

39. David Rechter, *The Jews of Vienna and the First World War* (Oxford, Portland (Oregon):

Rumors had it that the old Emperor would be prepared to open the palaces of Schönbrunn and the Hofburg for them if no other accommodation was available.[40] That story perfectly fit with the veneration for Francis Joseph shared by most of his Jewish subjects, but one may doubt whether it rested on true fact. No doubt was permissible as to the immediate hostility with which the Viennese met their new coresidents. Anti-Semitism had been rampant in Vienna since the fifteenth century. As the war dragged on, "Jew" once more became synonymous with "usurer," "war profiteer," and "exploiter." The writer Joseph Roth, himself a native of Eastern Galicia, noted a deplorable absence of solidarity with the innocent human flotsam on the part of Vienna's well-to-do, assimilated Jewry, newspapermen in particular.[41] In June 1916, a new Russian advance, the Brussilov offensive, triggered a second large wave of Jewish emigration to the West. But this time, only a fraction of the 200.000 refugees were admitted to Vienna, and swift repatriation together with a planned effort to distribute those who stayed more evenly within the Austrian half of the Empire soon limited the number of permanent settlers in the capital to between 20.000 and 40.000.[42] Hatred of the Jews outlasted both the Viennese refugee problem and World War I. In 1922, Hugo Bettauer, a muckraker, philanthropist, and prolific author of novels critical of society wrote "City without Jews," a prophetic piece of fiction about the expulsion of all Jews from Vienna at the hands of a feckless "Christian" political caste. Bettauer's book finishes with a surprising twist: the Jews return, invited back by their repenting one-time neighbors. When Hitler in 1938 took to the task of "cleansing" Vienna of her Jews, there was no such happy ending.

Hunger

Among those who found refuge in Vienna from the second Russian onslaught towards the Carpathians was the Sperber family of Zabłotów: father, mother, and three boys aged five, ten, and fourteen. The middle one was Manès who would later come to fame as a disciple of the psychologist, Alfred Adler, and an author of political novels and essays.[43] Like most of the new arrivals from Galicia, the Sperbers moved into a dilapidated small apartment in the *Leopoldstadt*, formerly Vienna's Jewish Ghetto. Manès'

The Littmann Library of Jewish Civilization, 2008), 69-73.
40. Ibid., 72.
41. Hofmann, 161 f.
42. Rechter, 80.
43. A recent biography is Mirjana Stančić, Manès Sperber, *Leben und Werk* (Frankfurt: Stroemfeld, 2003).

parents were to stay there until 2 September 1939, the day following Hitler's assault on Poland.[44] In his Galician native province, Sperber Senior had been a bank clerk. Refusing to accept a similar job in Vienna for religious reasons (he would have had to work on Saturdays, a requirement unacceptable for pious Jews), social degradation was inevitable for himself and his family. It happened at a time when the procurement of food and fuel to heat one's home, ever more difficult as the war continued, would have required a solid financial basis. Lacking the means to tap the black markets which sprang up in different corners of the town, Mrs. Sperber and her sons were compelled, like most women and children of Vienna's poor and middle class neighborhoods, to spend long "windy, freezing, rain-soaked"[45] nights in streets without lighting, queuing up for the meager stocks of bakeries and greengrocers which would open in the early hours of the morning and sell out minutes later. Looking back in his memoirs, Manès would comment on the resemblance of Viennese wartime hunger crowds to the personnel of Schiele's expressionist portraits.

According to historian Andrea Brenner, Vienna's permanent food chaos was a combined effect of false expectations concerning the duration of the War, Allied blockade measures, military events on the Eastern front, rivalries between the Monarchy's administrative bodies (competing ministries, army and civilian bureaucracies), and unresolved tensions between Austria and Hungary.[46] As a pre-war net exporter of agricultural products, the Habsburg Monarchy had never given much consideration to preparing for times of food scarcity. Neither was there such a thing as a contractual basis for the supply of Vienna with Hungarian grain and meat. It was simply treated as given. Due to weather caprices, the 1914 wheat harvest of the Hungarian plains turned out to be disappointing, and Magyar authorities withheld parts of the usual Viennese share of the crop for home consumption. The same Russian military offensive that drove hundreds of thousands away from their Galician homes caused another major source of Vienna's grain supply, the fertile soils of the Monarchy's far East, to dry up. By the end of November 1914, Vienna's magistrate thought it indispensable to set price ceilings for grain and flour as a measure against inflation. To the surprise of everyone, both items ran into increasingly short supply as Austrian farmers converted grain fields into pasture or fed their harvest to animals instead of delivering into the unprofitable urban market. Food rationing in Vienna began in April 1915 with the distribution of vouchers for bread.

---

44. Manès Sperber, *Die Wasserträger Gottes* (München: dtv, 1978), 124.
45. Sperber, 159.
46. Brenner in Pfoser and Weigl, 143.

Sugar, milk, coffee, fat, and potatoes followed suit.[47] Rationing did not mean that people actually got what their vouchers promised them. More often than not, their claims were turned down by shop owners diverting stocks for more lucrative purposes, or stocks were actually depleted due to the intervention of some privileged class of recipients like the police or military. To make up for foodstuffs that were increasingly hard to find, war propaganda recommended the use of substitutes (*"Ersatz"*). There was "Ersatz" for, inter alia, meat, eggs, flour, fat, and oil. Sometimes "Ersatz" was added to the original product of limited availability (sawdust to flour, for instance). Sometimes it replaced the original entirely, as was the case with margarine and butter, or yeast and meat, or colored baking powder and yolk of an egg. Such were the sanitary consequences of the consumption of lesser "Ersatz" products that Karl Kraus, the satirist, ironically deplored their absence in August 1914. Had the warmongers of Berlin and Vienna tried the taste of "Dottofix" (imitation egg), wrote Kraus, war would surely have been avoided.[48]

Hunger was not equally manifested for everyone in wartime Vienna. In his memoirs written during the 1940s while in exile in the US, opera composer Ernst Krenek (*"Johnny spielt auf"*), a born Viennese with Czech roots, recalls how his mother managed to feed her family through the early war years without apparent difficulty. Father Krenek, an army officer on front duty in Austrian Poland, sent home enough of his pay (some of which went into the purchase of war bonds that became worthless paper when the fighting was over). Rationing is mentioned only in passing by Krenek, when he speaks of the indignation of the public at the sale of flour being placed under state control. According to Krenek, this put an end to the addiction to sweet cakes on the part of the Viennese.[49] As late as summer 1915, mother and son Krenek happily vacationed in Mariazell, a small Styrian town whose cathedral church is a famous place of worship for Austrian Catholics. "Food was plentiful and delicious everywhere, and traffic functioned pretty normally," Krenek remembered.[50] However, things got worse in 1916, and despite their continued privileged access to army food depots, the Kreneks in winter 1917/18 made acquaintance with "Ersatz" bread of straw and sawdust, and with wild garlic leaves growing in the Vienna woods and recommended by the authorities as a substitute for vegetables.[51] Meanwhile, Viennese working class families had to make do with no more than seven

---

47. Ibid., 143.
48. Ibid., 145.
49. Krenek, 112.
50. Ibid., 115.
51. Ibid., 132.

hundred calories per person and day, as opposed to the three thousand five hundred calories recommended for male manual workers of our time.[52] Undernourishment resulted in the reappearance in Vienna of tuberculosis on a mass scale, a disease that had been formally declared extinct by Lower Austrian Governor Erich Count Kielmansegg in 1903.[53] Together with TBC came kidney infections, intestinal disorders, rheumatism, heart diseases, and hunger edemas. Viennese adults on the average lost between twenty and thirty pounds of their weight in the war. Three quarters of all school children were unfit for any learning effort due to physical weakness. The number of births in the capital declined by one third compared to prewar years, and abortions soared. When the war was over, sanitary conditions in Vienna were truly desperate. Average life expectancy dropped four to six years below the level of 1913, provided one was still alive at the time of the armistice. An estimated 22.000 to 26.000 Viennese would never return from the battlefields.[54]

Lost certainties

One chapter of Stefan Zweig's nostalgic account of a vanished Central European universe is titled "The world of certitude."[55] Indeed, there were many things before 1914 of which a (male) resident of the Habsburg Monarchy who possessed a regular income and maybe some wealth, and who had enjoyed the benefits of education, could be fairly certain of. Public authority rested firmly with the Emperor, his army, and the civil service. The law was to be obeyed, and so were people who wore uniforms (all of them men). Constitutional rights were more or less granted, such as the right to express one's opinion, religious liberties, freedom of settlement and travel, and the freedom to choose one's own profession. Men enjoyed secure, often life-long employment in public administration, the army, or the private sector. Captains of industry and finance, at least in theory, obeyed traditional ethical standards and detested fortunes of doubtful or too recent origin. A woman's place was in the household, and children were reared by their mothers (or nannies). The proletariat was held in check by the entrepreneurial class, who could rely on authorities such as the police or army to protect their interests. Workers lived at a safe distance from the privileged ranks of society, and earned significantly less than bureaucrats, managers, and professionals. Reliance on gold-based currency kept the value

---

52. Weigl in Pfoser and Weigl, 66.
53. See Victor Loos, Der Kampf gegen die Tuberculose, *Fackel* Nr. 140 (Juni 1903), 5-7.
54. Boyer, 384; Weigl in Pfoser and Weigl, 69.
55. Zweig, 15-44.

of money stable. Ownership of tenement houses warranted social prestige and a solid income. Taxes were modest, and those who could afford it felt morally obliged to sponsor art and culture and to donate for charitable ends. Young men of the upper class were introduced to the world of sexuality either by maidservants or prostitutes, and then looked for a spouse whose social status matched their own. Permanent improvements in science and technology were taken for granted. War and revolution were considered remote theoretical possibilities, not an imminent threat.

The coming of World War I unsettled Zweig's idyllic world and finally destroyed it. To begin with, traditional gender relations proved untenable while the conflict lasted. As late as 1903, a young philosopher named Otto Weininger (son of a renowned Viennese goldsmith, and brother of Richard Weininger, who would later become a successful financial wizard of Wall Street) insisted upon the intellectual and moral inferiority of women and Jews.[56] Most of Weininger's enthusiastic upper-class readers—his book went through several editions and sold a record number of copies—were drafted into the army in summer or fall 1914, and "inferior" women took on the task of saving the Austrian *hinterland* from economic and social collapse. These women served as nurses, tram and bus drivers, handlers of the post, factory workers in the armaments and textile industries, harvesters, etc. Not everybody was grateful for the work women performed in the service of the belligerent state. A novelist from Trieste, Italo Svevo, wrote a moving wartime short story in which a young female tram driver bewitches an elderly man who is torn between love for the girl and nagging jealousy. He tries to tie her to him with money and little presents.[57] In Vienna, neither money nor presents were offered to female employees of the city's public transportation system. Instead, passengers admonished them to go and darn the socks of their poor husbands out in the trenches.

Lining up for food and coal became the most obviously female affair in wartime Vienna. Street markets and food queues were places were one could witness a marked change in what was seen as appropriate feminine conduct. Angry women hurled offenses at each other, at shop owners who failed to serve them or treated them with disdain, and at police charged with overseeing the potentially dangerous crowds. Elderly or pregnant waiters-in-line were refused the polite respect that had been common among the Viennese in peacetime. As the war entered its third year, the struggle for means of survival became increasingly violent. American historian Maureen

---

56. See Chandak Sengoopta, Otto Weininger, *Sex, Science, and Self in Imperial Vienna* (Chicago: Chicago University Press, 2000).
57. Italo Svevo, *La novella del buon vecchio e della bella fanciulla* (Milano: dall'oglio editore, 1954).

Healy, author of a pioneering study of Viennese society in wartime[58], reports an instance when thirty desperate women and children assaulted a food transport in Vienna's *Ottakring* suburb, shouting "hunger" and "bread."[59] Other women openly confessed to their pacifist leanings and encouraged bystanders to speak out against the war. Such behavior was not restricted to proletarian women, says Healy. Ladies of a middle-class background were sometimes equally outspoken.

In the giant armament factories of the Viennese periphery, female workers became a common sight. Up to 1914, women had been largely confined to work in the textile and clothing industries, to agricultural activities, and domestic services. Whereas the male workforce in the military-industrial complex subsequently got subjected to the same disciplinary regulations that applied to fighting units, women were never placed under military jurisdiction.[60] This gave them considerable leeway to partake prominently in strikes and other protest activities that gained momentum in the later stages of the war. Until then, both male and female workers were financially better off in the arsenals than in other industrial occupations, due to the fact that Austria-Hungary's perspectives of victory depended to a large extent upon their output. As the war drew closer to its end, labor discontent grew exponentially as a result of dwindling food rations, failure of the Austrian government to negotiate for immediate peace (a demand put forward by the workers), the impact of Russia's Bolshevik revolution on workers' morale, and the conclusion of the Treaty of Brest-Litovsk. January 1918 witnessed the largest workers' demonstrations hitherto seen[61], and in June of that year first the metalworking industry, and later many others, were forced to grant substantial pay increases to their personnel. Far from resolving the situation of an utterly exhausted labor force, these pay hikes fueled already existing fears of degradation on the part of Vienna's conservative middle classes.

The prevailing sentiment at the outset of the war had been one of national unity in the face of foreign aggression. But very soon it became obvious for everyone that instead of promoting consensus, war acted as a great divider of society. This was particularly true for the patchwork middle class "little folk" coalition which, before 1914, had endorsed Vienna's Christian Social government of both mayors, Lueger and Weiskirchner. With the decision to introduce the protective measure of "*Mieterschutz*" (a

58. Maureen Healy, *Vienna and the Fall of the Habsburg Empire. Total War and Everyday Life in World War I* (Cambridge: Cambridge University Press, 2004).
59. Healy in Weigl and Pfoser, 134.
60. Ernst Bruckmüller, *Sozialgeschichte Österreichs* (Wien: Verlag für Geschichte und Politik, Oldenbourg, 2001), 354-357.
61. Bonyhady, 197.

set of laws curtailing the right of landlords to expel tenants or to raise their rents at will, largely aimed at safeguarding soldiers who returned from the front[62]) in early 1917, the Christian Socials made the hard choice between homeowners and middle-class tenants, both of them potential supporters of political Catholicism. Similar choices had to be made between small manufacturers squeezed out of the market by lack of available raw materials and labor, and others who supplied the army and hence did enjoy privileged access to resources; or between civil servants pressing for "indexed," i.e. inflation-adjusted, salaries and those segments of the bourgeoisie for whom the public service and its privileges, imagined or real, had always been a thorn in the flesh.

Scapegoats

At the time of Lueger's death in 1910, a group of junior politicians of the Christian Social party already sensed the difficulty of catering to the expectations of a following that was becoming less and less homogenous over time. Men like Franz Spalowsky and Heinrich Mataja reacted by advocating a return to the "programmatic vigor" of the party's founding fathers, in other words, the fomenting of anti-Semitism to rally conservative Vienna in its entirety behind the party's leadership.[63] The war of 1914-18 provided anti-Semites of all shades with plenty of opportunity to stress what in their eyes was the detrimental impact of Jews on a beleaguered society. To begin with, the Galician refugees, in their majority poor *Chassidim* disinterested in worldly matters, were accused of hoarding food and fuel to benefit from the resulting rise in prices. Of course, the "Easterners" were not alone in attracting the scorn of Vienna's half-starved crowds. Other scapegoats were the governments of Austria and Hungary (for their alleged incapacity or unwillingness to combat foot shortages), Vienna's city council and mayor Weiskirchner, the military, the farmers of Lower Austria, the trade unions, and organizations charged with economic war planning like the earlier mentioned *"Kriegszentralen."*[64] Those were, in all but name, state-sponsored and privately run cartels, each one encompassing the most important domestic manufacturers or dealers in war-related products. The *Zentralen* would put at the disposal of the army whatever item was required at a given time. And their staff would include a fairly large number of men with Jewish backgrounds, thus mirroring the composition of big business in

---

62. Charles A. Gulick, *Österreich von Habsburg zu Hitler*, Band II (Wien: Danubia Verlag, 1948), 71 ff.
63. Boyer, 388.
64. Berger in Pfoser and Weigl, 215.

a country where Jews never had a great chance of pursuing careers in fields other than commerce, finance, or industry. One of the big names in the beer cartel was Josef Kranz, better known to the public as CEO of the powerful "Depositenbank." Kranz was ordered by the war ministry to supply, by way of the beer-*Zentrale*, front troops with fresh beer, and later got accused of having unduly profited from that business. A court of first instance in Vienna pronounced him guilty. But then the Supreme Court quashed the sentence and acquitted Kranz.[65] The Kranz affair may have been equally symptomatic of the pressure felt by Austrian prosecutors to show a firm hand in cases of purported infringements of the law by influential Jews, and of the bipartisanship of Austria's judiciary.

The *Zentralen*-men were by far not the only ones in a position to benefit from extraordinary business opportunities created by the war. The beginning of 1914 triggered the meteoric rise of a small group of investors, speculators, and wholesale traders of a relatively young age. Many but not all of them were Jewish and, much to the chagrin of moralists like Karl Kraus, they were able to skillfully manipulate public opinion in their favor. As a result, few questioned the origins of their immense wealth that, according to Kraus' satirical journal "*Die Fackel*," was extracted from "the blood of others."[66]

For example, Siegmund Bosel and Richard Kola had both been born in Vienna, Bosel in 1893, Kola in 1872. During the war, Bosel engaged in selling used garments to the imperial army against foreign currency, which earned him a fortune as the Austrian crown rapidly depreciated. Through a bank of his own, Bankhaus Bosel, he later gained access to cheap loans that he used to finance the purchase of equity. While Bosel's stocks rose, repayment of the loans became less and less onerous thanks to the accelerating inflation. Kola also ran a private bank trading in stocks.[67] More importantly, during the war he acquired a prominent stake in Austria's paper and printing industries and in 1920 set up a publishing house, the "*Rikola Verlag*." Like another famous wartime tycoon, Camillo Castiglioni, a native of Trieste and pioneer in the aircraft motor industry, Kola later made a name for himself as a benefactor of Viennese theater life. Of the three men, it seems that only Kola died rich (in 1939). Castiglioni lost most of his wealth following a misguided speculation in 1924 against the French Franc. Bosel, also a "victim" of the French Franc episode, served a prison term for bank fraud in 1937, was again brought behind bars in 1938, and finally got

---

65. Dieter Stiefel, *Camillo Castiglioni oder die Metaphysik der Haifische* (Wien: Böhlau, 2012), 54.
66. *Fackel*, 632-639, 150.
67. See Kola's autobiography, *Rückblick ins Gestrige* (Wien: Rikola Verlag, 1922).

killed by German Nazis on board a deportation train to the Baltic.[68]

Epilogue

"When the end of the Habsburg Empire came after four years of war, which for Vienna included almost three years of want and unfreedom, and when the capital of a large realm became overnight the capital of a small, isolated, defeated Republic of six million inhabitants, another Vienna rose from the shambles..." Ilsa Barea wrote in 1966.[69] This was Red Vienna of the Social Democrats who had conquered the city hall following victory at the first communal elections under universal (male and female) franchise in May 1919. It was the Vienna legally separated in 1922 from the rural province of Lower Austria whose majority of Catholic land folk would hardly have welcomed the social experiments now launched by the Viennese socialists: banning compulsory religious education at public schools, legalizing divorce, seizing "excess" living space from apartment owners to accommodate the homeless, introducing luxury taxes to pay for a vast program of construction of flats for workers, etc., etc. It was the Vienna of a timidly defensive bourgeoisie, unsettled by the departure of the old gods (throne, altar, and uniform), and chafing at the "social disorder" caused by the apparent emancipation of the working class, and by soaring inflation which in a few hours destroyed savings it had taken years to accumulate. In his beautiful account of the Viennese atmosphere in the August days of 1914, Edmund de Waal speaks of "two speeds" discernible in the imperial capital: a fast one of the soldiers' marching feet, and a slower one of the food lines shuffling along in front of groceries, tobacco stores, and warm rooms for homeless persons.[70] In the early 1920s, there reigned a third speed, that of the rattling calculators behind the counters of banks or shops adding up millions, then billions and trillions to amounts equivalent of a worker's daily pay, or the cost of a few bottles of drink. No wonder the question of whether Austria would be capable of surviving within her new boundaries occupied the minds of her contemporaries. According to the composer, Ernst Krenek, everyone from the secretary of state down to the last chimney sweep was convinced that Austria could not last.[71] According to Krenek, Pan-Germanic and Nazi "*Anschluss*" propaganda easily fed on this general sentiment.

While the war caused the number of people residing in Vienna to swell

---

68. Matthias Auer, Der Trillionär von Kaisers Gnaden, *Die Presse* (Jan. 5 2014), 20.
69. Barea, 366.
70. De Waal, 194.
71. Krenek, 200.

from 2.15 to 2.4 million, a reverse trend set in following the collapse of Habsburg rule. Many who lived in Vienna left the city for one of the new successor states who offered passports and jobs to those who, as ethnic Czechs, Slovaks, South Slavs, etc., chose to return to the land of their forebears. Some twenty thousand Jewish ex-refugees from Galicia, however, remained—to the intense dislike of Vienna's anti-Semites. Viennese façades looked dull and impoverished, partly due to wartime neglect, and partly because homeowners did not bother to invest in objects that, because of new rent regulations, failed to produce returns on capital. As a heritage of the war years, undernourishment and tuberculosis continued to plague the urban population. As late as 1919, more people died than were born in Vienna. The rate of underfed schoolchildren amounted in 1920 to an estimated seventy-five percent. An average Viennese child in the 1920s could not hope to exceed the height of children of equal age living around 1800.[72] Countries that had remained neutral in the World War I took pride in hosting Viennese "war children" for a period of several weeks or months of abundant diet and medical care. The number of children invited to Denmark, The Netherlands, and Switzerland is reported to have been 90.000.[73]

And yet, Vienna rose again. It did so, with lasting effect and visibly for everyone, only in my lifetime, to be precise: during the 1960s. I recommend to those who wish to sense a distant echo of the feelings shared by a generation who went through World War I and its aftermath to visit Vienna's ninth district. There, at the feet of the "*Strudlhofstiege*" (a stairway leading from the baroque gardens of the aristocratic Liechtenstein dynasty to the one-time residence of Count Berchtold, Francis Joseph's foreign minister in 1914) a memorial plaque bears the lines of a poem by the novelist Heimito von Doderer: "When the leaves lie on the steps/Autumn breath arises from the old staircase/What has walked on it ages ago./Moon within two closely/Embraced, light shoe and heavy steps/ The mossy vase at its core/Outlives years between wars./Much has fallen to our sorrow/And the beautiful lasts the shortest."[74]

---

72. Data are from Weigl in Weigl and Pfoser, 70.
73. Oliver Rathkolb ed., *Außenansichten. Europäische (Be)Wertungen zur Geschichte Österreichs im 20. Jahrhundert* (Innsbruck: Studienverlag, 2003), 81.
74. English translation of the German original text found at www.tourmycountry.com/ austria/strudelhofstiege.htm (accessed Feb. 7, 2014).

Bertha v Suttner Portrait, veiled as a widow, 1906, Pf 3437:C(5), Photo Carl Pietzner, Austrian National Library - Picture Archives and Graphics Department, Vienna

Resistance Against the War of 1914–1918

Gerhard Senft

By general consent, World War I is today perceived as the disaster that launched the catastrophic 20th century. Even though several international conflicts had begun to heat up already at the turn of the century, nobody believed in the feasibility of a belligerent event that would envelop the whole world and take several years. The soldiers mobilized in mid-1914 were told that their service would be limited in time and that they would be back home "before the trees shed their leaves"[1]. Among the imponderables was the social transformation which had occurred globally in the course of the 19th century, driven by the strengthening of pacifist ideas and a growing unwillingness to solve conflicts by military means. The international peace conferences held in The Hague in 1899 and 1907, while not yielding any genuine steps towards disarmament, nevertheless caused the adoption of some preliminary rules to limit the consequences of war. The conferences also paved the way for an international arbitral tribunal which was intended to resolve future conflicts.

The peace movement reached an astonishing degree of diversity before 1914. Bourgeois pacifism, socialist antimilitarism, and peace studies using figures and statistics all contributed different but useful approaches that could be applied in theory as much as in programs. The war enthusiasm in 1914 is a myth which, while frequently cited, cannot be maintained as recent research has discovered.[2] Efforts to suppress protests against armament and war, first begun in the Danube Monarchy by the Kriegsleistungsgesetz (War Services Act) of 1912, did not go down well. Already in the first year of the war, the ranks of refuseniks swelled and it required considerable

---

1. Wilhelm II in Hans-Ulrich Wehler, *Deutsche Gesellschaftsgeschichte, vol. 4: Vom Beginn des Ersten Weltkrieges bis zur Gründung der beiden deutschen Staaten 1914–1949*, 3rd ed., (Munich: C.H. Beck, 2008) 3.
2. Jeffrey Verhey, *Der "Geist von 1914" und die Erfindung der Volksgemeinschaft* (The Spirit of 1914: Militarism, Myth, and Mobilization in Germany), trans. Edith Nerke and Jürgen Bauer (Hamburg: HIS Verlag 2000), 231 et al. Thomas Raithel, *Das "Wunder" der inneren Einheit. Studien zur deutschen und französischen Öffentlichkeit bei Beginn des Ersten Weltkrieges*, Pariser Historische Studien, 45 (Bonn: Bouvier 1996).

efforts to bring them under control. Due to the continuation of the war, the inexorably rising loss of lives, and the deterioration of living conditions back home, riots and strikes began to spread. The dynamism of revolution in Russia in 1917 made its way to the other countries. Its revolutionary spark quickly ignited the German Reich, Austria-Hungary's closest ally, where it tore apart the Social Democrats. Towards the end of the war, desertion grew to dramatic dimensions in all the countries at war. Once the potential to resist reached a critical mass, the European continent irrevocably changed its face.

The following chapters attempt to paint the early peace efforts at a global level, the pacifist activities at the start of the war and, chiefly, the antiwar mood in the population of the warfaring countries between 1914 and 1918. An obvious approach is to go beyond the borders of the Habsburg Monarchy since many of the events can be explained only in an international context.

The modern peace movement

Modern pacifism has its roots in the United States at the time of the Napoleonic wars. In 1814, Noah Worcester published his manifesto *A Solemn Review of the Custom of War*.[3] This was followed by an—initially modest—flourishing of peace-oriented structures and publications. After the Civil War, influential thinkers such as Ralph Waldo Emerson or Walt Whitman entered the fray. Independently of the American situation, the London Peace Society was formed in 1816 as the first European peace movement. The first of the pacifist unions on the continent was created in Geneva in 1830. The goal was to get large standing armies dissolved, international arbitration established, and information on measures to secure peace disseminated.[4]

Conferences and meetings began to multiply, taking the peace concept to a global audience. From the mid-nineteenth century onwards, the labour movement, still in its infancy, began to take an interest in the idea, although the antimilitarism practiced by workers' organizations differed in key elements from the bourgeois "petition pacifism" due to the former's greater readiness to take action (strikes, boycotts) and to link it to social

3. *A Solemn Review of the Custom of War Showing that War is the Effect of Popular Delusion and Proposing a Remedy by Philo Pacificus* (Noah Worcester, the "Friend of Peace"), 11th American edition, revised by the Author: stereotyped by Lyman Thursdon and Co., published by S. G. Simpkins 1833. Oberlin, Ohio: www.nonresistance.org 7007. Complete version on the internet: http://www.nonresistance.org/docs_pdf/A_Solemn_Review.pdf (accessed Aug. 24 2013).
4. Karl Holl, *Pazifismus in Deutschland* (Frankfurt/M.: Suhrkamp 1988): 221 et. seq.

issues.[5] Serious setbacks for the peace movement were the Crimean war and the German-French war. With the onset of the global economic crisis in 1873, economic rivalries between the states accelerated and the tone of communications between foreign offices became distinctly hostile. In spite or perhaps because of the ever noisier sabre rattling, peace efforts increased at an international level. In Russia, Leo Tolstoy, who had been skin-deep into the horrors of battle as an officer in the Crimean war, emerged as a prominent peace activist.[6] By the early 1890s, there were supraregionally active peace societies in the United States, Great Britain, France, Italy, Denmark, Sweden, Belgium, Switzerland, and the Netherlands. The movement arrived in the Danube Monarchy with the publication of Bertha von Suttner's book *Die Waffen nieder!* in 1889.[7] The Austrian peace society founded by her in the autumn of 1891 started out with some 2.000 members.[8] The "International Peace Bureau" was set up in Berne in 1892. By that time, world peace conferences were regular events. Also in 1892, the Deutsche Friedensgesellschaft was created in Berlin.[9] An important mentor in the German-speaking countries was Eduard Loewenthal, a lawyer who published his paper *Der Militarismus als Ursache der Massenverarmung in Europa* in 1870.[10]

The economic aspect of warfare was emphasised by Ivan S. Bloch, a Russian-Polish railway financier and banker. Drawing on statistical calculations and supported by numerous scientific arguments, Bloch showed in his momentous work *Der zukünftige Krieg*[11] that in an age of large-scale technologies war would not generate any economic benefits for any of the parties involved. Bloch inspired Alfred Hermann Fried, publisher

5. Cf. Pierre Ramus, *Der Antimilitarismus als Taktik des Anarchismus* (1908) in Pierre Ramus, *Erkenntnis und Befreiung. Konturen einer libertären Sozialverfassung.* (Vienna: Monte Verita, 2000), 41-43.
6. Romain Rolland, *Das Leben Tolstois* (La Vie de Tolstoï), trans. O.R. Sylvester (Zurich: Diogenes, 1994): 55 et seq.
7. Bertha von Suttner, *Die Waffen nieder! – Eine Lebensgeschichte* (Dresden: Pierson ~ 1900).
8. More details on Bertha von Suttner: Beatrix Müller-Kampel, "Bürgerliche und anarchistische Friedenskonzepte um 1900. Bertha von Suttner und Pierre Ramus," in *"Krieg ist der Mord auf Kommando". Bürgerliche und anarchistische Friedenskonzepte. Bertha von Suttner und Pierre Ramus.* ed., Beatrix Müller-Kampel (Nettersheim: Verlag Graswurzelrevolution, 2005): 7-95.
9. Cf. Dieter Riesenberger, *Geschichte der Friedensbewegung in Deutschland. Von den Anfängen bis 1933* (Göttingen: Vandenhoeck & Ruprecht, 1985).
10. Eduard Loewenthal, *Der Militarismus als Ursache der Massenverarmung in Europa und die europäische Union als Mittel zur Überflüssigmachung der stehenden Heere. Ein Mahnruf an alle Freunde bleibenden Friedens und Wohlstandes* (Lütze: Potschappel, 1870).
11. Jan Gotlib Bloch, *Der Krieg. Der zukünftige Krieg in seiner technischen, volkswirtschaftlichen und politischen Bedeutung*, vol. 1-6 (Berlin: Puttkammer & Mühlbrecht, 1899). The Russian first edition had been published the previous year.

of the Austrian magazine *Die Friedens-Warte*. In contrast to the ethical pacifism represented by Tolstoy and Bertha von Suttner, Fried looked at peace from a scientific point of view. He was convinced that an expansion of the commercial, transport, and communications networks and an increasing cultural exchange would, in the long term, foster peace efforts. He felt that international conflicts should be resolved by arbitral tribunals, setting out his ideas in his *Handbuch der Friedensbewegung* in 1905.[12]

The killing spree starts

Yet in spite of all this a belligerent spirit pervaded the world in 1914, fueled by the traditions of a patriarchal culture of obedience and ever stronger hatemongering, the effects of which were felt even by basically pacifist natures.[13] Stefan Zweig acknowledged that "there is something grand, electrifying and seductive in this first sallying-forth of the masses."[14] It was mostly the intellectual elites who were susceptible to the "spirit of 1914" conjured up by the conservative press and who were prone to become enthusiastic about the war.[15] Thomas Mann felt the war to be "cleansing", and Carl Zuckmayer celebrated the "August experience" as "Liberation! Liberation ... from everything that we—consciously or not—had felt to be saturation, sticky air, petrification of our world. [...] it had become serious, bloody, holy serious and at the same time an enormous and intoxicating adventure."[16] The "Association of International Understanding", which had enjoyed the support of celebrities such as Ernst Haeckel and Max Weber, ceased to exist in 1914.[17] Hysterical advocates of war in Austria included Hermann Bahr, Hugo von Hofmannsthal, Franz Theodor Czokor, Felix

---

12.   Alfred Hermann Fried, *Handbuch der Friedensbewegung* (Wien, Leipzig: Friedens-Warte 1905). Full text available on the internet: http://archive.org/stream/handbuchderfrie00friegoog#page/n2/mode/2up (accessed Aug. 24 2013). First published in 1905, revised edition in 1911, extended edition in 1913.

13.   Barbara Tuchman, *August 1914* (The Guns of August), trans. Grete and Karl-Eberhardt Felten, 4th ed. (Frankfurt/M.: Fischer 2011), 327.

14.   Stefan Zweig cited in Beate Schlanstein, Gudrun Wolter and Gerold Karwath (eds.): *Der Erste Weltkrieg* (Berlin: Rowohlt 2004), 168.

15.   Cf. Sigmund Paul Scheichl, "Journalisten leisten Kriegsdienst. Die Neue Freie Presse im September 1915," in *Österreich und der Große Krieg 1914-1918. Die andere Seite der Geschichte*. ed. Klaus Amann, Hubert Lengauer (Vienna: Brandstätter, 1989), 104-108. Peter Broucek, "Das Kriegspressequartier und die literarischen Gruppen im Kriegsarchiv 1914-1918", in *Österreich und der Große Krieg 1914-1918. Die andere Seite der Geschichte*, ed. Klaus Amann, Hubert Lengauer (Vienna: Brandstätter, 1989), 132-138. For the Austrian war press headquarters see also: Eberhard Sauermann, *Literarische Kriegsfürsorge. Österreichische Dichter und Publizisten im Ersten Weltkrieg* (Vienna: Böhlau, 2000), 30-37.

16.   Thomas Mann, Carl Zuckmayer cited in Schlanstein, Wolter, Karwath, *Weltkrieg*, 61.

17.   Holl, *Pazifismus*, 104.

Salten, Franz Karl Ginzkey, and Ottokar Kernstock.[18] Albert Einstein, steadfastly pacifist, was amazed: "All the learned men at the universities have accepted military services or jobs."[19] Herbert Lüthy got it exactly right when he talked of the "delirious intellectual elites" in Europe.[20] In a similar vein, the labour parties and trade unions, which made efforts to integrate in a system they had once fought, were unable to escape the martial frenzy and submitted to the demands of the warmongers.[21] By their action, their leaders expected to improve the climate for future social and political reforms. Moreover, some of them felt that (war-driven) "stricter discipline" among workers would be quite desirable.[22]

Yet a closer look confirms that talk of all parts of the population becoming intoxicated with the idea of war is just a myth. The poorer, ordinary people in particular experienced the outbreak of war as a calamity. Away from the jubilant crowds, people were worried. In the towns and cities, there was a general feeling of gravity and dejection. In the rural parts, many villagers were less than happy to be forced to leave their home and community for a questionable adventure.[23] A citizen of Hamburg remembers: "The agitation, first expressed in a panicky run on savings banks and food shops, grew. Most people were dejected, as if they were scheduled to be beheaded on the next day."[24] A boy from Bremen noted in his diary: "The railway station is packed full with people. It is like one great hangover, […] mothers, women and brides […] bring the young men to the trains and cry. All feel that they are being led directly to the slaughterhouse."[25] With national institutions and the press all brought into line, the previously influential pacifist strain was substantially weakened and counter-opinions had a hard time reaching a greater audience.

One bastion of pacifism that remained steadfast for a long time was

18. For more details: Franz Schuh, "Krieg und Literatur. Vorläufige Thesen zu einer Bewußtseinsgeschichte des Ersten Weltkrieges," in *Österreich und der Große Krieg 1914-1918. Die andere Seite der Geschichte*, ed. Klaus Amann, Hubert Lengauer (Vienna: Brandstätter, 1989), 8-15. Sauermann, *Kriegsfürsorge*, 340-366.
19. Albert Einstein cited in Schlanstein, Wolter, Karwath, *Weltkrieg*, 123. Among the well-known opponents of war were Albert Einstein, Alfred H. Fried, Rudolf Goldscheid, Hermann Hesse, and Romain Rolland. The latter met with Einstein at Lake Leman in 1915.
20. Herbert Lüthy, "Schicksalstragödie?" in *Der Monat* 16, no. 191 (1964), 28.
21. Wolfgang Abendroth, *Sozialgeschichte der europäischen Arbeiterbewegung* (Frankfurt/M.: Suhrkamp, 1965), 79 et seq.
22. Alfred Pfabigan, "Austromarxismus und Kriegsgesinnung" in *Österreich und der Große Krieg 1914-1918. Die andere Seite der Geschichte*, ed. Klaus Amann, Hubert Lengauer (Vienna, Brandstätter, 1989), 90-95.
23. Hannes Leidinger, Verena Moritz, *Der Erste Weltkrieg* (Cologne: UTB, 2011), 33.
24. Cited in Schlanstein, Wolter, Karwath, *Weltkrieg*, 26.
25. Ibid.

the USA. There, a very strong peace movement remained current which spanned an astonishing range within the overall social spectrum, including bourgeois industrialists as much as advocates of anarchism. Important players in this respect were Andrew Carnegie, the steel baron who had set up his Endowment for International Peace in 1910[26], and Emma Goldman, factory worker and libertarian activist, who gave fulminating speeches against war and patriotism to large audiences while being observed by government agencies.[27]

That the United States entered the fray so very late was thus due not just to the fact that they were insufficiently prepared for such an event in 1914 but also to the circumstance that the national peace movement was able to delay the decision for war by the political leaders for a long time. Actually, Woodrow Wilson was elected president on the basis of an antiwar programme in 1916.

Ordinary people and their "obstreperous rationality"

There are many appraisals of the World War I[28], but much more to the point is what J. William Fulbright pithily and succinctly noted in his work *The Arrogance of Power*: "In 1914 all Europe went to war, ostensibly because the heir to the Austrian throne had been assassinated at Sarajevo, but really because that murder became the symbolic focus of the incredibly delicate sensibilities of the great nations of Europe. The events of the summer of 1914 were a melodrama of abnormal psychology: Austria had to humiliate Serbia in order not to be humiliated herself but Austria's effort

26. Tuchman, *1914*, 466. Carnegie followed in the footsteps of Ivan Bloch who had set up his peace foundation in ca. 1900.
27. Emma Goldmann, *Gelebtes Leben* (Living my Life), vol. 2, trans. Renate Ory and Sabine Vetter (Berlin: Karin Kramer-Verlag, 1979), 501 et seq. Emma Goldman, "Patriotismus als Kriegsgrund", trans. Michael Gingrich and Johann Heiss, in *Falsche Helden. Frauen über den Krieg*, ed. Daniela Gioseffi (Frankfurt/M.: Suhrkamp, 1988), 112 et seq.
28. The anniversary year 2004 threw up a cornucopia of new literature on the Great War: Stephan Burgdorff, Klaus Wiegrefe (ed.), *Der Erste Weltkrieg. Die Ur-Katastrophe des 20. Jahrhunderts* (Munich: C. H. Beck, 2004). John Horne, Alan Kramer, *Deutsche Kriegsgreuel 1914. Die umstrittene Wahrheit* (German Atrocities, 1914. A History of Denial), trans. Udo Rennert (Hamburg: Hamburger Edition, 2004). Gerhard Hirschfeld, Gerd Krumeich, and Irina Renz ed., *Enzyklopädie Erster Weltkrieg* (Paderborn: Ferdinand Schöningh Verlag, 2004). Hew Strachan, *Der Erste Weltkrieg. Eine neue illustrierte Geschichte* (The First World War: A New Illustrated History), trans. Helmut Ettinger (Munich: C. Bertelsmann Verlag, 2004). Michael Howard, *Kurze Geschichte des Ersten Weltkrieges* (The First World War), trans. Helmut Reuter (Munich: Piper Verlag 2004). Wolfgang J. Mommsen, *Der Erste Weltkrieg. Anfang vom Ende des bürgerlichen Zeitalters* (Frankfurt/M.: Fischer, 2004). Volker Berghahn, *Der Erste Weltkrieg* (Munich: C. H. Beck, 2003). Also of note: Jean Jacques Becker, Gerd Krumeich: *Der Große Krieg. Deutschland und Frankreich 1914-1918*, trans. Marcel Küsters and Peter Böttner (Essen: Klartext Verlag, 2010).

at recovering self-esteem was profoundly humiliating to Russia; Russia was allied to France, who had been feeling generally humiliated since 1871, and Austria in turn was allied to Germany, whose pride required that she support Austria no matter how insanely Austria behaved and who may in any case have felt that it would be fun to give the German Army another swing down the Champs-Élysées. For these ennobling reasons the world was plunged into a war which took tens of millions of lives [...] and set in motion the events that led to another world war [...]."[29] Even though Austria-Hungary's expenditure on arms, at about 16% even before the War Services Act of 1912 was enacted, took up a large share of total public spending, the Habsburg Empire still very much depended on Germany's goodwill, since a comparably small part of its population only was under arms.[30] The German imperial government, in the fullness of its power and secure in its conviction of Germany's dominant role in the world, was not only ready to confer every support on its ally. In its "security-imperialist" efforts to prevent any further powers from accruing to France and to keep Russia away from the German border, it was the actual driver in the drama. Fritz Fischer, who vividly describes the active role of the German Reich in the "July crisis" of 1914 and its war programme in *Griff nach der Weltmacht*, must be agreed with when he assigns the chief responsibility for the disaster of the world war to the German imperial government.[31]

After Austria-Hungary declared war on Serbia, several countries started to mobilize their armies almost simultaneously. The German general staff implemented the so-called Schlieffen Plan which envisaged rapid deployment at the western front so that neutral Belgium was invaded already on August 4. Next, there followed a shower of declarations of war. The swift advance provided for by the German plan, however, soon had the army grappling with supply problems. Quite quickly, France put a stop to the German invasion and initiated a successful counter-attack ("Miracle of the Marne"). This brought the mobile war to a halt and, after bloody fighting in Flanders, led to the stalemate of trench warfare.

Emergency laws and targeted disciplinary measures were used to nip in the bud all schemes to resist mobilization. Labour's right to unionize and strike had already been abolished in the War Services Act of 1912. Next came restrictions of the right of assembly, stricter censorship, bans on publications, and targeted seizures of publications. Known peace activists had to expect that they would be monitored, searched, restricted in their

---

29. J. William Fulbright, *The Arrogance of Power* (New York: Random House, 1966), 7.
30. Daniel Marc Segesser, *Der Erste Weltkrieg in globaler Perspektive* (Wiesbaden: Marix, 2010), 14.
31. Fritz Fischer, *Griff nach der Weltmacht*, 4th ed. (Düsseldorf: Droste, 1984).

travelling and, quite frequently, apprehended. In July 1914, all political crimes in Austria were placed under the jurisdiction of military courts. At an antimilitarist demonstration on the Schmelz in Vienna in May 1914, one speaker was activist Rudolf Großmann aka Pierre Ramus, who called upon his listeners to ignore their conscription order.[32] Once war was declared, Großmann was detained and spent the war years first at a prison run by the Army Division Court of Vienna, then under house arrest and, lastly, in exile.[33] In Great Britain, famous philosopher Bertrand Russell called upon men to refuse military service and advocated an active peace policy. For disseminating his views in leaflets and newspaper articles he lost his teaching job in Cambridge and went to prison.[34] Edmund Morel similarly agitated against the war. Branded as a "traitor" by the British press, he was sentenced to solitary confinement where he sewed mail bags during the war years while under a strict ban on speaking.[35] In order to achieve "internal pacification" in the longer term, efforts were made to quiet the population by way of targeted welfare measures. Thus Austria countered the war-driven price inflation by food subsidies and a lock on rents. Such measures were part and parcel of a system of government whose war and emergency laws were almost entirely based on the notorious "dictator clause": Section 14 of the December Constitution of 1867, which was at best alleviated by occasional sloppiness.[36]

Resistance "from below", "inner desertion", a widespread "not with me" attitude among conscripts, however, typically met with helplessness on the part of the superior officers. Immediately upon the start of war, there were numerous cases of people disobeying their calling-up order; many deserted

---

32. "Unsere Agitation und Bewegung," *Erkenntnis und Befreiung. Organ des herrschaftslosen Sozialismus 2*, no. 23 (1920), 4.
33. Pierre Ramus, *Friedenskrieger des Hinterlandes* (Mannheim: Verlagsbücherei "Erkenntnis und Befreiung im Sinne Leo Tolstois", 1924).
34. Achim von Borries, *Rebell wider den Krieg – Bertrand Russell 1914-1918* (Nettersheim: Verlag Graswurzelrevolution, 2006).
35. Philipp Blom, *Der taumelnde Kontinent – Europa 1900-1914* (Munich: Carl Hanser Verlag, 2009), 149. According to Christoph Jahr, more than 70 antimilitarists died in British prisons between 1914 and 1918. Christoph Jahr, *Gewöhnliche Soldaten. Desertion und Deserteure im deutschen und britischen Heer 1914-1918* (Göttingen: Vandenhoeck & Ruprecht, 1998), 126.
36. Hans Hautmann, "Kriegsgesetze und Militärjustiz in der österreichischen Reichshälfte 1914-1918," in *Justiz und Zeitgeschichte: Veröffentlichungen des Ludwig-Boltzmann-Instituts für Geschichte der Gesellschaftswissenschaften I*, ed. Erika Weinzierl, Wolfgang Huber (Vienna: Jugend & Volk, 1977), 102.

at the first opportunity.[37] Aided by local police forces, the imperial military authorities rigorously pursued all those that had missed the general mobilization or had gone AWOL. The files on deserters made available to the investigators contained detailed information on the wanted person's appearance and belongings. Authorities had many ways and means to put people under pressure: a deserter's family lost all state benefits, and all of his own assets, savings, and property could be seized and impounded.

Obviously, there was no such person as the typical deserter. Motifs and reasons that caused persons to desert varied considerably.[38] Yet one circumstance is striking: it was mostly people from the lower strata of society that developed an inclination to desert.[39] One exemplary case in the Habsburg monarchy illustrates this situation. Upon being seized, infantryman Leopold Oberger explained his disappearance from the Sopron barracks by the continual "bullying from his superior officers." Even though he managed to hide at his sister's in Wiener Neustadt, he was—as stated in the records of the investigating court—in such an exceptional mental state ever since his escape that he was considered suicidal.[40] In a majority of the cases it can be assumed that the men did not leave their military unit on frivolous grounds.

In spite of state aid, the war-induced loss of a male worker could threaten the very existence of a family. From mid-1914, high-ranking military men had their desks filled with letters from desperate wives who begged that their husbands or sons be given an "easy service."[41] From the file of deserter Franz Stefan Jirkas, soldier in the dragoon regiment no. 15

---

37. The extent to which conscription and its implementation in Austria-Hungary affected people's attitudes towards the war is the subject of a study carried out by Christa Ehrmann-Hämmerle and entitled "Die allgemeine Wehrpflicht zwischen Akzeptanz und Verweigerung: Militär und Männlichkeit/en in der Habsburgermonarchie (1868-1914/18)," findings of which are pending. A project of the Österreichischer Fonds zur Förderung der wissenschaftlichen Forschung (P 15234).

38. According to Jahr's study, "self-demobilization" was more likely among newbies and front oldtimers. It appears that frequently it was the microclimate in a given unit that was responsible for desertion, while political reasons for desertion were relatively rare. Jahr, *Gewöhnliche Soldaten*, 132, 148, 138, 175 et seq. Court files, however, provide only part of the story because it was inadvisable for apprehended deserters to give the military judge political reasons for what they had done.

39. Nevertheless it should be assumed that the desertion of officers tended to be hushed up. Jahr, *Gewöhnliche Soldaten*, 151.

40. File of Leopold Oberger, court decision in the criminal case of infantryman Leopold Oberger of infantry regiment no. 76 of 23 June 1914. Österreichisches Staatsarchiv (ÖstA), Kriegsarchiv, Militärgerichtsarchiv, k. u. k. Divisionsgericht Vienna 1914, box no. 1264/1.

41. Cf. the petition by the Bochner family to have their 16 year old son discharged from military service: No. 21 740. ÖstA, Kriegsarchiv, Kriegsministerium, Exhibitenprotokolle 1915. Petition by the Plonka family to have their 15 year old son discharged from military service: No. 24 345. ÖstA, Kriegsarchiv, Kriegsministerium, Exhibitenprotokolle 1915.

based in Lemberg/Lvov, it can be seen that following his leave in Vienna he failed to return to his unit but instead took up a job in order to "alleviate the financial distress of his family," as he explained after being arrested.[42] Deserters who escaped without adequate funds survived as casual labourers. Some were even willing to sleep rough. On 8 December 1914, Peter Catoiu took French leave from his troops, the imperial and royal infantry regiment no. 31, in order to retreat into an impassable mountain region. He hid in the mountains until the early days of September 1915, occasionally venturing into a nearby hamlet in order to scavenge for food, surrendering only when the next winter was afoot. His voluntary return was allowed as a mitigating circumstance by the military court.[43]

Finding a hideout quickly was a piece of luck for a deserter. In February 1917, the trial of lance-corporal Friedrich Imre "for the crime of desertion" commenced at the Vienna Division Court.[44] As can be seen from the charge sheet, Imre had left his troops on his own accord on 5 December 1915 and stayed with his mistress in Vienna until he was arrested by the military police on 18 July 1916. An informer appears to have squealed on him. Apart from having deserted his post twice already he had no police record, a fact that helped him get a relatively lenient sentence. The lance-corporal was demoted and sentenced to three months incarceration, "aggravated by two fasts per month and a hard bedstead on the holidays", as is scrupulously stated in the sentence.[45]

Hiding a deserter was a dangerous venture for civilians. People who helped absconders ran a high risk of being caught up in the wheels of justice themselves, as is exemplified by the Lukasek/Leyrer case. Oskar Lukasek was called up on 20 November 1914 and was instructed to report to his unit on 1 February 1915. However, he preferred—to quote the charge sheet—to "stay away from every military subunit" and remain at the flat of his girlfriend Marie Leyrer in the 10th district of Vienna until he was

42. File of Franz Stefan Jirka, prosecution order in the criminal case of dragoon Franz Stefan Jirka of dragoon regiment no. 15 of 17 July 1914, including exhibits. ÖstA, Kriegsarchiv, Militärgerichtsarchiv, k. u. k. Divisionsgericht Vienna 1914/15, box no. 1264/2.

43. File of Peter Catoiu, charge sheet of reservist Peter Catoiu of the imperial and royal infantry regiment no. 31 of 14 November 1915. ÖstA, Kriegsarchiv, Militärgerichtsarchiv, k. u. k. Divisionsgericht Vienna 1915, box no. 1267.

44. In the hinterland, military jurisdiction was exercised by the landwehr divisional courts whereas so-called field courts (drumhead courts-martial) were competent for the "army in the field". Death sentences were mostly passed by field courts. For the organization of military jurisdiction and procedural issues in Austria-Hungary see: Hautmann, "Kriegsgesetze", 113 et seq. On the procedure in the German army: Jahr, *Gewöhnliche Soldaten*, 183 et seq. On the procedure in the British army: Jahr, *Gewöhnliche Soldaten*, 205 et seq.

45. File of Friedrich Imre, court decision in the criminal case of landsturm lance-corporal Friedrich Imre. ÖstA, Kriegsarchiv, Militärgerichtsarchiv, k. u. k. Divisionsgericht Vienna 1914, box no. 925.

arrested on 9 April 1915. Lukasek was handed over to his unit even before preliminary proceedings had been concluded whereas separate criminal proceedings were initiated against Marie Leyrer. Hiding deserters was a "crime under Section 220 of the Criminal Law."[46]

This also explains the conduct of Leopold Wietrowsky, an electrics apprentice from Vienna who, just about 17 years old, was conscripted into the infantry in early August 1914. On 28 August 1915, the young man, who had no previous record, deserted for the first time. The bureaucratic mills of the investigation authorities worked quickly and efficiently. Already on 27 September, Wietrowsky was recognized by policemen at a barbershop in the 13th district of Vienna and promptly apprehended. At the police station he was handed over to a military patrol who took him to a landwehr detention unit. There, Wietrowsky took advantage of a moment of inattention by his guards to make his escape again. Shortly afterwards, on 2 October he was again caught by a patrol. The military court sentenced him to altogether two years of strict confinement. Still, his incarceration was deferred to a time after demobilization, as was the custom in many such cases. In mid-January, Wietrowsky, on his way to the eastern front, lost his unit and returned to Vienna on his own accord, where he went underground until he was seized on 12 February. Asked by the police where he had hidden all that time he steadfastly refused to tell because he did not want to "get somebody into trouble" as he correctly put it.[47] The file does not clarify how this type of noncooperation was punished. Desertion became easier towards the end of the war when confusion began to spread at the various frontlines. Josef Tuschak, born in Vienna in 1900, had been one of the last conscripts in 1918. At the front he met with a war-weary officer who enabled him to abscond, saving him from becoming cannon fodder.[48]

The list of crimes under Austrian military criminal law included mutiny, sabotage, breach of duty while on guard duty, insubordination (breach of the

46. File of Oskar Lukasek, charge sheet against landsturm recruit Oskar Lukasek of infantry regiment no. 4 of 11 June 1915 and exhibits. ÖstA, Kriegsarchiv, Militärgerichtsarchiv, k. u. k. Divisionsgericht Vienna 1914, box no. 1265/2.
47. File of Leopold Wietrowsky, imperial and royal infantry regiment no. 84. 2nd reserve company: file no. 120/M., recorded on 19 February 1916 with infantrist Leopold Wietrowsky from the 2nd /84th reserve company. ÖstA, Kriegsarchiv, Militärgerichtsarchiv, k. u. k. Divisionsgericht Vienna 1914, box no. 1267.
48. "'... überall hat's schon gegärt ...' Josef Tuschak über Hungerstreiks und Desertion im 1. Weltkrieg" ('... turmoil was brewing everywhere ...' Josef Tuschak on hunger strikes and desertion in the First World War), interview of 17 July 1982 in *Widerstand gegen Krieg und Faschismus in Österreich*, ed. Forum Alternativ (Vienna, 1982), 11. Other cases of refuseniks are documented in Olga Misař, Martha Steinitz, and Helene Stöcker: *Kriegsdienstverweigerer in Deutschland und Österreich* (Berlin: Die Neue Generation, 1923).

duty to obey), and self-mutilation.[49] Among the crimes that grew more frequent in the course of the war were absence without leave (Section 212 of the Military Criminal Act M.St.G.), which was judged to be a non-aggravated breach of the duty of service ("prolonged leave"), and desertion (Section 183 M.St.G.) The latter, punished much more severely, was defined as an act committed with the intention to permanently escape the duty of service.[50] For the field courts such a differentiation was irrelevant because they could sentence a soldier to death by firing squad just for a conduct classified as cowardice.[51] The Imperial and Royal Army Divisional Court, domiciled at Hernalser Gürtel 6-12 in Vienna, imposed several weeks of incarceration for crimes under Section 212 M.St.G. but anything from three months of incarceration (if there were alleviating circumstances) to the death penalty in cases of desertion. Individuals considered to be shirkers, gripers, misfits, and scaremongers had the option of submitting to painful "cures" in one of the army's psychiatric wards. Rudolf König, a repeat deserter, was sentenced to "death by firing squad" by the Vienna divisional court on 22 September 1916. The sentence was later commuted to six years of incarceration.[52] The file is not clear about the grounds but the man appears to have profited from a wave of amnesties a few months later. In the spring of 1917, the regime's belligerent absolutism was slightly modified in order to counter the beginning collapse of the Danube Monarchy.

As already noted, the serving of a sentence was generally postponed to a time after demobilization. The need for cannon fodder was simply too urgent

---

49. Self-inflicted wounds could lead to draconian punishment meted out especially by field courts. Some soldiers in the World War I practiced a type of "concealed self-mutilation" which was difficult to punish, by intentionally contracting a venereal disease. Jahr, *Gewöhnliche Soldaten*, 125.

50. Under the military criminal law enacted in 1855 in the Habsburg empire, a deserter was a person "who, after taking the oath, leaves his regiment, corps or service or place of residence allotted to him without authorization and with the intention to permanently abstract himself from his duty of service, or who keeps away with the same intention." Extract from: Oswald Überegger, *Der andere Krieg: die Tiroler Militärgerichtsbarkeit im Ersten Weltkrieg. Tirol im Ersten Weltkrieg*, vol. 3 (Innsbruck: Wagner, 2002), 232. For the military court the factor deciding which clause was to be applied was not the duration of the absence but the "credibility" of the arguments submitted in the man's defence.

51. Section 252 of the Military Criminal Act included a clause on so-called justifiable defence in a war situation: "In cases where the refusal to fight the enemy or where the desertion of a subordinate soldier could immediately endanger the service or the spirit of the troops, each superior officer shall be obliged to promptly and personally kill such highly culpable person or to order his immediate execution." Extract from: Ferdinand Schmid, *Das Heeresrecht in der Österreichisch-Ungarischen Monarchie* (Vienna, Leipzig: Tempsky, 1903), 529.

52. File of Rudolf König, report to the head of the k. u. k. Garnisonsarrest of 12 February 1918. ÖstA, Kriegsarchiv, Militärgerichtsarchiv, k. u. k. Divisionsgericht Vienna 1916, box no. 925.

to afford the luxury of jam-packed prisons in the hinterland.[53] Moreover, the individual was to be given an opportunity to have his sentence reduced by his especially courageous conduct in the field, as is frequently noted in the records. A consistent trait of the military courts appears to have been to permanently brand those unwilling to serve. The normal procedure was to keep the deserter's file on record for several decades and in some cases until the 1950s/1960s.[54] The new republic, while pardoning all deserters after 1918, nevertheless did not grant the frequent request to have the registration as a deserter expunged in order not to suffer disadvantages at work.

As regards the number of desertions in the Danube Monarchy, there are only estimates available today.[55] Austrian military historian Manfried Rauchensteiner talks of hundreds of thousands who absconded between 1914 and 1918: "There was nothing comparable in England, France, or the German Reich."[56] Desertion increased towards the end of the war, when troops were called back home to be deployed against insurgents. The comparatively high losses of the Austro-Hungarian army were, not least, caused by nationalistic conflicts, which, albeit in a weaker form, were also experienced by Great Britain (Irish) and Germany (Alsace-Lorraine). Uncertainties of a similar scope are found when it comes to the total number of military court cases in the Habsburg empire, since many files were lost at the end of the war. Estimates put the figure of individuals prosecuted by the field courts at three million as a minimum, albeit this includes civilians (accused of espionage and high treason).[57] It is not possible to give an exact figure of the executions performed since many were carried out without any court judgment. Karl Kraus specified the Habsburg Regime

---

53. Of the 8 million soldiers deployed by the Habsburg empire over the course of the war, only about 600,000 were at the front towards its end. Manfried Rauchensteiner: "Eine k. u. k. Leiche" (An imperial and royal corpse), *Die Presse*, Spectrum, 29 July 2006, 7.

54. This type of stigmatization was also used on refuseniks in Germany and Great Britain. Jahr, *Gewöhnliche Soldaten*, 201.

55. Sources with regard to desertion figures are better in Great Britain. For a detailed discussion see: Jahr. *Gewöhnliche Soldaten*, 167 et seq. An assessment of the situation in the German field army, on the other hand, is fraught with uncertainties. Jahr has made projections, cf. Jahr, *Gewöhnliche Soldaten*, 149 et seq. Note the figures in: Georg Richard Plaschka, *Avantgarde des Widerstandes. Modellfälle militärischer Auflehnung im 19. und 20. Jahrhundert*, vol. 2 (Vienna: Böhlau, 2002), 90 et seq.

56. Rauchensteiner, "Eine k. u. k. Leiche," 7.

57. Georg Leweler, "Die Militärpersonen" in *Krieg und Kriminalität in Österreich, Carnegie-Stiftung für internationalen Frieden. Abteilung für Volkswirtschaft und Geschichte. Wirtschafts- und Sozialgeschichte des Weltkrieges. Österreichische und ungarische Serie*, ed. Franz Exner (Vienna: Hölder-Pichler-Tempsky, 1927), 119 et seq, as cited in Hans Hautmann, "Habsburg-Totenrummel und vergessene Vergangenheit," *Mitteilungen der Alfred Klar Gesellschaft* 18, no. 3, 2011, 2.

was responsible for 11.400 executions in 1919.[58] This figure also appears in *Krieg dem Kriege* published by German pacifist Ernst Friedrich in 1924, and a similar one is given in *Erkenntnis und Befreiung*, a magazine published by Rudolf Großmann.[59] Other sources furnish figures that substantially exceed those named here.[60]

First war protest that reached the masses

By December 1914 it was clear that the war would not end quickly. Neither party would be able in the foreseeable future to win the trench war at the western front, given the means of war technology they had. All the signs pointed towards a long-lasting war of matériel and attrition. The frontline at the Ypres bow had Belgian, French, and English soldiers entrenched, in unbearable weather conditions, against the Germans who were at places themselves entrenched only 60-70 meters away. Temperatures in the trenches, muddy and fenced in by barbed wire, turned frosty. After some particularly harrowing butchery on December 18, the enemy troops agreed on a short armistice in order to bury their dead in the no-man's land. This agreement caused the men on both sides spontaneously to cease all hostilities. The soldiers, who had just faced each other as mortal enemies, crawled out of their trenches, showed each other photographs of their families, exchanged cigarettes and food, drank each other's hot toddies, and

---

58. Karl Kraus, "Nachruf," *Die Fackel* XX, no. 501-507, 1919, 45.

59. Ernst Friedrich, *Krieg dem Kriege* (Berlin: Freie Jugend, 1924), 135. "Bund der Kriegsdienstgegner," *Erkenntnis und Befreiung. Organ des herrschaftslosen Sozialismus* 6, no. 24, 1924, 4.

60. Thomas G. Masaryk, "Austria under Francisco Joseph," in *The New Europe* 7, vol. 1, 1916, 201, as cited in: Imre Gonda, *Verfall der Kaiserreiche in Mitteleuropa. Der Zweibund in den letzten Kriegsjahren (1916-1918)* (Budapest: Akad.. Kiadó, 1977), 193, as cited in: Hautmann, "Habsburg-Totenrummel", 2. For figures on executions in Great Britain, France, Italy and the German Reich see: David Stevenson, *1914-1918. Der Erste Weltkrieg* (1914-1918: the History of the First World War), trans. Harald Eckhardt and Ursula Vones-Liebenstein (Mannheim: Marix, 2010), 261 et seq. Military justice in the German army appears to have been rather mild compared to Great Britain and France as well as compared to the Habsburg regime which clearly committed war crimes. Death sentences in the British and French armies became rarer as the war progressed while the German side unhesitatingly continued its problematic course. The 2,000 volt fence between occupied Belgium and free Holland, designed to prevent German deserters from escaping, had cost some 2.000 lives by 1918. Roman Sandgruber, "Lichter aus für Lebzeiten" (Lights out for life), *Die Presse*, Spectrum, 24 July, 2004, 5. It should also be noted that Great Britain had two systems of norms, one for the civil society and one for the army, while Germany and the Habsburg Empire were ruled by authoritarian systems that extended to all spheres of life. Jahr, *Gewöhnliche Soldaten*, 248 et seq.

joined in the singing of songs.[61] Although not all the arms fell silent along the western front at the turn of 1914/1915, the armistice was mostly maintained throughout the front. Most cases of refusals occurred at a line of some 50 kilometers around Ypres, between Diksmuide and Neuve Chapelle. The wish for peace, articulated "from below", spread and fraternisation occurred at the Carpathian front as well, this time between Habsburgian and Russian soldiers.[62] For the general staff and troop commanders this unexpected silence must have been uncanny. Officers had to threaten terrible sanctions to get their men back into the trenches and restart the killing.

At the start of 1915, negative trends accelerated. In February, the German Reich commenced upon unlimited U-boat warfare. Fighting reached a particularly cruel dimension when the Germans deployed poison gas for the first time during the second battle of Ypres in late April. On a six-kilometer section of the front near Ypres, some 100.000 kg of poisonous gas were released from 6.000 cylinders to drift towards the enemy line.[63] The Germans had hoped to break open the rigid frontline through this surprise attack. But they failed due to lack of reserve troops, and their opponents promptly responded with a poison gas attack of their own. The deployment of chemical weapons, with their devastating effects, was not restricted to the western front.[64] Research labs in the combatant countries raced to discover ever more powerful weapons of mass destruction. Yet all the large-scale battles of matériel in 1916 failed to make an indention in the rigid western front. Through months of combat, the Germans aimed to "bleed white" the opponent. Between February and July, the fighting over just a few square kilometers of ground slaughtered some 420.000 mostly young men on both sides and left another 800.000 wounded.[65] The fighting over Verdun ended in mid-December in 1916 when French troops occupied Fort Douaumont.

"I can't bear the war any more"

The year 1917 was a turning point in several respects: On April 6 the United States declared war on the German Reich.[66] In mid-August China joined on the side of the Entente.[67] In Europe the slaughter continued

61. Michael Jürgs, *Der kleine Frieden im Großen Krieg. Westfront 1914: Als Deutsche, Franzosen und Briten gemeinsam Weihnachten feierten* (Munich: C. Bertelsmann, 2003).
62. Wolfdieter Bihl, *Der Erste Weltkrieg 1914-1918* (Vienna: Böhlau, 2010), 92.
63. Eberhard Strohal, *Erster Weltkrieg* (Vienna: hpt-Verlag, 1989), 84.
64. On the poison gas deployment in Italy: Bihl, *Weltkrieg*, 19.
65. Leidinger, Moritz, *Weltkrieg*, 38.
66. The US declaration of war on Austria-Hungary was issued on 7 December 1917.
67. Tilemann Grimm, "Weltwende auch in Ostasien?" in *Weltwende 1917. Monarchie · Weltrevolution · Demokratie*, ed. Hellmuth Rößler (Berlin: Musterschmidt, 1965), 189.

unabated. The offensive launched in Flanders by the British and French in late July (Battle of Passchendaele) took almost four months and produced a succès d'estime against the Germans. On 19 August the 11th Battle of the Isonzo, which produced notable territorial gains for Italy, began.[68] By the end of the year, however, it became increasingly difficult to continue the war due to the haemorrhaging of the troops on both sides.[69] Confronted with a shortage of troops, the combatant states responded by lowering the recruiting age and conscripting older cohorts.[70]

The overall situation changed with events in Russia. Badly bleeding from the war and unable to cope with the military challenges in socioeconomic or technological terms, Russia suffered dramatic defeats from 1915 onwards. Poland, Lithuania, and Kurland had to be vacated. On 8 March 1917, the February revolution broke out, led by workers and soldiers and leading to the abdication of Tsar Nicholas II.[71] The situation remained volatile even after a bourgeois government took over since the new political masters failed to consider the peasants' hunger for land and the war-weariness pervading all segments of the population. A second revolution in the latter half of the year brought the Bolsheviks to power who entered into armistice negotiations with the Central Powers in December 1917. When these negotiations broke down, the German side attacked in February 1918 and found no resistance on the part of Russia. On 3 March 1918, a peace treaty was signed at Brest-Litovsk which involved further territorial losses for Russia.

With the supply situation in the warring states worsening, problems in their respective hinterlands began to multiply. Growing bitterness among the population was given a voice in demonstrations and strikes. In May

---

68. With Italy declaring war on the Habsburg Empire in late May 1915, a new front was created which ran through mostly alpine terrain. Starting at the Stilfser Joch on the border to Switzerland in the west it was drawn across South Tyrol and the Dolomite mountains to the Carnic and Julian Alps from where it moved southwards to merge with the so-called Isonzo frontline. This was also mostly of an alpine nature, running along the Isonzo river to the Adriatic Sea. This frontline was the theatre of altogether twelve major battles between 1915 and 1917, which turned into a trench war similar to that along the western front. Dieter Storz, "Alpenkrieg," in *Enzyklopädie Erster Weltkrieg*, ed. Gerhard Hirschfeld, Gerd Krumeich, and Irina Renz (Paderborn: Ferdinand Schöningh Verlag, 2004), 331-334.
69. Hans Meier-Welcker, "Die militärischen Planungen und ihre Ergebnisse 1917/18" in *Weltwende 1917. Monarchie · Weltrevolution · Demokratie*, ed. Hellmuth Rößler (Berlin: Musterschmidt, 1965), 12. Regarding the troops deployed by the British from their colonies see: Brigitte Hamann, *Der Erste Weltkrieg* (Munich: Piper Verlag, 2009), 69 et seq.
70. An imperial decree of 18 January 1916 extended military service in the Habsburg empire up to age 55. Cf. Imperial Law Gazette 1916, no. 18.
71. Stevenson, *1914-1918*, 349 et seq.

1916, Vienna experienced its first hunger riots.[72] The grain harvest in Austria-Hungary yielded only half the quantity of peacetime production.[73] Racketeers and speculators achieved spectacular profits on the black market. The unbearable conditions caused physical decline in ever more people. Famine oedemas and wasting diseases such as consumption and rickets spread at a rapid pace. In Germany, food shortages first began to be felt in late January 1915.[74] The distribution of food stamps helped alleviate the situation only temporarily. By mid-April 1917, "hunger strikes" occurred in Berlin, Leipzig, Hannover, Dresden, and other German cities, which increasingly took on a political character.[75] What had started in Russia threatened to spread to other countries. In France, the wheat harvest reached its lowest level so far, at 40% of the pre-war volume.[76] By the end of the year, the food crisis reached Great Britain, and the queues at the shops became ever longer.

Slowly, the antimilitarist movement began to come out of its paralysis. In 1914 it had been easy to drown out pacifist voices by the din of the war. Paul Scheerbart, trailblazer of Dadaism, died in 1915 after going on hunger strike to protest against the war.[77] Socialist Jean Jaurès was assassinated by a nationalist in late July 1914. Poet Hedwig Lachmann had to put up with social ostracism when she wrote against the global catastrophe.[78] But gradually the opponents of war began to get a hearing. "I can't bear the war any more" was how German Expressionist Carl Einstein summarised a widespread mood after his own frontline experience. "Everything is collapsing; all that was valuable to me has been destroyed."[79] Oskar Maria Graf resolved to

---

72. Manfried Rauchensteiner, *Der Tod des Doppeladlers. Österreich-Ungarn und der Erste Weltkrieg* (Graz: Böhlau, 1997), 325. Stevenson, 1914-1918, 344.

73. Bihl, *Weltkrieg*, 124.

74. The walkout of young workers in Brunswick in April 1916 was a protest against the cutbacks ordered by the military command. When the strike began to escalate, the austerity orders had to be retracted.

75. Walkouts first occurred at Berlin factories in early February 1917, i.a. at torpedo maker Schwartzkopff, turbine maker AEG, at Löwe & Co. and at Stock & Co. By April, the strike movement in Berlin involved some 300.000 participants. The creation of workers' councils was countered with massive repression measures. By 23 April, the strikes were broken, but the sailors' riot in August 1917 became the signal for new unrest, Comment in Scharrer, *Vaterlandslose Gesellen*, 293 et seq.

76. Bihl, *Weltkrieg*, 175.

77. Paul Scheerbart, *Die Entwicklung des Luftmilitarismus und die Auflösung der Europäischen Land-heere, Festungen und Seeflotten. Eine Flugschrift* (Berlin: Oesterheld & Co. Verlag, 1909).

78. Hedwig Lachmann, *Gesammelte Gedichte. Eigenes und Nachdichtungen*, ed. Gustav Landauer (Potsdam: Gustav Kiepenheuer Verlag, 1919).

79. Carl Einstein, "Brief vom Frühjahr 1917," in Christoph Braun, *Carl Einstein: zwischen Ästhetik und Anarchismus. Zu Leben und Werk eines expressionistischen Schriftstellers* (Munich: iudicium, 1987), 231.

refuse serving in arms and could not be prevailed upon to reconsider even by the most serious threats of punishment.[80] Karl Kraus fought against the unintellectual mobilization by a sort of "reversed silence," relentlessly attacking the phraseology of war propaganda.[81] Rudolf Goldscheid, a financial economist from Vienna, kept denouncing the method of solving conflicts between states by violence as being typical of a low culture.[82] George Bernard Shaw deplored patriotism, calling upon the opponents to immediately enter into peace negotiations.[83] Of some importance was the women's conference in The Hague in 1915 which adopted a comprehensive programme for peace.[84] Austrian delegates were Rosa Mayreder and Olga Misař. Alfred Hermann Fried, who was forced to precipitately leave for Switzerland after his public protest in 1914, assiduously continued his work for peace from his new home. Frenchman Romain Rolland similarly chose Switzerland as his exile because he believed the country to offer the best prerequisites for uncensored publication of his antimilitarist works.[85] The circle of opponents was increased by Albrecht Mendelssohn Bartholdy, a reputed expert in international law from Hamburg who, focusing on development, interpreted events as an educational endeavour towards peace.[86] British economist Norman Angell, who had undertaken a peace mission through many states shortly before the outbreak of war, in 1916 began, jointly with Bertrand Russell, to help refuseniks at their trials. Through such activities the two of them managed to gather some 5.000 supporters.[87]

At the German Reichstag plenary, critical voices multiplied when the discussion concerned expenditures for arms. Initially just two of the Social Democratic MPs, Karl Liebknecht and Otto Rühle, voted against war

---

80. Oskar Maria Graf, initially confronted with a death sentence, was taken to the Lida military hospital after a ten-day hunger strike in January 1916. He spent the next months at psychiatric wards, first at Görden/Brandenburg and then at the Haar institute near Munich. In early December he managed to be graded "unfit for military service" and was discharged. Oskar Maria Graf, *Wir sind Gefangene: Ein Bekenntnis* (Vienna: Kurt Desch Verlag, 1965), 198-209.

81. Karl Kraus, "In dieser großen Zeit," *Die Fackel* XVI. no. 404 (1914): 1-19.

82. Rudolf Goldscheid, "Krieg und Kultur. *Die Lehren der Krise*," *Die Friedens-Warte. Zeitschrift für zwischenstaatliche Organization* 13, no. 12 (1912): 441-446.

83. George Bernard Shaw, *Der gesunde Menschenverstand im Krieg* (Common Sense about the War) (1914), trans. Siegfried Trebisch (Zurich: Max Raser Verlag 1919).

84. Rosa Mayreder, "Der Haager Frauenkongress im Lichte der Frauenbewegung," *Neues Frauenleben: Organ der freiheitlichen Frauen in Österreich* 17, no. 5 (1915): 98-101.

85. Romain Rolland, "An die freien Geister aller Länder!" *Erkenntnis und Befreiung. Organ des herrschaftslosen Sozialismus* 1, no. 21 (1919): 3. Rolland had been awarded the Nobel Prize for literature in 1915.

86. Albrecht Mendelssohn Bartholdy, *Bürgertugenden in Krieg und Frieden* (Tübingen: Verlag von J. C. B. Mohr/Paul Siebeck 1917).

87. Jahr, *Gewöhnliche Soldaten*, 126.

loans, but by 1916 almost two dozen MPs of that party showed that they had reconsidered. A party that had once led the workers' movement was increasingly torn apart by the issue of whether to continue to participate in the murderous political decision-making. It became ever more obvious that, the same as other major social institutions, it had screwed up and was in danger of breaking up. April 1917 saw the foundation of the Unabhängige Sozialdemokratische Partei (Independent Social Democratic Party USPD). The Spartacus League had been formed in January 1916.[88] New organizations emerged on the political scene, the result of an increasing inability of political and administrative institutions to cope. During the last phase of the war, councils of commissars and similar organizations at local level gained in importance for political decision-making processes and supply issues in many of the countries at war. The commissar system spread as a type of direct democracy in Germany, Austria, Hungary, and other countries.[89] The shop stewards movement, active in the British mining and metal industry and aiming to install workers' control over companies, experienced a notable influx of new members from 1917 onwards.[90]

In Austria, one event in particular contributed to spreading an antiwar mood. On 21 October Friedrich Adler, son of the Social Democratic party chairman Victor Adler, went to the Hotel Meißl & Schadn at Neuer Markt in Vienna and shot and killed Count Carl von Stürghk, the Austrian Minister-President who was having breakfast at the hotel. Adler had chosen Stürgkh because he saw him as one of those chiefly responsible for the war disaster in absolutist Austria. His trial began in May 1917 and he impressively used it as a stage to call the creaking Habsburg regime to account.[91] Adler was sentenced to death, a sentence which was later commuted to eighteen years imprisonment, and finally amnestied in early November 1918 even before the new state formally came into being. The social democratic *Arbeiterzeitung*, which had initially condemned the assassination in the strictest terms, now celebrated Adler as a "hero and martyr." In a later assessment, Otto Bauer, leader of the Social Democratic party between the wars, recognized the assassination as a decisive "turning

88. According to Wohlgemuth, an illegal organization had been set up already in late 1914. By mid-1915, some 300 places were organised in the network. In early 1918, representatives of the Spartacus League were active in some 3.000 towns and cities. Heinz Wohlgemuth, *Burgkrieg, nicht Burgfriede! Der Kampf Karl Liebknechts, Rosa Luxemburgs und ihrer Anhänger um die Rettung der deutschen Nation in den Jahren 1914-1916* (Berlin: Dietz Verlag, 1963), 255.
89. Cf. Hannah Arendt, *On Revolution* (New York: The Viking Press, 1963).
90. Abendroth, *Arbeiterbewegung*, 89.
91. Johann Wolfgang Brügel, ed., *Friedrich Adler vor dem Ausnahmegericht* (Vienna: Europa Verlag, 1967).

point" in the period before the downfall of the Danube Monarchy.[92] The "Leftist Manifesto" at the Social Democratic party convention in Vienna on 19-24 October 1917 initiated the party's shift away from its policy of "war Marxism."

Breakdown of the old order

The prolonged war brought to the civilian population ever greater sufferings in the form of food scarcity, repercussions, deportations, detentions, forced labour, hostage-taking and executions. "Frontline" and "hinterland" began to merge. The number of war crimes committed by the imperial and royal army in the Balkans, Poland, and Russia increased by the day.[93] The taboo had been broken already in 1914, just three weeks into the war, when Austrian soldiers perpetrated their first massacre of Serbian civilians.[94] Whether in Serbia and Montenegro, in Croatia, Bosnia, along the Adriatic coast, in Bukovina and Galicia, troop commanders invoking the "justifiable defence in war law" had thousands of men and women summarily executed by court-martial or field court, frequently without any trial. A suspicion of "high treason", "Russophilia" or "collaboration with the enemy" sufficed. In Galicia, it was mostly the Ukrainian and Jewish civilians who were victimized.[95] Fear of independence movements, of "subversive plots" by some nations, and of espionage got to be near-paranoid. Soon the only object was to set a warning example. For the sake of deterrence, the bodies of the hanged were left rotting for days on trees and gas lamp posts in the center of towns and villages. The scorched-earth policy was also applied in Bohemia and Moravia where civilians accused of treason were detained for years and where some 5.000 death sentences were imposed in the course of the war.[96] In such cases, the trial was a short affair. Cesare Battisti, a social democratic publisher and member of the k. u. k. Reichsrat, was arrested by the Austrians as an Italian soldier and sentenced to death for "treason and high treason" after a trial of just two hours. His execution

---

92. Norbert Leser, "Der Abgesang des alten Österreich," *Wiener Zeitung*, 27 October 2007, 4.
93. Bihl, *Weltkrieg*, 4.
94. Hellmut Butterweck, "Zeitgeschichtlicher Schocker in Bildern. Das Lächeln der Henker: Dokumente zum Wüten der k. u. k. Massenmörder," *Wiener Zeitung*, 2 December 2008, 10. Mark Mazower writes: "[…] mass executions, concentration camps and deportation of the Serbian élite were all used by Franz Josef's military to ensure order in the occupied territories." Mark Mazower, *The Balkans. From the End of Byzantium to the Present Day* (London: Phoenix, 2000), 119.
95. Hamann, *Erster Weltkrieg*, 182, 341.
96. Hautmann, "Kriegsgesetze", 107.

took place immediately afterwards.[97]

Supply and distribution problems increasingly derailed the situation in the combatant states. Civilian resentment was voiced particularly in the industrialised conurbations. In May 1917, 15.000 workers went on strike at the Vienna Arsenal and quickly won their main demands for more food and a reduction of working hours. More strikes followed: at the Škoda works in Pilsen/Plzeň, at the ammunition factories along the Steinfeld, at Witkowitz/Vítcovice in Mährisch Ostrau/Moravská Ostrava; from 31 May onwards, strikes broke out regularly in Prague, and supraregional railway lines began to feel the effect of insurgencies on their operations.[98] Hanna Sturm, a worker in one of the ammunition factories of Blumau near Wiener Neustadt since 1912, reports of the beginnings of resistance schemes against the war. Blumau had four large state-owned operations where altogether 65.000 workers from all corners of the monarchy produced military goods. Starting in 1915, according to Hanna Sturm, some matériel was intentionally damaged before it was sent to the front. Moreover, pamphlets were placed in the boxes which called upon soldiers to cease hostilities. Even though conditions for underground activities were less than favourable, workers managed to stash away small quantities of explosives and carry out acts of sabotage by blowing up warehouses stocked with arms. Suspected of contributing to such an insurgency scheme, Hanna Sturm was arrested in August 1917. Even though no proof was forthcoming, she was not released until 21 January 1918.[99]

In the German Reich, the April strikes in Berlin and Saxony and a new wave of strikes in the Ruhr district and Upper Silesia in mid-1917 were followed by a cumulation of sabotage acts: signaling equipment and shunts important for railway operation were disabled, the brakes of trains and railway cars used for military transports were destroyed, prominently placed large-scale banners such as "Down with War" went up, clearly expressing what the people wanted.[100] In the spring of 1917, social unrest reached France, where strikes enveloped arms factories and other operations. A key role was taken on by the women workers who did not run the danger of being conscripted as a punishment for unruly behavior. Political demands played a rather subordinate role in France at the time. What was important was to

---

97. Hamann, *Erster Weltkrieg*, 189. Karl Kraus used a photograph of Cesare Battisti, who had been sentenced to death by hanging by an Austrian military court, as a frontispiece in his *Letzte Tage der Menschheit*.
98. Bihl, *Weltkrieg*, 154.
99. "'… the Polish were strongest also when it came to placing nitroglycerine on rails …' Hanna Sturm on resistance in the World War I," interview of 27 July 1982 in *Widerstand gegen Krieg und Faschismus in Österreich*, ed. Forum Alternativ (Vienna, 1982), 13f, 16.
100. Jahr, *Gewöhnliche Soldaten*, 162 et seq.

achieve specific improvements in the working conditions. The government quickly managed to defuse the situation by getting employers to accept far-reaching compromises with the workers. In this way, obstructionism was much less pronounced in France than in Russia or Germany.[101]

The strike of January 1918, starting in Hungary and Galicia, rang in the end of the war catastrophe. Next to mining operations, the strike extended to arms factories, railway car factories, and wharfs. Between Linz and Temesvar, from Trieste to Cracow, some 700,000 people laid down their tools between the start and the end of January 1918. In Austria, it was mostly the workers in Vienna, Lower Austria, Upper Austria, and Styria that fell in line. The coast and Bohemia were affected as well. In the coal fields of Moravia and Silesia the strike continued right into February.[102] Towards the end of January, large-scale mass strikes broke out in the ammunition factories in Berlin and other German cities. In Berlin alone, some 400.000 went on strike.[103] Workers were supported by large parts of the general population who joined impressive demonstrations on the streets. This time around, the fight was no longer just for better wages and working conditions, but the goals were "bread" and "peace"; the call was for fundamental political rights and it got louder. What they demanded was the right to strike and the freedom of assembly, democracy and participation, women's suffrage, and the release of political prisoners. Military authorities threatened to court-martial participants and an aggravated state of siege.[104] But when the strikes reached the industrial centers of Donawitz and Leoben on 12 May Hungary (mining, metal, and transport operations) in late July and Bohemia and Moravia (mining, metal, and armament operations) in late September it became all too obvious that the instruments of martial law no longer sufficed to dam up the growing revolutionary ambitions in the population.[105]

The uprisings had turned into a serious threat for the regime. Amongst its leaders, panic spread, cabinets were overthrown, and generals attempted to take control. Increasing numbers of soldiers were rerouted to the hinterland to be deployed against strikers. But outrage among civilians became mixed up with a growing discontent among the troops. In spite of being threatened with severe punishments, cases of desertion and mutiny

---

101. Segesser, *Erster Weltkrieg*, 196.

102. Bihl, *Weltkrieg*, 175.

103. Commentary in Scharrer, *Vaterlandslose Gesellen*, 303.

104. In the German Reich, the January strike was accompanied by mass detentions and forced recruitment; in Hamburg, strikers were court-martialed. Commentary in Scharrer, *Vaterlandslose Gesellen*, 305 et seq.

105. Bihl, *Weltkrieg*, 209, 224, 237 et seq.

multiplied.[106] Towards the end of the war, incidences of cease-fire and fraternization invoked "from below" again grew at several front sections.[107] When mutiny spread among French units between April and June 1917, the army leaders managed to restore order only by practising unrelenting harshness (courts-martial, death sentences).[108] But the tide began to turn in 1918.

At the imperial and royal naval port of Cattaro, where the battle cruiser division and flotilla of torpedo boats were stationed, sailors rose in revolt in early February 1918, their action triggered mostly by drastic disciplinary measures and a bad supply situation. The insurgents presented a catalogue of requests that were anything but apolitical: announcement of an immediate general peace based on the Russian proposals, serious discussion of the Fourteen Points for securing peace presented by U.S. President Woodrow Wilson on 8 January 1918, implementation of the right of self-determination of the nations, and democratisation of the administrative structures.[109] One last time the army command managed to crush the mutiny. Of the 392 men prosecuted forty were court-martialed and four of the mutineers were sentenced to death. The naval port command order no. 12 issued at Castelnuovo on 14 February 1918 notes: "Convicts Franz

---

106. The greatest numbers of desertion in the World War I were found in the armies of Austria-Hungary and the Ottoman Empire. In Hungary alone, there were 200,000 deserters in the first three months of 1918, as can be seen from statistical figures of the Honved ministry in Budapest. Ludwig Jedlicka, "Das Ende der Monarchie in Österreich-Ungarn," in *Weltwende 1917. Monarchie · Weltrevolution · Demokratie*, ed. Hellmuth Rößler (Berlin: Musterschmidt, 1965), 72. In late October 1918, another wave of deserters from the imperial and royal army was reported. According to estimates made by Colonel Ratzenhofer, deputy head of military railways, some 250.000 soldiers had deserted. Bihl, *Weltkrieg*, 235. Wild rumours about the numbers circulated in the Reichsrat in Vienna, but were promptly denied by the supreme army command. Yet based on serious figures, some 50.000 soldiers were missing among the reserve units in mid-1918. These were men who refused to obey their conscription order, absconded or openly refused to serve. Leidinger, Moritz, *Weltkrieg*, 62. Official reports made frequent mention of the disloyal conduct of Czech soldiers in the army. This accusation, coupled as it was with the crime of "high treason," is discussed in a recent study by Richard Lein, who concludes that official reports by the supreme army command were given to much distortion in this respect in order to divert from their own failures. Added to this was the anti-Czech agitation by the German Nationalists who tried to prevent any concessions by the Habsburgs to the population of Bohemia and Moravia. Richard Lein, *Das militärische Verhalten der Tschechen im Ersten Weltkrieg*. Diss., University of Vienna, 2009. Typical of the German situation is the content of a telegram sent by a colonel general to Field Marshal von Hindenburg on 28 October 1918: "Am appalled to report current situation to Your Excellency: [...] more than 30 divisions refuse to continue fighting! Parts of some regiments absent themselves without leave [...]. Commanders are powerless. [...] Provision of reserves or replacement is impossible since troops can no longer be transported to the front." Telegram to von Hindenburg, cited in Bihl, *Weltkrieg*, 270.
107. Jahr, *Gewöhnliche Soldaten*, 95.
108. Segesser, *Erster Weltkrieg*, 196 et seq.
109. Jedlicka, "Ende der Monarchie," 74 et seq.

Rasch, Anton Garbar, Jerko Sisgoric, and Mate Bernicevic were executed at 6 am on 11 February 1918."[110] On 23 October Croatian soldiers of the infantry regiment no. 79 rose in mutiny in Fiume. Rioting spread rapidly, ultimately forcing Austria-Hungary to abandon its navy.[111] In late October 1918, units of the German deep-sea fleet in Wilhelmshaven refused to sail. The rebellious spark jumped over quickly: in Kiel, sailors rebelled in early November.[112]

A good description of the proliferating refusenik attitude on board the German "suicide steamers" is provided by Theodor Plivier, who at the start of the war was forcefully recruited in the navy and who spent most of the war on the *Wolf*, an auxiliary cruiser, in his book *Des Kaisers Kulis* (The Kaiser's Coolies).[113] The uprising of the fleet spread like wildfire. Started without any particular organizational preparations, the workers' and soldiers' councils quickly took over key posts in administrative and supply line sectors. Over the next days, the revolutionary movement took hold in all of Germany. Sailors, deserters, and radical leftists chased away the old elites.[114] Apart from objectives such as socialising the economy, the main goal was to immediately end the war. Austria, Hungary, and Italy were also caught up in the radicalisation process. In late 1918, the political order in Central Europe broke down. Even before a cease-fire between Austria-Hungary and the Entente powers had been agreed in Padua on November 3, the multinational Danube Monarchy had dissolved into several successor states.[115] On 9 November Kaiser Wilhelm II and his crown prince abdicated, opening up the way for the proclamation of the German Republic. Two days later, the last cease-fire agreement was signed. After more than fifty months, the butchery finally ended.

The legacy of the war

An account of the years between 1914 and 1918 yields a devastating

---

110. "K. und K. Kriegshafenkommando Cattaro, Reservat. Kriegshafenkommandobefehl 1, no. 12, Castelnuovo, 14 February 1918. 1. Res. No. 3170," in Kurt Kläber (ed.), *Der Krieg. Das erste Volksbuch vom großen Krieg* (Berlin: Internationaler Arbeiter-Verlag, 1929), 113.
111. Rauchensteiner, *Tod des Doppeladlers*, 612.
112. Karl-Heinz Janßen, "Der Untergang der Monarchie in Deutschland" in *Weltwende 1917. Monarchie · Weltrevolution · Demokratie*, ed. Hellmuth Rößler (Berlin: Musterschmidt, 1965), 105 et seq.
113. Theodor Plivier, *Des Kaisers Kulis* (Berlin: Malik Verlag, 1930): 331 et seq.
114. Janßen, "Untergang," 104.
115. The Czechoslovak Republic was proclaimed on October 28; on the next day, the southern Slavic territories merged into the Kingdom of Serbs, Croats, and Slovenes (SHS), and on October 31 the new government of Hungary proclaimed its separation from the House of Habsburg. Strohal, *Erster Weltkrieg*, 113.

picture. Almost ten million soldiers—mostly young men—did not return from the killing fields. About double were severely wounded. Taking into account all consequential effects and the influenza epidemic of 1918 which rapidly decimated an exhausted civil population, total losses amounted to over 60 million individuals.[116] A proper account of the legacy of the Great War must not ignore the economic consequences. Calculated at purchasing power values of 1914, military operations alone are estimated to have swallowed US$ 180 to 230 billion by 1918. Added to this were the material losses caused by the war, set at some US$ 150 billion.[117] Kurt Eisner, representative of the Independent Social Democrats, noted in one of the revolutionary assemblies after the war that the billions wasted for the military could have been used to create quasi-paradisiacal conditions.[118] The national debt, enormously grown during the war, and the reparations imposed after peace had been made placed great hurdles in the path towards economic health on the European continent. The combatants had their production structure severely distorted by the increasing dominance of the armament industry, and Europe's share of global production and global trade was perceptibly reduced. The massive growth in the inequality of wealth within the population was confirmed by Rosa Luxemburg's assessment: "Dividends rise, proletarians fall."[119] Added to this, money depreciated dramatically thanks to peculiar ways to finance the war, impacting the post-war years until the 1920s. Economic follow-up problems caused states to erect fire walls against each other and to pursue an isolationist policy, thus preparing the way for another disastrous war.

116. Stevenson, *1914-1918*, 637.
117. Wirtschaftsgeschichte, Modul 3, www.wu.ac.at/vw3/downloads/telematik/wirtschaftsgeschichte3.pdf (accessed 9 Aug. 2013). For the long-term impact of the war see: Herbert Matis, Dieter Stiefel, *Die Weltwirtschaft. Struktur und Entwicklung im 20. Jahrhundert* (Vienna: Ueberreuter, 1991), 88-96.
118. Kurt Eisner, "Wahlrede," in *Die Müncher Räterepublik – Zeugnisse und Kommentar*, ed. Tankred Dorst (Frankfurt/M.: Suhrkamp, 1967), 44.
119. Rosa Luxemburg cited in: Schlanstein, Wolter, Karwath, *Weltkrieg*, 43. Profiteers of the war had been mostly the large armament operations and supplier companies. Another wartime profiteer was the sector of the big banks which thanks to better opportunities for disposition knew how to avoid the pitfalls of the inflation crisis (the Austrian crown had fallen to one fifteen hundredth of its original parity by 1922).

Ein Seeheld! Keinen echter'n
Umvreb je Glorienschein!
Er wird den Adrianvächtern
Ein strahlend Vorbild sein.   Th. Waldau

Egon Lerch, Portrait in uniform as a lieutenant, Postcard "Austrian Heroes at Sea of the World War 1914-1915, Pf 33.836:C(4), artist, Harry Heussler, Austrian National Library - Picture Archives and Graphics Department, Vienna

'Our Weddigen.' On the Construction of the War Hero in the k.u.k. Army.[1]
The 'Naval Hero' Egon Lerch as an Example

Nicole-Melanie Goll

General der Infanterie Emil von Woinovich, who was in charge of the War Archives in Vienna during the First World War, published an essay in the Österreichische Rundschau in 1910, in which he dealt with the exigencies that a "modern" war would create. He argued that:

> One must also remember that modern warfare relies not only on the armed forces deployed in the field but also reflects on all the strengths of the state and the people, on the material, intellectual, moral powers and so on. However, the population must be convinced of this from the start so that people are not surprised by the demands that war places upon them.[2]

Woinovich recognized that, besides the necessary equipment and provisions for the army and a well-functioning transport system, a *"certain spirit"*[3]—which must take hold of the civilian population in particular—was critical to a war's success, and that future wars could only be won with the help of the *"willing cooperation of the entire population"* on the "home front."[4] New challenges, brought on by mass warfare that required mobilization at all levels throughout the state, could only be met by controlling and

---

1. This article is based on the author's project for her doctoral thesis conducted at the University of Graz, which analyzes the construction of War Heroes of the Austro-Hungarian Monarchy during the First World War. The author would like to thank the translator Anne Kozeluh for transferring the German manuscript into English. The author, however, translated the endnotes.
2. Emil von Woinovich, *Gedanken über den modernen Krieg*. (Vienna: Fromme, 1910), 4.
3. Ibid., 3.
4. Ibid., 6.

214   Goll: 'Our Weddigen': On the Construction of the War Hero
in the k.u.k. Army.
The 'Naval Hero' Egon Lerch as an Example

influencing the population as a whole.[5] When the First World War broke out five years later, the Austro-Hungarian Empire was one of the first of the warring nations to hastily introduce surveillance measures and to declare a state of emergency, along with a drastic restriction of the political and social rights of the population, thus placing military affairs above those of civilian society.[6]

The state had to meet the challenges this created in a way that was publicly effective, since "Our own population must be united and morally reinforced in order to promote fighting strength and the will to persevere."[7] The definitive instruments chosen for this purpose were the portrayal, interpretation, and heightening of the war—a task that was to be carried out by a state propaganda agency—in order to ensure the loyalty of the civilian population, among other things. In this way state propaganda developed into an indispensable element of both "internal" and "external" war conduct. With the reintroduction of censorship, a state-controlled media system was created, which encompassed all types of media and was designed to uphold the utopian idea "that the Central Powers cannot be defeated." [8] The 'Kriegspressequartier' (KPQ) and the "literary group" within the war archives of the Austrian State Archives were responsible for controlling this

---

5.   Stefan Kaufmann, *Kommunikationstechnik und Kriegsführung 1815–1945. Stufen telemedialer Rüstung*. (Munich: Fink, 1996); Martin van Creveld, *Technology and War: From 2000 B.C. to the Present*. (New York: The Free Press, 1989); Klaus-Jürgen Bremm, *Propaganda im Ersten Weltkrieg*. (Darmstadt: Theiss, 2013); Rolf Spilker ed., *Der Tod als Maschinist: Der industrialisierte Krieg 1914–1918* (Ausstellungskatalog des Museums Industriekultur Osnabrück, 1998), (Bramsche: Rasch, 1998); Mark Cornwall, *The undermining of Austria-Hungary: the battle for hearts and minds*. (Basingstoke: Palgrave, 2000); Anne Lipp, *Meinungslenkung im Krieg. Kriegserfahrung deutscher Soldaten und ihre Deutung 1914–1918*. (Göttingen: Vandenhoeck&Ruprecht, 2003).
6.   Gernot D. Hasiba, *Das Notverordnungsrecht in Österreich (1848–1917)*, (Vienna: Verlag der Akademie der Wissenschaft, 1985); Tamara Scheer, *Die Ringstraßenfront: Österreich-Ungarn, das Kriegsüberwachungsamt und der Ausnahmezustand während des Ersten Weltkrieges*, (Vienna: Heeresgeschichtliches Museum Wien, 2010).
7.   Harold D. Lasswell, *Propaganda Technique in the World War*, (London: reprint, MIT Press, 1971), cited as in Eberhard Sauermann, *Literarische Kriegsfürsorge. Österreichische Dichter und Publizisten im Ersten Weltkrieg*, (Vienna: Böhlau, 2000), 341.
8.   *Militär-Zeitung*, 22 April 1915, 49.

apparatus and all state propaganda activities.[9] Both had lasting influence and control over the information system in Cisleithania during the First World War. They were to create a certain perception within the population and influence people in specific directions. It was up to the propaganda and censorship apparatus to decide which news items and events, and therefore information, would be made public at which time and to what extent. They decided who would receive special attention and took care of disseminating the image they had created of the chosen person to the media. They made "heroes" out of individuals and effectively created the heroic figures of the First World War.[10]

During the "Great War" in particular there was a "renaissance of heroism," which had its roots in the changes brought about by mechanized mass warfare that faced the soldiers on the front. Although a certain "quiet heroism" on the home front was acknowledged, it was mainly military heroic figures that took on an important function in wartime society. These

9. The Kriegspressequartier (KPQ, War Press Quarters) was installed as a subgroup of the Supreme Command of the Army (Armeeoberkommando) in 1914 and was responsible for the entire military press services. With its mediation function between the military and the home front it had far-reaching influence on the Monarchy's entire information system. Literates, journalists, and artists had to be accredited with the KPQ in order to proceed with their professional activities—all in line with the war efforts. They supplied newspapers with articles about the frontlines sided by photographs; they published propagandistic writings and held speeches. Many of the known Austro-Hungarian artists and writers supported with their craftsmanship the "duty for the fatherland." The "literary group" (Literarische Gruppe) in the War Archive, which was mainly involved with publishing military historical writings before the outbreak of the First World War, was now also included in the propaganda apparatus. The members of this group published various propagandistic works. Most publications of the "literary group" were aimed at "leading" the population into the "correct" direction by transmitting values such as self-sacrifice, bravery, or love to the fatherland, illustrated via numerous examples. Klaus Mayer, *Die Organisation des Kriegspressequartiers beim k.u.k. Armeeoberkommando im Ersten Weltkrieg*, PhD. diss, University of Vienna, 1963; Jozo Džambo ed., *Musen an die Front. Schriftsteller und Künstler im Dienst der k. u. k. Kriegspropaganda 1914–1918. Begleitband zur gleichnamigen Ausstellung*, (Munich: Adalbert Stifter Verlag, 2003); Eberhard Sauermann, *Literarische Kriegsfürsorge. Österreichische Dichter und Publizisten im Ersten Weltkrieg*, (Vienna: Böhlau, 2000); Peter Broucek, "Das Kriegspressequartier und die literarischen Gruppen im Kriegsarchiv 1914–1918," in *Österreich und der Große Krieg 1914-1918. Die andere Seite der Geschichte*, ed. Klaus Amann, Hubert Lengauer (Vienna: Brandstätter, 1989), 132-139; Peball Kurt, "Literarische Publikationen des Kriegsarchivs im Weltkrieg 1914–1918," in *Mitteilungen des Österreichischen Staatsarchivs*, No. 14 (1961): 240-260.

10. The "literary group" published several books with special emphasis on singular heroic acts. They were based upon the so-called "Belohnungsanträge" (applications for rewards) which were sent to the War Archive. See for example: Alois Veltze, *Unsere Offiziere. Episoden aus den Kämpfen der österreichisch-ungarischen Armee im Weltkrieg 1914/15*, (Vienna: Manz, 1915); Alois Veltze ed., *Unsere Soldaten. Episoden aus den Kämpfen der österreichisch-ungarischen Armee im Weltkrieg 1914/15*, (Vienna: Manz, 1916); Emil von Woinovich, Alois Veltzé eds., *Helden des Roten Kreuzes. Aus den Akten des k.u.k. Generalinspektorates der freiwilligen Sanitätspflege*, (Vienna: Manz, 1915).

216   Goll: 'Our Weddigen': On the Construction of the War Hero
in the k.u.k. Army.
The 'Naval Hero' Egon Lerch as an Example

heroes were expected to personify values such as self-sacrifice, loyalty, and love of the fatherland for the rest of the population to reinforce the will to persevere and to encourage young men to emulate them.[11]

It is, therefore, particularly worthwhile to consider which men were chosen to be "made" into heroes, and why. Studying the establishment and acceptance of these war heroes, their media coverage and their veneration, allows us to draw conclusions about the degree of militarization within society. This exposition will focus on those changes that were a crucial influence on the fabrication of heroes during the First World War. The mechanization of the war was central to the rise of a new type of hero: the submarine hero. This type of hero was consciously created to represent the antithesis of the "unknown masses" of land warfare. One individual, the Austro-Hungarian "naval hero" Egon Lerch, will stand as an example for this new type of hero.

War and Heroism

Within the first few months of the war, the idea of "war" that had been valid before 1914 was already completely outdated. The use of modern weapons systems, created to effectively eradicate large numbers of soldiers with one strike, would alter the face of war forever. The increased effectiveness of these weapons, combined with their expanded range and improved accuracy, changed the manner of combat and, with it, the experiences of the soldiers.[12] For the soldier on the ground, the enemy became effectively

---

11. Regarding the construction of masculinity in wartime see for example: David H.J. Morgan, "Theater of War: Combat, the Military and Masculinities," in *Theorizing Masculinities*, ed. Harry Brod, Michael Kaufmann (Thousand Oaks: Sage, 1994), 165–182; Ulrike Brunotte, "Martyrium, Vaterland und der Kult der toten Krieger. Männlichkeit und Soteriologie im Krieg," in *Perspektiven des Todes in der modernen Gesellschaft*, ed. Klinger, (Vienna: Böhlau, 2009), 55-74.

12. The individual experiences were coined by inadequate supplies, wounding, psychic stress, trauma, and death. See for example: Tony Asworth, *Trench Warfare 1914–1918: The Live and Let Live System*, (London: Pan Books, 2000); Rolf Spilker, Bernd Ulrich eds., *Der Tod als Maschinist. Der industrialisierte Krieg 1914–1918*, (Bramsche: Rasch, 1998). Bernd Ulrich, Benjamin Ziemann, *Frontalltag im Ersten Weltkrieg. Wahn und Wirklichkeit*, (Frankfurt/M.: Fischer Taschenbuch-Verlag, 1994); Gerhard Hirschfeld, Gerd Krumreich, Dieter Langewiesche, Hans-Peter Ullmann (eds), *Kriegserfahrungen. Studien zur Sozial- und Mentalitätsge-schichte des Ersten Weltkrieges*, (Essen: Klartext, 1997); Hans-Georg Hofer, "Gewalterfahrung, Trauma und psychiatrisches Wissen im Umfeld des Ersten Weltkrieges," in *Terror und Geschichte*, ed. Helmut Konrad, Gerhard Botz, Stefan Karner, Siegfried Mattl (Vienna: Böhlau, 2012), 205-221; Hans-Georg Hofer, "Was waren Kriegsneurosen?" "Zur Kulturgeschichte psychischer Erkrankungen im Ersten Weltkrieg," in *Der Erste Weltkrieg im Alpenraum. Erfahrung, Deutung, Erinnerung*, ed. Hermann Kuprian, Oswald Überegger (Innsbruck: Wagner, 2006), 309-321.

"invisible."[13] Ultimately, the use of these new weapons systems lead to a higher frequency of killing and consequently to a higher death rate than in any military conflict that had gone before:

> One was not crouched in a muddy trench, while someone, who was not a personal enemy, five miles away, fired a gun and shot one to pieces and was not even aware of it! This was no longer honest fighting; it was murder. Senseless, brutal and base.[14]

The soldiers in the trenches experienced this mechanized war as a shock. The Great War had, within the briefest time, made century-old military patterns of behavior obsolete. It was the common soldier who had to come to terms with this altered concept of war, a concept in which it was not he himself, but rather the mass of soldiers and material that was important.[15] This modernization went hand in hand with a loss of the significance of the actions of the individual. Due to the situation at the front, the common soldier was hardly able to prove himself as an individual combatant in hand-to-hand combat. [16]The duel, historically part of the "gentlemanly codes of warfare and killing,"[17] was no longer applicable in the age of mass armies.

Nevertheless, it was necessary to create an incentive to uphold the individual's "morale" and his willingness to make sacrifices.[18] The possibility of becoming a hero, of the resulting veneration, was considered extremely motivating for the individual soldier. Of course, this not only made it possible to influence the individual's self-perception, it was also a way of dealing with the horrors, that is, the reality of war.[19]

This modern but impersonal form of warfare and the use of mass

---

13. An impressive document is the poem by Wilfried Owen, "Dulce et Decorum est," which portrays a gas attack and the death of a soldier and uncovers the apothegm of Horace's "dulce et decorum est pro patria mori" as a lie.

14. Cecil Lewis, *Schütze im Aufstieg. Eine autobiographische Erzählung*, (Berlin: Rowohlt, o.J.), 50.

15. See: Joanna Bourke, *An intimate history of killing: Face to face Killing in Twentieth-Century Warfare*, (New York: Basic Books, 1999).

16. On the meaning of the duel see Ute Frevert, *Ehrenmänner. Das Duell in der bürgerlichen Gesellschaft*, (Munich: Beck, 1991).

17. Davis H.J. Morgan, "No more Heroes? Masculinities, Violence and the Civilizing Process" in *State, Private Life and Political Change*, ed. Lynn Jamieson, Helen Corr (New York; St. Martin's Press, 1990), 13-30, 13.

18. The meaning of the fitness for military service for the interpretation of masculinity is depicted on the many different picture postcards published before and during the Great War. See for example: Heinrich Hartmann, *Der Volkskörper bei der Musterung. Militärstatistik und Demographie in Europa vor dem Ersten Weltkrieg*, (Göttingen: Waldstein, 2011).

19. Cf. Omar Bartov, "Man and the Mass, Reality and the heroic image of War" in *History & Memory*, 2/1989, 99–122, 100.

218   Goll: 'Our Weddigen': On the Construction of the War Hero
in the k.u.k. Army.
The 'Naval Hero' Egon Lerch as an Example

armies thus increased the need for "heroes" during the First World War. The population longed for heroes who offered the means to come to terms with the industrialized, inhuman war. The government was also aware of this. By resorting to something "old" which had worked in the past, there was a way to make the present more tangible and comprehensible. By cultivating heroic figures, the war could be made less terrible. To do this, the old values and patterns of interpretation were revived and efforts were made to fit them into the framework created by the war. The new "heroes" were found in new branches of service that had been deployed in this war for the first time; it seemed possible for pilots and submariners to engage in heroic single combat again. Attempts were made to combine the old moral concepts with this "new" element and to allow men the opportunity to prove themselves. The novelty was in the combination of "old" moral concepts and new technology. The success of "flying aces" and of submarine heroes depended on their effective interaction with machines. The ideas of "knights of the air" and "naval heroes" were consciously propagated in an attempt to obfuscate the atrocities of the war. Battles in the air and at sea were always portrayed as battles between two equal opponents. Although reality presented a different picture, this unquestioned image still exists today. This portrayal was an attempt to pander to the widespread desire to return to combat between two opponents, and at the same time to make sure that cruelty and atrocities were only connected with the war on land. Especially in Germany, the fabrication of aviation and marine heroes functioned extremely well, focusing increasingly on pilots like Oswald Boelcke, Max Immelmann, and particularly Manfred von Richthofen, as well as the submarine commander Otto Weddigen. Heroic legends were built up around these men within their lifetimes, sustained and propagated by the military, the government, and the general population, and culminated in countless decorations, celebrations, publications, and memorabilia. They were to have a lasting effect on the heroic legends of other military powers.[20]

Although the k.u.k. Army was a pillar of the Austro-Hungarian State, only in exceptional cases was it possible to create a military hero cult. This is surprising, since the army and its martial heroes had played a significant role in the creation of a (national) identity and mobilizing the population, particularly in the 19th century.[21] Regionally, hero cults had also grown

20. So far, Rene Schilling has published the most extensive study to the topic. Rene Schilling, *"Kriegshelden." Deutungsmuster heroischer Männlichkeit in Deutschland 1813–1945*, (Paderborn: Schöningh, 2002); see also: Florian Schnürer, "'But in death he has found victory': the funeral cere-monies for the 'knights of the sky' during the Great War as transnational media events" in *European Review of History* 15, no. 6 (2008): 643-658.
21. See especially the works of Karen Hagemann. For example: Karen Hagemann, "Of 'Manly Valor' and 'German Honor': Nation, War, and the Masculinity in the Age of

up in the multinational Austro-Hungarian Empire, for example the cult around Andreas Hofer in Tyrol, but these had not been intended or indeed desired by the government. In fact, to counter them the government created a cult around the Emperor Franz Joseph I, who was portrayed as the one unifying figure for all the Empire's peoples. Occasionally military heroes—like Radetzky and Prince Eugen—were also developed, but they did not have the same relevance for all the nationalities.[22] When general conscription was introduced, the government missed an opportunity to create military heroes who could have become the unifying figures for all the men who were involved with the military. Instead, the State clung to old structures and habits and the aristocratic "heroic leader" remained the primary heroic figure. This focus gradually changed over the course of the First World War, a development that was significantly influenced by the new branches of service in the mechanized war and their protagonists. The veneration of Egon Lerch is one example of this gradual change. Since he combined old military traditions with the new technology, he appeared to be the ideal case.

"Our Submarine Hero: Egon Lerch"

Linienschiffsleutnant Egon Lerch[23] took over command of the U-XII, one of the k.u.k. Navy's seven submarines, at the beginning of the First World War in 1914[24]. He was stationed with the submarine in Pola. Although the k.u.k. Navy could have lessened the head start that the Allied Forces had in this sector with its development program prior to 1914, most of their financial means had been pumped into the construction of the so-

the Prussian Uprising against Napoleon" in *Central European History* 30/1997, 187-220; Karen Hagemann, "'Heran, heran, zu Sieg oder Tod!' Entwürfe patriotisch-wehrhafter Männlichkeit in der Zeit der Befreiungskriege," in *Männergeschichte – Geschlechtergeschichte. Männlichkeit im Wandel der Moderne*, ed. Thomas Kühne (Frankfurt/M: Campus, 1996), 51-68.

22. Laurence Cole, "Der Radetzky-Kult in Zisleithanien 1848–1914," in *Glanz – Gewalt – Gehorsam. Militär und Gesellschaft in der Habsburgermonarchie (1800 bis 1918)*, ed. Laurence Cole, Christa Hämmerle, Martin Scheutz (Essen: Klartext, 2011): 243–268.

23. Egon Lerch, whose father Richard had served from 1871 to 1909 in the Austro-Hungarian Navy, was born on 18 June 1886 in Trieste. After having visited the military secondary modern school in Güns and the Navy Academy in Fiume/Rijeka he was accepted into service as Navy Cadet on 1 July 1904. In October 1909 he was assigned to the submarine station in Pola/Pula. At this time, the Austro-Hungarian submarine fleet had been in service for merely a year. Initially Lerch served on *U-V* and *U-VI*, but was reassigned at the turn of the year 1912/1913 to Torpedo Boat 16. In 1913, he also was promoted to "Linienschiffsleutnant." At the outbreak of war in 1914 Lerch took over the command of the submarine *U XII*, a sister ship of the submarines he had already been serving aboard.

24. On the submarine fleet see: Wladimir Aichelburg, *Die Unterseeboote Österreich-Ungarns*, (Graz: Akademische Druck- und Verlagsanstalt, 1981).

220   Goll: 'Our Weddigen': On the Construction of the War Hero
in the k.u.k. Army.
The 'Naval Hero' Egon Lerch as an Example

called "dreadnoughts," leaving little room for other acquisitions which were urgently needed if the navy wished to engage in modern maritime warfare. The submarines, which had only been put into service shortly before the war, were seen more as a defensive measure and did not play a significant role in wartime planning. As with the war on land, the expectation was that this war would be over soon and that *one* decisive battle would be all that was needed to end it. At the beginning of the First World War the k.u.k. Navy came up against the French and British naval forces. Austria-Hungary would never have been able to stand up to a coordinated advance by the two powers, but since the British Navy was being held in check by the German Navy, leaving the French naval force operating off Malta almost unaided, the k.u.k. Navy was able to attempt to confront their ships. The Kingdom of Italy's declaration of neutrality exacerbated the situation geo-strategically, since the possibility that Italy would join the war hung like a Damocles sword over the k.u.k. Navy: its operational radius was confined to the Adriatic. The k.u.k. ships were given the task of protecting the Adriatic coastline from incursions and enemy attacks and to support the army from the sea. Then, on December 21, 1914, the "impossible" happened: the *U-XII* was able to damage the *Jean Bart*, the flagship of the French Navy—a battleship of the Courbet class—near Antivari in the Otranto Strait with a torpedo. The ship was able to reach the harbor of Malta but it was deemed "disabled" for a considerable length of time.[25] Although the submarine had not been able to sink the ship, this operation had an effect on the strategy of the Entente.[26] The strength it revealed resulted in the marine forces of the Entente having to send battleships as anti-submarine escorts for their supply convoys for the Allies in Montenegro. After their experience with the Austro-Hungarian Navy, the French felt that advancing into the Adriatic was too risky. Consequently, French ships ceased to operate in the Adriatic.[27] This event was, for propaganda purposes, proclaimed and touted by the Austro-Hungarian media as a huge success over France.[28] The k.u.k. fleet command made the following public announcement regarding Lerch's "heroic deed": "Our Submarine 12—Commander Linienschiffsleutnant Egon Lerch [in the original document highlighted—author's note]—attacked, on 21.d. in the morning, in the Otranto Strait, a French fleet comprising 16 large ships,

---

25. Cf. *Heldenwerk* 1917 (Vienna: Heldenwerkverlag, o.J.), 135f and 228.

26. Lawrence Sondhaus, *The Naval Policy of Austria-Hungary 1867–1918* (West Lafayette: Purdue University Press, 1994), 265.

27. Ibid.; Wladimir Aichelburg, *Die Unterseeboote Österreich-Ungarns*, (Graz: Akademische Druck- und Verlagsanstalt, 1981), 75f.

28. Different newspapers reported on the sinking of the "Riesenschlachtschiffes" (giant battleship), a false report, as it was to turn out later on. Cf. *Neue Freie Presse*, 22 Aug. 1915, 14.

launched two torpedoes at the "Courbet" type flagship and hit both times. The resulting confusion within the enemy fleet, the dangerous proximity of several ships and the high seas and poor visibility prevented the submarine from knowing what then happened to the ship."[29] Some daily newspapers carried numerous reports on this event. The whole crew of the *U-XII* was subsequently awarded the Gold or Silver Medal for Bravery.[30]

Less than a year later, on 8 August 1915, the *U-XII* hit a mine while attempting to gain entry into the heavily guarded harbor of Venice and sank.[31] All seventeen crewmembers died. The Italian Navy had the wreck salvaged and the remains of the entire crew were interred at the San Michele cemetery.

The Construct of the "Submarine Hero"

A cult had been built up around Egon Lerch immediately after the *Jean Bart* was torpedoed but it grew significantly after his "heroic" death. In many ways, he was this ideal subject for this type of hero worship.

Egon Lerch represented the new generation of officers whose rise was connected with the changes that the First World War brought on many different levels. He came from a new branch of service, which was used for the first time during the First World War, took war to a new dimension, and initially carried with it no expectations whatsoever. The use of submarines was only implemented shortly before the war and they, like air force planes, were initially regarded with indifference. Their function as crucial instruments of warfare was not yet acknowledged. It was not until Italy entered the war, which blocked the k.u.k Navy from entering the Mediterranean and limited its sphere of action to the Adriatic, that submarines, working with seaplanes and torpedo boats, began to play a role in combat.[32] Subsequently, the "secondary theater of war" underwater became increasingly important. Lerch's "surprise victory" in torpedoing the *Jean Bart* revealed new possibilities that had clearly not even been considered and were certainly not planned, even though submarines—along with aircraft—were the most modern war machines available, the high-tech weapons of their time, and as in Germany should have represented the means to technological superiority over the enemy. The "masters" of these machines were highly specialized

---

29. *Grazer Tagblatt*, 15 Aug. 1915, 5.
30. Vgl. *Neue Freie Presse*, 15 Aug. 1915, 8.
31. On the loss see *Laibacher Zeitung*, 14 Aug. 1915, 1854 and *Triester Tagblatt*, 14 Aug. 1915, 1.
32. The introduction of this weapon also underlined the changing strategy in naval warfare. The need to send smaller, faster and more maneuverable units into combat increased steadily.

222   Goll: 'Our Weddigen': On the Construction of the War Hero
in the k.u.k. Army.
The 'Naval Hero' Egon Lerch as an Example

soldiers, technically trained and skilled men who came from the ranks of the NCOs, a level that, prior to the First World War, had been of little significance in a war. Now, the changes in combat methods had made the subaltern officer, some of whom came from the (upper) middle class and had worked their way up through the ranks, far more important.

Egon Lerch's "victories" in battle quickly brought him the necessary acclaim within the military. The relatively hasty awarding of decorations and special attention in reports can be seen as signs of "hero worship" within the military world. For torpedoing the *Jean Bart*, "a record achievement that is almost magical,"[33] Lerch received the Knights Cross of the Order of Leopold with War Decoration.[34] Although Lerch's attack had not sunk the enemy battleship, the episode was immediately picked up and exploited for propaganda purposes. One statement claimed that: "The Entente fleet was seized by terror after this spirited deed. Austria's small navy is too dangerous after all. The Adriatic has been avoided since that day. And this must be the most glorious victory of Lerch's heroic deed, to have freed our own beloved sea, the beloved Adriatic, from the enemy [highlighted in the original text—author's note]."[35] The reporting that followed in the media made Lerch famous on the home front as well, but it was his death that ultimately brought the heroic cult built up around him to a peak.

The Death of a "Naval Hero"

The report that the *U-XII* had been lost was published in the media after a delay. The Marburger Zeitung wrote: "Our submarine *XII* has not returned from a battle mission in the Northern Adriatic."[36] On 14 August 1915 the *Neue Freie Presse* reported on the "glorious demise of the *U-XII*" and the "Heroic Death of Linienschiffsleutnant Lerch."[37] Numerous letters of condolence were sent to the officer's family and obituaries were printed

---

33. *Egon Lerch UXII*, ed. Österreichische Flottenverein (Vienna: St. Stefan Wiener Verlagsgesellschaft, 1915), 63.
34. Already shortly after the introduction of submarines Egon Lerch was assigned to this new weapon. He was awarded the medal "Militärverdienstmedaille am roten Bande" for no military achievements, but for the rescue of a person from drowning. *Egon Lerch UXII*, ed. Österreichische Flottenverein (Vienna: St. Stefan Wiener Verlagsgesellschaft, 1915), 53f.
35. *Egon Lerch UXII*, ed. Österreichische Flottenverein (Wien: St. Stefan Wiener Verlagsgesellschaft, 1915), 65.
36. *Marburger Zeitung*, 13 Aug. 1915, 3.
37. *Neue Freie Presse*, 14 Aug. 1915, 2.

in the daily newspapers.[38] In the one year that Lerch served as wartime commander of a submarine, apart from torpedoing a French battleship, which was massively exploited for propaganda purposes, he only chalked up one confirmed sinking. However, after his death he was glorified in the media in a way that has seldom been seen. The reports that were quickly published exhibit all the characteristics of the fabrication of a war hero. This is not surprising, since the k.u.k. Navy, its sphere of action restricted to the Adriatic, needed a victory to relieve the plight it was in as a result of war events. Building up Egon Lerch as a war hero can therefore be seen on the one hand as a strategy to improve morale in the navy, which was suffering due to its limited field of operations in the Adriatic, and on the other hand to relieve the pressure on the fleet. It was essential for the new weapon, which had hardly been tested yet, to be successful in order to silence the voice of criticism. At the same time, by choosing Linienschiffsleutnant Lerch, the new branch of service could be shown to be open to men from all levels of society: a place where any man could become a hero. And the newspapers were actively involved in this construct. Most of the articles about Lerch contained a lively portrayal of his "heroic deed" during his brief period of service, for which Lerch received the necessary military recognition in the form of the Knights Cross of the Order of Leopold with War Decoration and the Iron Cross. Although the collaboration of the whole crew was essential for the performance of a submarine, in the majority of the articles that appeared when the *U-XII* sank the emphasis was on Linienschiffsleutnant Lerch as its commander.[39] The fact that Lerch fell in the line of duty also made him particularly interesting for exploitation as an instrument of propaganda. He had crossed the threshold from the traditional "Führerheld" ("heroic commander")—which he certainly was due to his command of the *U-XII*, and which had, in the course of the First World War, been expanded to include lower grade, non-aristocratic officers—to a "Opferheld" ("heroic victim") who gave his life "for the Fatherland, for our Kaiser"[40] and could thus take his place in the Austro-Hungarian canon of heroes and become "immortal"—at least until the demise of the Empire.

---

38. For example in *Kleinen Zeitung*, 15 Aug. 1915, 2; *Grazer Tagblatt*, 15 Aug. 1915, 5; *Grazer Tagespost* 15 Aug. 1915, 9. The strong media interest in the city of Graz in the crown land Styria was maybe due to the fact that the greater part of Lerch's family was living here.

39. In several articles, as for example in the newspaper *Kleine Zeitung*, also the fate of the 2nd officer, Fregattenleutnant Ernst Zaccaria, and of the crewmembers was covered. Still, they were an exception. See *Kleine Zeitung*, 15 Aug. 1915, 2.

40. *Egon Lerch UXII*, ed. Österreichische Flottenverein (Vienna: St. Stefan Wiener Verlagsgesellschaft, 1915), 79.

224   Goll: 'Our Weddigen': On the Construction of the War Hero
in the k.u.k. Army.
The 'Naval Hero' Egon Lerch as an Example

Another reason for Lerch's use as an instrument was that, with the k.u.k. Monarchy taking its time to come to terms with the implementation of technological innovations, he demonstrated the possibilities inherent in this new weapon. In many ways, Egon Lerch took on a pioneer role, and due to his first-time achievement particular attention was centered on him. He was not only the first to "enter into battle with a powerful enemy fleet" but "was also the first seaman to heroically sacrifice his life for the Fatherland".[41] The *Neue Freie Presse* wrote:

> Lerch was the first, and nowhere is it more important or advantageous to be the first than as a war hero. He gloriously breaks through the darkness of uncertainty, releases the fiercest tension and is singled out for all the glory becoming of a hero. For today he is still the one, the only one, who leaps from obscurity. Tomorrow perhaps there will be more, who will repeat familiar deeds and whose heroism, however great, will always appear to be emulations of his example.[42]

Classic elements were used for the hero construction that now began. Lerch had died a hero's death "in the bloom of youth." In the newspaper articles that were published he was always described as young, even though at the time of his death he was already twenty-nine years old. However, the emphasis on the youth of the "war hero" was designed to appeal to young men in the Austro-Hungarian Empire who were willing to make sacrifices, to encourage them to follow his example, and at the same time to illustrate that the "hero" was one of them. He was used as a shining example of a branch of service that had not yet emerged as a particularly successful element in the war: "Lerch has really provided an example, so wonderful and great, so significant for the future, that it hardly seems possible to the human imagination that it could ever be surpassed."[43]

In descriptions of his appearance, Egon Lerch was also always portrayed as heroic looking. Reports always labeled and described him as good looking; he was "tall, blond, blue-eyed and well-built" and could therefore "serve well as the model for a Viking"[44] and according to the *Neue Post* and the *Grazer Tagespost* he was "the archetypical soldier."[45] The majority of reports described him as blond and blue-eyed. Whether this was true or not, this

---

41. *Neue Freie Presse*, 22 Aug. 1915, 14.
42. *Neue Freie Presse*, 14 Aug. 1915, 2.
43. Ibid.
44. Ibid., 3.
45. Ibid., 2.

description of his "Germanic" appearance linked him with the heroic figure that had already been created in a German context.[46]

Apart from these external advantages, as an "adept naval officer" he combined virtues such as "ruthless daring," "an iron will," and "physical resilience."[47] Egon Lerch was said to be highly skilled, dashing, spirited in the attack, and self-castigating.[48] In addition, he was described as a "dare-devil" who fought the enemy with enthusiasm and risked all to do so—even his life. "When an opportunity arose to take part in a dangerous task, he was right there."[49] All these attributes can be found in earlier construction of heroes. The new element was the use of technology. In this connection, Lerch was portrayed "as if he were one with the submarine."[50] Comparisons with the battle between David and Goliath were also very popular. In this context, Lerch was described as a man with "nerves of steel"[51] who had fought a battle-ship from a "nutshell" and been victorious: "Egon Lerch was the personification of calm. It is wonderful to think that in this day and age there are still people who are not 'nervous.'"[52]

Along with these values and virtues, which were so crucial in wartime, Lerch was also described in newspaper articles as having an impeccable character, being extremely popular. and as a "good buddy" who was already ready to join in any escapades.[53] He was said to have stood out from the crowd before the war already and in one article he was described as a "lifesaver" as he was alleged to have saved a man from drowning.[54]

His description as a "soldier, seaman, and engineer in one" is particularly interesting. In this way, old traditional heroic patterns—those of the naval hero—were combined with new patterns—those of the technological hero—a combination that was typical for the constructed heroes of the German Empire but less so for the Austro-Hungarian Empire, which makes it all the more surprising. In the Habsburg Monarchy, technology only played a secondary role. Austria-Hungary could not be a pioneer in this field because it had neither the financial means nor the political will. Although the idea of progress was present in some parts of the military, its

---

46. Rene Schilling points in this context to a link with the reichs-national War Hero. Schilling, *Kriegshelden*, 258.

47. *Neue Freie Presse*, 14 Aug. 1915, 2.

48. *Egon Lerch UXII*, ed. Österreichische Flottenverein (Vienna: St. Stefan Wiener Verlagsgesellschaft, 1915), 52.

49. *Tagespost*, 15 Aug. 1915, 9.

50. *Egon Lerch UXII*, ed. Österreichische Flottenverein (Vienna: St. Stefan Wiener Verlagsgesellschaft, 1915), 59.

51. Ibid., 93.

52. Ibid., 63 und 93.

53. *Neue Freie Presse*, 14 Aug. 1915, 3.

54. *Neue Freie Presse*, 20 Dec. 1915, 6.

226   Goll: 'Our Weddigen': On the Construction of the War Hero
in the k.u.k. Army.
The 'Naval Hero' Egon Lerch as an Example

leaders still adhered to its old, tried-and-trusted course.

All the newspaper reports used associations to other heroes, in particular the German submarine hero Otto Weddigen.[55] Like Lerch, Weddigen had very quickly illustrated, for both the military and the general public, the deployment possibilities of the new weapon. He was also someone who had "died a hero's death in the line of duty for his Fatherland" and around whom a heroic cult was quickly built up:

> Let us admit it, he was to us what Weddigen was to the Germans, the personification of lighthearted bravery and the height of seamanship, able to look terrible danger in the face with cold calm, he was beloved, like Trapp, Singule and others we know, a hero chosen by the people, because they need him, because they need a representation of the facts they receive, because they like to know who is defending their homeland and on whose brow they may place the laurels.[56]

This association was to make it clear that Lerch's achievement was equal to

---

55. Born in 1882, Weddigen was descendant from a bourgeois family. After a poor school record he decided to pursue a Navy career. At that time the German Navy was seen, as Rene Schilling puts it, as the "armed force of the bourgeoisie" and had won prestige since the 1890s. Joining the Navy appeared to have been very attractive for young bourgeois men who hoped for career opportunities. Weddigen joined the new German submarine fleet in 1908 and was promoted to Kapitänleutnant in 1912. As the commander of the submarine *U-9* he and his crew managed to sink a total of three British battle cruisers in a short period of time on 22 September 1914—an achievement that had seemed impossible until then and dominated the media for days. As a consequence, Weddigen was decorated with the Iron Cross 1st class as well as with the medal Pour le Merite. His "career" as a hero terminated as fast as it had begun: on 18 March 1915 *U-9* was sunk by a British battleship with its ram, killing the entire crew. Rene Schilling, "*Kriegshelden,*" 40-42.

56. *Neue Freie Presse*, 14 Aug. 1915, 2. Rudolf Singule and Georg Ritter von Trapp were among the most successful submarine commanders of the Austro-Hungarian Navy. Singule was born in Pula/Pola in 1883, studied at the Navy Academy in Rijeka/Fiume and subsequently served on various vessels before he was assigned to the submarine fleet in 1909 and was given the command over *U-IV* in 1915. Singule sank 15 merchant vessels and one battle cruiser (for which he was decorated) and damaged several more ships. Georg Ritter von Trapp was born in 1880 in Zara and was offspring of a family of sailors. After his training he was assigned in 1908 to the submarine fleet and two years later took over the command of *U-VI*. During the First World War he was commanding *U-V* and became known for sinking the French battle cruiser "Leon Gambetta" and the Italian submarine "Nereide." Finally he took over the command of a prize, the modified French submarine "Curie." Trapp sank an additional 12 merchant vessels. Both never became as popular as Lerch in the monarchy. Nevertheless, Trapp's military achievements were overlapped by his later career as the head of the famous "Trapp family singers" (*The Sound of Music*). See: Georg Ritter von Trapp, *Bis zum letzten Flaggenschuß, Erinnerungen eines österreichischen U-Boots-Kommandanten*, (Salzburg: Pustet, 1935).

that of Weddigen, but it was also intended to imply that the "victories" of the k.u.k. Navy were also equivalent to those of their German allies. Like Weddigen, Lerch had "proved himself a true hero"[57] because, despite the restrictions put on the Austro-Hungarian Navy due to Italy entering the war, the Neue Presse argued that "All our submarines fought bravely just like the German submarines."[58] This sentiment echoes the underlying feelings of inferiority apparent in the k.u.k Navy in comparison to the German Navy. However, it is an often-overlooked fact that the German Navy was actually in a similar situation to the Austro-Hungarian Navy. It was directly threatened by the maritime power of Great Britain, was in a serious plight, and was in great need of a victory. In a very short time, Weddigen had shown what this new weapon could achieve in a war. It is also interesting to note that in later publications associations were also drawn with the Austro-Hungarian "seaplane hero" Gottfried von Banfield, who at this time also held the status of a "hero." In the so-called "Heldenwerk," created by members of the "Literarische Gruppe" of the war archives, attention was drawn to the fact that Banfield and Lerch had been childhood "friends" since they both grew up in Pola.[59] While Banfield was glorified as a "hero of the skies," by the time of his death at the latest, Lerch had become the first "submarine hero." Connecting the two was intended to consolidate each one's role and status and ensure that some of their "heroism" rubbed off.

Construction and Lobby

Lerch's death provided a new impulse for the heroic construction built up around him. Lerch was the only k.u.k. "war hero" to be worshiped in a similar way to the war heroes of the German Empire, in particular Otto Weddigen, with whom connections were drawn. Unlike, for example, the aviation troops, the navy had a "lobby" behind it, which quickly became actively involved in the hero worship building up around Lerch and was to a certain degree also involved with the seaplane pilot Gottfried von Banfield.[60] The Österreichische Flottenverein, a maritime society founded in 1904 with the idea of promoting seafaring interests, which by 1914 already

---

57. *Kleine Zeitung*, 15 Aug. 1915, 2.
58. *Neue Freie Presse*, 14 Aug. 1915, 2.
59. *Heldenwerk* 1917, 201.
60. It was also intended to build a hero-cult around the person of Gottfried von Banfield, the most successful Austro-Hungarian Navy pilot, which finally was realized with a strong regional bias. His "heroism" was founded mainly upon his fame as "savior" of Trieste. He profited from the background agitation of the Navy-lobby, but at the same time actively contributed to the design of the heroic cult around his person.

228   Goll: 'Our Weddigen': On the Construction of the War Hero
in the k.u.k. Army.
The 'Naval Hero' Egon Lerch as an Example

had more than 44.000 members, formed the basis of this hero worship.[61]
Its members were initially mainly wealthy aristocrats and industrialists but
as the society began to offer more advantages, membership extended to a
broader section of the population.[62] Although commercial matters were its
priority, another goal of the association was to promote the development of a
powerful modern naval fleet. Before the First World War the Flottenverein
had already begun to sell various kinds of merchandise. These were now
expanded and used to raise money for various charitable organizations. A
range of items was produced and sold for donations, the proceeds going
to the navy and naval dependents. Sales of books, badges, brooches,
sealing bands, writing paper, postcards, as well a special uniform and the
publication of a special magazine, were quite lucrative. During the war, the
Österreichische Flottenverein was able to finance one submarine and two
naval aircraft from donations.[63] It was also this society that instrumentalized
Lerch after his death, not only by producing various medallions and badges,
but also by publishing a comprehensive written memorial. This is the only
hero's memorial published about an Austro-Hungarian war hero during the
First World War and it is very reminiscent of those published in Germany.[64]

The "Austrian Wartime Welfare Service" (Österreichische
Kriegsfürsorge) also sold various articles, the proceeds going to a number
of welfare organizations. The items sold included the so-called "Vivat" or
"Vivant" ribbons. These silk ribbons, originally made for specific celebrations,
were already extremely popular before the First World War. Initially made
on private initiative, they were now taken over by the wartime welfare
service. A total of eighty-eight different ribbons were produced by the
official welfare service.[65] Various artists, mainly from the Kriegshilfskomitee
of the fine arts founded in 1914, provided the artwork.[66] One of these Vivat
ribbons was dedicated to the navy, depicting Egon Lerch with his *U XII* in

---

61. Sondhaus, *The Naval Policy of Austria-Hungary*, 194.

62. The Austrian Flottenverein offered inter alia also travels to the Adriatic Sea.

63. On 10 August 1915 the Austrian Flottenverein published an appeal, which was intended
to animate the populace to support the so-called "U-Boot-Spende" (submarine donation)
with the purchase of a submarine badge for the price of two crowns. The newspaper *Neue
Freie Presse* published on August 11, 1916 a sum of 795.679 crowns and 74 hellers, to which
the submarine campaign of the Austrian Flottenverein had amounted until then. *Kleine
Zeitung*, 10 Aug. 1915, 5; *Neue Freie Presse*, 11 Aug. 1916, 10.

64. *Otto Weddigen und seine Waffe. Aus seinen Tagebüchern und nachgelassenen Papieren*,
bearbeitet von Hermann Kirchdorff, (Berlin: 1915); Otto Weddigen, *Unser Seeheld Weddigen.
Sein Leben und seine Taten dem deutschen Volke erzählt*, (Berlin: 1916).

65. Tristan Loidl, *Andenken aus Eiserner Zeit. Patriotische Abzeichen der österreichisch-
ungarischen Monarchie von 1914 bis 1918*, (Vienna: Militaria, 2004), 172-182.

66. Kriegshilfskomitee bildender Künstler Wien 1914 –1916, Tätigkeitsbericht, (Vienna:
1916).

particular.[67]

One pavilion at the 1916 War Exhibition in Vienna, the largest event of its kind in the Austro-Hungarian Empire, which was put on for the purpose of "educating the public, to give them an insight into the way the war is being conducted and show them how the enormous resources need to successfully get through the war are used" and exhibited "a selection of genuine trophies and captured items, which provide eloquent testimony of the many heroic deeds of our Army and their victorious activities"[68] was dedicated to the navy. Here a wooden submarine was set up for "Kriegsbenagelung." The practice of paying donations to hammer nails into an effigy, which had originated in Vienna, became extremely popular during the First World War and was therefore copied in many different cities.[69] The battle submarine at the Viennese War Exhibition was donated by the industrialist Krupp von Bohlen and Halbach "to benefit the widows and orphans of the fallen, with special attention to members of the k.u.k. Navy."[70] By allowing people to hammer various iron and gold nails into the wooden statue, money was raised for charity. The submarine form was unique to this exhibition and illustrates the special importance this weapon had after 1915. Apart from this focus on the submarine, two photographs of Lerch and the *U XII* and a painting from the Österreichische Flottenverein by the naval artist Harry Heusser, entitled *The Heroes of the U 12*, were also exhibited.[71]

Conclusion

In many ways Lerch was a special case. After his first success, "hero machinery" was set in motion, which—unlike that of other heroic figures,

---

67. This is the case with ribbon no. 17 *Vivant die Helden von U 12*, dedicated with "our grateful memory to the marine hero Egon Lerch with his brave crew of *U XII*." Ribbon no. 16 was dedicated to U-5 and Georg Trapp, another one (no.15) to the entire Navy. All three ribbons were designed by Alfred Offner. By comparison, there existed only one Vivant-ribbon dedicated to the flyers (co.64). It was designed by Josef von Diveky. See Tristan Loidl, *Andenken aus Eiserner Zeit*, 186 und 194.
68. *Offizieller Katalog der Kriegsausstellung Wien 1916*, ed. Vom Arbeits-Ausschuss, (Vienna: 1916), 5.
69. So far, no detailed analysis of the number of these "Kriegsnagelungen" in Austria-Hungary was presented. For the German Empire see: Gerhard Schneider, *Zur Mobilisierung der "Heimatfront." Das Nageln sogenannter Kriegswahrzeichen im Ersten Weltkrieg* (MS Bielefeld 1999); Michael Diers, "Nagelmänner. Propaganda mit ephemeren Denkmälern im Ersten Weltkrieg", in *Mo(nu)mente. Formen und Funktionen ephemerer Denkmäler*, ed. Michael Diers (Berlin:Akademie-Verlag, 1993), 113-135.
70. *Offizieller Katalog der Kriegsausstellung Wien 1916*, ed. Vom Arbeits-Ausschuss, (Vienna: 1916), 91.
71. Ibid., 92f.

230   Goll: 'Our Weddigen': On the Construction of the War Hero
in the k.u.k. Army.
The 'Naval Hero' Egon Lerch as an Example

for example the pilots—actually worked. Lerch profited from the lobby standing behind the k.u.k. Navy, which upheld maritime interests and helped to boost the popularity of the navy. "Our Weddigen," as Lerch was called in the title of his memorial, was able, due to his heroic death, to take his place in the canon of heroes of the Austro-Hungarian Empire and "live on forever in the people's memory."[72] The Flottenverein, with his memorial book and numerous articles, forced the construction and heightening of the "naval hero." Lerch was also the only one for whom, after the sinking became public, an appeal for donations was published in the Neue Freie Presse in order to finance a memorial stone.[73] A committee for the erection of the Egon Lerch Memorial was also formed and within a short time had received so many donations that they considered setting up an Egon Lerch Foundation, primarily to support the dependents of the *U XII* crew but to be expanded later to support the families of other submarine crews.[74]

A number of memorial services were held across the territories of the Danube Monarchy.[75] Like Banfield, Lerch came from the navy and was deeply rooted there, not only due to his family history. His career in the navy seemed almost to have been preordained. "This boy could only become a naval officer" it said in his written memorial.[76] Both Lerch and Banfield also had the "home advantage." They were both stationed where they had grown up and fought in the same area. Like the majority of the k.u.k. Navy, they came from the coastal regions of the Habsburg Empire, had built up a good network, and knew the geographical conditions well. They had grown up bilingual and were well anchored in the navy. The location of their activities was crucial to the construction of both heroes and was very instrumental in their popularization. The entrance to the Adriatic had to be held at all costs and Lerch's objective was to prevent the enemy from entering the Adriatic. A contemporary postcard was inscribed: "A naval hero! Never was a more genuine hero crowned with a halo! He will be a shining example to the guardians of the Adriatic."[77] Lerch was subsequently depicted on picture postcards and immortalized as a motif in various welfare articles so that he also became well known on the "home front."

This clearly demonstrates the level at which the construction of this hero

---

72. *Kleine Zeitung*, 15 Aug. 1915, 2.
73. Vgl. *Neue Freie Presse*, 22 Aug. 1915, 14.
74. Vgl. *Neues Wiener Journal*, 6 May 1916, 9.
75. A well-visited commemorative mass was held for the family of the deceased in Graz on 30 August 1915.
76. *Egon Lerch UXII*, ed. Österreichische Flottenverein (Vienna: St. Stefan Wiener Verlagsgesellschaft, 1915), 21.
77. This picture postcard can be found among the sources of the Picture Archive of the Austrian Na-tional Library in Vienna.

was accomplished. The important factors in this case were the appropriate lobby and the regional connection. This formed the necessary perception but did not lead to general veneration throughout the Empire, as it did in the allied German Empire. Attaching the "new hero construction" to the new branches of service and their protagonists did not happen by chance. Germany's example was ever-present to the Austro-Hungarian Empire, and demonstrated capabilities that in mechanized mass warfare would soon become essential. The ideas that were borrowed from the German Empire, the images projected onto the Austro-Hungarian "heroes," are obvious but they did not lead to a comprehensive hero construction because the creator was not the State but rather semi-private institutions and individual regions, for which and in which the "heroes" were to gain importance. In Austria-Hungary, the importance of a comprehensive military hero cult went unrecognized, and with it the opportunities that were certainly represented by the pilot and the submarine commander. If nothing else, this is evidence of how poorly the State was able to adapt to the requirements of modern mass warfare.

Russian spies executed under martial law, ca. 1916, 154.908-B,
Austrian National Library - Picture Archives and Graphics Department, Vienna

The Treatment of Prisoners of War in Austria-Hungary 1914/1915

Verena Moritz[1]

The Historiography of Prisoners of War in the Late Habsburg Empire

Historians have long ignored the treatment of prisoners of war (POWs) in the Danubian Monarchy during World War I.[2] World War I prisoners of war only started to receive some scholarly attention in the 1990s, when POWs in Austria-Hungary became the focus of research.[3] Since then a number of surveys have appeared, mostly addressing the issue in the Austrian half of the Dual Monarchy.[4] The bulk of works on POW

---

1. Günter Bischof translated this essay from German into English.
2. The fate of POWs in Austria-Hungary is the subject matter of a large research project (P 25968-G16 running from 2014 to 2017) funded by the Austria Science Fund (FWF). Verena Moritz is heading this research project and the Austrian State Archives in Vienna is hosting it. The focus of the project will be the treatment of POWs and their work deployments. Some initial results of this research are presented in this essay.
3. Hannes Leidinger, "Gefangenschaft und Heimkehr: Gedanken zu Voraussetzungen und Perspektiven eines neuen Forschungsbereiches," *Zeitgeschichte*, no. 11/12 (1998): 333-342. An example of early research is the collection of essays on WW I by Peter Pastor/Samuel R. Williamson, eds., *POWs Essays on World War I: Origins and Prisoners of War* (Boulder: Social Science Monographs, 1983).
4. Hannes Leidinger/Verena Moritz, "Verwaltete Massen: Kriegsgefangene in der Donaumonarchie 1914-1918," in Jochen Oltmer, ed., *Kriegsgefangene im Europa des Ersten Weltkriegs* (Paderborn: Schöningh, 2006), 35-66. For a broader perspective on the topic, see Verena Moritz/Hannes Leidinger, *Zwischen Nutzen und Bedrohung: Die russischen Kriegsgefangenen in Österreich 1914-1921* (Bonn: Bernard & Graefe, 2005), as well as Julia Walleczek, "Hinter Stacheldraht: Die Kriegsgefangenenlager in den Kronländern Oberösterreich und Salzburg im Ersten Weltkrieg," PhD. diss., Innsbruck University, 2012; see also Peter Hansak, "Das Kriegsgefangenenwesen während des 1. Weltkrieges im Gebiet der heutigen Steiermark," PhD. diss., Graz University, 1991.

treatment during World War I deals with specific prison camps.[5]

During the 1920s and 1930s Austrian military historians almost exclusively concentrated on the history of World War I. They failed to cover important fields of research that did not deal with operational and strategic or technical military issues. Former military officers of the Royal and Imperial (k. u. k.) Army during World War I were mainly interested in drawing a rosy picture of the "merits" of the Army, leaving no room for critical perspectives of the war.[6] In the first decade after World War II a positive image of the Habsburg Monarchy became part of Austrian historical constructions and the formation of Austrian identity.[7] First attempts to initiate a drawn-out public discourse about the responsibility of the Army's leadership were stopped dead in their tracks soon after the end of the war in 1918.[8] Heated debates about the "war guilt question" (*Kriegsschuldfrage*) consumed Germany but hardly touched the small Austria left over from the Habsburg Monarchy.[9] The First Austrian Republic failed to launch a critical discourse on World War I, let alone master these events. So the treatises of the former officers who refused to accept any critique of the "old Army" found no adversaries. This kind of historiography also influenced the

5. A number of dissertations and MA theses deal with the Austrian half of the Habsburg Monarchy, mostly dealing with regional or camp studies. See Stefan Brenner, "Das Kriegsgefangenenlager in Knittelfeld: Eine Untersuchung der Akten des Kriegsarchivs Wien von den ersten Bemühungen Otto Zeilingers zur Errichtung des Lagers Knittelfeld bis zur Umwandlung des Kriegsgefangenenlagers in ein Militärspital," MA thesis, Graz University, 2011; Rudolf Koch, *Das Kriegsgefangenenlager Sigmundsherberg 1915-1919* (Wien: Verband der Wissenschaftlichen Gesellschaften Österreichs, 1981); Ernst Mihalkovits, "Das Kriegsgefangenen- und Interniertenlager des 1. Weltkriegs in Neckenmarkt mittleres Burgenland 1915-1919," PhD. diss., Vienna University, 2003; Petra Rappersberger, "Das Kriegsgefangenenlager Freistadt 1914-18," MA thesis, Vienna University, 1988; Franz Wiesenhofer, *Gefangen unter Habsburgs Krone. K.u.k. Kriegsgefangenenlager im Erlauftal* (Purgstall: F. Wiesenhofer, 1997); Julia Walleczek, "Das Kriegsgefangenenlager Grödig bei Salzburg während des Ersten Weltkriegs," MA thesis, Innsbruck University, 2005.
6. For a useful case study of the memory of World War I in the Tirol region, see Oswald Überegger, *Erinnerungskriege: Der Erste Weltkrieg, Österreich und die Tiroler Kriegserinnerung in der Zwischenkriegszeit* (Innsbruck: Wagner, 2011).
7. Anton Pelinka, "Tabus in der Politik: Zur politischen Funktion von Tabuisierung und Enttabuisierung," in Peter Bettelheim, ed., *Tabu und Geschichte: Zur Kultur des kollektiven Erinnerns* (Wien: Picus, 1994), 21–28.
8. In December 1918 a "Commission for the Recording of Breaches of Duty" (*Kommission zur Erhebung militärischer Pflichtverletzungen*) was started, see Wolfgang Doppelbauer, *Zum Elend noch die Schande: Das altösterreichische Offizierskorps am Beginn der Republik* (Wien: Österreichischer Bundesverlag, 1988); Peter Melichar, "Die Kämpfe merkwürdig Untoter: K.u.k. Offiziere in der Ersten Republik," in *Österreichische Zeitschrift für Geschichtswissenschaften*, no. 1 (1998): 51–84.
9. See Patrick Houlihan, "Was There an Austrian Stab-in-the-Back Myth? Interwar Military Interpretations of Defeat," in Günter Bischof/Fritz Plasser/Peter Berger, eds., *From Empire to Republic: Post-World War I Austria* (*Contemporary Austrian Studies* 19) (New Orleans: UNO, 2010), 67-89.

treatment of the POW issue. POW treatment in the Danubian Monarchy was either entirely glossed over by historians or covered as a trip to paradise.[10] These works stressed the humanitarian treatment of POWs by the k. u. k. military authorities. Since former high officials in the Austrian-Hungarian POW administration were part and parcel in drawing this positive image of POW treatment in the Habsburg Monarchy, these published texts were designed to justify their actions during the war.[11]

The postwar exculpatory treatment of POW handling during the war can best be discerned from assigning POW to activities directly related to the conduct of the war in direct violation of international law. The excuse was that former enemies had done so too. The "principle of reciprocal treatment" was the flimsy excuse for all things related to POWs. All critical charges that the living conditions of all POWs in Austria-Hungary were deteriorating in 1916/17 due to the general crisis in provisioning the civilian population during these years were dismissed to the outside world as "enemy propaganda." In their interior, communications officials were quite aware of these charges levied by not only POWs themselves, but also by both members of neutral welfare commissions and k. u. k. Army officers inspecting the POW camps. In the writing of the history of the POW treatment these internal critiques were simply glossed over. On top of this, those responsible for POWs in the wartime military administration looked down condescendingly on POWs "from the East." From their elevated perch of "cultural" superiority, they perceived these Slavic soldiers as "rough and uneducated." Additionally, they also engaged in a "discourse on personal hygiene." In particular, Slavic and Italian POWs were reputed to be unclean and disorderly. From their "German (-Austrian) perspective, the principal figures in the Austrian-Hungarian POW administration thus redefined their job as a chance to improve the lot of these men from "an

---

10. The "Federal Association of Former Austrian Prisoners of War" (*Bundesvereinigung ehemaliger österreichischer Kriegsgefangener*) promoted a positive image of the POW experience, especially the experience of k. u. k. soldiers in Russian captivity, in contrast to the imprisonment on the home front in Austria-Hungary. The important work in this respect is Hans Weiland/Leopold Kern, eds., *In Feindeshand: Die Gefangenschaft im Weltkriege in Einzeldarstellungen*, 2 vol. (Wien: Bundesvereinigung der ehemaligen österreichischen Kriegsgefangenen, 1931); for a history of Federal Association of Former Austrian Prisoners of War, see Hannes Leidinger/Verena Moritz, eds., *In russischer Gefangenschaft: Erlebnisse österreichischer Soldaten im Ersten Weltkrieg* (Vienna: Böhlau, 2008), 30-35.
11. Ernst Streeruwitz, who later became Austrian chancellor, as well as Heinrich Raabl-Werner contributed texts for the 2-volume *In Feindeshand*. Both had been leading administrators in the Tenth Department in the War Ministry in Vienna, responsible for POW Affairs, and thus shaped the entire Austrian-Hungarian POW treatment. Maximilian Ronge, the wartime intelligence chief of the Imperial and Royal Army, also contributed to this publication in his new postwar role as second in command of the new Office of POW and Civil Internees.

East without culture."[12]

Between the wars, imprisonment in Austria-Hungary was often contrasted with POW treatment in Russia, which was considered particularly rough and inhumane. It was indeed the case that mortality rates were much higher among POWs in Russia when compared with the Central Powers.[13] In the course of World War I a few hundred thousand k. u. k. soldiers ended up in Russian captivity. Numerous reports about their treatment circulated during the war. After the war many former POWs wrote down their experiences in factual accounts (*Tatsachenberichte*), as well as memoirs and novels for a broader audience. These negative comparisons with Russian POW treatment seemingly were seen as evidence of the correct handling of POWs by Austria-Hungary. Conversely, few POWs in Habsburg camps penned memoirs about their experience in Austrian-Hungarian captivity after the war. Moreover, the bulk of prisoners in Austrian-Hungarian camps were men from the Russian Empire captured on the Eastern front. In many cases the "October Revolution" and postwar events quickly crowded out their memories of the war.[14] In Italy and other countries, prisoners of war were often seen not as "victims" of the war, but rather as "traitors to the fatherland."[15] Under the pall of such views, men showed little interest after the war in recording their experiences in Austrian-Hungarian captivity. No counter narratives were written to challenge the tales of the former officers in the Imperial and Royal Army regarding the living conditions of enemy POWs in Austrian-Hungarian custody during the war.

---

12. The newspaper of the POW camp in Reichenberg/Liberec (Bohemia) wrote in this vein: "The prisoners learn here what they never saw at home. They will carry a light to the East – into their homeland lacking any culture. Thus these 'legions of useless devourers of food' may become one day a blessing in the distant understanding among peoples." (*Die Gefangenen lernen bei uns, was sie zuhause nie gesehen haben. Sie werden ein Licht nach dem Osten tragen in ihre kulturarme Heimat und so werden die 'Legionen unbequemer Fresser' vielleicht noch zu einem großen Segen für das fernere Verstehen der Völker werden [...]*), see *Reichenberger Kriegsgefangenen-Lagerzeitung* (Doppelheft März-April 1916), 18.

13. On POW treatment in Russia during World War I, see Hannes Leidinger/Verena Moritz, *Gefangenschaft, Revolution, Heimkehr: Die Bedeutung der Kriegsgefangenenproblematik für die Geschichte des Kommunismus in Mittel- und Osteuropa 1917–1920* (Vienna: Böhlau, 2003); Alon Rachamimov, *POWS and the Great War: Captivity on the Eastern Front* (Oxford: Berg, 2002); see also Georg Wurzer, *Die Kriegsgefangenen der Mittelmächte in Russland im Ersten Weltkrieg* (Göttingen: V&R unipress, 2005), and Reinhard Nachtigal, *Russland und seine österreichisch-ungarischen Kriegsgefangenen 1914-1918* (Remshalden: Greiner, 2003).

14. On this issue, see Verena Moritz, "Zwischen allen Fronten: Die russischen Kriegsgefangenen in Österreich im Spannungsfeld von Nutzen und Bedrohung (1914-1921)," PhD. diss., Vienna University, 2001, 325-335.

15. On the issue of Italian views of their soldiers in enemy captivity, see Alan Kramer, "Italienische Kriegsgefangene im Ersten Weltkrieg," in Hermann J. W. Kuprian, ed., *Der Erste Weltkrieg im Alpenraum: Erfahrung, Deutung, Erinnerung* (Innsbruck: Wagner, 2006), 247-258.

Housing the POWs

During the course of the war some fifty large POW camps sprung up in the hinterland of the Habsburg Empire. As a rule, these camps were designed for a few thousand POWs. But given the growing numbers of men being cooped up, they were expanded in the first two years of war. During peak times these POW camps were crowded with many more men than the camps were originally planned for. Take the camp in Knittelfeld, Styria as a case study. By mid-December 1914 the camp's population swelled from 600 to 19.000 POWs in a matter of eleven days.[16]

Apart from these camps in the Monarchy's hinterland, so-called "prisoner of war stations" were put into place close to the front lines, open field enclosures[17] designed to be reception centers for soldiers just taken prisoners. The number of these POW stations differed according to the changing front lines of the war. The number of camps in the hinterland kept changing too. New ones were added as needed or were closed after a while like the POW camp in Oświęcim (Auschwitz). According to the regulations of the 1907 Hague Convention on land warfare, officers received privileged treatment and were separated from common soldiers. They were concentrated in "officer stations" and kept in separate "officer sections" in the big camps next to the regular barracks. During the initial months of the war, officers were even housed in hotels and private tourist quarters.[18]

Prisoner Numbers and Problems of Administration

The significance of the POW topic can be discerned from the sheer mass of prisoners captured by the k. u. k. troops. The total numbers given by World War I POW administrators and later scholars, however, differ widely. While k. u. k. military offices talked of some 1.3 million POWs they registered, later estimates arrived at between 1.86 million and 2.3 million POWs in captivity in the Habsburg Monarchy in the course of World War

16. Moritz, *Zwischen allen Fronten*, 79.
17. Little information exists about these "prisoner of war stations"— some of them may have been open field enclosures like the controversial "Rhine Meadow Camps" at the end of World War II. A the end of World War II half a million of German POWs were cooped up by the U.S. Army close to the front lines; enclosed by barbed wire fences under open skies, these POWs were without shelter, food and water, see Günter Bischof/Stephen E. Ambrose, eds., *Facts against Falsehood: Eisenhower and the German P.O.W.'s.* (Baton Rouge: Louisiana State University Press, 1992); Rüdiger Overmans, "'Ein untergeordneter Beitrag im Leidensbuch der jüngeren Geschichte'? Die Rheinwiesenlager 1945," in Günter Bischof/ Rüdiger Overmans, eds., *Kriegsgefangenschaft im Zweiten Weltkrieg: Ein vergleichende Perspektive* (Ternitz-Pottschach: Verlag Gerhard Höller, 1999), 233-264.
18. Moritz, *Zwischen allen Fronten*, 66-78.

I.[19] These vast discrepancies most likely are both the result of the registration procedures of enemy soldiers and the tendency to manipulate the number of POWs who died in captivity. All official figures of mortality rates among POWs need to be questioned.[20]

Until 1916/1917 the entire complex of POW affairs in the Habsburg Monarchy were handled by the 10th Department of POWs.[21] Late in the war the k. u. k. Army High Command, commands in the rear as well as the new chief of the reserves army designated by Emperor Karl, all took away competencies from the War Ministry.[22] This produced serious consequences in the registration of POWs. Starting in August 1914, the information office for POWs of the "Joint Central Evidence Bureau" of the Austrian and Hungarian Red Cross estimated in April 1916 that 160,000 enemy prisoners had not been properly registered in the previous two years due to the deficiencies in "POW Registration Affairs." In spite of attempts to harmonize the registration process, these deficiencies could not be entirely corrected in 1917/1918. Many enemy prisoners of war were kept by the army behind front lines and forced to do various jobs; as a result they never showed up in any central registration. Even those bureaus determined to register the POWs taken according to the rules were not capable of reporting reliable data. Due to the fluctuation of POW numbers in the POW stations behind front lines, the numbers of registered enemy soldiers from the Entente-powers remained incomplete at all times. The very broad deployment of POWs for work duty made the entire effort to maintain control of prisoner numbers even more complicated. In the course of 1915 the POWs kept in "internee stations" in the hinterland were increasingly assigned both to sites for military production and private employers. The "labor offices" (*Arbeitsämter*) of the various crown lands were designated to supervise the POWs to keep track of the available enemy soldiers inside and outside of the camps.

K. u. k. prisoner affairs thus were increasingly fragmented and the comprehensive work deployments of enemy soldiers made the supervision of POW treatment difficult if not impossible. Inspection tours both by representatives of protection powers such as the Red Cross and the k. u. k. Army only covered a small number of POWs. Those enemy soldiers laboring

---

19. *Österreich–Ungarns letzter Krieg 1914–1918*, vol. VII: *Das Kriegsjahr 1918* (Vienna: Government Printing Office, 1938), 45; *In Feindeshand*, vol. 2, 214.

20. Moritz/Leidinger, *Zwischen Nutzen und Bedrohung*, 193-195.

21. Ernst von Streeruwitz, "Kriegsgefangene im Weltkrieg," unpublished manuscript, 6 volumes, here I, 67f.

22. See Rudolf Hecht, "Fragen zur Heeresergänzung der gesammten bewaffneten Macht Österreich-Ungarns während des Ersten Weltkrieges," PhD diss. University of Vienna 1969, 437.

for the "Army in the field" were at the mercy of the local commanders.

The overwhelming majority of enemy POWs captured were Czarist Army soldiers. The most reliable figures we have mention 1.269.000 Russians, 369.000 Italians, more than 150.000 Serbs, and 50.000 Rumanians in captivity on the territory of the Habsburg Monarchy. Prisoner numbers from Montenegro, Albania, France, and the United States were comparatively small.[23]

For k. u. k. military authorities the national background of POWs determined their treatment. A number of propaganda activities initiated during the first months after the war's beginning serve as proof of this. Ukrainian and Polish POWs from the Czarist army received preferred treatment compared to the rest of the POWs. This was a means to incite them against Czarist Russia. Their privileged position was made apparent by their access to better housing, food rations, as well as better educational offerings and leisure time activities in the camps. Yet such privileged treatment of enemy POWs did not last very long as a scarcity of resources prevented their further training in propaganda activities to fight eventually on the side of the Central Powers. In addition, political concerns seemed to make such propaganda activities questionable. As a case in point, the propaganda campaigns targeting the Ukrainians produced few results. The k. u. k. Foreign Ministry thought to inspire in them "a separate national consciousness" (*Bewusstsein der nationalen Sonderart*) as well as a "racial difference" (*Rassengegensatz*)[24] between "*Kleinrussen*" and "*Grossrussen*."[25] When it came to nationalism, Austria-Hungary, the fragile multinational empire, could hardly serve as a good mentor. The propaganda directed at the

---

23. Franz Scheidl, *Die Kriegsgefangenschaft von den ältesten Zeiten bis zur Gegenwart* (Berlin: Ebering, 1943), 97. Scheidl was an Austrian National Socialist who denied the Holocaust after 1945. Given his ideological inclinations, his prisoner numbers and POW mortality rates may not be so reliable either.

24. The racial-anthropological studies of the medical doctor and anthropologist Rudolf Pöch in the POW camps of the Habsburg Monarchy need to be mentioned here, see Andrea Gschwendtner, "Als Anthropologe im Kriegsgefangenlager – Rudolf Pöchs Filmaufnahmen im Jahre 1915," in *Wissenschaftlicher Film*, no. 42 (April 1991): 105–118, and Maureen Healy, *Vienna and the Fall of the Habsburg Empire. Total War and Everyday Life in World War I* (Cambridge: Cambridge Univ. Press, 2004), 112-113.

25. Moritz, *Zwischen allen Fronten*, 125-141; concerning the Ukrainians, see Rappersberger, *Das Kriegsgefangenenlager Freistadt*; Elisabeth Olentchouk, "Die Ukrainer in der Wiener Politik und Publizistik 1914–1918: Ein Beitrag zur Geschichte der österreichischen Ukrainer (Ruthenen) aus den letzten Jahren der österreichisch-ungarischen Monarchie," PhD. diss., Vienna University, 1998; Wolfdieter Bihl, "Einige Aspekte der österreichisch-ungarischen Ruthenenpolitik 1914–1918," in *Jahrbücher für Osteuropäische Geschichte*, 14 (1966), 539–550; Wolfdieter Bihl, "Das im Herbst 1914 geplante Schwarzmeer-Unternehmen der Mittelmächte," in *Jahrbücher für Osteuropäische Geschichte*, 14 (1966), 362–366; Wolfdieter Bihl, "Österreich-Ungarn und der Bund zur Befreiung der Ukraine," in *Österreich und Europa: Festgabe für Hugo Hantsch* (Graz: Styria, 1965), 505–526.

Muslim POWs of the Czarist army showed even fewer results.

Excessive Demands on the Military Authorities

The military authorities of the Habsburg Empire did not expect to have to deal with a few hundred thousand POWs in the course of the war. Expectations were also similar among the other warring nations. Nobody expected to have to house and take care of so many people over a period of a few years.[26] Given the lack of facilities to house and take care of prisoners during the opening months of the war, the situation in the POW camps was nothing short of catastrophic. Sanitary facilities were missing in most camps, which only aggravated the situation. The authorities had not been prepared to accommodate such a mass of humanity. These conditions left plenty of opportunity for infectious diseases to spread quickly.[27]

In 1914/15 the worst reports came from the POW camps in Knittelfeld (Styria), Kleinmünchen (Upper Austria) and Boldogasszony (Hungary), as well as the internee-and-refugee camps in Thalerhof/Graz (Styria) and Nezsider (Hungary). Conditions in the POW camp in Marchtrenk (Upper Austria) were a cause for concern too; typhus was spreading there. Conditions also were dire in the Mauthausen camp in Upper Austria, where 14.000 prisoners were penned up, most of them Serbs. Within a few months thousands of men died in Mauthausen. A spring 1915 report from a k. u. k. inspection officer noted that 5.600 POWs were buried in the camp cemetery. But there are other reports mentioning even more deaths.[28] As a consequence of the epidemics in Mauthausen, the majority of barracks were incinerated after the first winter of the war. The surviving barracks were disinfected and new ones added.[29] After Italy's declaration of war against the Habsburg Monarchy in the summer of 1915, Mauthausen became a camp for Italian POWs.[30]

The mass death of Serbs in Mauthausen is a classic example for the inability of the Habsburg authorities to house and take care of enemy soldiers. Nobody has yet investigated in detail whether the perishing of

26. Taking care of hundreds of thousands of refugees came with the same problems, see Walter Mentzel, "Kriegserfahrungen von Flüchtlingen aus dem Nordosten der Monarchie während des Ersten Weltkrieges," in Bernhard Bachinger/Wolfram Dornik, eds., *Jenseits des Schützengrabens: Der Erste Weltkrieg im Osten: Erfahrung – Wahrnehmung - Kontext* (Innsbruck: Studienverlag, 2013), 359-390.
27. Robert Mateja, "Oberösterreich im 1. Weltkrieg 1914–1918," PhD. diss. Linz University, 1948, 227.
28. Leidinger/Moritz, *Verwaltete Massen*, 35-36.
29. Mateja, *Oberösterreich im 1. Weltkrieg*, 227.
30. In December 1915, 267 Italian officers and 8.061 Italian soldiers were kept in Mauthausen camp, as well as 1.945 Serbs and 46 Russians.

Serbian POWs in Mauthausen might also have rested on a conscious decision by authorities *not* to contain the epidemics in the camp. This thought is not so far-fetched for at the same time k. u. k. military authorities were confronted with reports of miserable treatment of Habsburg soldiers in Serbian captivity.[31] In this context one might also ask whether officers on the front failed to remind their soldiers to treat captured enemy soldiers decently.[32]

While a spirit of vengeance among k. u. k. military authorities may have been possible, it is more likely that logistical challenges explain the abuse of POWs. The transport of captured enemy soldiers from the frontlines to the rear areas was chaotic during the first months of the war.[33] Many of these men, crowded for days on end into cattle cars bursting at the seams, already carried viruses and/or pathogens. Frequent deaths accompanied these POW transports to rear areas. No sanitary measures were undertaken during the beginning months of the war. Few doctors were available for medical treatment in the POW camps once prisoners arrived. Most of the available doctors served on the frontlines of the war or in the rear echelon areas of the military districts.[34]

To their credit, in the camps in the hinterland responsible military authorities tried to improve camp conditions. They improved hygiene and sanitary conditions and also sped up the building of proper camp facilities. They tried to prevent an overcrowding of barracks, built shower and washing facilities, initiated steam disinfection programs, and built "isolation barracks" for infected POWs. New detailed rules were issued on improvement of sanitary conditions. POWs were to be "energetically deloused" upon arrival in camps. Camp personnel was ordered to "pay very special attention towards scrupulously enforcing cleanliness."[35]

In the spirit of humane accommodation of prisoners of war some planners, for a brief while, also went overboard in mapping out "ideal" camp conditions for prisoners. Luxurious new camp complexes were also built

31. Alan Kramer, *Dynamic of destruction: culture and mass killing in the First World War* (Oxford: Oxford Univ. Press, 2007), 67.
32. Brian K. Feltman has looked at such treatment of German soldiers, see "Tolerance As a Crime? The British Treatment of German Prisoners of War on the Western Front, 1914-1918," in *War in History*, no. 17 (2010), 435-458.
33. Elisabeth Dietrich,"Der andere Tod: Seuchen, Volkskrankheiten und Gesundheitswesen im Ersten Weltkrieg," in Klaus Eisterer/Rolf Steininger, eds., *Tirol und der Erste Weltkrieg* (Innsbruck: Studienverlag, 1995), 255–275, 256–258.
34. Manfried Rauchensteiner, *Der Tod des Doppeladlers: Österreich-Ungarn und der Erste Weltkrieg* (Graz: Styria, 1993), 140.
35. Emerich Bjelik,"Das Los der Kriegsgefangenen in Österreich-Ungarn,"in *Österreichisch-ungarische Kriegskorrespondenz*, no. 100 (1917) 3–4; Wiesenhofer, *Gefangen unter Habsburgs Krone*, 177–180.

with the idea to utilize them after the end of the war. It defies imagination that the War Ministry approved the application of the Knittelfeld camp commander to build an enclosed and heated indoor swimming pool. The costs for this indoor pool amounted to 100.000 crowns, which made this camp one of the most expensive ones built in Austria/Hungary.[36] The building set aside for the camp command in Wieselburg also was top notch. The Army administration was proud of these "tidy barracks" (*schmucken Barackenlager*) and noted that "large segments" of the Monarchy's own population lived in more constricted and much worse living conditions than the enemy prisoners.[37] In Kleinmünchen a fountain graced the park-like camp. The seemingly lavish layout of the camp also impressed neutral foreign visitors who came for inspection tours.[38]

The Habsburg Monarchy's military bureaucracy thus responded to the initial chaos in POW affairs with a series of new instructions and orders. In 1915 these new directives were all included in the official primer "*Dienstbuch* J-35." All directives were printed in more than 200 pages of guidance for the k. u. k. prisoner of war camps, with distinctions between officers and regular soldiers. Nothing was left to chance any longer. If in the first months of the war the War Ministry had lost control of POW affairs, now it insisted on total control. The directives were quite fastidious in listing point by point the guarding of enemy soldiers, the detailed standardization of food rations and the correct cleaning of chimneys in the POW barracks. In 1916 and the following years further ordinances were issued. Together all these rules became known as "the blue POW-book", which served as the basis for the entire complex of k. u. k. POW affairs. Yet this flood of schematized POW directives left those executing them quite skeptical. The adjutant of the Josefstadt camp commander in Bohemia felt that many of these detailed directives were impracticable. These directives amounted to the "locking away" of masses of POWs. This "camp reality" by 1915 had become incompatible with the "reality of war." This "reality of war" increasingly dissolved the strict borders between the home front and the fighting fronts. The worsening reality of the war came to define the fate of the POWs in the Habsburg Monarchy.[39]

Some camps tried to simulate "normal life" outside the camps by setting up bakeries and coffee houses and offering prisoners libraries and movie

36. Hansak, *Das Kriegsgefangenenwesen während des I. Weltkrieges*, 91.
37. Bjelik, *Das Los der Kriegsgefangenen*, 3.
38. Thorsten Wennerström, "Besuch von Kriegsgefangenenlagern in Österreich-Ungarn," in *In Feindeshand*, vol. 2, 214–224.
39. Verena Moritz/Hannes Leidinger, "Aspekte des 'Totalen Lagers' als 'Totale Institution'" - Kriegsgefangenschaft in der Donaumonarchie 1914-1915, in Wiener Zeitschrift zur Geschichte der Neuzeit, no. 1 (2008), 86-101.

houses. Yet these "tidy worlds" behind barbed wire left few lasting impressions among the POWs. More and more enemy soldiers were drafted for work duty in the back areas of the front lines and the Monarchy's hinterland. The camp barracks thus became increasingly empty. The POW experience as life behind barbed wire in camps only defined the years 1914/15. In the later years of the war prisoners were only kept in the camp enclosures during the winter months, or in case of ill or wounded and disabled. Only the small minority of enemy soldiers that were instructed in propaganda activities remained in the camps.

Prisoners of War on Work Details

In the second half of 1915 on an average only 30 to 40 percent of enemy prisoners were stationed in camps. The reasons were quite obvious. In the early months of the war the number of unemployed people rose rapidly in the Habsburg Monarchy. As soon as the spring of 1915 this trend reversed. Most branches of industry suffered scarcities of labor. The war economy soon boomed in many branches – the initial economic downturn was replaced by an accelerating upswing.[40] Hundreds of thousands of workers being drafted into the armed forces soon were missing as workers in the economy. In 1916, 4.9 million men had been drafted and armed. In the Hungarian half of the empire a whopping two-thirds of the male work force was missing in the factories and fields.[41] In 1915 the Habsburg authorities were forced to respond to these drastic labor shortages. The Army High Command stressed vis-à-vis the War Ministry that prisoners of war and refugees "can and must provide the equivalent of their labor in return for their provisioning at public expense."[42]

In February 1915 the k. u. k. Minister of Public Works organized a conference in Vienna "concerning the employment of prisoners of war." Representatives of the Ministries of Agriculture and Railroads and the Ministry of Public Works agreed on a work plan. Enemy soldiers were to be deployed in a number of ambitious projects such as in coal mining and in the running of railroads.

The War Ministry initially prohibited the use of POW workers in territories with majority Slavic populations. Apparently the authorities

40. Robert J. Wegs, *Die österreichische Kriegswirtschaft 1914–1918* (Wien: Schendl, 1979), 53.

41. Ivan Berend/György Ránki, "Ungarns wirtschaftliche Entwicklung," in Adam Wandruszka/Peter Urbanitsch, eds., *Die Habsburgermonarchie 1848–1918*, vol. 1: *Die wirtschaftliche Entwicklung* (Wien: Österreichische Akademie der Wissenschaften, 1973), 462–527, 522.

42. Cited in Moritz, *Zwischen allen Fronten*, 107.

were afraid of Russian POWs "fraternizing" with Slavic people. Yet as the work shortages became more drastic, the War Ministry slowly eased these restrictions. Thus the Army High Command and the War Ministry permitted the unencumbered utilization of POWs in "purely Polish" territories such as Western Galicia as early as spring 1915. Apparently the authorities were confident that the Polish and Ukrainian native population there would not be "Russophile." A tinge of mistrust remained though and the surveillance of the relationship between locals and enemy POWs continued to prevent "fraternizations."[43]

POWs meanwhile were deployed in all kinds of different jobs. For one, there was a very controversial debate on the highest level about the distribution of the POWs in the Austrian and Hungarian halves of the Dual Monarchy. Particularly the k. u. k. and the Hungarian Agricultural Ministries clashed. The Austrian side felt that the Hungarian side demanded too many POWs to be assigned to agricultural labor.[44]

Meanwhile the crisis created by the lack of provisions for the home front, the soldiers in the field, as well as the POWs and refugees became so severe that it had consequences with the entente prisoners. Military authorities guessed that the increase in POW escapees from the enclosures of "the army in the field" was related to the growing scarcity of food among its own military personnel. Yet an increase in the rations for POWs totally exhausted from the drudgery of hard physical labor and severe nutritional deficiencies was out of the question. The command of the 11th Army suggested alternatively to refrain from "the uninterrupted work deployment" of POWs, or at least to grant them longer breaks in their work schedules. Numerous POWs perished as a result of their work deployments on the front or rear areas. Contrary to the rules and regulations of the Hague Conventions the POWs were bunched into labor-companies and deployed in "road-building and earth works behind the frontlines"; they also toiled as carriers of heavy loads and in mine-sweeping duties, as well as in special "work details cleaning battlefields." Hundreds of POWs perished as a result of avalanches and other "work accidents" and many thousands due to exhaustion and starvation.[45] The actual number of deaths can only be estimated. For the k. u. k. Interior and War Ministries agreed as early as fall 1915 that both cases of disease and deaths among Army personnel and POWs in the areas where war raged should not be divulged in any public news bulletins. After the end of the war, the "Ministry in Charge of Liquidating the War" was no longer capable of arriving at any precise

43. On this and work details, see ibid., 100-125.
44. Hecht, *Fragen zur Heeresergänzung*, 276.
45. Moritz, *Zwischen allen Fronten*, 100-125.

figures of enemy POWs that had died in the Austro-Hungarian captivity.[46]

Conclusion and Prospective Scholarship

After the mass deaths of POWs induced by epidemics in half-finished camps in 1914/15, k. u. k. POW Affairs constructed a camp system in the hinterland of the Monarchy designed to offer proper treatment of enemy soldiers. The Habsburg authorities tried to abide by the Hague Conventions on POW treatment during the latter parts of the war. Only months after the beginning of the war, however, requirements of international law and the actual treatment of POWs began to drift apart both in housing and provisioning the enemy soldiers. In the course of mass labor deployments of POWs, k. u. k. POW affairs began to fall apart. It became impossible to adhere to the growing body of rules and directives in maintaining control over POWs.

Only further research into the extant materials of the Austrian State Archives will explain how the authorities dealing with POW affairs in the War Ministry confronted the erosion of directives protecting enemy prisoners in Habsburg captivity. POW scholarship has hardly even tackled the complex life circumstances of those prisoners kept in temporary enclosures close to the frontlines. Unlike the POWs kept in the permanent camps in the hinterland, these prisoners were not subject to controls through the protecting powers or even inspections by the k. u. k. Army. All retrospective assessments about the treatment of enemy POWs in the Dual Monarchy by k. u. k. officers usually excused maltreatment with the basic rule of "reciprocity" ("I treated your POWs like you treated ours") in order to dismiss all deficiencies and grievances that might have occurred during the war.

Future research will have to determine whether the k. u. k. officer corps was guided in its treatment of enemy prisoners by deeply entrenched ideas of Social Darwinism and condescending views of superiority vis-à-vis Slavic POWs. Did preconceived "enemy images" of Serbs prior to the war determine the treatment of captured Serb soldiers during the war? The same questions need to be asked about the treatment of Russian POWs, especially since the public perception of Russia changed in the course of the war due to its specific development (two Revolutions in 1917).[47] The

---

46. Leidinger/Moritz, *Verwaltete Massen*, 53-54.
47. On the question of the composition and state of mind of the k. u. k. officer corps during World War I, see some tentative answers in Verena Moritz/Hannes Leidinger, "Eine Nachbetrachtung," in Wolfram Dornik, *Des Kaisers Falke: Wirken und Nach-Wirken von Franz Conrad von Hötzendorf* (Innsbruck: Studienverlag, 2013), 201-222.

question of whether the dynamics of a worsening scarcity of resources during 1916/17 led to the deterioration in the treatment of enemy prisoners of war both by the military authorities and the civilian population in the hinterland that got into close contact with POWs is also one that needs to be addressed.

The scholarly assessments of the treatment of prisoners of war during World War I differ widely. Richard Speed, for one, argues that in spite of the descent into total war the treatment of POWs was not brutalized in the course of the war.[48] Other scholars have stressed continuities between the treatment of POWs from World War I to World War II[49], even though the absence of intentional systematic killing of POWs during World War I has not been ignored.[50] Some see continuities with the 19th century in POW treatment, others the nexus with later radicalization of POW abuse. Depending on what questions scholars pose about the treatment of enemy soldiers during World War I, they see both continuities and breaks with previous and later military conflicts.[51] We are still in the middle of sorting out discourses related both to general developments in POW treatment and individual case studies. In addition, we have not yet arrived at a consensus about the policies individual warring powers applied towards POW treatment. The dynamics of the conflict have not produced a homogeneity of perspectives but rather a multitude of "First World Wars."[52] Only further research will tell where the Habsburg Monarchy and its "POW policies" will fit into these larger contexts.

---

48. Richard B. Speed, *Prisoners, Diplomats and the Great War: A Study in the Diplomacy of Captivity* (New York: Praeger, 1990,) 65.

49. On the treatment of German POWs during World War II, see the magisterial survey by Rüdiger Overmans, "Das Schicksal der deutschen Kriegsgefangenen des Zweiten Weltkrieges," in Rolf-Dieter Müller, ed., *Das Deutsche Reich und der Zweite Weltkrieg*, vol. 10/II: *Der Zusammenbruch des Deutschen Reiches/Die Folgen des Zweiten Weltkrieges* (Munich: DVA, 2008), 379-507 (on continuities with World War I, see 379-382).

50. Representative of such scholarship are Uta Hinz, *Gefangen im Großen Krieg: Kriegsgefangenschaft in Deutschland 1914–1921* (Essen: Klartext, 2006), 20–22; Reinhard Nachtigal, *Kriegsgefangenschaft an der Ostfront 1914 bis 1918: Literaturbericht zu einem neuen Forschungsfeld* (Frankfurt/Main: Lang, 2005), 136–138; Wurzer, *Die Kriegsgefangenen der Mittelmächte*, 30–33.

51. Particularly useful in this regard is Heather Jones, "A Missing Paradigm? Military Captivity and the Prisoner of War, 1914-1918," in Matthew Stibbe, ed., *Captivity, Forced Labour and Forced Migration in Europe during the First World War* (London, New York: Routledge, 2009), 19-48.

52. Heather Jones/Jennifer O'Brien/Christoph Schmidt-Supprian, Introduction: "Untold War," in idem, eds, *Untold War: New Perspectives in First World War Studies* (Leiden: Brill, 2008), 1–20.

Gathering War:
The Collection Effort by the Imperial Court Library in Vienna during World War I

Hans Petschar[1]

On August 4, 1914, *Hofrat* (Court Councillor) Josef Ritter von Karabaček, the director of the Imperial Court Library k. k. (*Kaiserlich Königliche* [Imperial Royal] *Hofbibliothek*)[2], corrected the draft of a handwritten missive to the Imperial Royal Court and State Printing Office (*k.k. Hof- und Staatsdruckerei*), filing the record in the state bureaucracy. On the same day Austria-Hungary also began the general mobilization of its Army and the first troops deployed under lively participation of the population with "flags, flowers, and brass bands."[3] Othmar Doublier, responsible for the division of Legal and State Affairs, as well as of the Scandinavian and Dutch Languages and Literatures section, had drafted the Director's letter:

---

1. Günter Bischof has translated this essay from German into English.
2. The Imperial Court Library in Vienna was the predecessor of the Austrian National Library until the collapse of the Habsburg Monarchy in 1918. After the *Ausgleich* of 1867, the prefix k. k. was used for all imperial institutions in the Austrian part of the Monarchy, while the prefix k. u. k. (Imperial and Royal) was reserved for the common institutions in the Austrian and Hungarian parts of the Monarchy. (eg. the *k. u. k. Armee*).
3. Manfried Rauchensteiner, *Der Erste Weltkrieg und das Ende der Habsburgermonarchie 1914 – 1918* (Vienna: Böhlau, 2013), 172f. On Friday, 31 July 1914 and Saturday 1 August, the posters announcing the general mobilization were put up. 4 August was the first day of mobilization of troops (ibid., 149, 171).

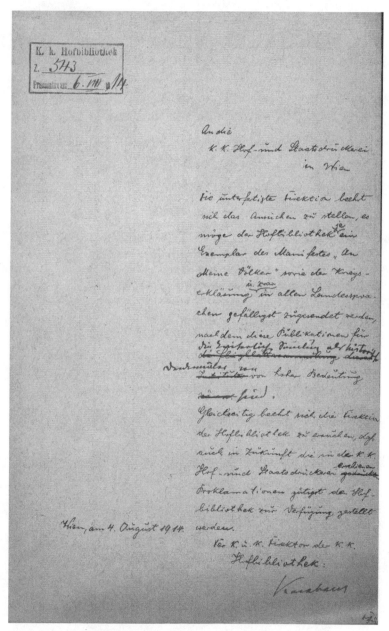

Requesting from the k.k. Court- and State Printers the delivery of the proclamation "To My Peoples," Aug. 4, 1914 HB 543/1914,
Austrian National Library – Picture Archives and Graphics Department, Vienna

To the Imperial and Royal Court and State Printing Office:

The Director's Office has the honor to request that the Court Library receive copies of the [emperor's] manifest "An Meine Völker" as well as a declaration of war issued in all [the empire's] languages. These publications are of the greatest importance to the poster collection of this institution. At the same time the Director of the Court Library kindly requests that in the future all proclamations published by the Imperial and Royal Court and State Printing Office be made available to the Court Library.

The Imperial and Royal Director of the Imperial and Royal Court Library, August 4, 1914.[4]

Karabaček crossed out the neutral and self-referential formulation "these publications are of the greatest importance to the poster collection of this institution", and replaced it with one much more laden with historical meaning: "they are of great importance for the imperial collections as historical monuments" ("*für die kaiserliche Sammlung als historische Denkmäler von hoher Bedeutung sind*") and signed the file.[5]

---

4. HB 543 /1914, 6 August 1914, Archives of the Austrian National Library [hereinafter cited as ÖNB Archives]. The one-of-a-kind "Habsburg bureaucratese" of the original language is impossible to translate: "*An die k. k. Hof und Staatsdruckerei Die unterfertigte Direktion beehrt sich das Ansuchen zu stellen, es möge der Hofbibliothek je ein Exemplar des Manifestes 'An Meine Völker' sowie der Kriegserklärung in allen Landessprachen gefälligst zugesendet werden, nachdem diese Publikationen für die Flugblättersammlung dieses Institutes von hoher Bedeutung wären. Gleichzeitig beehrt sich die Direktion der Hofbibliothek zu ersuchen, dass auch in Zukunft die in der k.k. Hof- und Staatsdruckerei erschienenen Proklamationen gütigst der Hofbibliothek zur Verfügung gestellt werden. Der k. u. k. Direktor der k.k. Hofbibliothek Wien, am 4. August 1914.*"
5. Ibid.

Poster "To My Peoples," 1914
KS 16216363,
Austrian National Library – Picture Archives and Graphics Department, Vienna

The director of the Court Library recognized the world historical importance of the imperial proclamation *"An meine Völker"* instantly. Due to his relentless efforts, the emperor's manifest was collected in all the languages of the Habsburg Empire, along with the declaration of war.

These priceless documents constitute the foundational stone of the Court Library's war collection.

The Director of the Government Printing Office actually turned the request down for legal reasons, since "the office was not authorized to pass on official publications, as long as they were not scheduled to be thrown away."[6] Karabaček would not be denied and turned to the Imperial and Royal Treasury Department ("*Oberstkämmereramt*") in charge of the Court Library for help.[7] With his excellent contacts in the higher ministerial bureaucracy in the Interior Department, he managed to have an order issued to all higher offices in the state bureaucracy to send the Court Library a copy of all declarations, proclamations and public appeals related to the war effort.[8] The relentless activism by the director's office to establish and maintain a war collection are the exact opposite of the massive restrictions the Court Library faced throughout the entire war of 1914 to 1918.[9] In the very early days of the war the Court Library director's office sent a report on securing and possibly removing valuable objects for safekeeping to the Treasury Department.[10] When in August six librarians and nine men servants were drafted into the Army, a September 12 order closed the reading room of the Court Library for the use of the public for the rest of the war.[11]

The Court Library Director's Office was in agreement with the Habsburg Empire's ruling elites—being fully aware of living *in great times*—and systematically began collecting from the early days of the conflict all material history related to the war for all posterity. It was the stated goal to comprehensively document and legitimate the anticipated victorious ending of the war. It was this very hope for final victory that determined both the Court Library's collecting impetus and guided the expectations of the German elites of Austria-Hungary. These expectations continued to blossom in spite of the military setbacks and disasters suffered by the Austro-Hungarian Army during the early months of the war in late 1914/ early 1915; only the massive support of the German ally prevented a total

---

6. Aug. 20, 1914, HB 543 /1914, ÖNB Archives.
7. Sept. 4, 1914, HB 543/1914, ÖNB Archives.
8. Nov. 26, 1914, HB 652/50/1914 – 1918, and HB 106/1915, ÖNB Archives.
9. On the Imperial Court Library during World War I and its War Collection see Manfred Rauchensteiner, ed., *An meine Völker: Der Weltkrieg 1914 – 1918* (Vienna: Amalthea 2014).
10. Othmar Doublier, "Ein Vierteljahrhundert aus der Geschichte der Hofbibliothek 1891 – 1916: Die Direktionen Hartel, Zeissberg, Karabacek," in: *Festschrift der Nationalbibliothek in Wien*, ed. zur Feier des 200 jährigen Bestehens des Gebäudes, vol. 1 (Vienna: Government Printing Office, 1926), 163-210 (here 207).
11. Ibid.

collapse on the battlefields.[12] The ideological purpose of the Court Library's determination to collect everything did not differ from the German Reich's. In August 1914, the Royal Library in Berlin initiated a number of collections relating to the war.[13]

Whereas some 500 public and private collections were gathering materials regionally dispersed throughout the German Reich, in Austria-Hungary the collecting effort was centered in the German-speaking provinces of the Monarchy and in the imperial capital city. In Vienna, next to the Court Library the Imperial War Archives, the municipal libraries and archives also began gathering war-related materials.[14] The Court Library, however, continued to be the most active central collecting point in the entire Monarchy. In agreement with the Imperial and Royal Treasury Department, all state offices and libraries in the Austrian ("*Cisleithania*") and Hungarian halves of the Monarchy were asked to assist in collecting war-related materials.

On October 30, 1914, Karabaček sent out a circular letter to the Cisleithania university libraries in Prague, Innsbruck, Graz, Cracow, and the regional study libraries in Linz, Salzburg, Klagenfurt, Olmütz, and Görz, as well as the library of the k.k. Trade and Nautic Academy in Trieste, to remind them of the historical importance of these imperial collections being gathered. He also appealed to their "patriotic assistance"[15], imploring them to "only with such patriotic assistance of all state offices will it be possible to secure the valuable and interesting witnesses of our great times for future generations and thus preserve these historical materials from destruction and ruin."[16]

In Hungary he asked the university library and the library of the National Museum in Budapest, as well as the university library in Kolosvár/Klausenburg, to cooperate in this endeavor. When Karabaček received positive responses from the university libraries in Prague, Klagenfurt and Kolosvár/Klausenburg and the National Museum in Budapest, he thanked them expressing his hope for "lively interaction."[17] The Court Library's most active contacts in terms of mutual visits and exchange of documents,

12. Rauchensteiner, *Erste Weltkrieg*; on elites, see Petra Ernsted., *Der Erste Weltkrieg im Diskurs der Moderne* (Studien zur Moderne 20) (Vienna: Passagen-Verlag, 2004).
13. Aibe-Marlene Gerdes, "Sammeln. Dokumentieren. Erinnern? Die österreichischen Kriegssammlungen des Ersten Weltkrieges," in: Wolfram Dornik/Julia Walleczek-Fritz/Stefan Wedrac, eds., *Frontwechsel: Österreich-Ungarns "Großer Krieg" im Vergleich* (Vienna: Böhlau, 2014), pp. 139–161.
14. Ibid. On Vienna during World War I, see also Alfred Pfoser/ Andreas Weigl, eds., *Im Epizentrum des Zusammenbruchs: Wien im Ersten Weltkrieg* (Vienna: Metro, 2013).
15. Nov. 3, 1914, HB 652/68/1914 – 1918, ÖNB Archives.
16. Ibid.
17. Nov. 16, 1914, HB 652/68/1914 – 1918, ÖNB-Archives.

however, developed with the "sibling collection" in the Budapest at the Hungarian National Library.[18]

The Cisleithanian libraries showed themselves ready to cooperate too. They served more as collecting points for the Court Library rather than accumulating their own war-related holdings. The only exception was the university library in Lvov/Lemberg, right in the middle of the hotly contested Galician front. With the outbreak of the war they began collecting documents and asked the director of the Court Library in May 1916 to help them put order into their material and catalogue it.[19]

The Court Library's efforts went beyond its traditional institutional and library connections. It tried hard to make the public at large aware of its collecting strategies. To gather the visual history of the war, the director corresponded with the Austrian Photographic Society as well as the photo agencies Kilophot, Angerer-Göschl, and the Budapest newspaper agency Az Est, which regularly exhibited photos from the various war fronts in its Vienna subsidiary. The Court Library also placed ads in all the important newspapers to encourage people to send in personal documents and photos relating to the war.[20]

Officers' apartments on the Russian front, front and back side
Newspaper Agency AZ Est Budapest, 1915/16, Pk 3002, 7832,
Austrian National Library – Picture Archives and Graphics Department, Vienna

18. Second report by Doublier, HB 285/1915, Jan. 6, 1915, ÖNB-Archives.
19. June 5, 1916, HB 652/1914 – 1918, ÖNB-Archives.
20. Nov. 21, 1914, HB 652/6/1914 – 1918; Feb. 23 and 25, 1915, HB 652/16/1914 – 1918; Jan. 4, 1916, HB 652/70/1914 – 1918, ÖNB-Archives.

Ruthenian refugees, Russian frontlines
Newspaper Agency AZ Est Budapest, 1915/16, Pk 3002, 7833,
Austrian National Library – Picture Archives and Graphics Department, Vienna

In November 1914, Karabaček wrote to the Bureau of War Aid (*Kriegshilfebüro*) on the Interior Ministry. He noted "the earth shattering events that are affecting our fatherland so profoundly," and asked the *Kriegshilfebüro* for its support in submitting all the "publications, public appeals and announcements, picture postcards, war calendars, etc."[21]

In January 1915, Karabaček turned to the Justice Ministry and urged them to send a directive to all the chief prosecutors to remind them of their duty to submit all the outlawed pieces of writings to the Court Library, referencing a public decree from 1888 that had fallen into oblivion.[22]

Karabaček's extensive correspondence and the director's massive endeavor to gain the support of all public offices in the collection of official documents were crowned by success. Even villages and district offices were ordered to submit all the printed matter that did not make it to bookstores but were still crucial as "historical materials for the future."[23]

As early as March of 1915 Karabaček composed a first report about the state of the incipient war collection to the Treasury Department. The

21. Nov. 6, 1914, HB 652/8/1914 – 1918, ÖNB-Archives.
22. Letter from Karabaček, Jan. 13., 1915, and reply from the Justice Ministry, Feb. 12, 1915, HB 652/18/1914 – 1918, ÖNB-Archives.
23. Nov. 6, 1914, HB 652/8/1914 – 1918, ÖNB-Archives.

report was drafted by Dr. Othmar Doublier, the chief curator tasked with the inventory and the systematizing of the war collection, and his assistant Dr. Otto Brechler. The director coupled the report with the request to dispatch Doublier and Brechler for a seven-day study trip to Berlin and Leipzig "in order to visit the Royal Library in Berlin and the German Library in Leipzig, familiarize themselves with the existing war collections there, and return with the insights gained for improving the Court Library collections."[24]

In March 1915, the inventory of the war collection included 738 files, among them 231 legal deposit submissions[25], 450 purchased acquisitions, 57 donated exemplars of printed matter, as well as 380 posters and public announcements, 94 individual sheets with poetry, and 2,420 picture postcards.[26] Karabaček pointed out that the exchange of duplicates was working well with the k. u. k. War Archives, the Polish War Archives in Vienna[27], both the German Library in Leipzig and the Royal Library in Berlin; only the submission of *Pflichtexemplare* was laggard.

Doublier wrote his second report on July 1, 1915.[28] In only a few months the Court Library doubled the size of its war collections: 1,924 printed works (among them 493 *Pflichtexemplare*, 1,314 purchases, 118 donations), 1,044 posters, 70 artistic prints, 554 photographs, 39 pictorial war narratives (*Bilderbögen*), 53 individual sheets, 118 sheets with poetry, 22 handwritten war-related musical compositions, 53 handwritten poems, 59 celebratory ribbons (*Vivatbänder*[29]), 134 maps of the various theaters of war, a large number of sundry official announcements and documents, 3,842 picture postcards (558 of them from enemy territory).

The systematic acquisition of books, brochures, art prints and picture postcards by way of book suppliers such a Gerold & Co went off without a hitch. Doublier also stressed quite proudly that they bought subscriptions for the duration of the war of a number of important political newspapers and magazines from neutral and enemy countries, and added: "future historians will surely welcome finding these in the k.k. Court Library." Among them were: *Der Bund* (Berne, Switzerland), the London *Times*, the *Temps* (Paris), *Nowje Wremy* (St. Petersburg), *Samouprava* (Belgrade, Serbia), the politically satirical *Le Rire Rouge* (Paris), and the picture magazines

---

24. March 27, 1915, and Report and Letter Karabaček to Royal Treasury Department, March 24, 1915, HB 140/1915, ÖNB-Archives.
25. According to the legal deposit law the Imperial Court Library received copies of all printed publications in the Austrian part of the monarchy.
26. Ibid.
27. Formerly a part of the k. u. k. War Archives.
28. July 1, 1915, HB 285/1915, ÖNB-Archives.
29. "*Vivatbänder*" were linen ribbons celebrating battle victories with a patriotic fervor.

L'Illustrazione (Rome), and *Russkaja Illustracija* (St. Petersburg).[30]

Les apôtres du "Gott" [God's apostles], caricature by Charles Léandre, *Le rire rouge*, Oct. 23, 1915, 510.570-C,
Austrian National Library – Picture Archives and Graphics Department, Vienna

The selection of foreign newspapers was quite remarkable. Next to important daily newspapers, their interest concentrated on collecting illustrated newspapers and satirical magazines to gauge and document public opinion formation in both the neutral states and the entente powers.

In the second report they mentioned positively the exchange of experiences with their colleagues in Berlin and Budapest and the bartering of materials resulting therefrom. However, they also complained that the

30. Ibid.

required delivery to state offices on all levels of all print forms such as art posters, picture postcards and public announcements was not as prompt as they wished.

Only when the Court Library started recruiting soldiers, doctors and front officers during the war years 1915 to 1917 did they achieve a major breakthrough in the mass delivery of print products. They also had success in making public calls in the press to appeal to the civilian population on the home front.

In March 1915 Karabaček asked the Treasury Department to persuade the Welfare Office in the War Ministry, which organized the delivery of so-called "gifts of love" (*Liebesgaben*) from the home front to the frontline soldiers, to assist the Court Library with its war collection with a summary appeal. The Treasury Department responded enthusiastically and offered to pay for printing the notice to be included in all parcels with these "gifts of love" to the soldiery:

The Court Library in Vienna is collecting all proclamations, posters, individual prints, public calls, war-and-fortress-related newspapers. Each and every one of these pieces is intended to constitute the material for the accomplishments in the war of the Austro-Hungarian and German armies for future historians and writers. Therefore we extend the urgent and heartfelt request to every officer and interested soldier, who might be in the possession of such printed matter relating to the war, to keep this collection effort in mind and to send it to the "Court Library's War Collection in Vienna" after gaining permission from the military.

Vienna, March 9, 1915

k&k Court Councillor and Director of the k.k. Court Library Karabaček[31]

With this very clever move the director's office managed to include important decision makers on the frontlines in the Court Library's collection efforts. In the coming years – until the end of the war – numerous members of the armed forces, including Archduke Eugen, the army command Rohr, as well as many officers, doctors and soldiers sent war materials to the Court

31. March 11, 1915, HB 113/1915, ÖNB-Archives.

Library.[32]

The command of the k. u. k. Army of the Balkans, Peterwardein/Petrovaradin, May 19, 1915, PORT 00067686/01,
Austrian National Library – Picture Archives and Graphics Department, Vienna

The Court Library managed to lay down the cornerstone for its very effective publicity campaign about its collection activities with its public calls in the press in the fall of 1914. After these appeals in the newspapers both private citizens and various associations (*Vereine*) sent documents to the Court Library. Beginning of December the "Viennese Associations of Waiters" wrote to the Court Library's director's office that it had noted the press announcement on the "Collection of War Literature by the Court Library." It intended to send in printed matter designed further the distribution of receipts for the Red Cross. The Waiters' Association had collected and distributed half a million such Red Cross *receipts* since the beginning of the war. Until December, the Waiters' Association managed to collect and send 40,000 crowns to the Red Cross and 12,000 Crowns to the War Welfare Office.[33]

The public calls in the newspapers continued. The longer the war lasted, the more the sympathy and emotions of the population was directed toward

32. HB 652/82, 115, 165/1914 – 1918, ÖNB-Archives.
33. Dec. 7, 1914, HB 652/1914 – 1918, ÖNB-Archives.

situation reports from the frontlines and the individual fate of soldiers.

Distribution of letters to the front in the battalion III/85 in Damber near Salcano/Solkan, 1917, WK1/ALB004/01067,
Austrian National Library – Picture Archives and Graphics Department, Vienna

On November 14, 1914, Karabaček wrote to Julius Tauber, a journalist of the *Illustrierte Kronenzeitung* and asked him to donate the field postcards from the front lines and the "wishes of love" (*Liebeswünsche*) to the War Collection of the Court Library that was coming into being.[34] As early as January 1915, he thanked the editorial office of the *Illustrierte Kronenzeitung* for the "donation of all field postcards, drawings, and original photographs they received."[35]

The *Kronenzeitung* subsequently used the postcards soldiers sent to the editorial office as their preferred form of advertisement. The field postcards sent to the *Kronenzeitung* and acquired by the Court Library documented the frontline soldiers' greetings during the Christmas and Easter seasons, usually including photos of their comrades in the field. They asked for publication in the newspaper to demonstrate that they were still alive and doing well.

34. Nov. 14, 1914, HB 652/72/1914 – 1918, ÖNB-Archives.
35. Nov. 14, 1914, [HB 652/72/1914 – 1918, ÖNB-Archives.

The Collection Effort by the Imperial Court Library in Vienna during World War I

Front and backside of a field post card to the editorial office of the *Illustrierte Kronenzeitung*, KS16320303,
Austrian National Library – Picture Archives and Graphics Department, Vienna

Given the Court Library's active role in the media, numerous private submissions were sent to the War Collection of the Court Library. They provided an impressive picture of the mood and emotional state of the educated ethnic German middle and upper classes in the Habsburg Monarchy, who happened to be the main contributors to the War Collection.[36]

---

36. The directors of the War Collection systematically ordered and summarized the contents of the important and significant correspondences from state offices. However, the correspondences of private citizens and the replies from the director's office were only

One of the main focuses of submissions from private citizens was unpublished poems and writings manifesting and cementing enemy images and propaganda themes. The main topics in the war poetry were the hope for victory, faithful allies, and the glorification of Emperor Francis Joseph during the beginning months of the war, the "betrayal" of Italy in 1915, and the hope for peace as the war kept grinding on.

Some of the people who sent in their writings put pressure on the director's office to publish their work; so Karabaček felt duty bound to respond. On August 21, 1915, the Budapest writer Heinrich Krausz sent in the poem *Der Honved* and asked for a confirmation of receipt and for the poem to be published. When the director's office turned down the publication of the poem, Krausz asked submissively that "the distinguished compilation department of the k.k. Court Library accept the poem I composed, which experts have deemed 'beautiful', with an expression of full devotion, let me know as soon as possible about its acceptance."[37]

On Feb. 8, 1916, Karabaček wrote to the Baroness Anna Lachs and told her: "the constant, one is even tempted to say mass produced, submission of poems to our collection program has not been intended," and announced that he would return 134 poems. He did accept, however, a "Prayer for Peace" from the pharmacist Josefine Zfass sent from Jassy in Romania, yet could not meet her request to dedicate the prayer to Emperor Francis Joseph or Emperor Wilhelm.[38] After the many public press announcements, private citizens also sent the Court Library personal field postcards and diary entries written on the frontlines, frequently asking for the return of the originals after they had been copied. In March 1915, Louise Beier sent in a private letter from her spouse that she wanted returned.[39] In September 1915 Wilhelm Plettl from Graz submitted a letter from his son also requesting the return of the letter since it would be "a very dear memory" for the children and future offspring.[40]

Naturally, the changing fortunes of war, especially on the Eastern frontlines, left deep traces in the materials submitted to the Court Library. After the reconquest of the fortresses Premyśl and Lemberg by the Habsburg armies in 1915, a number of newspapers and official announcements made

referenced with a date under the main archival rubric 652 and deposited without being put into order in the Archives of the Court Library.

37. The stilted language of the time is impossible to render into suitable English: "[...] unterbreitete er die 'untertänigste' Bitte, 'die hochlöbliche Redaktion der k.k. Hofbibliothek möge mein von mir verfasstes Gedicht, welches von Fachmännern als 'schön' bezeichnet worden, mit dem Ausdrucke meiner tiefsten Ergebenheit entgegennehmen und mich von der Annahme ehestens verständigen'." Oct. 12, 1915, HB 652/47/1914 – 1918, ÖNB-Archives.
38. Feb. 8, 1915, ÖNB-Archiv HB 652/1914 – 1918, ÖNB-Archives.
39. Mar. 17, 1915, HB 652/1914 – 1918, ÖNB-Archives.
40. Sept. 15, 1915, HB 652/1914 – 1918, ÖNB-Archives.

it to the Library. The director's office even went a step further and sent librarians to the frontline areas of the war, to gather actively materials for the Library on the spot. After the taking of Belgrade in October 1915, the defeat of the Serbian Army on the Amselfeld, and their retreat via Montenegro into Albania in November 1915, Othmar Doublier was dispatched to Belgrade in December 1915. In Karabaček's letter of recommendation, also copied to the Treasury Department, he explained the collection mission of the Court Library: "The eminently historical and patriotic mission of the Court Library's endeavor enjoys the full support and cooperation of all levels of bureaucracy and all the military and civil administrations in the Monarchy; therefore the undersigned director's office suggests to give the widest of support to these gentlemen."[41] In Belgrade, Doublier assigned the book seller Géza Kohn to send war-related books to the Court Library; after overcoming some bureaucratic obstacles the book deliveries began in March 1916.[42] After the unconditional surrender of Montenegro in January 1916 and the invasion of Albania by k. u. k. troops, the Imperial Academy of Science dispatched a study "expedition" into the Balkans (May 22 – August 28, 1916), which was joined by the Court Library official Dr. Franz Kidrič.

In June 1915, Kidrič sent a postcard from Skutari in Albania to Karabaček, reporting about his successes: "Am well and very happy about results! Will travel tomorrow into the interior, only to return here after three weeks. During my absence here, 3 gentlemen will collect for us: my group commander, a monk, a teacher. Our scientific expedition has left both here and in Montenegro an excellent impression on the natives."[43]

---

41. Nov. 11, 1915, HB 431/1915, ÖNB-Archives.
42. Oct. 1, 1916, HB 9/1916, and Dec. 2, 1916, HB 73/1916, ÖNB-Archives.
43. Picture postcard Kidrič to Karabaček, June 6, 1916, Pk3741_76.

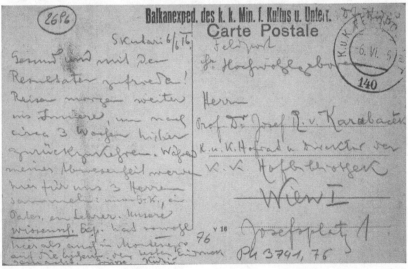

Front and backside of a picture postcard from Franz Kidrič to the director's office of the
k.k. Court Library, June 6, 1916, Pk 3741/76,
Austrian National Library – Picture Archives and Graphics Department, Vienna

Kidrič returned home to Vienna with quite a haul: posters, telegrams,
public calls for protest meetings after the assassination of the successor to
the Habsburg throne in Sarajevo, newspapers and photographs, among

them a picture of the assassin Gavrilo Princip, widely circulated in Serbia.[44]

Gavrilo Princip portrait, lithograph by M. Milošević, Belgrade, no date
Picture caption: "Born in 1895 in Grahovo, Crni Potoci (area in nortwest Bosnia bordering Croatia), from the nest of the old Vujadin, who on St. Vitus Day 1914 killed the successor to the Austrian-Hungarian throne and his wife with with two revolver bullets."
PORT 00014226/01,
Austrian National Library – Picture Archives and Graphics Department, Vienna

Two events decisively changed the character of the war collection: Italy's entry into the war in 1915 and the death of the 86-year old Emperor Francis Joseph in 1916. Italy's entry into the war sparked a new wave of submission from the new theaters of war in the South on the Isonzo River

44. ÖNB-Archiv HB 150/1917; see also Marianne Jobst-Rieder, "Die Kriegssammlung der Hofbibliothek," in: Marianne Jobst-Rieder/Alfred Pfabigan/Manfred Wagner, eds., *Das letzte Vivat: Plakate und Parolen aus der Kriegssammlung der k.k. Hofbibliothek* (Vienna: Holzhausen, 1995), pp 11–21 (here 12).

and the Dolomite mountains. The perception of the new enemy Italy became the topic of numerous items from the daily press as well as school children's drawings and school essays flooding the Court Library from the home front. What the submissions to the Court Library clearly demonstrated was that the "betrayal" of Austria-Hungary's ally Italy fed into a renewed and final flaring up of martial enthusiasm for the Monarchy contributing to a new wave of mental war mobilization. Francis Joseph's death, however, meant the irretrievable loss of the principal figure all ethnicities of the Monarchy could identify with.

There was no way the new Emperor Karl could fill this void, even with massive propaganda campaigns. After Francis Joseph's passing, his successor Karl initiated an intense program of visits to the various frontlines. His personal photographer Ludwig Schumann and sometimes a motion picture film team regularly documented these visits.[45] Schumann staged Emperor Karl as the supreme war leader – the monarchy's leader deeply loved and giddily welcomed by populations everywhere. Emperor Charles' efforts to stage himself in the media also caught the interest of the archivists and librarians in the capital city. Franz Schnürer, the director of the k. & k. dynastic family library (*Familien-Fideikommissionsbibliothek*), initiated a separate "Emperor Karl in the World War" collection, designed to run parallel to the Court Library's War Collection.[46] To accomplish this goal, on September 27, 1917, Josef Donaubaum, the new director of the Court Library, dispatched Schnürer to Villa Wartholz, suggesting to Emperor Charles to initiate a war collection in the *Familien-Fideikommissionsbibliothek* dedicated to him personally. Armed with Emperor Karl's agreement, Schnürer, following in the footsteps of Karabaček before him, contacted the Treasury Department, the War Archives, the Army High Command, and the Institute of Military Geography with the request to support him in launching the "Emperor Karl in the World War" collection.[47]

Schnürer's efforts produced a collection of some 7,000 photographs, a few hundred books, and various pictorial materials in the *Fideikommissionsbibliothek*. The premises of the *Fideikommissionsbibliothek* were adjacent to the Court Library, yet organizationally and financially it was a separate institution.[48] However, the buildup of the collection never gathered speed beyond the initial efforts, even though Schnürer received

---

45. Anton Holzer, Die andere Front: *Fotografie und Propaganda im Ersten Weltkrieg ; mit unveröffentlichten Originalaufnahmen aus dem Bildarchiv der Österreichischen Nationalbibliothek* (Darmstadt: Primus 2007, repr. 2012), pp. 52-75.

46. Nov. 16, 1917, HB 459/1917, and report by Schnürer, Oct. 16, 1917, ÖNB-Archives.

47. 69/1917, 71/1917, 74/1917, Archives of the *Familien-Fideikommissionsbibliothek* [hereinafter cited as FKB-Archives].

48. Apr. 4, 1918, 20/1918, FKB-Archives.

Emperor Karl I during the tenth battle of the Isonzo, May 17, 1917, WK1/
ALB060/16900, Austrian National Library – Picture Archives and Graphics Department,
Vienna

Das Interessante Blatt, May 24, 1917, 399.792-D,
Austrian National Library – Picture Archives and Graphics Department, Vienna

3,000 crowns from a private Habsburg family fund for its development.[49]

The Court Library continued its War Collection in the last years of the war 1917/18, albeit with reduced resources. Numerous documents kept arriving from the theaters of war in the East and in Italy. The Headquarters of the War Press announced that it would transfer its collection of newspapers and archival materials to the Court Library.[50]

By the end of the war the War Collection in the Court Library had swollen to 52,000 documents.[51] In terms of size, contents, and structure, the Court Library's collection resembled the large state holdings gathered in Berlin and Munich.[52] After the end of the war and with the collapse of the Habsburg Monarchy imperial institutions such as the Headquarters of the War Press and the Institute of Military Geography were dissolved. Their extensive war-related holdings were transferred to the Court Library in the 1920s. The collections of newspapers from the Headquarters of the War Press were handed over late in 1918. The Court Library refused to pay anything for it.[53] In the course of 1924 the books, archival materials and a collection of 26,000 photo prints were transferred from the Headquarters of the War Press.[54] In 1929, the Court Library acquired additionally 33,000 original photos on glass plates, along with 110 photo albums with photos from the Institute of Military Geography glued in.[55]

These books and photographs eventually were integrated into the catalogue of the Austrian National Library. However, the Court Library's massive War Collection was never really processed and/or utilized by scholars due to either a lack of interest or "pathological shyness"[56] to begin mastering the memory of a lost war—neither in the First Republic, nor in the Second. Only at the end of the 20th century did the Austrian National Library present a small selection of the War Library's collections in an exhibit to the public.[57]

Yet one hundred years after the outbreak of World War I, the busy

---

49. 17/1918, 25/1918, FKB-Archives.
50. Nov. 8, 1918, HB 652/238/1914 – 1918, ÖNB-Archives.
51. Doublier, "Vierteljahrhundert," p. 199.
52. Gerdes, "Sammeln."
53. Nov. 8, 1918, HB 652/238/1914 – 1918, and Dec. 21, 1918 & January 14, 1919, HB 482/1918, ÖNB-Archives.
54. HB 1627/1924, ÖNB-Archives.
55. Picture Archives and Graphics Collection of the Austrian National Library, archival holdings Urheberrecht 132/1929. On the picture collection of the Headquarters of the War Press, see Holzer, *Die andere Front*, and idem, "Mit der Kamera bewaffnet. Kriegsfotografien aus dem Ersten Weltkrieg," in: Uwe Schögl, ed., *Im Blickpunkt: Die Fotosammlung der Österreichischen Nationalbibliothek* (Innsbruck: Haymon 2002), p. 166-191.
56. Othmar Doublier, "Die Kriegssammlung der Nationalbibliothek," *Wiener Zeitung*, July 14, 1923.
57. Jobst-Rieder, ed, *Das Letzte Vivat*.

and assiduous efforts of the librarians and their staff to assemble a War Collection in the Court Library appear in a different light. From the very beginning of the war the Court Library's staff turned into a constituent part of the conduct of the war on the home front. Systematically including the civilian population via announcements and reports in the press, along with both communicating with the fighting soldiers in the field and institutionally anchoring the cooperation with the entire bureaucracy, all contributed to the success of the War Collection, so important for future generations. The War Collection offers profound evidence for the spiritual and emotional mobilization of the governing elites and the ordinary people in the Habsburg Monarchy during the long and difficult war years of 1914 to 1918.

Nontopical Essays

Yoichi Okamoto and the "Pictorial Section": Austrian-American Relations in Press Photography 1945 – 1955

Marion Krammer, Margarethe Szeless

In 1945, Austria was liberated by Allied troops and divided into four occupation zones within the borders that had existed until 1938.[1] Shortly after the arrival of U.S. troops and the establishment of U.S. High Command headquarters in Salzburg, the Information Service Branch (ISB hereafter) responsible for cultural and media policy, was set up. (It was later renamed the United States Information Services, USIS hereafter.) Alongside a press department and other services, the ISB also operated a picture service, the so-called "Pictorial Section." Succeeding his predecessor, Officer Howard Hollem, it was Yoichi Okamoto, head of the "Pictorial Section" from 1948-1954, who transformed this section into a thriving and successful picture service and photo archive. Of the original 35.000 or so items making up the USIS photo archive, around 16.000 photographs survive in the Picture Archive of the Austrian National Library, and have been scanned, key-worded and made available online.

Academic research has hitherto not dealt with the "Pictorial Section" and its protagonists in sufficient detail, but has focused instead on US cultural and propaganda policy more generally. The pioneering study on the American occupying power's political propaganda and media policy by historian Oliver Rathkolb is still up to date.[2] A further milestone in research

1. We would like to thank the Dietrich R. Botstiber Foundation, Pennsylvania, for supporting our project with a travel grant, enabling us to conduct extensive research in the USA in 2012/13. This article summarizes our major findings and describes the next stage of our research.
2. Oliver Rathkolb, "Politische Propaganda der amerikanischen Besatzungsmacht in Österreich 1945-50: ein Beitrag zur Geschichte des Kalten Krieges in der Presse-, Kultur, - und Rundfunkpolitik," PhD Diss. University of Vienna 1982. On the media and cultural policies of the Americans, see also Michael Schönberg, "Die amerikanische Medien- und Informationspolitik in Österreich von 1945 bis 1950," PhD Diss. University of Vienna 1976, and Andrea Ellmeier, "Von der kulturellen Entnazifizierung Österreichs zum konsumkulturellen Versprechen: Kulturpolitik der USA in Österreich 1945-1955," in Karin Moser, ed., *Besetzte Bilder: Film, Kultur und Propaganda in Österreich 1945-1955* (Vienna:

on American cultural policy, the work of the ISB, and the influence of its cultural propaganda on Austria was produced by Reinhold Wagnleitner in his 1989 thesis "Coca-Colonisation and Cold War: The Cultural Mission of the USA in Austria after the Second World War."[3] Finally, Günter Bischof must also be mentioned here, whose numerous articles and books since the 1980s have dealt primarily with US occupation policies.[4]

Despite the availability of source materials on US photographic production in Austria and the numerous traces it left in contemporary newspapers, an in-depth investigation of the "Pictorial Section's" impact on Austrian press photography is still lacking. However, all authors publishing on Austrian press photography after World War II emphasize the influence of American photojournalism and the importance of the "Pictorial Section" of the ISB for the development of Austrian press photography.[5] Underlining the exceptional role of the "Pictorial Section" and its reception as the "birthplace of modern photojournalism"[6] has become a widely accepted convention in the literature without ever having been adequately substantiated.

This lack of knowledge about the "Pictorial Section," its organization, staff, and impact on Austrian press photography indicated a very specific starting point for our investigation: the National Archives and Records Administration in Washington, D.C. Record Group 260 contains archival materials on all ISB sections operating in Austria during the occupation

---

Österreichisches Filmmuseum, 2005), 61-85.

3. Published in German as *Coca-Colonisation und Kalter Krieg: Die Kulturmission der USA in Österreich nach dem Zweiten Weltkrieg* (Vienna: Verlag für Gesellschaftskritik, 1991), and in English as *Coca-Colonization and the Cold War: The Cultural Mission of the United States in Austria after the Second World War* (Chapel Hill: The University of North Carolina Press, 1994).

4. Günter Bischof/Anton Pelinka/Dieter Stiefel, eds. *The Marshall Plan in Austria* (*Contemporary Austrian Studies* [*CAS*] 8) (New Brunswick, NJ: Transaction, 2000); Günter Bischof/Dieter Stiefel, eds., *Images of the Marshall Plan in Europe: Films, Photographs, Exhibits, Posters* (TRANSATLANTICA 3) (Innsbruck: StudienVerlag, 2009).

5. Leo Kandl, "Pressefotografie und Fotojournalismus in Österreich bis 1960," in Otto Hochreiter, ed., *Geschichte der Fotografie in Österreich* (Bad Ischl: Verein zur Erarbeitung der "Geschichte der Fotografie in Österreich," 1983), 312-324; Gerhard Schnabl, "Geschichte des österreichischen Photojournalismus vom Durchbruch der Autotypie bis zur Einführung des Fernsehens," PhD thesis University of Vienna 1983; Hans Petschar, " Der fremde, der eigene Blick: Amerikanisch-österreichische Bilddokumente 1945-55," in *Zeitgeschichte*, vol. 32, No. 4 (2005): 269-274; Hans Petschar/Herbert Friedlmeier, "The Photographic Gaze—Austrian Visual Lives during the Occupation Decade: A Cross-Section of Ordinary Austrians Photographed by American and Austrian Artists," in Günter Bischof/Fritz Plasser/Eva Maltschnig, eds., *Austrian Lives* (*CAS* 21) (New Orleans: UNO, 2012), 359-384.

6. Wolfgang Kos, ed., *Photo: Barbara Pflaum: Bildchronistin der Zweiten Republik* (Vienna: Exhibition Catalogue Wien Museum, 2006), 76.

period.[7] A preliminary evaluation of this data is the objective of this article and will be structured as follows:

A brief introduction of Yoichi Okamoto's personal and professional background will show that his Viennese period was the starting point of a very impressive career in press photography.

Using the NARA source material, we will outline the organizational and operating structures of the "Pictorial Section." How did this section work? Who worked for the "Pictorial Section"? Who gave the assignments? How were the pictures distributed? These are some of the questions we will provide answers to. Furthermore, we will address Okamoto's often claimed but never proven qualities as a teacher of press photography.

Last, we will introduce Inge Morath, another protagonist of postwar press photography who in the late 1940s also worked for USIS in Vienna as an editor for the picture magazine *Heute*, which was published by the US authorities in Germany. As NARA records show, there was extensive contact between Okamoto, Morath, and the *Heute* publishers in Munich in the second half of the 1940s. We will argue that *Heute* magazine played an important role in bringing a modern American style of reportage to Austria and that experts such as Okamoto and Morath intensively aimed to foster it.

Yoichi Okamoto's Career as Press Photographer

Yoichi Robert Okamoto was born in 1915 in Yonkers, N.Y., as the first of two sons of Japanese immigrants. His interest in photography dated from his undergraduate years at Colgate University. Graduating in 1938, he entered the professional field as a nightclub photographer in Syracuse, NY. Later he joined the *Syracuse Post Standard* as a staff photographer. Despite his American citizenship he was rejected when he volunteered for the army before Pearl Harbor. When he was finally accepted on Jan. 6, 1942, he became the first Japanese-American to join from the New York area.[8] In 1944, he came to Europe as a war correspondent and personal photographer

---

7. Following a systematic inspection of the ISB files for Austria, we studied all relevant materials on the "Pictorial Section" from this period, including correspondence, so-called daily reports, exact records of the photographers' daily assignments and workloads, staff lists, organigrams, invoices, telegrams etc. As a matter of fact, there is a lack of ISB material after 1950; the NARA material dates primarily from the period 1945-1950.
8. Yoichi Okamoto's CV, written by Franz Bader, Inc, 1705 G St, N.W, 11 Feb. 1956, Art & Artist File, Smithsonian American Art Museum/National Portrait Gallery Library, Washington, D.C.

for General Mark W. Clark, first commander of the US forces in Austria.[9] After four years of documenting the destruction of war and the first efforts at reconstructing Austria, Okamoto was appointed head of the "Pictorial Section" of the ISB in Vienna.

Fig. 1: Anonymous: Yoichi Okamoto, c. 1960, Private Collection

Okamoto's merits as head of this section will be discussed separately; here it has to be stressed that his activities as a photographer were not limited to his job for ISB. He organized workshops on photography and invited famous guests like Edward Steichen to visit Vienna.[10] Okamoto demonstrated how to use the camera in modern press photography at Vienna's Kosmos Theater in front of an interested public. And, last but not least, he was an active member of the Viennese art scene until his departure

9. See the biography Yoichi R. Okamoto, in Helen Zia/Susan B. Gall, *Asian American Biography* (New York: UXL 1995), 311- 313; Greg Robinson, *A Tragedy of Democracy: Japanese Confinement in North America* (New York: Columbia Univ. Press, 2009); Yumiko Murakami, *Hyakunen no Yume: Okamoto famirī no America (Their Dreams of Hundred Years: The Okamoto Family's America)*, (Tokyo: Shinchōsha, 1989). We are grateful to Gabriel Wartofsky for giving us a copy of the typewritten English synopsis of the book.
10. Kurt Kaindl, ed., "Okamoto sieht Wien (part 2)," in *fotoseite: Kommentierte Beiträge zur Fotografie aus der Wiener Zeitung EXTRA* (1990): 23.

in 1954. His sensitive portraits of Austrian artists were regularly displayed in a poster campaign called "*Schöpferisches Österreich*" in an attempt to shape postwar Austrian intellectual life.[11] In fact, Okamoto had developed his own personal style. He often used framing elements within the picture; he specialized in strong contrasts of black and white with asymmetric compositions designed to maximize the work's emotional impact. In 1954, the Austrian Art Club organized a show of Okamoto's personal oeuvre at the famous Würthle Gallery in Vienna.

When Yoichi Okamoto was transferred back to Washington in 1954 he had clearly become a distinguished artist and public figure in Austria; a photo showing the Austrian Foreign Minister Leopold Figl handing a farewell present to Okamoto attests to his reputation.[12] Beside Okamoto stands his wife Paula whom he had met at the Salzburg Festival only a few years earlier.[13] Together they left for the United States in 1954. Back in the U.S. after his years in Europe, Okamoto built a career as a freelance photographer for *Life, Look, Time, Collier's* and other leading magazines, and became the first White House photographer under President Lyndon B. Johnson.[14]

---

11. Petschar/Friedlmeier, "The Photographic Gaze," 359-384; Kurt Kaindl, ed., "Okamoto sieht Wien (part 1+2)," in *fotoseite: Kommentierte Beiträge zur Fotografie aus der Wiener Zeitung EXTRA* (1990): 22-23.

12. In 1954 Okamoto was also given the Silver Award of the Austrian Photographic Society for "contributions to the advancement of photography" in Austria, see "Gallery notes: A One-Man Photo Show," *Washington Post*, 5 Jan. 1958, clipping in Art & Artist File, Smithsonian American Art Museum/National Portrait Gallery Library, Washington, D.C.

13. Personal interview, Marion Krammer and Margarethe Szeless with Arda Rammler, Munich, 24 Nov. 2012 (interview in possession of the authors).

14. Okamoto's work is discussed in a recent publication, see John Bredar, *The President's Photographer: Fifty Years Inside the Oval Office* (Washington, D.C.: National Geographic, 2010). For Okamoto's years in the Oval Office, Mike Geissinger is a prolific source of information. Geissinger was a photographer and colleague of Okamoto's in the photo office of the White House between June 1966 and January 1969. Telephone interview Margarethe Szeless with Mike Geissinger, 21 June 2013 (interview in possession of the authors).

Fig. 2: Gottfried Rainer: Farewell reception for Yoichi Okamoto at the Austrian Foreign
Ministry, 1954, Private Collection

The "Pictorial Section": Organizational and Operating Structures

At the end of the war the essential mission of ISB and its "Pictorial
Section" was to educate the Austrian public about the horrors of National
Socialism. But in the absence of publication opportunities, the first
photographic reports documenting National Socialist mass murder
were displayed in the window of a Salzburg photographic supplies shop
in 1945. However, with the increasing expansion of the ISB's fields of
activity and the reorganization of the Austrian press, new opportunities
for publishing photos eventually arose. The photo reportages created by the
"Pictorial Section" staff were used primarily for wall newspapers, posters,
magazines, and, above all, in the daily newspaper *Wiener Kurier*, published
by the Americans since 1945. Since 1948 the "Pictorial Section" was also
responsible for producing the weekly pictorial supplement ("*Bildbeilage*") of
the *Wiener Kurier*. Moreover, since the "Pictorial Section" was also charged
with creating a photo archive, all photographic negatives with detailed
captions were systematically archived in order to allow access to the pictures
at any time. Photographic prints were made available at no charge to other
Austrian media outlets and institutions.

As can be seen in an early dissemination scheme from 1946, the task of the ISB Pictorial Section basically revolved around procuring (not producing) and redistributing pictures (cf. fig. 3). While the "Pictorial Section" exchanged pictures with the British and French ISB, there was no similar cooperation with the Russian ISB. Furthermore, the "Pictorial Section" distributed photos about the United States to other interested parties and bought pictures for distribution in Austria from Polish and German sources as well as other military agencies. By 1946, the photos produced by the ISB staff comprised only a small percentage of the incoming pictures. On the outgoing side, the scheme shows the picture exchange with other agencies. It also shows that Austrian newspapers in Vienna, Linz, and Salzburg were furnished with pictures (free of charge as mentioned before). Furthermore, the Information Centers in Salzburg, Linz, and Vienna regularly showed window displays prepared using photographic material for the "Graphic Display Section" with pictures by the "Pictorial Section." The "Pictorial Section" also handled special requests by writers, scientists, teachers, etc. who needed visual material for educational purposes.

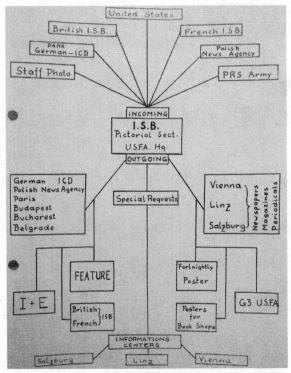

Fig. 3: ISB-Organigram, 1946, National Archives and Records Administration, Washington, D.C.

Due to an ever-increasing workload, the staff of the "Pictorial Section" steadily expanded over the years. On 28 February 1949, Yoichi Okamoto wrote to his former boss Herman Borzner at the *Syracuse Post Standard*. He proudly described his working conditions and professional environment in Vienna in considerable detail:

> Herm, it sure would be nice if by some miracle you could pop over here to see the setup we have. We got three American photographers, three Austrian photographers, a lab staff of ten Austrians translating, captioning, cutting, retouching and packaging people. In addition we have two staff-photographers in Salzburg. Just recently they threw the load of editing the roto section [printing technique of rotogravure—eds.] on me, so that involves a picture show and conference every morning from now on. The many things you taught me when I was there are sure coming in handy now [...] Anybody in or outside of the organization can give us an idea and then we build out from there. It works out pretty well. Most important to me is that I can shoot the stuff I want to, so I am not stuck behind this desk. Mostly I am concentrating on full-page features and use the Rollei most of the time. We use our own fine grain formula, DK 50, D-60a, and D11, in the developing room. The photographer turns in his film and after development contact prints are made and brought to my desk. With a cropping code that I draw on the contact prints using cropping T´s then all the stuff goes up to the dark room and is printed in the way we want it, muddy for roto, contrasty for news or magazines.[15]

A year later, in 1950, when the "Pictorial Section" was working intensively for the Marshall Plan's ECA (Economic Cooperation Administration) mission, additional picture editors, a pictorial researcher, and an ECA liaison man were employed.[16] The section also had verbal contracts with ten Austrian stringer photographers who regularly obtained assignments from the "Pictorial Section" (e.g. Wilhelm Appelt, Franz Kraus, Gottfried Rainer, and Robert Halmi). The archival documents contain no clues as to

15. Letter, Yoichi Okamoto to Herman Borzner, 28 February 1949, Folder 11 "Requests for Pictorial Service", Box 1, Pictorial Section, ISB, RG 260, NARA.
16. See the document "The ISB Pictorial Section as of 31 August 1950," Folder 1 "ISB policy", Box 1, Pictorial Section, ISB, RG 260, NARA.

how these photographers were recruited. They do indicate, however, the training of these Austrian photographers. Mostly they started out with training in the darkroom so they would learn how to print their own pictures. Martin Schindelar, for example, received ten days of darkroom training sessions at the Vienna office before he started working as a staff photographer and darkroom technician at the Linz office covering news in Upper Austria.[17]

With the incorporation of the "Pictorial Section" into the MSA (Mutual Security Agency) in 1951, the situation changed considerably and got more complex. By 1950, the USIS photo archive already contained around 35.000 negatives. The monthly output in photographic prints ran to around 7.000 pictures.[18] The "Pictorial Section" literally flooded the Austrian market with free pictorial material. This posed a considerable disadvantage to freelance Austrian press photographers. In fact, Okamoto repeatedly received letters from Austrian photographers who complained about unfair competition.[19]

In the course of 1950, it is noteworthy to point out, on the *incoming side* the emphasis shifted away from dealing with picture agencies towards the production of photos by "Pictorial Section" staff members and stringer photographers, as well as freelance photographers. On the *incoming side*, the "Pictorial Section" did not serve as the most prolific deliverer of news photos. On the *outgoing side*, the "Pictorial Section" was only a member, albeit an important one, in a chain of USIS and non-USIS government agencies, all working together to promote the Marshall Plan in Austria.

Teaching Photography

The materials in the National Archives in College Park are very eloquent on one issue in particular, namely Okamoto's constant efforts to improve the journalistic and artistic skills of his staff photographers and the pictorial quality of the printed picture in the Austrian press in general. Okamoto's ambitions as a teacher of photography become very obvious during his efforts to obtain an exhibition set of the show by the New York Museum of Modern Art "In and Out of Focus." He was determined to stage this show in Vienna as an excellent example of modern American

17. Memorandum Yoichi R. Okamoto to Kurt Hoffman, Director US Information Center Linz, 28 July 1949, Folder 8 "Correspondence with Information Center Linz," Box 1, Pictorial Section, ISB, RG 260, NARA.
18. Memorandum Yoichi R. Okamoto to Mr. Abraham N. Hopman, 31 August 1950, Folder 1 "ISB policy," Box 1, Pictorial Section, ISB, RG 260, NARA.
19. Letter Walter Hubeni to Yoichi Okamoto, 28 February 1949, Folder 7 "Correspondence with Info Center Salzburg," Box 1, Pictorial Section, ISB, RG 260, NARA.

photography.[20] Okamoto wanted to get sets of pictures of the following outstanding, mostly American photographers: Henri Cartier-Bresson, Ansel Adams, Edward Weston, Andreas Feininger, Paul Strand, Gjon Mili, Irwin Blumenfeld, and Berenice Abbot.[21] He even wrote a personal letter to Ansel Adams on 7 Feb. 1950: "My greatest difficulty is in training Austrian personnel in getting the most out of a negative. I have been studying your books 'Basic Photo Course' and find them most interesting and helpful. I should like to have one or two prints (11 x 14 or larger), illustrating your famous print quality, which we could frame and hold as an example of what we should strive for."[22]

Fig. 4: USIS: Yoichi Okamoto and staff at the office of *Wiener Kurier*, 1952, Picture Archives of the Austrian National Library

The best place to study the results of Okamoto's ambitious project of

20. Draft by Okamoto to the attention of Reuben Nathan, Chief N.Y. Field Office, Civil Affairs Division, Department of the Army [no date], Folder 15, "Department of the Army Correspondence," Box 1, Pictorial Section, ISB, RG 260, NARA.

21. Letter, Reuben S. Nathan to Mary Bundy Ford, 22 July 1949, Folder 15, "Department of the Army Correspondence," Box 1, Pictorial Section, ISB, RG 260, NARA.

22. Letter, Yoichi Okamoto to Ansel Adams, 7 February 1950, Folder 14 "General US Correspondence," Box 1, Pictorial Section, ISB, RG 260, NARA.

increasing the aesthetic quality of the printed picture is the *"Bildbeilage"* of the *Wiener Kurier*, the four page rotogravure pictorial supplement that was published once a week. For this weekly *"Bildbeilage,"* Okamoto would select the best photos he could get on a given topic; for this very purpose any photographer could submit pictures to the "Pictorial Section". In February 1949, Okamoto asked permission from his superiors to offer top prices for photographs of freelance photographers.[23] His measure paid off. In a July 1949 *Quarterly Report*, Yoichi Okamoto asserted: "The new system of paying good prices for pictures from outside photographers [...] has resulted in top-notch photographers giving us first look at their pictures. This we feel has resulted in a much more successful Bildbeilage."[24]

The *"Bildbeilage"* gradually represented the kind of approach to press photography that Okamoto identified with and strove for. This is why he would answer one Austrian photographer, whose pictures he rejected, as follows: "You will have to study the Wiener Kurier Bildbeilage and you will see that we buy only either very good news pictures or picture stories. Picture stories must present an idea or must say something to the reader rather than just show him something as the camera is seeing it. In other words we require individual interpretation by the photographer."[25]

The success of the *"Bildbeilage"* encouraged Okamoto in July 1950 to propose to increase the *Wiener Kurier* rotogravure section from four to eight pages. He argued that only in the longer format could photos be printed in adequate size as in American newspapers; larger photos would be more captivating and persuasive and better printing quality could be achieved. All of this would maximize the newsstand pull of *Wiener Kurier*.[26] Okamoto summarized the "Bildbeilage's" editorial policy in four principles, which he jotted down in a document in August 1950[27]:

1) Always tell the truth in pictures.
2) U.S. propaganda should be subtle, without losing reader interest.

23. Memorandum Yoichi Okamoto to Theodore Kaghan (Press Officer), 7 February 1949, Folder 4 "Correspondence Bildbeilage," Box 1, Pictorial Section, ISB, RG 260, NARA.
24. Memorandum Yoichi Okamoto to Norman E. Bloom (Research and Analysis Officer), 7 July 1949, Folder 16 , "Quarterly Historical Reports," 12 June 1949 to July 10, 1949, Box 1, Pictorial Section, ISB, RG 260, NARA.
25. Letter Yoichi Okamoto to Fritz Matl, 11 August 1950, Folder 13 "Various Correspondence," Box 1, Pictorial Section, ISB, RG 260, NARA.
26. Memorandum Yoichi Okamoto to Ray E. Lee (Chief of Branch), Folder 4 "Correspondence Bildbeilage," Box 1, Pictorial Section, ISB, RG 260, NARA.
27. See the document "The ISB Pictorial Section services the following agencies," Folder 1 "ISB policy," Box 1, Pictorial Section, ISB, RG 260, NARA.

3) All picture stories will present a fundamental idea rather than straight reportage. So that the reader is left with a mental impression of an idea.

4) Use new, modern and even radical approaches and uses of photo technique to carry on the American tradition of journalistic progressiveness.

Fig. 5: Bildbeilage *Wiener Kurier*, 01.10.1949

From the sources quoted so far it becomes obvious that Okamoto was not only an ambitious teacher of press photography but also a professional art director concerned with optimizing every aspect of the printed picture. He encouraged competitiveness within Austrian press photographers by paying high fees for the best photographs of an event submitted. He expected photojournalists to take a personal approach to their stories. Last but not least he was aware of the impact layout, captioning, and print quality have on a news story.

Though the archival material clearly documents Okamoto's important role in bringing American photojournalism to Austria, his influence on Austrian press photography after World War II has yet to be proven at the level of imagery. Further research[28] will allow us to gain a more complete

28. We plan to continue this work with a grant we received from the Austrian Science Fund (FWF), Austria's central funding organization for basic research. The project entitled "War of Pictures. Austrian Press Photography 1945-1955" will start in February 2014 and it will

picture of Austrian press photography during the occupation period. Our objective is to describe the "Pictorial Sections" of all four occupational powers and to conduct biographical research on all press photographers and photo agencies active in Austria between 1945 and 1955; we will also investigate the publication context of the press photographs. We will try to show that the Cold War can be visually manifested as a "war of pictures" in the daily newspaper *Wiener Kurier* and in the illustrated weekly magazines *Wiener Bilderwoche*, *Große Österreich Illustrierte*, *Wiener Illustrierte*, and *Welt-Illustrierte*. Our analyses of the pictures will prove (or disprove) our hypothesis that Okamoto's introduction of American *Life* magazine-style photography had a lasting influence on Austrian press photographers.

We have another hypothesis that we would like to elaborate on in the last part of this article. We believe that the magazine *Heute* edited by the American Military Government in Munich played a crucial part in bringing modern-style American reportage to Austria.

Heute: Between *Life* and *Look*

Efforts similar to those made by Okamoto concerning the pictorial quality and layout of "*Bildbeilage*" had already been undertaken on a much larger scale in Germany with the illustrated newspaper *Heute*. Published in Munich since 1945 by the American Military Government, *Heute* had been explicitly designed to bring American photojournalism to Europe. The related NARA documents on the founding and mission of this newspaper leave no doubt about this. Penned in a June 1947 official memorandum issued by the American Military Government, the editorial policy for *Heute* reads as follows:

> *Heute* is to be directed to the broad reading public. Its appeal should be to the moderately intelligent and informed reader, its approach should not be narrowly specialist or sensationally journalistic. Through its pictures and stories it should present a dignified coverage of material designed to interest and inform readers on matters relevant to the task of creating a democratic Germany. Its level of appeal should be somewhat between that of the American Magazine *Life* and *Look*.[29]

be carried out for three years at the *Institut für Publizistik- und Kommunikationswissenschaft* (Department of Communication) at the University of Vienna.

29. "The Development of Heute Policy," Folder 1 "Heute policy," Box 247, Publication Control Branch, Information Control Division, RG 260, NARA.

The last sentence of this quote is particularly noteworthy. "*Heute*'s level of appeal should be somewhat between that of the American Magazine *Life* and *Look*." This is the key to understanding what the editors of *Heute* were striving for journalistically and especially on the level of imagery: they were striving for a European version of *Life* and *Look*, the most successful American magazines of the interwar period. *Heute* magazine was also distributed widely in Austria, with 150.000 issues per month in the second half of the 1940s.[30] In addition, *Heute* had its own Austrian editor, namely Inge Mörath (Morath), who later became a world-famous photographer and member of the Magnum agency.

Inge Morath was twenty-two years old when she started working for the ISB in 1945. First she was hired as a writer and translator for ISB's "Feature Section" in Vienna. She worked there for two years. Following a short two-month intermezzo editing the satirical magazine *Der Optimist* with her friend Hans Weigl, a famous Viennese theater critic, the ISB promoted Morath to become the Austrian picture editor for *Heute* magazine. From Morath's personal letter to Weigl we know that she received editorial training at *Heute*'s central Munich office:

> I sit in the [Munich] office all day and observe how work is done here. I participate in all the meetings and I could already place two Austrian stories. If I am not around, nobody takes care of this. Anyway, I will come to Munich more often now and see to it that these less urgent topics will be dealt with. An Austrian issue does not exist yet, but at least they decided on 2 pages per issue. In any case, the financial aspects are taken better care of now. I get more photos and I have learned the secrets of the Munich editorial office. They now respect me more. I am curious to find out how all of these newly decided things will work out in Vienna.[31]

So what kind of picture stories of Austria was Inge Morath able to place in *Heute* magazine? Over a period of two years (1947-1949), when Morath took off to Paris to work for the Magnum agency, *Heute* published numerous illustrated articles on Austria. The authors of the articles are rarely mentioned but we can assume that Inge Morath wrote them. And we

---

30. See the photograph General Mark Clark in front of an exhibition display showing the distribution channels of the magazine *Heute*, Folder "Photographs," Box 4, Austria, ISB, News Operations (Editorial Section), General Records 1945-50, RG 260, NARA.
31. Letter Inge Morath to Hans Weigl, Munich, 20 June 1948, Papers of Hans Weigl, AB 22, ZPOH 847, Handschriftensammlung, Wienbibliothek, Vienna.

know that Inge Morath started a very fruitful cooperation with another Austrian photographer who would become world-famous, Ernst Haas. On 3 August 1949, *Heute* published a reportage by Ernst Haas called "*Und die Frauen warten....Die Geschichte jedes Krieges wird mit Tränen geschrieben*" (And the Women are waiting...The Story of Every War is written in Tears), a picture story of prisoners of war returning from the Soviet Union. This story became the starting point of Haas' subsequently highly successful international career as a photographer. It is worth mentioning that Haas's reportage was published in slightly modified form in *Life* magazine within a week of its first appearance in *Heute*.

Fig. 6: Ernst Haas, Inge Morath: "Und die Frauen warten...," *Heute*, no. 9, 03.08.1949, 16-23

Haas's pictures have become iconic, especially the one with a young returning prisoner of war passing an old lady showing him the picture of her son dressed in the uniform of the Wehrmacht.[32] It has often been pointed out why Haas' pictures had such an impact on his contemporaries

---

32. Ludger Derenthal, "'...und die Frauen warten': Ernst Haas 'Kriegsheimkehrer'," in: Katharina Sykora/Ludger Derenthal/Esther Ruelfs, eds., *Photographische Leidenschaften* (Marburg: Jonas, 2006), 189-193; Hans Michael Koetzle, "Ernst Haas: Wien," in idem., *Photo-Icons: Die Geschichte hinter den Bildern 1928-1991*, vol. 2 (Cologne: Taschen, 2002), 64-71; Albert Lichtblau, "Befreit, besetzt und in Trümmern: Nach dem Ende des Zweiten Weltkriegs," in Agnes Husslein-Arco, ed., *Ernst Haas: Eine Welt in Trümmern* (Weitra: Bibliothek der Provinz, 2005), 37-51.

even though his topic was conventional for the time: he did not show the fate of one soldier but a kind of collective fate of a generation. By cropping the pictures very tightly, he created the illusion that the spectator was part of the crowd. He put the emphasis on the waiting women and he showed an arsenal of emotions which every viewer could relate to. The appeal of these pictures lies in their deeply humane approach; they are essentially ahistorical and decontextualized. Inge Morath's text (even though the author is not mentioned we can assume that Inge Morath did write this text) adds to this decontextualization and generalization. The text does not include any background information on the returnees of war. Morath only mentions the *Südbahnhof* (southern railway station) in Vienna as the location where these photos were taken. She does not include any historical facts. Neither World War II nor National Socialism is referred to (except on the pictorial level with the soldier wearing the uniform of the Wehrmacht). Since parts of the text are used as captions, it is as if text and pictures refer to each other in a circular system that does not permit different interpretations.

Inge Morath and Ernst Haas' reportage made it to the Munich *Heute* office and to *Life* magazine and eventually earned them an invitation to the Magnum agency in Paris. So it is not surprising that Yoichi Okamoto took a vital interest in their work. We have Okamoto's personal account of how he met Ernst Haas:

> At this time a young photographer came to me and showed me his black-and-white photographs that I liked a lot. I told him this and I asked him if he did not want to show his pictures in my office. He accepted and we made an exhibition. His name was Ernst Haas. He was at this time teacher of photography for the GIs. He was so revolutionary, that he got kicked out of the Graphische Lehr-und Versuchsanstalt[33] [...] That all was before he made his photos of the returning prisoners of war.[34]

Okamoto was also personally acquainted with Inge Morath. A daily report of the "Pictorial Section" from October 1948 states: "Mr. Okamoto

33. Okamoto might be mistaken about the reasons why Haas was ejected from the *Graphische Lehr- und Versuchsanstalt*. According to Haas' sister-in-law, Haas was expelled because he was Jewish. Personal interview Margarethe Szeless with Eva Haas, 12 May 2012 (interview in author's possession). According to the roster of students enrolled, Haas attended the photography class at *Graphische Lehr- und Versuchsanstalt* in the winter semester of 1940/41. We are grateful to Klaus Walder from the Archive of the *Graphische Lehr- und Versuchsanstalt* for providing us with this information on Haas.
34. Michael Mauracher, "Interview with Yoichi Okamoto," in Camera Austria 18 (1982): 82.

had a conference with Miss Inge Möerath [*sic*], Austrian '*Heute*' editor. Miss Moerath was informed of our recommendation to expand the Pictorial Section to include photo-essay specialists."[35]

Inge Morath began her training at the Munich *Heute* office in June 1948; so only four months had elapsed before Okamoto sought her know-how on photo-essays. We know that staff photographers of the "Pictorial Section" were assigned picture stories for *Heute*, and *Heute* photographers in return did photo-essays for the *Wiener Kurier*'s "*Bildbeilage*." Our hypothesis is that the professional ties between the editorial staff of *Heute* and the "Pictorial Section" might have been very tight. But the nature of this important cooperation in Central European photojournalism after the war merits further scholarly investigation.

The close ties between *Heute* and the "Pictorial Section" must also be understood as another measure taken by Okamoto to convey American-style photo-essay techniques to his staff members and to improve their photographic approach. When in 1954 Franz Kraus and Gottfried (Jeff) Rainer, Okamoto's long-term staff members and trainees, won an American prize called the Christopher Award for their photo-essays on returning prisoners of war, it surely made their teacher proud. Their pictures demonstrate unmistakably how the Cold War was fought on the level of images. It is certainly not a coincidence that two photo series dealing with returning prisoners of war from Russian prison camps were awarded American prizes at the height of the Cold War in 1954. Compared to Haas' famous series on the same subject matter, which shows human emotions on a very general level, Kraus's picture depicting a returnee from Soviet prison camps who is paralyzed by shock takes a much more critical and explicit stance. It overtly accuses the enemy of abuse of POWs. This example reinforces our main hypothesis that the Cold War was fought with the help of press photography, namely as a war of pictures.

---

35. Daily Report: 7 October 1948, Folder 22 "Daily Reports 1949-1950", Box 2, Pictorial Section, ISB, RG 260, NARA.

A Local History of the 1938 "Anschluss" and Its Memory: Vienna Servitengasse[1]

Birgit Johler, Katharina Kober, Barbara Sauer, Ulrike Tauss, Joanna White

Introduction

Despite the unusually cold weather, numerous people gathered on 8 April 2008 for the ceremonial unveiling of the memorial *Schlüssel gegen das Vergessen* (Keys against forgetting), erected seventy years after the "Anschluss" in memory of the persecuted Jewish residents of the Servitengasse, a street in Vienna's 9th district. Julia Schulz, an Austrian transmedia artist, designed the memorial: A glass case set into the ground, into which used keys have been placed, each bearing a nametag engraved with the name of a former resident or business owner from the street who was murdered or driven away under National Socialism. The keys symbolize the fact that people lived in apartments and ran businesses here which they were forced to leave. Yet the glass case, with its 462 keys and nametags, also stands for the archeological dimension of the project: the rediscovery and remembrance of this local history.

Recent years in particular have seen numerous works published on the Nazi era in Austria. The "Anschluss" or "Annexation" of Austria to Hitler-Germany and its impact on the Jewish population in particular have also been dealt with from several different perspectives. The following article presents the results of a research project with a *micro-historical approach* that took place over several years. It aims to show how both detailed archival research and the inclusion of individual memories of this particular moment in the history of National Socialism—the "Anschluss"— can add to our understanding of how these events played out at a local level in

1. This article is based on the results of the research project "Servitengasse 1938 – Schicksale der Verschwundenen," which commenced in 2005 with funding from the Jubilee Fund of the Austrian National Bank. They have previously appeared in: *1938 Adresse: Servitengasse. Eine Nachbarschaft auf Spurensuche*, ed. Birgit Johler and Maria Fritsche (Vienna: Mandelbaum, 2007). This article also includes new research findings, in particular on synagogues and prayer houses in Vienna's 9th district, as well as incorporating aspects and issues arising from the study of cultural memory.

the everyday lives of those involved. The article also attempts to situate the "Servitengasse 1938" project, run by a group of local citizens, within both the general academic discourse on cultural memory and contemporary memorial practices.

Servitengasse 1938: History in Memory

Through the project "Servitengasse 1938," a group of individuals engaged with the history of National Socialism in a very specific and active way. Using Jan and Aleida Assmann's work, "Servitengasse 1938" could be described as a memorial project that conceptualizes history as being closely linked to memory. The interest in "digging where you stand," the impulse to remember, and the wish to break the silence are what motivates each individual member of the group to engage with local history in a more intensive way. These individual motivating factors reflect a broader social interest in the Shoah and in the processes of remembering and forgetting in a local setting.[2] Often this is accompanied by a strong desire to commemorate the victims of the Nazi regime, to bring them back into public awareness through "giving them a name" and researching their fates. Furthermore, the growing academic interest in those described as "perpetrators," "collaborators," "sympathizers" and "bystanders" is, increasingly, becoming a feature of memorial practices. Within this context, greater attention falls on those places that have a connection to the history of National Socialism. These are primarily the "topographies of terror," i.e. the places and locations directly linked to the organized persecution and extermination carried out by Nazi perpetrators.[3]

Yet anti-Jewish measures began in city apartment blocks, in shops, in the streets, and on the squares. And it is this that the research project on the Servitengasse takes as its starting point. The street itself is interchangeable. What was happening when and how in the Servitengasse was also taking place in many other parts of Vienna and the *Ostmark*, or had already taken

2. On current discourse on the functions of cultural memory, to which remembering and forgetting belong, see Aleida Assmann, *Das neue Unbehagen an der Erinnerungskultur: Eine Intervention* (Munich: Beck, 2013); Aleida Assmann, *Geschichte im Gedächtnis:. Von der individuellen Erfahrung zur öffentlichen Inszenierung* (Munich: Beck, 2007). And with particular reference to urban settings: Sharon Macdonald, *Difficult Heritage: Negotiating the Nazi Past in Nuremberg and Beyond.* (New York: Routledge, 2009); Jennifer A. Jordan, *Structures of Memory: Understanding Urban Change in Berlin and Beyond* (Stanford: Stanford University Press, 2006); Andreas Huyssen, *Present Pasts: Urban Palimpsests and the Politics of Memory* (Stanford: Stanford University Press, 2003).
3. *Topographie des Terrors: Gestapo, SS und Reichssicherheitshauptamt in der Wilhelm- und Prinz-Albrecht-Straße. Eine Dokumentation* (Berlin: Stiftung Topographie des Terrors, 2008).

place in Germany. What makes this street special is its connection to a civic participation project: out of a private initiative for a memorial plaque on a single house in the Servitengasse grew a larger group, formed with the aim of researching every house in the street and the biographies and fates of every Jewish person living there in 1938, and of commemorating those people.

A "Microscopic" View

Historiography therefore provides the foundation for the "Servitengasse 1938" project's engagement with local history. The research project of the same name, "Servitengasse 1938: Fates of the Disappeared," carried out research into the Jewish residents of this entire street, their lifeworlds before and after the "Anschluss" to Nazi Germany in 1938 and—to bring in cultural memory studies—drew from both cultural and communicative memory. On the one hand it made systematic use of the material traces of the past, i.e. the documents and registration forms etc., that have been preserved in archives. This form of cultural memory, characterized as "storage memory," is reactivated by targeting and selecting data collected in the archive and linking it together. On the other hand, the project takes into account forms of communicative memory. The recollections of witnesses contemporary to the events, often only passed on within the family, if at all, were recorded as part of the project and placed alongside the quantitative analysis of data from the archives, as well as other documented memories. Today it is survivor testimony in particular that introduces perspectives lacking in the "documents of power" stored in the archives. The "Servitengasse 1938" project, whose approach is rooted in the history of everyday life, in micro-histories, as well as in the interdisciplinary study of culture, sought to determine how both sides, Jews and non-Jews, reacted to structural changes and shifts in power relations, what actions they took, and what strategies they developed in order to live and survive.

1938: Address Servitengasse

It was, perhaps, a sense of already being used to something that meant sixteen-year old Frieda Feuerstein[4] found her way home to 20 Servitengasse without much difficulty on 15 March 1938, on the day of Hitler's speech on the Heldenplatz, despite the threatening omnipresence of the National

---

4. Frieda Feuerstein, née Fink, born 16 March 1922 in Vienna, died 24 Dec. 2013 in Tel Aviv. Birgit Johler and Barbara Sauer carried out a biographical interview with Frieda Feuerstein in August 2013, parts of which are published here for the first time.

Socialists. Rallies and demonstrations in the days before the "Anschluss" had already given rise to anti-Semitic incidents. These involved young people in particular and were judged by Jewish newspapers to be the result of the "Berchtesgaden Agreement" of 12 February.[5] Already as a child, Frieda Feuerstein had been made to experience the pain of discrimination through the anti-Semitic comments of her classmates at school. On 15 March so she tells, following a visit to the doctor in the 4th district, she was "no longer able to take the tram home. The trams were overcrowded because Hitler had come to Vienna and given a speech on the Heldenplatz… I started to walk home, I knew my way around Vienna very well because my parents went out for walks with me a lot. …I thought, I'll never get home, it was so full of Nazis. I can't forget it, it was terrible. All at once there were so many Nazis. There were no people any more, only Nazis!"[6]

In March 1938, the Jewish population of Vienna numbered some 206.000 people.[7] In Alsergrund, Vienna's 9th district, around a quarter of the population was Jewish in the interwar years and was thus, after the 2nd district of Leopoldstadt, the district with the second highest percentage of Jewish population.[8] Along with neighboring Berggasse and Porzellangasse, the Servitengasse lies in the center of a residential and shopping district formerly favored by Jews, which, in addition, is near to the Ringstraße and thus in attractive striking distance of the city center. The residents of the street were mostly self-employed, white-collar workers or mid-level public servants, and they had social and economic ties to other parts of the city. Often their apartments were located some distance from their places of work, something typical for the middle classes establishing themselves in Vienna's inner districts (II-IX) as a result of a period of increased building activity.[9]

---

5. "Die Volksbefragung," in *Die Stimme* 11 March 1938, 1. Concerned reports of organized Nazi parades and rallies were also coming in from other cities such as Graz and Linz. The "Berchtesgaden Agreement" between the Austrian chancellor Kurt Schuschnigg and Adolf Hitler resulted in the National Socialists' participation in the government, leading to Arthur Seyß-Inquart being named Security and Interior Minister.
6. Interview with Frieda Feuerstein, 12 August 2013.
7. According to Jonny Moser, the number of people in Austria with Jewish religious affiliation on 13 March 1938 was 181.882. These people were termed *Glaubensjuden* during the Nazi period. On the basis of this calculation, the number of Jewish people according to the Nuremberg Laws (*Volljuden, Rassejuden*) is given as around 206.000. Cf. Jonny Moser, *Demographie der jüdischen Bevölkerung Österreichs 1938-1945* (= Schriftenreihe des Dokumentationsarchivs des österreichischen Widerstandes zur Geschichte der NS-Gewaltverbrechen, 5) (Vienna: Dokumentationsarchivs des österreichischen Widerstandes, 1999), 16.
8. Leo Goldhammer, *Die Juden Wiens: Eine statistische Studie* (Vienna: R. Löwit, 1927).
9. Marsha L. Rozenblit, *Die Juden Wiens 1867-1914: Assimilation und Identität* (= Forschungen zur Geschichte des Donauraumes, 11) (Vienna: Böhlau, 1998), 82.

The historical research revealed that before 1938, over half of the 680 residents of the Servitengasse, namely 377 adults and children under eighteen, were of Jewish descent or were persecuted as Jews by the National Socialists after the "Anschluss" (around fifty-five percent).[10] Of the total of 111 businesses registered in the street, sixty-four can be allocated to Jews (around fifty-eight percent).

The "Anschluss" and Its Consequences for the Residents of the Servitengasse

"I remember the Servitengasse as a lively, popular shopping district, where an annual market took place," wrote Fritz Pojer, a survivor from Australia whose mother ran a knitwear and hosiery shop at 5 Servitengasse.[11] The grocery store run by Frieda's father at number 20 was also very popular and, from what she remembers, was frequented primarily by non-Jewish customers. That until the National Socialists seized power, Jewish and non-Jewish tenants were neighbors, met on the street or in the shops, and did business with one another should not distract from the fact that even before 1938, anti-Semitism was considered perfectly socially acceptable. Religiously-motivated anti-Jewish sentiment had a long tradition in Austria and, since the end of the nineteenth century, had combined with elements of "modern," racist anti-Semitism.[12] With Karl Lueger (1844-1910), the founder of the Christian Social Party, turn-of-the-century Vienna had a professed anti-Semite as mayor. After the First World War, anti-Semitic propaganda and measures increased. The "Aryan Clauses" that had already been introduced in some German nationalist fraternities were also now introduced by some branches of the *Alpenverein* (Austrian Alpine Association) and the Austrian Tourist Association, later also by cinema owners with anti-Semitic leanings.[13] The radicalization of the Vienna NSDAP (National Socialist Workers' Party of Germany) in the early 1930s, the devastating bomb attacks on Jewish businesses and business owners, and the rising level of aggression and discrimination against Jews in public life and Jewish students and staff at the universities, all attest to

---

10. 285 could be categorized as "non-Jewish." For eighteen people it was unclear whether they were of Jewish descent or were persecuted by the National Socialists as Jews.

11. Letter from Fritz Pojer to the "Servitengasse 1938" project group, 22 June 2006, Private Archives of the "Servitengasse 1938" project group, Vienna.

12. Thomas Albrich, "Vom Vorurteil zum Pogrom: Antisemitismus von Schönerer bis Hitler," in *Österreich im 20. Jahrhundert: Von der Monarchie bis zum Zweiten Weltkrieg*, Vol. I, ed. Rolf Steininger, Michael Gehler (Vienna: Böhlau, 1997), 309-365, 310.

13. For example, the headline in the Jewish newspaper *Die Stimme* ran "Films without Aryan Clause" in its edition of 11 February 1938, see *Die Stimme*, 11 Feb. 1938, 5.

the increasing threat to and exclusion of the Jewish population.[14]That the Austrofascist regime, despite its explicit anti-Semitism, was considered by the Jewish population as protector against National Socialist persecution— the constitution of 1934 granted Jews the same civil rights as well as freedom of religion[15]— could still be seen in 1938: "We say yes to Austria! Everyone to the ballot box" ran the headline on 11 March 1938 in *Die Stimme*, the official publication of the Zionist Committee of Austria.[16] To the last, Jewish organizations such as the *Israelitische Kultusgemeinde* (Jewish Community) supported, both ideologically and to a large extent financially, the plebiscite scheduled by Chancellor Schuschnigg for 13 March 1938 calling for a "free and German, independent and social, Christian and united Austria."[17]

As is well known, 13 March 1938, a Sunday, turned out rather differently from what the Austrian government had planned[18] and today, the events of 11-12 March—Schuschnigg's resignation speech, the formation of a new government under Seyß-Inquart, the entry of German troops without resistance—are anchored in collective memory as the "Anschluss" of Austria to National Socialist Germany. To these can also certainly be added the images of the enthusiastic crowds on the Heldenplatz cheering National Socialism, which were in fact taken at the Nazi rally and parade held in the early afternoon of 15 March, when Hitler gave his historic speech from the balcony of the Hofburg palace. However, between the raising of the border gates to the German troops and the cheering welcome given to the Führer on the Heldenplatz more than three days passed in which Jews across Austria were attacked in various ways by the general population, something scarcely documented by the Nazis, with the exception of the so-called *Reibeaktionen*, when citizens were forced to scrub the streets on their hands and knees.

Frieda Feuerstein was lucky—with her blonde hair she was not taken for a Jew. On 15 March, after a long journey on foot, she got home to the Servitengasse safe and sound. From what she remembers, during these

---

14. Erika Weinzierl, "Antisemitismus in der Ersten Republik," in *Verlorene Nachbarschaft: Die Wiener Synagoge in der Neudeggergasse. Ein Mikrokosmos und seine Geschichte*, ed. Käthe Kratz et al. (Vienna: Mandelbaum, 1999), 181-186, 184.
15. Emmerich Tálos, *Das austrofaschistische Herrschaftssystem Österreich 1933-1938*, 2nd ed. (Vienna: Lit 2013), 473.
16. *Die Stimme*, 11 March 1938, 1.
17. "Aufruf des Bundeskanzlers," in *Die Stimme*, 11 March 1938, 1. Recently, Edmund de Waal recalled this huge level of support for the Schuschnigg government, fuelled by desperate hope, see *The Hare with the Amber Eyes: a Hidden Inheritance*. (London: Vintage, 2011).
18. On this day notice was given of the announcement of the federal constitutional law of 13 March, 1938 on the reunification of Austria with the German Reich, B.G.Bl. Nr. 75/1938.

days she had to witness how Jews were stopped in the street and forced to clean off the *Vaterländische Front* (Fatherland Front) slogans from the pavements and walls with soap and water. Public humiliations like this and of other kinds were taking place all over Vienna. Following the "Anschluss," a simultaneity of order and caprice, of visible violence, discrimination and theft, of invisible appropriation, oppression, and exclusion prevailed in the streets and neighborhoods of Vienna, on its squares and in its parks, in its houses and apartments. In many places house searches, looting, and countless evictions were taking place with no prior warning. Witnesses tell of arbitrary expulsions from their apartments, often initiated by neighbors or landlords who wanted to make the house *judenfrei* (lit. "Jew-free").[19] Buoyed up by the propaganda slogans in a range of newspapers and borne along by the wish of numerous branches of the NSDAP to obtain flats for party members, the evictions—often unauthorized—of Jewish residents from their apartments continued and reached a new high-water mark with the staged pogrom of 9-10 November 1938.[20] We know about these evictions from the information found in the address registration forms dating from that time held in the Municipal and Provincial Archives of Vienna. Thus, the registration form for the manufacturer Karl Krishaber, a long-term resident of 6 Servitengasse, shows that he de-registered from this address on 10 November. On this day he felt compelled to move to a house in the 18th district that, at that time, still belonged to himself and his sister. Rosa Goldschmidt was also clearly forced to leave her flat in the same building, together with her son Paul. As became apparent later, she was able to find a home in an apartment one story below for a short time. A third tenant in house number 6, Gisela Reichsfeld, also had to give up her apartment at the time of the November pogrom. The 73-year-old had lived in this apartment since 1915. On November 12 she was ordered to move into apartment no. 10, one story higher, that had been the home of the

19. See the various witness statements in *Erzählte Geschichte: Jüdische Schicksale, Berichte von Verfolgten*, ed. Dokumentationsarchiv des österreichischen Widerstandes (Vienna: Dokumentationsarchiv des österreichischen Widerstandes, 1992); Günter Bischof, Austria's Loss—America's Gain: Finis Austriae—The "Anschluss" and the Expulsion/Migration of Jewish Austrians to the U.S, in: idem, *Relationships/Beziehungsgeschichten. Austria and the United States in the Twentieth Century* (= Transatlantica, 4) (Innsbruck: StudienVerlag, 2014), 57-82. on discourses related to the "Anschluss" as a place of Austrian memory, see Oliver Rathkolb, The Anschluss in the Rearview Mirror 1938-2008: Historical Memories between Debate and Transformation, in Günter Bischof/Fritz Plasser/ Barbara Stelzl-Marx, eds., New Perspectives of Austrians and World War II (*Contemporary Austrian Studies* 17) (New Orleans: UNO Press, 2009), 5-28.
20. Gerhard Botz, *Wohnungspolitik und Judendeportation in Wien 1938 bis 1945: Zur Funktion des Antisemitismus als Ersatz nationalsozialistischer Sozialpolitik* (Vienna: Geyer-Edition, 1975), 57f.

Deutsch family since 1916. It seems that Gisela Reichsfeld only remained there for a short time. Two months later she was forced to move again into what the National Socialists officially termed a *Wohngemeinschaft*[21] (shared apartment) in the Praterstraße in the 2nd district.

November 10, 1938: Registration form (*Meldezettel*) documenting the change of address in the course of the November pogrom
Municipal and Provincial Archives of Vienna (MA8), Vienna.

For the non-Jewish owner of the house at 6 Servitengasse, the days of the November pogrom were a busy time—she signed every change of address or de-registration form. And whilst SS units were destroying the synagogue in nearby Müllnergasse, the SA was looting apartments and shops throughout the area.[22] Also located at 6 Servitengasse, Moritz Lichtmann's shop was destroyed on November 10. The watchmaker's memoirs, written down in 1948, relate the devastating events of these days: "But in the area

---

21. From early 1939 onwards, evictions of Jews could be carried out "legally." The Reich Law on the Tenancy of Jews of 30 April 1939 repealed Jewish tenants' rights vis-à-vis non-Jewish landlords. Jews could now also be forced, at the order of the authorities, to take in Jewish tenants and sub-tenants. This led to the creation of numerous *Sammelwohnungen* (forced collective apartments), in particular in the 2nd and 9th districts. Jews living here were later transferred to so-called *Sammellager* (collection centers), located mainly in the 2nd district, before being deported. Cf. Johler, Fritsche, *1938 Adresse: Servitengasse*, 41, 42.
22. Robert Streibel, "Die Zerstörung der Tempel und was wir alles nicht wissen," in *Verlorene Nachbarschaft*, ed. Kratz et al., 187-198, 191f.

where I had my shop, up until this time, despite all the troubles that usually took place in Vienna, there were no disturbances. Even today it seems to me that there was no danger present... Then, at around 10:30 I saw a crowd opposite my shop and a man threw all the baskets containing fruit and vegetables that were outside on the stand into the green grocers. So I ran out to pull down the shutters on my shop, scared that my windows might be smashed. The man from opposite rushed over to me to stop me doing this. I retreated into my shop but I couldn't close the door. He ordered me to follow him but I refused. Only when he called a passing policeman, who persuaded me to give myself up, did I follow him, leaving my wife, near fainting and in fear, alone... The keys to my shop were immediately taken from me and that was the end of my career in Vienna, after thirty-two varied years as a watchmaker."[23] Moritz Lichtmann was subsequently imprisoned in a school in the Karajangasse in the 20th district before being transferred to "protective custody" and admitted to the feared Roßauer Lände prison—incidentally very close to the Servitengasse. During the ten days of his imprisonment Moritz Lichtmann had to endure hunger, harassment, and sleep deprivation and survived numerous interrogations. His family received no news of him during this time.

"I saw the *Reichskristallnacht*..."—Charles Kurt describes his impressions as a 12-year old— "and I saw three shops [in the Servitengasse] on the other side of the road and I saw how the SA came with trucks, with torches, it was already getting a bit dark and you could hear the SA singing, the Horst-Wessel Song. I know that: *Die Reihen dicht geschlossen ... marschieren ... festen Schritt*. Then they dragged people out of their shops by their hair and threw them onto the trucks and then they moved on to the next shops. So, that was the *Kristallnacht* and of course so many of the Jews were taken away."[24] The seemingly supernatural speed with which actions were taken against the Jewish population on November 9 and 10, and which resonates in Charles Kurt's memories, was part of the National Socialists' use of terror to spread fear. "Speed, that means: You are slung like a bale of hay into a dark truck, which, high up and with no footboard, posed a problem for the non-gymnasts and non-climbers, for the old and tired. ... Speed, that was the ringing slap that came whistling down on the cheek of the man sitting on my lap. ... And again—when we got out —what do I mean got out?—when we were whipped and chased out of the high truck with no steps—speed, speed!" This is how Ernst Benedikt, the

---

23. Unpublished memoir by Moritz Lichtmann, 1948, "Servitengasse 1938" Project Archives, Vienna.
24. Interview with Charles Kurt (né Karl Heinz Goldschmidt, born 7 June 1926 in Vienna), 16 September 2006.

former publisher and editor of the *Neue Freie Presse*, described the National Socialists' methods when he was arrested on 10 November 1938.[25]

Today, academic historians consider the November pogrom to have been a combination of "organization and spontaneity, of authority and the anti-Semitic majority."[26] It is known that the Nazi party leadership not only ordered the destruction of prayer houses and synagogues, but also house searches and actions against shops and apartments.[27] That large parts of the Viennese population looked on and that some Viennese were directly involved in the destruction, looting, and evictions can now be considered certain. This is also clear when one considers that, firstly, apartments and houses built before 1917 fell under the tenancy laws of 1922, which gave the tenants of these apartments special protection from eviction[28] and secondly, that the appropriation of privately owned apartments was not covered by law until 28 December 1938. This kind of expropriation ("wild Aryanization") was, therefore, only possible on one's own initiative and with the support of those living nearby. In the Servitengasse, at least fourteen Jews were evicted from their apartments during the November pogrom. Most of the evictions took place in houses owned by non-Jews.

Official expropriations targeting the Jewish population began already shortly after the "Anschluss" of Austria to the German Reich. At that time, newspapers announced new anti-Jewish measures daily and reported on successful "Aryanizations." "The Tandel market is Jew free" wrote *Die Reichspost*, for example, on 17 March 1938 in the name of the Vienna Association of Junk Dealers in order to dispel rumors circulating about the flea market located close to the Servitengasse.[29] With the "Order concerning the registration of property belonging to Jews" of 26 April 1938, Jews were given just two months to value and declare all their domestic and foreign property. This action was the prelude to the large-scale theft and expulsion

---

25. Ernst Benedikt was taken from his apartment in Grinzing to the police riding facilities in the Pramergasse, near the Servitengasse, and was held in inhuman conditions for 48 hours together with around 2.800 others, see Ernst Benedikt, *Erinnerungen an den Novemberpogrom 1938*. Manuscript, 36 pages, 10.
<http://www.doew.at/erinnern/fotos-und-dokumente/1938-1945/novemberpogrom-1938/wien> (accessed on 3 Jan. 2014).
26. Gerhard Botz, *"Volkszorn" und "Reichskristallnacht" im nationalsozialistischen Österreich*, quoted in <http://www.doew.at/thema/pogrom/kurz.html> (accessed on 31 July 2007). Due to the redesign of the DÖW homepage, this page is no longer accessible.
27. Ibid.; see also: "Auch die längste Geduld hat ein Ende! Eine Welle der Empörung gegen die jüdischen Meuchelmörder," in *Volks-Zeitung*, 11 November 1938, 7.
28. Georg Graf, *Der Entzug von Mietrechten: Ein rechtshistorischer und rechtsdogmatischer Bericht unter besonderer Berücksichtigung der Entwicklungen nach der Wiedererrichtung der Republik Österreich*. (Vienna: Historikerkommission, 2000), 4 ff.
29. "Der Tandelmarkt ist judenrein," in *Die Reichspost*, 17 March 1938, 14.

of the Jewish population that was to take just a few years and was actively supported by the Viennese population.

Before – After

For many survivors, looking back at the Vienna of the 1930s means looking back to their childhood, the "best period of their lives"— a memory that can also help in dealing with the traumatic events that followed.[30] That then, seemingly overnight, the social fabric became "totally different," is something witnesses report again and again. Charles Kurt remembers that, "[f]or example, one of our neighbors was a famous surgeon, he was a very very good friend of the family and one day after the "Anschluss," the swastika was already on his lapel and he had stopped speaking to us."[31] For the Jewish population the change meant a new "normality" that differed vastly from that before the "Anschluss" and from that of the "Aryan" population. Many recognized the danger inherent in the situation and tried to escape the Nazi terror. This led to information being exchanged and new contacts being formed. Frieda Feuerstein's father, Chaskel Fink, received a call in May 1938 from two shop-owners he knew from across the street who asked him, first verbally and then at his request in writing, to be out of his grocery store and apartment by the end of August. A neighbor in the street told the Finks about the possibility of escape to Palestine via Italy, a course Frieda's parents decided on after much debate. Chaskel Fink closed up his shop at the end of July and dropped the keys down the drain.

Of the 377 former residents of the Servitengasse of Jewish descent, 160 were, in all likelihood, able to leave Austria. The Fink family finally managed to escape to Palestine in 1939 after their first attempt failed—transit via Italy was suddenly no longer possible and the train on which the family, along with many others, was traveling was stopped at the Italian border and sent back to Vienna. 133 Jews from the Servitengasse were deported to the concentration and extermination camps, only eight of whom survived. The fates of sixty-five people remain unknown. The others remained in Vienna, died there during the Nazi period, or managed to survive in so-called *Mischehen* (mixed marriages). In terms of business and homeowners and their families (who often did not live in the Servitengasse), at least seventeen persons perished in the Holocaust; at least thirty were able to escape. In total, at least 462 people, who either lived or worked in the

---

30. Sabine Schweitzer, "Erinnerungen im Schatten der Schoa," in *Verlorene Nachbarschaft*, ed. Kratz et al., 162-180, 177.
31. Interview with Charles Kurt (né Karl Heinz Goldschmidt, born 7 June 1926 in Vienna), 16 September 2006.

Servitengasse, can be considered to have been the victims of persecution under the National Socialist regime.

The "Anschluss" and Its Consequences for Clubs and Organizations

Until 1938, Vienna boasted a vivid Jewish social life in the form of clubs, associations, and other organizations, ranging from sports clubs, charitable groups, and student fraternities to religious associations, some of which were registered in the Servitengasse and the nearby area. The "Anschluss" had far-reaching consequences for all of these clubs and associations. One of the first decrees concerning them required them to produce an exact statement of all their assets as of 31 March 1937 and 31 March 1938; the Nazi authorities were, of course, mainly interested in the larger and better-funded organizations. New—National Socialist—chairpersons were installed and, in most cases, their main task was to liquidate the association and secure any property, outstanding membership fees, and other assets for the Nazi regime.[32] The law on the transition and integration of clubs, organizations, and associations of 17 May 1938[33] was another of the measures taken by the Nazi regime to gain control over all aspects of people's lives. Many of the clubs were simply integrated into the appropriate Nazi institution, from charities to chess clubs, etc. Others were disbanded and their assets were either used to finance Jewish emigration and provide welfare for those unable to emigrate or directed into the Nazi system by bureaucratic means, such as the levying of special fees. In the following section, examples of student fraternities located in the Servitengasse and selected religious associations in the area around the street will be used to show proceedings in the months following 12 March 1938.

Student Fraternities and Youth Organizations

Three Jewish student and alumni clubs and one youth organization were located in the Servitengasse in March 1938. The Jewish-national *Emunah*

---

32. Katharina Kober, "Das jüdische Vereinswesen," in *1938 Adresse Servitengasse*, ed. Johler, Fritsche, 180.
33. Gesetz über die Überleitung und Eingliederung von Vereinen, Organisationen und Verbänden, 17 May 1938, AdR, Stiko Wien, Kt. 928, Nachrichtenblatt I, S. I. GBIÖ 44/1938, Austrian State Archives (ÖSTA), Vienna.

J.V.A. Aktivitas und Altherrenverband,[34] founded in 1896 as a summer association in Bielitz, had its club house in Servitengasse number 4. According to its articles of association, it upheld the "principle of faithful friendship" and promoted interest in Jewish and Zionist topics. Two years earlier, *Libanonia*[35] had been founded in Vienna and was affiliated to *Emunah*[36] and enjoyed a *Gastrecht* (hospitality rights) at *Emunah*'s club rooms in the Servitengasse. It viewed the preservation of Jewish identity and Jewish literature as essential. Another fraternity, *Jordania*,[37] founded in 1904, had grown out of a student association founded in Bukovina. In its clubrooms in the house at Servitengasse number 8 it promoted Jewish-national ideals by cultivating Jewish art, science, and education. *Emunah* and *Libanonia*'s Viennese branches were disbanded in the second half of August 1938 and were removed from the official register of associations (Vereinsregister) as per the law of 17 May 1938.[38]

The youth organization *Akiba*[39] was founded in Vienna in 1934. With its headquarters likewise in the house at Servitengasse number 4, the organization sought to promote the communal life and strengthen the Jewish identity of children and youngsters aged twelve to twenty-four years. By September 1938, the organization had already been incorporated into the *Zionistische Jugendverband* (located in the 1st district). One month later the Nazi authorities disbanded it and struck it off the register of associations.

The exact proceedings of the disbandment of these clubs, the confiscation of their movable and immovable property, and the extent to which the residents in the area were aware of it happening is not known. What is better documented and more present in public awareness, however, is the synagogue in the Müllnergasse—a street running parallel to the Servitengasse—and its destruction in 1938.

---

34. Harald Seewann ed., *Zirkel und Zionsstern: Bilder und Dokumente aus der versunkenen Welt des jüdisch-nationalen Korporationswesens. Ein Beitrag zur Geschichte des Zionismus auf akademischem Boden* (Graz: Eigenverlag H. Seewann, 1990), 139. Also cf. Fritz Roubicek, *Von Basel bis Czernowitz: Die jüdisch-akademischen Studentenverbindungen in Europa* (Vienna: Österreichische Verein für Studentengeschichte, 1986).
35. M.Abt. 119/Serie A 32/Standort 203/15/9548/37, Municipal and Provincial Archives of Vienna (MA8), Vienna. Cf. *Seewann, Zirkel und Zionstern*,135; cf. Roubicek, *Von Basel bis Czernowitz*, 82.
36. M.Abt. 119/Serie A 32/Standort 203/15/2812/21, MA8, Vienna.
37. M.Abt. 119/Serie A 32/Standort 203/15/1100/21, MA8, Vienna. Cf. Seewann, *Zirkel und Zionstern*, 135; also Roubicek, *Von Basel bis Czernowitz*, 82; The residents of Servitengasse number 8 were predominantly Jewish.
38. Gesetz über die Überleitung und Eingliederung von Vereinen, Organisationen und Verbänden, 17 May 1938, AdR/Stiko Wien, Kt. 928, Nachrichtenblatt I, S. I. GBIÖ 44/1938, ÖSTA, Vienna.
39. M.Abt. 119/Serie A 32/Standort 203/15/4001/34, MA8, Vienna.

Religious Associations

From the available sources, thirteen Jewish religious associations have been identified in the 9th district, although not all were still active by 1938.[40] Whilst these sources do not tell us about the religious views of the inhabitants of the district or their everyday religious practices, they do reflect the fact that Jewish religious life in Vienna was divided roughly into two strands, one more orthodox and the other more liberal or "assimilated." Some synagogues were run by the *Israelitische Kultusgemeinde*, Vienna's Jewish Community, which was a rather orthodox organization. Also, many immigrants from Galicia and other areas of the Austro-Hungarian monarchy adhered to a stricter, orthodox faith. In some cases, they rented an apartment in which to hold their services, eventually founding an association to support it administratively and financially. Other synagogues, such as the Müllnertempel, were founded by associations whose members were more liberal in their views and practices, preferring a modern service in a more modern ambience.[41] In any case, any new association pursuing (Jewish) religious purposes needed the approval of the *Israelitische Kultusgemeinde*.[42]

The synagogue in the Müllergasse, the Müllnertempel, was the most visible place of Jewish worship in nineteenth and twentieth century Alsergrund, being the only detached synagogue in the district. Interestingly, it is situated not far from the Roman-Catholic church in the Servitengasse, and the spires of the church and the synagogue seemed almost to be communicating with one another. The Müllnertempel was set on fire in the so-called *Reichskristallnacht* on November 9 and 10, 1938, as documented in the *Brandprotokoll* (fire service protocol): "Center fire! The interior fittings

---

40.   For details, see: Ulrike Tauss, "Ein Beitrag zur Erforschung der Synagogen und Bethäuser im 9. Wiener Gemeindebezirk (Alsergrund) vor dem Jahr 1938 (Militärsynagoge in der Rossauerkaserne, Betpavillon im Alten AKH, Privatbethaus des Großrabbiners Israel Friedmann aus Husiatyn)," unpublished manuscript, Vienna 2013. (Funded by the Municipal Department of Cultural Affairs (MA7), Science and Research Grants). And Katharina Kober, "Eine Skizze zu den Synagogen und jüdischen Bethäusern im 9. Wiener Gemeindebezirk und den mit ihnen verbundenen Vereinen," unpublished manuscript, Vienna 2012. (Funded by the Municipal Department of Cultural Affairs (MA7), Science and Research Grants). Further associations were Adass Jeschurun and Thoras Chajim at 5 Pfluggasse and Beth Jakob at 5 Rotenlöwengasse.

41.   Verena Pawlowsky, "Einschluss und Ausschluss: Österreichische Vereine nach 1938," in *Jüdisches Vereinswesen in Österreich im 19. Und 20. Jahrhundert*, ed. Evelyn Adunka, Gerald Lamprecht, and Georg Traska, (Innsbruck: Studien Verlag, 2011), 272.

42.   Angelika-Shoshana Duizend-Jensen, *Jüdische Gemeinden, Vereine, Stiftungen und Fonds.: Arisierung und Restitution* (= Veröffentlichungen der Österreichischen Historikerkommission. Vermögensentzug während der NS-Zeit sowie Rückstellungen und Entschädigungen seit 1945 in Österreich, vol.21/2: Vereine, Stiftungen und Fonds im Nationalsozialismus) (Vienna: Historikerkommission, 2004), 23.

in the central aisle of the Jewish temple and the altar burned. One hose line positioned in the interior and a second to protect the neighboring stable and hay store. After some time doused the fire inside the temple, no further danger."[43] Thus was the synagogue in the Müllnergasse, with its high symbolic value for the Viennese Jewish community and its artistically valuable interior, destroyed. Very few of the families of those interviewed seem to have attended services in the Müllnergasse synagogue regularly, apart from on high feast days.[44] For this reason it is even more remarkable that the events of 9 and 10 November are so present in their memories.

Felice Schrager, née Bruckner, mentions that, outwardly, her father was not very religious and ate non-kosher foods, but that he did visit the Müllnertempel with his daughter on Friday evenings. During the night of the pogrom her father was able to go down to the street to watch the fire at Müllnertempel without being molested. "I can remember. … November, …we saw the synagogue and we heard and everything. … And my father …—strangely enough—went down, and had a look at everything. And *nothing* happened to him."[45] Perhaps it would have been better, added Felice Schrager, if something had happened during this evening stroll that would have made her father see the urgency of leaving Austria. However, Alfred Bruckner decided to rely on his popularity and remain in Vienna for the time being in order to help his wife and daughter leave the country. A few months later Alfred Bruckner was evicted from his apartment and on 15 May 1942 he was deported to Izbica.

The synagogue at 21 Müllnergasse was run by *Chewra Beth Hatfilah*, an association that had convened at another address before buying a piece of land to build its own temple on. The open-mindedness of this community is illustrated by the fact that it was one of only five synagogues in Vienna equipped with an organ, a musical instrument strongly disapproved of in the orthodox tradition.[46] *Chewra Beth Hatfilah* was disbanded in early 1939,[47] the Müllnertempel having made it the only group to own the property where it convened.

43. Brandjournal 1938, 2. Teil, Archive of the Vienna Fire Service Museum, Municipal Department of Fire Services and Disaster Relief (MA68), Vienna.
44. Johler, Fritsche, eds., *Adresse 1938: Servitengasse*, 28 ff.
45. Interview with Felice Schrager (née Bruckner, 1924, Vienna) in New York, 1 August 2006.
46. Evelyn Adunka, "Religiöse jüdische Vereine in Wien vor der Shoa," in *Jüdisches Vereinswesen*, ed. Adunka et al., 47.
47. AdR, ZNsZ Stiko Wien, 31-A 9/5, ÖSTA, Vienna.

Notification of disbandment (Auflösungsbescheid)
Chewra Beth Hatfilah, AdR ZNsZ Stiko Wien, 31-A 9/5, Austrian State Archive.

Ohel Abraham Beth Hamidrasch is an example of a very orthodox group in the 9th district. They had their meeting rooms in 28 Grünentorgasse, around the corner from the Servitengasse. Founded in 1902, its agenda focused on "holding Jewish, religious-moral and Hebrew-scientific lectures."[48] The file for this organization was closed on 5 January 1940. Documents name Eugen Blau, who lived at 16 Servitengasse, as a member of the board in 1936 and 1938.[49] However, his daughter Lilly Capek[50] did not mention any activities her father engaged in specifically in relation to this when interviewed. The chairman of the organization was Siegmund

---

48. AdR, BKA-I, BPDNB-I 377, ÖSTA, Vienna.
49. AdR, ZNsZ Stiko Wien, 31-A 9/4, ÖSTA, Vienna.
50. Personal interview with Lilly Capek (née Blau, born 24 January 1925 in Vienna), in New York, 1 August 2006.

Kohn, a merchant living at 22 Servitengasse.[51]

Esrath Jisroel, based at 5 Stroheckgasse in the same district, also followed an orthodox tradition—the articles of incorporation, dating from 1907, explicitly state the requirement that at least six of the twelve members of the board adhere to orthodox Jewry. The disbandment of this organization is dated August 1938.[52]

Jonny Moser, a historian who has carried out extensive research into the history of the Nazi era in Vienna, was a twelve-year-old living in the Servitengasse in 1938. Speaking of the situation in the Servitengasse area after November 1938, he recalls that a friend of the family, a deeply religious man, took him to services which, after the synagogues and prayer houses had been destroyed, were held in a room in the Seegasse in the 9th district,[53] amongst other places.[54] Sources on religious associations are often difficult to obtain[55] and existing research on them is scarce.[56] The research carried out as part of this project is a first step towards closing that gap for the 9th district, and the interview material gathered as part of the "Servitengasse 1938" project adds a further layer to the archival material, helping to build a picture of how patterns of everyday life—such as where to go to attend a religious service—changed in 1938.

"Servitengasse 1938" – The Process of Remembrance

"[W]ho would have believed it … . That these people are taking the

---

51. Kober, "Skizze Bethausvereine," 33ff.

52. 1.3.2.119.A32, 2019/1924, MA8, Vienna and AdR, ZNsZ Stiko Wien, 31-A 9/3, ÖSTA, Vienna.

53. This refers to the hospital and old people's home at 9-11 Seegasse run by the *Israelitische Kultusgemeinde* until 1972. Cf. Elizabeth Anthony, Dirk Rupnow, "Wien IX, Seegasse 9: Ein österreichisch-jüdischer Geschichtsort," in *nurinst: Beiträge zur deutschen und jüdischen Geschichte* 5 (2010): 98–113.

54. Interview with Jonny Moser (born 10 December 1925 in Parndorf, died Vienna) in Vienna, 16 February 2006.

55. Exact statistics concerning associations and similar organizations are almost impossible to obtain as archival sources are scattered in many different locations, the material varying in content as well as in dates. Furthermore, most sources are incomplete, which allows only very few organizations to be traced completely from their founding to their disbandment. The material held in the archives of the Jewish Community is mainly based on originals in Tel Aviv, only some of which have been put onto microfilm, meaning these sources were only partially available in the course of this project.

56. Adunka, "Religiöse jüdische Verein in Wien vor der Shoa," 45-58.

initiative to do something, even if it comes very late."[57] This half-sentence,
uttered by Hedy Grandville at a meeting of the "Servitengasse 1938" project
group, is symptomatic of a social process of remembrance that is "bottom
up," that was initiated by local residents and is still continued by them.
These people, who gradually came together to form a group with the aim
of remembering those Jewish residents of the Servitengasse who had been
expelled and murdered during the Nazi era, these people were few in number
at first. It had all started on a very small scale, in a family context. Barbara
Kintaert, a resident of the Servitengasse since the 1980s, was interested not
only in the fate of the Jewish relatives of her father-in-law, but also in the
history of the house she lived in, Servitengasse number 6. With the support
of some of her neighbors in the house, the cultural historian Birgit Johler
was brought on board to research the names and the fates of the former
residents and the decision was taken to erect a memorial plaque to them on
the facade. At first this scheme met opposition from the house owner and
other residents, but with help from Agenda 21[58] the private initiative was
finally able to unveil a memorial plaque situated in the pavement—i.e. on
public ground—in front of the house in September 2005.[59]

The *BürgerInnenbeteiligungsprojekt* (civic participation project) that
had been established—"Servitengasse 1938"—attracted not only residents
of the Servitengasse and the immediate neighborhood, but those simply
interested in the topic as well as members of the Jewish families concerned.
Group meetings, which were moderated by Agenda 21, were open to all
and operated on grassroots, democratic principles. Proposals and ideas
developed into the plans that gave the project its current shape, widening
its scope to encompass all the houses in the street and to incorporate the
research project "Servitengasse 1938—Fates of the Disappeared."[60]

Even in its early stages, project members identified strongly with

57. Discussion between the "Servitengasse 1938" project group and Hedy Grandville, 17
October 2005. Hedy Grandville is the wife of Kurt Grünwald, who changed his name to
Kenneth Grandville in Great Britain. He lived with his parents Helene and Fritz Grünwald
at 19 Servitengasse until 1938 when, at the age of just 13, he was sent to London on a
Kindertransport.
58. Agenda 21 is a program for the politics of development and environment for the twenty-
first century and a nonparty platform, aimed at citizens' participation, which was founded
by 178 countries at a conference of the United Nations Conference on Environment and
Development (UNCED) in Rio de Janeiro (1992). On a community level, this is implemented
by the local Agenda 21, which strives towards sustainable (urban) development. Its merits
lie in the creation and moderation of project workshops and opening up the initiatives to
a broad basis of interested locals, thereby supporting and strengthening public action in
general. See: <http://de.wikipedia.org/wiki/Agenda_21> (accessed on 25 Nov. 2013).
59. Permission to site the memorial plaque on public ground was approved by the head of the
district council. The unveiling took place in the presence of the survivor Paul Lichtman.
60. For the research findings see above.

the aims of "Servitengasse 1938," with members volunteering to take on a variety of roles and responsibilities. Members saw networking as vital, and they helped the project to become well-known both nationally and internationally by distributing information at cultural events, speaking about the project at conferences and symposiums, and placing adverts in relevant papers calling for witnesses, documents, and photographs. Furthermore, the group set up a website, which is updated regularly and draws attention to group events.[61] The development, activities, and group dynamics of the project are reflected in the one-hour documentary film *Unter dem Alsergrund: Servitengasse 1938*,[62] which came about through contact with the film producer Kurt Mayer. In addition, the 2007 book *1938: Adresse Servitengasse. Eine Nachbarschaft auf Spurensuche* not only documented the research findings and presented some of the individual fates of former residents, but also included reflections written by members of the project group. This created a multilayered picture of the project that interwove the internal and external views of the many dedicated people involved.

The common aim of the group—to advocate the remembrance of the Jewish residents of the street who had been persecuted, expelled, or murdered and, in doing so, to take a stance against forgetting the horrors of National Socialist terror—strengthened its solidarity in the face of the conflicts that arose. Hanging on through long periods of planning and decision-making, as well as overcoming bureaucratic and financial obstacles, also required a great deal of perseverance. This perseverance finally resulted in the unveiling of the memorial *Schlüssel gegen das Vergessen* in April 2008. From the beginning, one of the group's central concerns had been to create a visible symbol of remembrance in public space, to inscribe the memory of those forced to leave into the history of the district. The search for a fitting means to represent this hidden and suppressed history led, in 2006, to the decision to carry out a two-stage student competition in cooperation with the University of Applied Arts Vienna. Together with the "Servitengasse 1938" project group, guidelines were developed for the memorial's design. For example, the guidelines stipulated that it should include all the names of the victims and provide the opportunity for placing stones, as is traditional on Jewish gravestones. From a total of twenty-three entries, a professional jury selected three winning projects, and the memorial *Schlüssel gegen das Vergessen* by Julia Schulz was chosen to be realized.

---

61. http://www.servitengasse1938.at.
62. Tobias Dörr and Henri Steinmetz, *Unter dem Alsergrund: Servitengasse 1938*. Documentary film (Vienna, 2006). (with English and French subtitles).

Servitengasse 2008: Keys against Forgetting (Schlüssel gegen das Vergessen)
Photo: Johannes Stern

The unveiling ceremony took place in April 2008. Alongside members of the project group, representatives from local government, and those who had funded the memorial, Charles Kurt spoke as a survivor from the street. The General Secretary of the Jewish Community of Vienna recited a prayer for the dead. The guests of honor, however, were those former residents of the Servitengasse who had been found through the project; Charles Kurt, Lilly Capek, Walter Feiden, and Felice Schrager from the United States, as well as Sophie Hirn from Vienna. Indeed, what most of the members considered to be the driving force behind the project, or the most important parameter, was personal contact and dialogue with survivors.

Since its unveiling, the memorial has become an important meeting place for survivors and descendants of the victims who come to Vienna; the moment when someone finds their relative's name is a very moving one.

It has also become a destination for visitors, who come either individually or as part of a guided tour, and recently the memorial was documented in Claude Lanzmann's film *Der Letzte der Ungerechten*.[63] Nearly all the reactions to it have been positive and, in the six years since the unveiling, there have been no attempts to damage the memorial. Rather, it has been used as a focus for remembrance by the group, with commemorative events held there to mark the November pogrom. Public awareness has also been raised through exhibitions,[64] workshops in schools, courses at the local adult education college, and guided walks.

As can be seen from the above, history, memory, and remembrance are interwoven in the "Servitengasse 1938" project. Rather than try to separate these things, the project shows how each is enriched or even "entangled" with the other.[65] Firstly, at the research stage, the project group combined archival research with oral history interviews. Next, the group used the results of that research as the basis for their commemorative activities and, in the form of the names, it became part of the memorial itself. Finally the memorial makes certain histories visible and becomes a means through which history is communicated—both that of the street and perhaps of the work that went into its creation.

"Servitengasse 1938" and Memorial Culture

This type of memory work[66] has become more prevalent in Vienna in recent years, and several local projects have been initiated that have successfully created visible markers of the past in public space.[67] Heidemarie Uhl writes that "such location-related memorial projects are manifestations

---

63. Claude Lanzmann/Iris Wegschneider (director/producer), *Der Letzte der Ungerechten*, 218 min. (France/Austria: Dor-Film, 2013).

64. Exhibitions: *Servitengasse 1938. Spurensuche in der Nachbarschaft.* June - July 2010 in the Galerie Fortuna and in the Servitengasse itself (shop windows), and from March - April 2012 in the Alsergrund adult education centre.

65. Marita Sturken writes that "I would posit cultural memory and history as *entangled* rather than oppositional," See Marita Sturken, *Tangled Memories: The Vietnam War, the Aids Epidemic, and the Politics of Remembering* (Berkeley: University of California Press, 1997), 5.

66. Iwona Irwin-Zarecka, *Frames of Remembrance: The Dynamics of Collective Memory* (New Brunswick: Transaction, 1994).

67. For example: Steine der Erinnerung <http://www.steinedererinnerung.net>; Herklotzgasse 21 und die jüdischen Räume in einem Wiener Grätzel <http://www.herklotzgasse21.at/>; Erinnern für die Zukunft <http://www.erinnern-fuer-die-zukunft.at>; Steine des Gedenkens Wien III <http://www.steinedesgedenkens.at>; Arnezhoferstraße. Ein Straßenname als Mahnmal <http://arnezhoferstrasse.currentlynowhere.com/>; Große Stadtgutgasse 34 <http://www.grossestadtgutgasse34.at/index.html> (accessed on 28 Jan. 2014).

of a transnational European culture of remembrance that began to evolve in the late twentieth century."[68] In post-Waldheim Austria, the memorial culture of the 1990s built on the new historical consciousness of the 1980s and on the official recognition of Austrians' complicity in and responsibility for the Shoah by Chancellor Vranitzky in 1991 and 1993. There was both an increase in the number of Shoah memorials and a critical reexamination of existing memorials.[69] Much of the decade was dominated by debate on the *Mahnmal für die österreichischen jüdischen Opfer der Shoah* on Vienna's Judenplatz, which was finally unveiled in 2000. However, the discussions were no longer on whether or not to commemorate victims of the Shoah, but on the form that commemoration should take.[70]

Indeed, by 2000, it seemed that remembering the victims of National Socialist persecution had become part of official Austrian political culture, enshrined in the coalition governing statement of that year.[71] Facing up to a difficult past, in particular the *Zivilisationsbruch Auschwitz*,[72] had also become a key element of international memory politics and a marker of a nation's democratic maturity.[73] In practical terms this meant an increase in funding for memorial projects through bodies such as the *Nationalfonds der Republik Österreich für die Opfer des Nationalsozialismus* and the *Zukunftsfonds der Republik Österreich*, who funded the "Servitengasse 1938" publication in 2007 and the 2010 exhibition, for example.[74]

It also meant that there has been virtually no political opposition to these memorials. While some politicians are actively supportive—and much can be achieved in Vienna at a district level due to the de-centralized *Bezirk* system with local administrations able to spend culture and research

---

68. Heidemarie Uhl, "Local and European: The Turner Temple Memorial Project in the Context of a new Culture of Remembrance," in *Memory Site Turner Temple. Searching for a Reflexive Archaeology*, ed. Is Andraschek et al.(Vienna: Kunst im öffentlichen Raum, 2012), 47-49, 47.

69. Biljana Menkovic, *Politische Gedenkkultur: Denkmäler – Die Visualisierung politischer Macht im öffentlichen Raum* (Vienna: Braumüller, 1999), 133-151.

70. Dietmar Seiler, "Im Labyrinth der Geschichtspolitik: Die Erinnerung an die Shoa im öffentlichen österreichischen Gedächtnis," *Zeitgeschichte* 24, no. 9-10 (1997): 281-301 (here 295).

71. Wolfgang Schüssel, "Regierungserklärung"

<http://www.demokratiezentrum.org/fileadmin/media/pdf/regierungserklaerung.pdf> (accessed on 28 Jan. 2014), 15.

72. Heidemarie Uhl, ed., *Zivilisationsbruch und Gedächtniskultur: Das 20. Jahrhundert in der Erinnerung des beginnenden 21. Jahrhunderts* (Innsbruck: StudienVerlag, 2003).

73. Heidemarie Uhl, "'Wann fahren Sie endlich mit den Kindern nach Mauthausen?' Transformationen der Österreichischen Gedächtniskultur seit 2000," in *Die Beschämte Republik. 10 Jahre nach Schwarz-Blau in Österreich*, ed. Frederick Baker and Petra Herczeg (Vienna: Czernin, 2010), 7-34.

74. Project codes P06-0063 and P10-0614. See: <http://www.zukunftsfonds-austria.at> (accessed on 28 Jan. 2014)

budgets as they choose—others merely remain silent. What opposition there is from house owners who refuse permission for memorial plaques to be mounted on their property, as was seen in the case of 6 Servitengasse.[75]

These newer projects share various features. Firstly, they are all rooted in *civil society*. While each got started in a different way—some by private individuals or groups, others by local councilors interested in the topic who used their position to initiate and carry out a project—all encourage and rely on civic participation. In their work on collective remembrance, Jay Winter and Emmanuel Sivan highlight the role of civil society, suggesting "that the dialogue between agents working within civil society and state institutions, an ongoing process of contestation, is and is likely to remain one of the permanent features of remembrance."[76] In the Viennese context, the experience of the "Servitengasse 1938" project shows that this is not only a process of contestation, but one of cooperation, with many different agencies interacting. This leads to group members gaining a certain expertise in this kind of public participative project; in Vienna, members of different memorial groups formed a networking initiative to make sharing experience and information easier.[77] Frequent inquiries to the "Servitengasse 1938" email address from people initiating a memorial project of their own or planning to do so illustrate how this project has become a point of reference for others of its kind. Furthermore, the expertise gained in doing this kind of biographical research led three members of the original team to teach a course titled "In the archive of memory" at the local adult education centre.[78] This nascent institutionalization of memory work raises questions about the ways in which grassroots initiatives become a fixed part of a city's cultural and heritage landscape, and the relationships between the concerned citizen as "memorial entrepreneur,"[79] an emerging type of "expert memory worker,"

---

75. See above. This was also the experience of the "Erinnern für die Zukunft" project: Ulli Fuchs, "Projektbeschreibung" in Kilian Franer and Ulli Fuchs, ed., *Erinnern für die Zukunft: Ein Projekt zum Gedächtnis an die Mariahilfer Opfer des NS-Terrors* (Vienna: echomedia, 2009), 54-64, 55.
76. Jay Winter and Emmanuel Sivan, eds., *War and Remembrance in the Twentieth Century* (Cambridge: Cambridge University Press, 1999), 39.
77. Institut für historische Intervention, founded in 2008. See: <http://www.iehi.eu> (accessed on 28 Jan. 2014).
78. See: <http://www.servitengasse1938.at/vermittlung/kurse/kurse.php> (accessed on 28 Jan. 2014).
79. This term comes from Jennifer Jordan and her work on Berlin. She writes: "I find that collective memory shapes the urban landscape in part at the observable intersection of four specific factors: land use, landownership, the resonance of the site's meaning with a broader (often international) public, and the presence of absence of what I call a 'memorial entrepreneur', which is to say, someone willing to lobby on behalf of memorialization." Jennifer A. Jordan, *Structures of Memory: Understanding Urban Change in Berlin and Beyond* (Stanford: Stanford University Press, 2006), 2.

and state authorities and official agencies.

This new type of memory work is also intrinsically place-based; each project grew out of and is centered around a particular location—be it a house, a street, or a district. This is often a feature of social memory, which Karen Till describes as "an ongoing process whereby groups map understandings of themselves onto and through a place and time."[80] In other words, memory work needs a location to "take place" in, in turn inscribing that place with new meanings and affects. For as Uhl writes, "[i]t is apparent that the logics governing the field of memory are not only determined by intentional acts of cultural preservation or political calculation, but also through the dimension of the emotional and the affective."[81] This can be seen in the memorial *Schlüssel gegen das Vergessen* in two ways. Firstly, its use of the victims' names focuses attention on the individuals before they became numbers in a camp—naming on memorials is a frequent trope and the individualization of memory is a powerful way of making seemingly incomprehensible events more concrete.[82] Secondly, its presence marks the street as a historical site, a site of suffering, and thus as an "authentic" site of the Shoah, with the "aura" or "antaeic magic" this evokes[83]—particularly for those involved in the project who also live there. Yet the presence of the memorial means the site is per se no longer "authentic"— it has already been changed. It is this interplay of the familiar, the historic, and the authentic that makes local sites so dynamic and enables them to remain active, used sites within the urban landscape even after their unveiling.

The notion of "active remembrance" is also important here. While in some senses a "buzzword" for politicians,[84] the range of activities undertaken

80. Karen E. Till, *The New Berlin: Memory, Politics, Place* (Minneapolis: University of Minnesota Press, 2005), 13.

81. Heidemarie Uhl, "Kultur, Politik, Palimpsest. Thesen zu Gedächtnis und Gesellschaft," in *Schauplatz Kultur - Zentraleuropa: Transdisziplinäre Annäherungen*, ed. Johannes Feichtinger et al. (Innsbruck: StudienVerlag, 2006). 25-35, 33.

82. Aleida Assmann, *Der Lange Schatten der Vergangenheit: Erinnerungskultur und Geschichtspolitik* (Munich: Beck, 2006), 249. Examples of naming in memorials range from the Vietnam Veterans Memorial in Washington, D.C., to the Atocha Station Memorial in Madrid. Individualization is also used as a strategy at memorial museums, for example the *Ort der Information* at the Memorial to the Murdered Jews of Europe in Berlin, where the exhibition opens with large-format photos of just six people.

83. Aleida Assmann notes that traumatic places possess an "antaeic magic," referring to the myth of Antaeus, who possessed great strength as long as he maintained contact with the earth. It suggests there is something in the ground that can be "felt." See Assmann, *Der Lange Schatten*, 223.

84. Cf. "Mailath fordert 'aktives Erinnern'", APA OTS Originaltext-Service for 17 May 2009.

<http://www.ots.at/presseaussendung/OTS_20090517_OTS0024/mailath-fordert-aktives-erinnern> (accessed on 17 May 2009). Andreas Mailath-Pokorny is Vienna's Executive City Councilor for Cultural Affairs.

by the "Servitengasse 1938" project group show that remembrance can be a powerful focus for civic and community engagement. The increase in such participative processes as "Servitengasse 1938," which aim to strengthen democracy by turning away from authoritative structures and towards a sense of social responsibility, give rise to the hope that remembering and remembrance, as integral aspects of how historical knowledge is dealt with, will ultimately contribute to sustaining open and democratic social structures. In Vienna's Servitengasse, researching the local history of the "Anschluss" revealed to what extent those structures had failed, but through recovering the names of neighbors who had vanished, new meanings were given to the neighborhood.

Book Reviews

Review of Robert Kriechbaumer, *Zwischen Österreich und Großdeutschland: Eine politische Geschichte der Salzburger Festspiele, 1933-1944* (Vienna: Boehlau Verlag, 2013)

Michael P. Steinberg

Robert Kriechbaumer, a professor of history at the Salzburg Paedagogische Hochschule, has written a conscientiously researched and informative history of the political context of the Salzburg Festival during the twelve years of the Third Reich. Reasonably, the book's two parts address local and national concerns before and after the *Anschluss* of March 1938, concluding with an account of the abrupt cancellation of the 1944 festival in the context of the declaration of total war.

Founded in 1920, the Salzburg Festival strove to present "the Austrian idea" (to use founder Hugo von Hofmannsthal's key phrase) to Europe and the world following the collapse of the Habsburg Empire and the declaration of the First Austrian Republic, the so-called "republic that no one wanted." Compensating for economic as well as political defeat, the festival claimed to inherit the mantle of a German-centered culture grounded not in Prussian militarism but in the soft power of the central European baroque. Hofmannsthal reconfigured his morality play *Jedermann* as the festival's mascot, staging it, under Max Reinhardt's direction, in front of the city's cathedral, where it has remained in place. Though the festival's globalization proceeded apace, *Jedermann* has continued to occupy its ideological core, with many in its audiences continuing to appear—as Hermann Broch famously observed in his 1947 study *Hofmannsthal und seine Zeit*—in local costume, or *Tracht*. The festival's musical anchor was and remains Mozart, the city's most famous native son, reviled and miserable during his youth there (like Thomas Bernhard two centuries later) but celebrated as the ultimate local-global product ever since. The musical-dramatic bridge between Mozart and Richard Strauss, a festival cofounder with Hofmannsthal and Reinhardt, was girded by the institution's abiding joint emphasis on the operas of the two composers. In 1927, Hofmannsthal himself radicalized his "Austrian idea" by placing it under the mantle of "conservative revolution." His theories etched a cultural ideology that contributed to the significant conceptual difficulty historians faced when attempting to place Austrian politics between the two fascisms of Germany and Italy, especially since an indigenous Austrian fascism was instituted in 1934 as a play for national independence.

As Kriechbaumer rightly emphasizes in his opening chapter, Salzburg and its economy were badly shaken by the 1000-Mark tax imposed by the National Socialist government in 1933 on all Germans crossing into Austria. The festival's survival depended on the determined internationalization of its elite visitors, a process that accumulated measured but substantial success by 1937. The book then turns to Austrian-Italian relations and Chancellor Dollfuss's ill-fated effort to share Mussolini's building of ballast against Hitler. To that end, Dollfuss's government unsuccessfully pressured the Salzburg Festival to complement its planned dose of Strauss and Mozart with Verdi's *Don Carlo* and *Julius Caesar*—the latter in the version not by Shakespeare but by Mussolini himself (59). In this same philo-Italian context, Arturo Toscanini conducted *Falstaff* in Salzburg from 1935-37, refusing to return in 1938 in a post-*Anschluss* gesture that repeated his disavowal of Bayreuth in 1933. As Kriechbaumer accurately states, Toscanini championed Italian opera as a ballast *against* fascism and German opera, especially Mozart, Beethoven, and Wagner (*Tristan* and *Die Meistersinger*), as heralds of Europeanness and freedom (257). Toscanini resigned from Salzburg in February 1938, within days following the so-called Berchtesgaden Agreement between Hitler and Austrian Chancellor Schuschnigg, one month prior to the actual *Anschluss*. His signature opera for Salzburg, Verdi's *Falstaff*, remained in the repertory in 1938 and 1939, conducted in 1939 by Tullio Serafin and heralded (along with Rossini's *Barber of Seville*) as a token of German-Italian solidarity, while in the nearby hotel *Oesterreichischer Hof* the Italian military role in the imminent invasion of Poland was being negotiated (299). From year to year, the allegorical status of works constant to the repertoire, such as *Falstaff*, shifted considerably, along with the productions and their clear political valences (leading with *Die Zauberfloete*), as well as, most clearly, with the replacement of signature works and productions—such as *Faust* with *Egmont*.

The chapter on "The Festival and the Jews" [*Die Festspiele und die Juden*] lacks a certain subtlety in both language and classification: the claim that the Salzburg Festival was "apparently dominated by Jews" [. . . *der angeblich von Juden dominierten Salzburger Festspiele* . . .] includes cofounder (along with Richard Strauss) Hugo von Hofmannsthal in this category. Although

Hofmannsthal was deeply curious about his Jewish ancestry, he lived his life as a third-generation Catholic (his grandfather had married a Milanese aristocrat) (178,186). Similarly, Sigmund Freud's disclosure to his son Ernst that Austro-fascism is to be preferred to National Socialism doesn't validate his inclusion among the so-called "Dollfuss-Jews," as the author suggests (185). Neither does Jewish preference for the Austrian authoritarian state as a ballast against National Socialism account for the deep attraction to Catholicism among so many (not, of course, including Freud), an attraction grounded emotionally and aesthetically in an Austrian idea both older and deeper than either political Catholicism or the emergency politics of the mid-1930s. For many, the cultural roots of conversion desire remained in place in the 1930s, even if the social and political results were no longer palpable.

Between 1938 and 1944, the Salzburg Festival's international face morphed into a national one, the face of *Grossdeutschland*, though always second in symbolic significance to Hitler's attentions to Bayreuth, whose ideology it now largely ventriloquized. The history of *Gleichschaltung* imposed ideological and aesthetic constraints, and Kriechbaumer tells the story of that grim process reliably and with some interesting biographical vignettes along the way. He reminds us that Richard Strauss's comportment was often more distasteful than neutral. For example, in response to a letter from Stefan Zweig, Strauss provides an agitated self-defense of his opportunistic replacement of the expulsed conductors Bruno Walter and Arturo Toscanini in Berlin and Bayreuth (182). Strauss's opportunism was matched by Clemens Krauss, the so-rumored illegitimate Habsburg scion who became Strauss's factotum and champion. Krauss replaced Fritz Busch for the Dresden premiere of *Arabella* in July 1933. Kriechbaumer seems incongruously generous to Karl Boehm, however, who took over most of Busch's Dresden assignments, including the 1935 premiere of *Die schweigsame Frau*, whose libretto had been conceived by the now-banished Zweig. In June 1944, Boehm conducted Strauss's *Ariadne auf Naxos* at the Vienna State Opera in honor of the composer's 80th birthday and in the presence of the Gauleiter, Baldur von Schirach. No one's comportment during these excruciating years broached the leonine integrity of Toscanini, who functioned as an autonomous outsider with regard to Germany and Austria to be sure, but who had also left Italy out of nothing other than conviction.

A somewhat platitudinous final chapter on Salzburg as a *lieu de memoire* to everyone's taste seems out of place in the context of the precise empirical accounts that marked the shifting political terrain surveyed in the book's body. Salzburg's pliability to the demands of twentieth-century politics is not an inspiring phenomenon, and it leads one to suspect a certain falseness at its core.

In this respect, Kriechbaumer's informative study does not explore where historiography still fears to tread, namely into the deep ideological structures and motivations for Austrian acceptance and enthusiasm for two fascist systems: so-called Austro-Fascism in 1934 and the Third Reich as of 1938. In the context of the Salzburg Festival and its revival of baroque theatricality as a principle of Austrian identity, this ideology has to do with the profound affinity between spectacle and power. This relation has been cogently analyzed in the context of Italian fascism, for example by Simonetta Falasca-Zamponi in her well-known study *Fascist Spectacle: The Aesthetics of Power in Mussolini's Italy* (2000). It was also the question that concluded my 1989 study of *The Meaning of the Salzburg Festival: Austria as Theater and Ideology* (second edition 2000 and translated as *Ursprung und Ideologie der Salzburger Festspiele*, 2000). It is not unreasonable to set "Catholic-baroque Salzburg" starkly against the "German Rome" of the Third Reich (272). On the other hand, the architecture of neo-Roman imperialism was not owned by Berlin alone. It had multiple sources, including, well, Rome: the baroque Rome to which baroque Salzburg has itself offered consistent architectural, if not always ideological, homage.

Heidi Hintner/Donatella Trevisa/Luise F. Pusch, eds., *Frauen an der Grenze: 13 Frauenbiographien aus Süd- und Osttirol und dem Trentino / Donne di frontiera: 13 biografie di donne tirolesi e trentine* (Innsbruck: StudienVerlag, 2012)

Christina Antenhofer

This edited collection of female biographies is the second volume that results from the cooperation between the feminist author-collective TANNA and the FemBio-Institute. FemBio provides a database, which continues to collect biographies on Notable Women International (www.fembio.org) hosted in Hannover and Boston and directed by Luise F. Pusch and Joey Holsey. Luise F. Pusch is a pioneering figure of the early feminist movement and is considered to be the founder of German feminist linguistics. One of her most groundbreaking works is her collected essays on German as a male language.[1] TANNA, on the other hand, is an autonomous regional group of six women living mostly in South Tyrol. According to their slogan "TANNA—*eigenmächtige frauen /donne tenaci/ëiles liedies*," TANNA women consider themselves powerful and autonomous, sharing a culture of three languages: German, Ladin, and Italian. Looking at their short biographies, it becomes clear that they are a generation of women who have now reached considerably powerful positions in South Tyrolean cultural life, working as journalists, teachers, translators, school principals, or even in political institutions. All of them have an academic background. Thus TANNA fulfils several requirements of feminist critique: it strengthens female solidarity, creates female networks and clubs, and provides mentoring for women. In a similar way, male networks and clubs push the careers of young men.

This book, then, comes with a feminist and regional heritage that must be discussed before turning to its content. In the short introduction, the editors state that they want to make the lives and works of women visible

---

1. Luise F. Pusch, *Das Deutsche als Männersprache: Aufsätze und Glossen zur feministischen Liguistik* (Frankfurt/Main: suhrkamp, 1984).

from a feminist point of view, as well as pass on their own knowledge and experience. In particular, they aim to reveal the conditions of women's lives and careers in a still male-dominated world. The book is bilingual, German and Italian, and focuses on women who lived in today's South Tyrol, Eastern Tyrol, and the Trentino. The selected biographies cover thirteen women from the age of Ötzi to 2011; each of them written by one of the TANNA women, with Astrid Kofler writing three chapters.

The first six portraits are dedicated to historically more distant figures. The book opens with the fictitious biography of Ötzi's mother, followed by the Vita of St. Notburga of Rattenberg, a prominent regional female saint of the 13th century. Her veneration began shortly after her death but increased considerably from the 17th century on due to the billing of Tyrol as the "Holy Catholic Land." The third portrait is given to Verena von Stuben, the famous 15th century abbess of monastery Sonnenburg near Bruneck. Von Stuben is noted for her quarrels with humanist bishop Nikolaus Cusanus on the secular rights and possessions of her monastery as well as the aristocratic lifestyle of her nuns. With the chapter on Steffa de Ley, we turn to the profile a woman of the early modern period declared to be a witch, beheaded, and burnt. Maria Hueber is honored as founding figure of the female Third Order of St. Francis and thus one of the pioneers of female school education. The final chapter of this section is dedicated to Anna Ladurner Hofer, well known as Andreas Hofer's tough wife since the anniversary celebrated in 2009 of the Tyrolean upheaval 1809.

With chapter seven we jump into the contemporary age. The portraits in this section are significantly enriched by background information collected via interviews. This is certainly the more interesting and innovative part of the book. The series starts with the inspiring figure of Ernesta Bittanti Battisti, journalist and highly intellectual pioneer of the Italian resistance of the early 20th century. She was remarkable both as the widow of the political victim Cesare Battisti and as one of the first women to graduate from an Italian university and fight for women's rights. Rather pale are the portraits of the textile artist and decorator May Hofer and the poet Maria Ditha Santifaller— they leave the reader with no real impression of the women. Angela Nikoletti's portrait, one of the clandestine elementary school teachers during the fascist regime in South Tyrol, remains hagiographic. She became one of the most famous victims, since she died at the age of 25 from the hardships and time in prison she endured. The chapter on Frida Piazza, author and pioneering autodidactic linguist of the Ladin language, is more articulate. The communal politician of Eastern Tyrol, Hirlanda Micheler, stands out as one of the few women in this collection who is not from an elite or academic background. Micheler was born as an illegitimate child and scandalized people by frequenting bars and consuming alcohol in the still-male rural public world of the second half of the 20th century. The book closes with Ingeborg Bauer Polo, communal politician of Bozen and school principal who scandalized practioners of the bourgeois urban lifestyle by living together with an Italian married man. She was only allowed to marry him when Catholic Italy allowed people to divorce and remarry in 1970.

All together the portraits collected in this volume are very heterogeneous: some of them remain pale while others make the reader think and want to know more. All of the portraits remain, however, *exempla* rather than stand as biographies. They provide a very short synopsis of these women's lives, a procedure which tends to render them idiomatic figures rather than individual people: the mother, the abbess, the saint, the witch, the intellectual, the poet, and so forth. In this respect, the collection resembles the antique genre of the *exempla* (*prodesse aut delectare*). The genre particularly flourished in the Renaissance, providing collected examples of famous (*illustris*) men and women. One wonders if this antique and conservative genre is really apt for the feminist attitude of the 21st century. Although it is an honorable project to make women visible, this collection very much echoes the spirit of the early feminist generations that overemphasized the gap between men and women. In fact, no men contributed to this book. Collecting and writing biographies of single women is, of course, still on the agenda of feminist studies today. But the focus these days lies more on their interaction with their male surroundings and the specific conditions of their womanhood in a given historical situation. It is no longer merely about the retelling of famous women's lives. In the current of postcolonial studies, feminists now tend to point out discriminations in a variety of fields that do not focus only on women, and even less on famous women.[2] While this is a rather general critique of the methodological approach of this book, a more specific one regards the title, which can be roughly translated as "women at the frontier." Nowhere in the book do the editors make clear if these women share an experience because of their lives on the frontier, and what they consider to be the frontier in their lives. They also do not reflect on the much-touted field of "frontier or border studies." We only learn that those women lived in today's South and Eastern Tyrol and the Trentino. However, from the age of Ötzi to the 21st century, one needs to ask where the border or the frontier in this region was. How did it change over time? And did/do these women's biographies reflect the geographical and political situation of this area? Did the multiethnic and multilingual area affect women's lives in a

---

2. Claudia Opitz-Belakhal, *Geschlechtergeschichte* (Frankfurt/Main: Campus, 2010).

particular way? A final caveat needs to be made about the editor's statement that the biographies are based on "exhaustive research in libraries and archives" (p. 8). In fact, it is a pity that the very short texts rely mostly on selected secondary literature and are largely journalistic pieces. To give three examples: the portrait on Anna Ladurner Hofer does not mention the two pioneering books by Andreas Oberhofer on the letters and life of Andreas Hofer, which are actually the source for what we know today about his wife.[3] The fictitious portrait of Ötzi's mother does not mention the most prominent regional academic discourses of the so-called matriarch theory and patriarchal critique by the key figure Claudia von Werlhof. Finally, the life of St. Notburga does not mention nor reflect on the many feminist readings of medieval Vitae of Saints, which have vitally contributed to a rereading of medieval texts from a gendered and feminist perspective. Apart from these critiques, these essays certainly are interesting to read. However, this book might tell us more about how powerful and intellectual women in the region of today's South Tyrol, Trentino, and Eastern Tyrol build their identities now and whom they consider to be their "role models."

---

3. Andreas Oberhofer, *Der andere Hofer: Der Mensch hinter dem Mythos* (Innsbruck: Wagner, 2009); idem, *Weltbild eines "Helden": Andreas Hofers schriftliche Hinterlassenschaft* (Innsbruck: Wagner, 2008).

Nicole M. Phelps, *US-Habsburg Relations from 1815 to the Paris Peace Conference: Sovereignty Transformed* (Cambridge: Cambridge University Press, 2013)

Kurt Bednar

You have to know the facts before you tell a true story. And is history not the story of "How it really was"? At least that is the pretension of one school of modern history. Writing about the relationship (was there one?) between the U.S. and Austria (which one?) at a moment when memory strikes hard can be tricky.

To begin with one certain fact that has escaped the author's attention again (since this grave mistake has already appeared in her University of Minnesota dissertation *Sovereignty, citizenship, and the new liberal order: US-Habsburg relations and the transformation of international politics, 1880-1924*, Ann Arbor 2008), in June 2014 the world will memorize the assassination of Franz Ferdinand in Sarajevo, and not in Belgrade as Nicole Phelps wants us to believe (p. 222). Unless U.S. historians finally accept another truth: that Serbia (and her capital has been and still is Belgrade) was responsible for the murderous act.

The book is "about the relationship between two of the world's most famously diverse countries": Thus Phelps opens her narrative. It is an excellent book not only because it covers an area that has been neglected for too long. Also, most of the literature available today does deal with Germany only if it covers Germanic issues. The author has combined a huge amount of interesting details to argue a debatable theory: that the U.S. and Austria stand for diverse methods of diplomacy.

But—to begin with—does the title satisfy? First, the relationship exists between states and not dynasties and since Habsburg (does the U.S. finally accept the original name with a "b"?) heads a state the other end would correctly be addressed as Austria (in whatever dress she appears). Secondly, why start the relationship with 1815 since it did not begin before 1838? Finally, why end it with the Paris Peace Conference in 1919 where Austria-

Hungary (that was the correct name before her demise) was not present (even had she still existed she would not have been allowed to take part)?

Relations between the two countries were dismantled in 1917 when Sweden took over the interests of the Dual Monarchy. Victor Mamatey, in a still recommendable observation, has pointed out that although the U.S. in the end denied Austria-Hungary her diplomatic existence the victorious parties had to find a body to deal with (*Austria History Yearbook*, vol. III, 1967, 236: "They insisted on concluding peace with the Austro-Hungarian empire, which did not exist any more and on distributing its territory to the Successor States, which were already in possession of it.")

It is indeed difficult for many historians to grasp the identity of the conglomerate in the middle of Europe. When the relationship finally commenced, it was called Austria proper and was one of the great powers of the Old World, strengthened by the victory over Napoleon and, in due course, enlargement of her territories and peoples. The U.S. first became aware of this construction when Vienna needed the Russian Tsar to defeat the revolution in Hungary in 1849. When Kossuth had been dragged from the Ottoman Empire to receive a hearty welcome in the New World the relationship suffered a first blow.

Phelps surmises that only a dozen of years later Washington again gave proof of her inexperience by fearing Vienna might recognize the Confederates because never would the court here deal with revolutionaries. At the end of the Civil War we see unofficial Austria step-toed in Mexico in what can only be called a huge blunder although—as Phelps makes clear—the U.S. identified France to be blamed for Maximilian's adventurous trip.

By then, however, the Danubian Monarchy had changed wardrobes and turned into Austria-Hungary in 1867, the Dual Monarchy which gradually became a second-rate power. Nothing much happened between Washington and Vienna (besides the Keiley affair—a diplomat destined for Rome and in the midst of the journey redirected to Vienna without the necessary agreement—expertly narrated on p. 75) until the former's "splendid little war" with Spain and the latter's efforts to secure the rank of the Spanish monarchy.

Yes, the U.S. press reacted furiously when Vienna did not take time to send condolences upon McKinley's assassination and yes, there was the Storer affair (a diplomat who, due to his wife's intrigues, had to be recalled without informing Vienna about it, nicely described on pp. 93ff.), and a, retired Theodore Roosevelt visited the Emperor (neglected in his memoirs and biographies), but the main development before the outbreak of the Great War received less attention: mass migration.

Beginning in 1890 many thousands of emigrants from the Dual Monarchy travelled America (via the entry point Ellis Island) to find a job or even a new home. Here Phelps overestimates the size of return migration (it surely was not 50 percent as she claims in the introduction, p. 6). Also one should not forget that because of the Contract Labor Law, hiring in the mother country was forbidden (p. 119 creates the impression U.S. companies fished in Croatia). Of course, dual citizenship made possible by mass migration caused enormous troubles even before the war shut down borders and shipping lines. Austrian consuls were busy helping their countrymen but also opposing activities from non-German speaking folks laying foundation for later activities and ultimately the demise of the monarchy. Phelps (like everybody else working in this field) must (and does indeed) thank Rudolf Agstner for his basic work on the organization of Austrian consulate services in the United States (although it may not be correct to address him as "amateur historian", see hint on p. 108n13; also p. 153n6; maybe calling him an "antiquarian" who collects basic facts from the archives might be more appropriate).

Taking into account that some three thousand deaths occurred annually among Austrian immigrants in Pennsylvania alone (p. 194, as of 1908), one does not wonder that consulates could not work miracles. Having said so, however, it is difficult even today for Americans to distinguish between Germans and Austrians as well as between Austrians and other people from the Danube Empire. Need proof? On p. 217n50 Phelps freely acknowledges that Alison Frank (see her *Oil Empire*) assisted her in explaining the religious split between the Slavs. In mentioning this race one wonders why a person like Emily Greene-Balch (p. 233) and author of *Our Slavic Citizens* has not been considered to join The Inquiry. She had lots of data ready that she could have shared with The Inquiry; but the group of men gathered by Col. House chose to collect their own information on the Dual Monarchy. Academics like Isaiah Bowman (p. 236) may have been experts at home but even in organizing The Inquiry they proved—politely expressed—innocent. Phelps (p. 237) acknowledges this by mentioning that no committee has been set up which dealt with Austria-Hungary as a whole—an empire that was just about to be dismembered not without sympathy in Washington. Putting the historian Archibald Cary Coolidge aside, who slid into a pro-Austrian position in 1919, the Dual Monarchy had no advocates in the inner circles of the Inquiry; but it featured avengers like Kerner, who despised the Habsburg Monarchy and who did not even try to hide his bias.

Old Europe supposedly saw the size of its population as an indication for success, vitality and progress (p. 179) or strength and prestige (p. 206). Therefore emigration of huge numbers has not been considered a welcome trend in Vienna especially when a destination like the U.S. developed some attraction although remigration has always been remarkable (but not as high as 50 per cent, (p. 6)). In connection with military service consuls saw as their job keeping the kinship together, keeping the old citizenship and working against naturalization. Furthermore once people settle in a new environment they tend to stop sending money home which of course hurts the economy there.

Toward the end of this sad ending of U.S. – Habsburg bilateral relations one may guess how events might have developed had the United States supposedly (according to Phelps, p. 8) not left conventional diplomacy, or, as she writes, had "norms of the international political system" not shifted. First, Austria could have recognized Ireland (p. 260) to answer the Allies' efforts regarding the independence of "suppressed Slavic people". Secondly, in not receiving Ambassador Tarnowski, President Wilson kept Austria from doing conventional diplomatic business with the United States (p. 8). Thirdly, to prepare for the Paris Peace Conference, Wilson directed Col. House to set up The Inquiry and in so doing sidelined the usual diplomatic channels in Secretary of State Lansing's State Department, where expertise on the Habsburg Monarchy resided.

But one could easily argue against it because Austria-Hungary would never recognize a rebellion, Tarnowski was not received because war became immediate und the Inquiry did not get a diplomatic role.

This is not to mention the behavior of America at the end of the Great War when against all traditions she used recognition as a diplomatic weapon to destroy the Habsburg Monarchy. Neither did the Czech-Slovak National Council have a territory (p. 259), nor a well-defined people (Wilson learnt of minorities on his way to Paris), nor a democratically empowered administration. These had all been criteria of old diplomacy. It was ironic to consider the "democratic character" of the Czecho-Slovak leaders, considering the motto of the U.S. "to make the world safe for democracy". What saved the day for Czechoslovakia was her army—in Russia.

Summarizing this valuable work one has to go back to its thesis. Are the United States and the Dual Monarchy so diverse? America has been founded on a revolution whereas Austria always has been the opposite of it. The U.S has from the beginning demonstrated her different views of nearly everything, politically by having started out as a democracy, economically by inventing capitalism. Austria on the other hand stayed behind in democratic and commercial issues. But other European powers did as well remain monarchies and hinder free enterprise for too long a time. England might have become a constitutional monarchy early on but her Irish, Boer and Indian politics cannot have warmed American hearts either. Still she had a different kind of relationship to the U.S. than continental Austria (a fact which might become the topic of another thesis). Phelps has told many aspects in the story of the strange relationship between old glorious Vienna and newly powerful Washington very well.

Maybe it is the melting pot idea that supports best the thesis of Phelps' book. Whereas the Czechs of Austria insisted on having their own historic state the Czechs in the U.S. completely forgot about it and assimilated into the American society. How this came into being might yet become another (hi)story.

Coffeehouses as a "Distilled Form of Modernity"

Charlotte Ashby, Tag Gronberg and Simon Shaw-Miller, eds., *The Viennese Café and Fin-de-siècle Culture* (New York: Berghahn Books, 2013)

William M. Johnston

Themed collections of scholarly articles have become a staple of today's historical scholarship, yet few guidelines exist about how to review these compilations or indeed how an editor, in this case Charlotte Ashby, ought to write an introduction to such a miscellany of insights. The editors of the present volume invited eleven inventive scholars to explore disparate aspects of coffeehouses in Vienna, Kraków, Zagreb, and Lemberg between 1890 and 1930 but did not impose any conceptual or methodological template upon the authors. The result is eleven highly stimulating articles, including several dazzling ones that nevertheless do not quite add up to a coherent volume. Too many readers are likely to come away from this collection stimulated but disoriented. The volume lacks the unifying focus that a body of shared concepts might have provided. This review will argue that the book blazes not too few but almost too many paths into a topic rather casually titled "The Viennese Café and Fin-de-Siècle Culture." Prioritizing is badly needed.

Since the 1980s the institution of the coffeehouse in the Dual Monarchy and its aftermath has attracted an enormous amount of scholarship, the bulk of it in German, Hungarian, or Slavic languages. Much of this literature takes pains to explore coffeehouses in provincial capitals like Zagreb, Kraków, or Trieste rather than solely in Vienna or Budapest, while a few comparative works draw on Paris, Italy, or Latin America as well. The panorama of comparisons can range very widely indeed, extending unexpectedly in this volume to Virginia Woolf's London. Overall, at least a half dozen theses have achieved consensus: 1) By any definition the coffeehouse was a pan-European phenomenon and not just an Austro-Hungarian one. 2) Nevertheless, the coffeehouses of the Habsburg Monarchy exemplified certain traits that made these institutions carriers of Habsburg specificity, however difficult that may be to define. 3) The institution reached its apogee between 1890 and 1918 and then for at least two decades thereafter continued to offer a simulacrum of pre-1918 amenities. 4) Certain groups of writers and artists in Habsburg cities, but above all in Budapest, and also in Paris, Berlin, and Munich liked to claim a specific coffeehouse as their forum. 5) After 1918 coffeehouses mattered enormously to émigrés (such as the Hungarians in Vienna) and to any others who wished to keep alive the culture of the pre-war era, either at home or in exile. 6) The interior design of coffeehouses offers abundant material for cross-cultural comparison, as the six chapters by art historians in this volume demonstrate.

The present collection of eleven articles includes six exclusively on Vienna and another four on Central Europe in the broadest sense, including Kraków, Zagreb, and Berlin, as well Edward Timms' virtuosic comparison between Freud's Vienna and Virginia Woolf's London. The editors and contributors are almost all British, having participated in a research project that culminated in an exhibition and a conference in London in 2008 (p. xi). The bibliography assembles seventy-five secondary works in English and German plus three in French (pp. 224-227). Unfortunately, only Schachar Pinsker—writing on Jewish cafés—appears to have used the remarkable volume to be discussed later edited by Michael Rössner, *Literarische Kaffeehäuser, Kaffeehausliteraten* (Vienna, Cologne, Weimar: Böhlau, 1999). That compilation suggests that it might have made more sense to plan a volume on coffeehouses *throughout* the Dual Monarchy, focusing on the two primary models of Vienna and Budapest, with variants in Prague, Kraków, Lemberg, Ljubljana, Zagreb, and Czernowitz among others. As we shall see, Rössner's volume comes close to achieving this goal. In any event, like Rössner's, the present volume contains a meticulous index. The publishers are to be commended for facilitating every sort of cross-reference.

Because the present volume abounds in hypotheses of wide potential use, this review will offer what Joseph Schumpeter used to call a "review of the troops." Here is an outline of eight of the articles that throw up wide-ranging theses in cultural history. This summation omits the three articles that deal chiefly with matters of interior decoration, on the grounds that the pieces by Tag Gronberg on Orientalist motifs, Mary Costello on the décor of Adolf Loos's American-style, all-male Kärntner Bar (1907-1908), and Richard Kurdiovsky on the "Viennese Café as an Extended Living Room" pertain more to the art history of Vienna than to the general cultural history of the Dual Monarchy. The forty black-and-white illustrations confirm that this volume will appeal especially to art historians. Indeed, the entire volume, edited as it is by three art historians, suggests that another such collection might profitably explore "How Are Art Historians Reshaping the Cultural History of the Dual Monarchy?" That inquiry deserves at least as much attention as do coffeehouses.

Editor Charlotte Ashby opens the volume with a lengthy overview, "The Cafés of Vienna: Space and Sociability," which draws all too predictably on Peter Altenberg, Stefan Zweig, and Karl Kraus to establish the distinctiveness of Viennese cafés as "counter-sites," what Foucault called "heterotopias" (p. 22). Unfortunately, no one else in the volume adopts this terminology, even though several synonyms for it emerge in other articles. Instead, in chapter 2, entitled "Time and Space in the Café Griensteidl and the Café Central," Gilbert Carr performs the initial task of surveying journalistic and literary accounts of coffeehouses from two periods, the late 1890s and the 1920s. In a memorable page and a half, Carr dissects Franz Werfel's portrayal in *Barbara oder die Frömmigkeit* (1929) of the Café Central as "part of a larger-scale diagnosis of Habsburg decline" (pp. 44-45). Surprisingly, instead of praising Vienna's literary output about coffeehouses, Carr finds most of it disappointing. His survey of the "memoir genre's own self-deconstructing myth-making" argues that "only a few writers [Anton Kuh, Alfred Polgar, Karl Kraus] experimented successfully in depicting such a purportedly creative milieu" (p. 46) Arguing against a view held by many including the Viennese Germanist, Wendelin Schmidt-Dengler, our author asserts that very few literary evocations of coffeehouses in Vienna achieved a creative breakthrough. Carr's disillusionment makes the categories introduced in other articles of this volume all the more enticing. Already one can discern one of the thrusts of this book: to interpret the coffeehouse requires international frames of reference, the more the better. Strange as it may seem, this book shows that although the Viennese may have excelled at eulogizing their signature institution, they neglected to conceptualize it.

As if aware of this challenge, Steven Beller writes the shortest chapter in the book on "Jews, Central Europe and Modernity." Tinged by a mood of loss, his elegy states some of the volume's most far-reaching theses. The pluralistic space of the literary coffeehouse nurtured across Central Europe "the possibilities and varieties of human thought in a way that narrow purviews of 'pure' national, conventional cultures" did not (p. 57). Beller's insistence on "the high level of Jewish predominance" in these milieux echoes, perhaps unconsciously and with milder rhetoric, the lifework of an earlier displaced child of Austria, George Steiner.

In a word, coffeehouses provided the core of a network of sites for networking. Beller's apt description of a "network of [literary] coffeehouses extending across Habsburg central Europe and beyond" deserves quoting at length. This network "provided not so much a 'republic of letters' but rather a sort of 'consociational' federation of coffeehouses....It was a culture that connected the region together, and connected the region with the rest of the world, but it was not heavily rooted in the 'soil' [*Boden*], it was a culture and a community that consisted of its connections, not of its roots – it is almost as though it hovered slightly above the territorial reality of central Europe, not so much as a Tower of Babel as rather a network of 'castles in the air.' It was this almost 'free-floating' network of connected 'spaces of freedom' that provided the setting, the space of Central European culture" (p. 57). One could hardly make bolder claims for the significance of the coffeehouse.

Of course, other candidates for inclusion in a Bellerian network of "connected 'spaces of freedom'" come to mind. These include the editorial offices of newspapers and literary journals, art schools, and exhibition spaces. Arguably these other forums extended the role of the coffeehouses in servicing a "community that consisted of its connections, not of its roots." In other words, all these counter-sites served individuals who were fleeing their origins. Beller's tantalizingly brief chapter abounds in further concepts awaiting development, including not least a distinction taken from Yuri Slezkine between agrarian peoples, whom the latter calls Apollonians, and trading peoples, whom he calls Mercurians (p.57). Beller's profusion of suggestions deserves to overflow into a book of its own.

In chapter 5, Schachar Pinsker demonstrates the value of examining a narrow population in his article "Between 'The House of Study' and the Coffeehouse: The Central European Café as a Site for Hebrew and Yiddish Modernism." With massive documentation he integrates the cafés of Lemberg, Vienna's Leopoldstadt, and Berlin into an incipient phenomenology of the coffeehouse. This is one of the most theoretical chapters in the collection. In ways that echo Beller, this chapter affirms that particularly for Jews who grew up in a *shtetl* and then moved to a metropolis such as Lemberg, the coffeehouse performed the crucial function of urbanizing them. Authors who wrote in Yiddish and Hebrew while living in a "tentative and provisional [urban] home" declared how cafés provided "a site of negotiation between inside and outside, public and private, real and imaginary, men and women, Jews and gentiles, 'the local' and the immigrant" (p. 94). In order to characterize this liminal space Pinsker adapts a notion coined by the political geographer Edward Soja, who in 1996 spoke of a "thirdspace" where everything comes together in a ceaseless process of hybridization. Although it would be too much to claim that Vienna's or Berlin's cafés of the 1920s achieved the degree of *hyper-*

hybridity that Soja has discerned in today's Los Angeles, Pinsker does us all a service by canvassing the parallels. As Beller's essay also shows, the relevance of the notion of "thirdspace" to Habsburg Studies deserves an essay all its own, for it was not just coffeehouses that supplied "thirdspaces," but other consociational spaces as well like art schools and galleries, publishing houses, and aristocratic salons. What was it about the Monarchy's sociability that provoked such diverse sites of dissent from official culture?

In chapter 6, the longest and most densely documented in the book, Katarzyna Murawska-Muthesius explores the unusual topic of coffeehouses as sites for fostering caricature, in both literature and the visual arts. Having asserted the role of the coffeehouse in many cultural capitals (Paris, Berlin, Vienna) as a quintessential site of modern "experiment, synaesthetic impulse, performativity and subversion" (p. 98), she goes on to examine Kraków's coffeehouses as locales for launching caricature between 1895 and 1918. Thus caricature becomes a lens for comparing cultures and their favorite modes of artistic inventiveness. How, she asks, did coffeehouses and caricature interact so as to "foster modern urban identities"? (p. 98). Both manifested "the new modes, conducts and themes of modernity," and by privileging distortion and irony, both exemplified "'the ephemeral, the fugitive, the contingent,' as Baudelaire famously put it" when writing about the prints of Constantin Guys (p. 100). She insists that café-art as embodied in *chansons* and cabaret performance gravitated toward parody. Nor was this proclivity confined to Kraków, for it was not only there that a literary sketch written at a café table could be used to pay the bill (p. 101).

When Murawska-Muthesius moves on to the local issue of anti-Semitic caricatures produced in specific coffeehouses of pre-1914 Kraków, her earlier pan-European perspective inevitably jars with a focus on individual cafés. An article which proffers a *tour d'horizon* of the symbiosis of coffeehouses and caricature throughout Europe devolves into a debate about which coffeehouse in Kraków produced the most telling anti-Semitic caricatures. As the discussion moves from the general to the disconcertingly local, the author wants the hyper-local to evoke universal trends. The historian's problem of balancing the particular and the universal here reaches agonizing intensity. Who, one wonders, is to establish what is universal in certain suburbs about which few outsiders know anything? Vienna's coffeehouses, supposedly the model for those elsewhere, recede into pale reflections of an Empire-wide template or indeed a Europe-wide template, centered on Paris. In the end, Murawska-Muthesius argues that not Vienna but Paris may supply the most pertinent conceptualizations for understanding Kraków's coffeehouses.

Maintaining a similar focus on the French capital, Ines Sabotić bases chapter 7 on her Paris dissertation *Les cafés de Zagreb de 1884 à 1914: sociabilités, normes et identités* (Paris, 2002). In comparing Zagreb *kavanas* to models that she chooses from Vienna and Paris (but not Budapest), she singles out as agents of this cultural mimesis not Jews but "a German-speaking bourgeois society that linked urban centres across the region" (p. 135). The "facilitating medium of the German language" promoted "cultural transfer between members of the bourgeoisie" (p. 135). In corroboration of such a Bellerian "community of connections, not roots," she could have cited the satires of the Croatian writer Miroslav Krleža, who from the 1920s on ridiculed as "*agramstvo*" the barbarous mixture of German and Croatian spoken by aspirational middle-class Zagrebians. Sabotić discerns an ideology bubbling up in Zagreb's cafés, whereby *imitation* of a distant center by people on the periphery provided a "way of proclaiming allegiance to a specific cultural sphere," one that was broader even than that on offer in Vienna and Budapest, and thus was "finding a way towards modernity and Europe." This last statement adumbrates a topic that no one else in the volume explores, for it was notably in Budapest that journals such as *Nyugat* ["The West"] (1908-1941) proclaimed the allegiance of coffeehouse intellectuals not to Vienna or Berlin but rather to Paris, Brussels, and London. Unlike the largely apolitical Jung Wien writers but very much like the hyper-political Hungarians, Zagrebians debated the politics not of local but rather of national identity. In aversion to Hungarian overlordship, clients of coffeehouses no longer craved a Zagrebian identity but rather a Croatian one.

In chapter 9 on interactions between graphic and interior design as "distilled forms of modernity," Jeremy Aynsley explores how the Viennese designer of fonts, Rudolf von Larisch (1856-1934), became one of the first practitioners anywhere to recognize the potential of "effective design" for conveying the "*commercial* identity of a company." While opposing the use of *Fraktur*, he established himself as a pioneer of today's ubiquitous exploitation of design in corporate image-making. Aynsley's final pages on the frontages of coffeehouses demonstrate that the signage, often featuring "calligraphic flourishes," preferred the French word "café" to the German one "coffeehouse" (p. 174). Even as Larisch was striving to internationalize Vienna's signage, he was foreshadowing the future direction of commercial design.

Like Larisch, this book too recognizes the significance of the coffeehouse for conveying the *cultural* identity both of Vienna and of the Dual Monarchy. Additional signifiers included the Ringstrasse, the waltz, the operetta, and after 1910 Vienna's municipal housing. Two challenges emerge, which this volume poses but cannot resolve: first, how is one to compare and contrast emblems of "Viennese-ness" and second, how is one to coordinate these Viennese tropes with emblems of the Dual Monarchy as such. Far from being chiefly Viennese, did not operetta, as Péter Hanák and Moritz Csáky have argued, bridge Austro-German and Magyar culture? Did not certain writers like Ferenc Molnár function equally well in Vienna and Budapest? Inevitably, the present volume veers between the two foci of Vienna and the Empire. Ashby, Carr, Aynsley, and Timms as well as the three art historians focus on Vienna, while Murawska-Muthesius and Sabotić treat two other cities, Kraków and Zagreb, leaving only Beller and Pinsker to address the Empire more or less as a whole. It is no coincidence that it is a focus on Jews that spurs these two to address the entire Dual Monarchy.

In a final chapter, "Coffeehouses and Tea Parties: Conversational Spaces as a Stimulus to Creativity in Sigmund Freud's Vienna and Virginia Woolf's London," Edward Timms formulates one of his ingenious alignments of seemingly incongruous sites and personalities around a central theme of cultural history. Timms construes both "coffeehouses and teaparties" as "integrative nexuses" in a "society in the throes of modernization" (p. 202). Embodying the "more open public spaces of modernity," these "discursive spaces"—he might equally well have said "thirdspaces"—created "the potential for the emergence of new forms of anti-establishment culture." As he has done elsewhere, Timms includes an almost surreal diagram consisting of fifteen overlapping circles that chart a "condensed system of micro-circuits" (p. 207) which made "the whole system so interactive" (p. 208). More than half of this article examines in highly original fashion certain Bloomsbury intellectuals and their reception of psychoanalysis (pp. 208-217). However eye-popping this examination of "integrative nexuses," it wanders perhaps too far from the ostensible topic of "The Viennese Café and Fin-de-Siècle Culture."

Tellingly, nearly all of Timms' general descriptions of anti-Establishment "discursive spaces," whether in intellectual Vienna or the Woolfs' Bloomsbury, apply with equal or perhaps even more force to coffeehouses in Budapest. Indeed throughout this book, one misses references to the coffeehouses of the Dual Monarchy's other capital. Pál Deréky's article in the Rössner volume discloses some of what the editors have forfeited through this omission. In particular, waiters in Budapest served not just as dispensers of food, drink, and newspapers, but even more flamboyantly than in Vienna, as enablers of writers' quirks, as if a coffeehouse were at once an office, a home, and a club. Budapest waiters supplied banking services, delivered last-minute manuscripts to publishers, and distributed alms to writers' needy friends. A neglected topic for comparative study beckons.

To be sure, the task of a review is to evaluate the book in hand, not some dream-alternative that no one has yet written. Because this collection lacks an introduction which locates the book's innovations in relation to previous scholarship, it may help us to gauge the contribution of this volume if we juxtapose it to another collection of articles concerning the two chief topics that intersect here: coffeehouses and the culture of Habsburg Central Europe. Accordingly I shall align the articles in the present book with two unusually rich ones from Michael Rössner's *Literarische Kaffeehäuser, Kaffeehausliteraten* (1999). I have chosen Wendelin Schmidt-Dengler's "Inselwelten: Zum Caféhaus in der österreichischen Literatur des 20. Jahrhunderts" (pp. 66-81), and Claudio Magris's sparkling essay on Trieste's "Caffè San Marco" (pp.226-250). At the very least, these two cornucopias of insight suggest how our authors might have enriched their perspectives by collating them with this earlier exploration of how literary coffeehouses throughout the Dual Monarchy *differed* from one another.

As one might expect from the editor of Heimito von Doderer's notebooks, Wendelin Schmidt-Dengler synthesizes exceptionally wide-reading with an analysis of how the novelists Werfel and above all Doderer *integrated* descriptions of coffeehouses into the structure of major novels. As a result, Schmidt-Dengler achieves a stunning synthesis, constructing a genealogy of how literary participants interpreted the role of coffeehouses in social intercourse. Moreover, his stylistic analyses call into question Gilbert Carr's reservations about the merits of this literature.

Schmidt-Dengler starts with Stefan Zweig's *Die Welt von gestern* (1943), arguing that this book disseminated after World War II an "ideology of the coffeehouse," which identified it with literature as such. For Zweig the coffeehouse comprised a "small cosmos," which by fostering communication and openness to the world combated provinciality (pp. 66-67). Schmidt-Dengler notes that at the same time the institution offered a haven for would-be decadents. He argues further that after 1920 the coffeehouse attracted nostalgics who wished to bask in reminders of a pre-war world. Indeed the coffeehouse became the principal bastion of the rituals and "Formalia" of pre-1918. Yet at the same time at least one Hungarian emigré in Vienna, the future film theorist Béla Balázs, began to prefer going to the moviehouse instead of the coffeehouse (p. 67). Like Gilbert Carr in chapter 2, Schmidt-Dengler goes on to analyse the "stylized pandemonium" that Franz Werfel depicted in the "Schattenreich" portion of his novel *Barbara* (1929). This descent into the underworld—dark, seductive, unholy—seems to have unhinged a displaced author who treasured the "sacral pathos" of a rural idyll that he remembered from childhood. In contrast to Zweig, for Werfel intellectuals hunkered down in the counter-world of coffeehouses in order to indulge in thought-experiments about the end of the world (p. 70).

In seven pages Schmidt-Dengler writes a subtle analysis of how Heimito von Doderer (1896-1966) integrated both of these views into various narratives (pp.71-77). Above all, for Doderer the café preserved privacy in a post-1918 era when the public domain seemed to be invading everywhere else. Already in *Divertimento No 1* (1924), a café survives a catastrophe of smashed windows and manages to remain an enclave (p. 72). In Part I of *Die Dämonen*, written during the 1930s, Doderer deployed different coffeehouses as social markers to differentiate various groups of friends. The Café Kaunitz, a locale inserted into the novel during the early 1950s, supplies a counterworld that lacks the seclusion (*Abgeschlossenheit*) of earlier cafés. Noise and screaming now drown out speaking (p. 75). In the *Strudlhofstiege* (1951), written just after World War II, cafés become once more a "world of islands" (*Inselwelt*), where tables are widely spaced and visitors relish distance from others (p. 76). In the later portions of *Die Dämonen* written during the early 1950s, the disorder manifested by the cafés of the 1920s has become a *beau désordre*. By the 1950s, the mellowing author, like the coffeehouses he depicts, had outgrown the crisis of the totalitarian 1930s and now once again allowed these meeting places to furnish a haven for individuality. In Doderer's fiction, the depiction of coffeehouses charts the ups and downs of his confidence in the capacity of institutions to sustain civilized values.

In 1997 a champion of such values, Claudio Magris, wrote a metaphor-rich essay about his own favorite coffeehouse, the Caffè San Marco, founded in the fateful year of 1914 in his hometown of Trieste. Happily, the Rössner volume printed a German translation of the Italian text two years later. With an ebullience that sometimes palls, Magris canvassed the almost innumerable functions that such a gathering place can fulfill for a spectrum of human types that range from aristocrats, brokers, and synagogue-goers to writers, sailors, and retirees. He compared this one coffeehouse, the quintessential old Austrian time-capsule, to a series of predicates. It becomes in turn Noah's Ark (p. 226), a "magic notebook" (p. 228), and a "periphery of history" (p. 230). It can be a haven of plurality (p. 230), a "Platonic academy ...of sociability and disenchantment" (p. 234), and a salon for eliciting metaphors (p. 234). Last but not least, it offers an asylum for the broken-hearted (p. 236) and a den of smoky air which veils distance (p. 238). Magris celebrates a sense of continuity, which almost any visitor may feel still vibrating in this inconspicuous spot, bridging many eras and many coffeehouses. Yet one cannot help but feel that analytical categories like those of Foucault, Slezkine, and Soja or Beller, Pinsker, and Timms seem forced when applied to this beloved space. For Magris insists that by its very nature this multicultural refuge, as distinct from a "pseudo-coffeehouse" that attracts only the like-minded (p. 230), will thwart the ambition of social scientists to collate data and to formulate hypotheses. As Doderer also implies, such a sanctuary of singularity exists above all to nurture idiosyncrasy. Magris wants his archetype to be evoked but not dissected.

The Triestine essayist isolates a crucial issue that will shape our conclusion. The eleven authors in the volume under review rightly celebrate the pluralistic and gregarious character of coffeehouse culture. They all affirm that, as Beller asserts, this "culture and community ...consisted of its connections, not of its roots" (p. 57). For us today who no longer can step across a threshold into such a network of networks—except electronically via the internet—what kind of scholarly volume, one may ask, will best convey this interactive potential? To what extent can an institution that favored individuality be mined by literary scholars, social scientists, and phenomenologists for categories of analysis? In the present book, tension between cherishing the micro-local (as in Zagreb, Kraków, or Bloomsbury) and announcing the universal (as in coffeehouses for Jews or for caricaturists) remains unresolved. If a century ago Habsburg coffeehouses offered to all and sundry, as well as to clusters of the like-minded, a refuge from an ever increasing urban chaos, why does it remain so hard for us to condense analyses of these functions into a coherent volume? Does our lack of daily forums for networking diminish our feel for coffeehouses?

In the end one must ask: how effectively does this collection of stimulating but discordant articles, chiefly by art historians, provide a platform for articulating the cultural significance of Habsburg coffeehouses? At least two responses are possible. On the one hand, one could wish that a single author had tackled the cities and milieux treated here in order to apply across the entire Dual Monarchy such ingenious analyses as those of Beller, Pinsker, and Timms. Only a single author, or perhaps two or three working together, could hope to achieve the seamless conceptualization that a phenomenology of the coffeehouse would require. On the other hand, one can rejoice that the eleven authors have done justice to the particularity of the milieux that they tackle. Perhaps the loose rein of our editors, art historians all, better suits our own era's heterogeneity of views. If, as Schmidt-Dengler argued, the Viennese coffeehouse of the 1920s offered a refuge for fanciers of pre-war lifestyles, the multifariousness of the Habsburg coffeehouse as both haven and link challenges us cultural historians more acutely than ever. Even without propounding an overview of its own contributions, the present volume addresses the challenge of synthesis by proposing fascinating but disconnected answers to crucial issues. Discourse on "connected 'spaces of freedom,'" on "sites of negotiation" among opposites, and on "condensed systems of microcircuits," as well as on the closely interrelated notions of "counter-sites," "heterotopia," and "thirdspace," supplies fresh terminology for articulating, without pathos or nostalgia, the potential of this subject. The same can be said about this book's theses concerning the tendency of Habsburg coffeehouses to shelter such self-regarding activities as diagnosis of decline, the art of parody, and "self-deconstructive mythmaking."

At the same time, the present book reclaims discourse about coffeehouses from once prevalent temptations. What Magris hails as a Noah's ark for the broken-hearted surviving on the periphery of history emerges here not as a pretext for lament or for caricature or for mythmaking but rather as an invitation to analysis. The volume investigates how these gathering place for shapers of modernity in Vienna, Zagreb, Kraków, Lemberg, and in the Dual Monarchy at large worked to construct intellectual and artistic networks as well as to design highly decorated spaces that nurtured these "communities of connections, not roots," all the while resisting pressures not always conducive to such endeavors. Even if not rigorously coherent, this volume nevertheless offers one of the most constructive, least lachrymose treatments that the subject has ever received.

"The Odd Couple"

Jean-Paul Bled, *Franz Ferdinand: Der eigensinnige Thronfolger*, trans. Susanna Grabmayr and Marie-Therese Pitner (Vienna: Böhlau, 2013)

Wolfram Dornik, *Des Kaisers Falke: Wirken und Nach-Wirken von Franz Conrad von Hötzendorf*, with afterword comments by Verena Moritz and Hannes Leidinger (Innsbruck: StudienVerlag, 2013)

Samuel R. Williamson, Jr.

In November 1906 Emperor/King Franz Joseph acceded to the wishes of his nephew and *Thronfolger*, Archduke Franz Ferdinand, and appointed Franz Conrad von Hötzendorf as chief of staff of the Austro-Hungarian Army. The two men—Conrad and Franz Ferdinand—worked together, often tempestuously, until the gunshots at Sarajevo. From the start they formed an "odd couple," one strong willed and mercurial, the other hawkish and prone to bouts of almost manic-depressive behavior. Both agreed on the need for a strong and effective Habsburg army. But the archduke wanted the army to shore up the monarchy and be ready for a confrontation with the Hungarians. The general, by contrast, wanted the army for preventive war against a neighboring state, sometimes Serbia, sometimes Italy, and only against Russia if a war with Serbia created that danger. Though the two men dined together in Sarajevo on the evening of Saturday, 27 June, following the army maneuvers, and parted on reasonable terms, the general knew that the archduke wanted him replaced and was only waiting to find a suitable general. Paradoxically, the next day brought the opportunity for war with Serbia that Conrad had so long advocated and he got his war. But he did not rescue the monarchy, indeed he condemned it to dissolution.

Jean-Paul Bled's biography of Franz Ferdinand, first published in Paris in 2012, is the most serious study of the archduke ever undertaken. It makes excellent use of the full archival sources in Vienna and adopts a careful and balanced assessment of a man who is, to be frank, not very likeable. Bled sets the stage and tracks the events that led to Franz Ferdinand's surprising emergence as the heir-apparent, while paying careful attention to the psychological impact that his long struggle with ill health and tuberculosis had upon his temperament. By the time he became the designated *Thronfolger* in March 1898, his determination to have his own way had become a habitual approach to any issue. The impact of this willfulness upon his relations with his uncle over his desire to marry Sophie Chotek receives extensive attention. Nor does Bled ignore the later frictions with Franz Joseph that emerged during the following years, over the 1907 election law changes in Austria, over the failure to confront Hungarian on the renewal of the *Ausgleich*, and almost certainly over the numerous little humiliations the Court inflicted upon his wife. Indeed, over time the nephew seldom saw his uncle and spent little time in Vienna. Still, if the two men were often in conflict, they agreed upon the most fundamental principle of statecraft: peace was preferable to war.

By contrast Conrad saw war as the only way to restore the monarchy's fortunes. Deeply influenced by Social Darwinist thoughts and the work of Arthur Schopenhauer, he viewed international politics as a struggle for state survival that only the strongest would survive. Wolfram Dornik's study examines the impact of these ideas upon Conrad's role as chief of staff before and during the war. In some instances he explores new ground, especially in describing the enemies that Conrad accumulated along the way among fellow officers, members of the aristocracy, and with the Social Democrats. His long rivalry with General Oskar Potiorek, whom many thought would be the chief of staff in 1906, is tracked until its conclusion with the ouster of Potiorek in the winter of 1914. Like the recent monograph by Lawrence Sondhaus, *Franz Conrad von Hötzendorf: Architect of the Apocalypse* (Boston: Humanities Press, 2000), the two scholars assess the impact of Gina von Reininghaus upon Conrad's psyche and the emotional instability that lay behind many of his demands for war. Interestingly, however, both fail to note that he would do nothing until his aged mother, Barbara, died on 1 August 1915. Then he wasted no time; on 19 October he married Gina and she soon joined him at the army headquarters at Teschen. For a few short months, until the military reverses of 1916, they were a happily married couple. The rest of the story, which Dornik and then Moritz and Leidinger in after remarks describe, was less happy. As Conrad sought to salvage his reputation with his memoirs, he merely convinced most historians that he bore a unique responsibility for the decisions taken in Vienna in July 1914.

Bled does not, of course, discuss the war decision and Dornik gives only modest attention to it. Still, Dornik fails to recognize how Conrad's "harvest leave" disrupted the timing of the ultimatum to Belgrade, a point made by this reviewer more than two decades ago. Nor does he grasp perhaps the simplest explanation for why Conrad implemented Plan B even as he knew the Russians were mobilizing: he wanted to be sure he got his war. Staying on the defensive against Serbia and awaiting the long delays of a Russian campaign might allow mediation to intrude; that above all, he did not want.

The deaths in Sarajevo brought the war; they also ended the strange relationship between two very complex men, one eleven years older than the other, that had existed from the fall of 1906 to June 1914. In many ways they shared many of the same beliefs: the monarchy needed to reform itself into order to survive, the army would be crucial to this reform, neither much cared for Prussians though Kaiser Wilhelm II treated Sophie with great courtesy, and both were intensely suspicious of Italy. They also agreed on the value of the offensive strategy and of the need for larger military budgets and recruit contingents. And, even as they might distrust the Prussians, both men fully appreciated the Habsburgs' need for the German alliance.

But the two men differed far more than they agreed, which shows that for all of his fickleness toward his colleagues, Franz Ferdinand saw Conrad as an asset. Still there were huge ideological and political differences. The *Thronfolger*, an ardent Roman Catholic in the strictest sense of the term, disliked Conrad's allowing Alfred Redl to commit suicide after his treason was discovered, then castigated Conrad for failing to attend church during a maneuver exercise in September 1913. Franz Ferdinand saw the army as a domestic instrument, the general an instrument to be used in war. The archduke liked to press the case for a Habsburg navy; the general saw it chiefly as a waste of money. And while both men were not modernists, Franz Ferdinand's appreciation of the role of technology in naval construction far outpaced Conrad's rather inattentive views on artillery and even aviation. He wanted the new instruments, but forts and infantry were his true passions.

In the realm of foreign policy they also differed. Franz Ferdinand favored stronger relations with Romania and overtures to Russia; he paid less attention to the threat posed by Serbia to the monarchy than did Conrad. And the heir-apparent returned repeatedly to his hope that a *Dreikaiserbund* might be negotiated with the Russians, a view that the Russians totally failed to appreciate. Furthermore, each time Conrad argued for a preventive war, in 1909 against Serbia, in 1911 against Italy, and again in 1913 against Serbia he found the archduke firmly opposed.

Both Bled and Dornik recount the one time that Franz Ferdinand switched positions on the question of war. In December 1912, with the First Balkan War still underway and Austro-Russian troops confronting each other, he got Franz Joseph to bring Conrad back as chief of the general staff, though he had to sacrifice his favorite Moritz von Auffenberg as war minister. Dornik sees the move as a clever way to impress both Belgrade and St. Petersburg that Vienna might go to war. Indeed, in early December Franz Ferdinand went to Schönbrunn to plead the case for war against Serbia with his uncle, only to find that Franz Joseph sided with Count Leopold Berchtold in arguing for a diplomatic, not a military approach. A chastened heir apparent never again varied from his earlier position: peace at almost any price. It should be noted that Moritz and Leidinger wonder if an archduke who survived Sarajevo would have maintained that peaceful pose, a point they find doubtful.

Conrad had his likes and his dislikes among people, ideas, and military strategy. But no general could survive as long as he did without elementary political skills in negotiating the complicated Austro-Hungarian governance structure and his relationships to the military chancelleries of both Franz Joseph and Franz Ferdinand. Conrad pressed, took defeat, and pressed again, careful not to burn too many bridges at least until the fall of 1911. Moreover, he always remained respectful of the aged Franz Joseph though he believed him weak and timorous. By contrast, the heir-apparent seethed with hatred for his uncle, found his court colleagues impossible, and left few doubts that he disliked them and his carefully orchestrated exclusion from the final levers of power. He found, repeatedly, that in the end Franz Joseph kept his own counsel and his control of the possibly tottering monarchy. There would be only one emperor/king despite the café talk otherwise.

Nor could the aged monarch have been entirely confident of what might happen upon his death. Bled examines in crisp detail the degree to which the archduke hated the Hungarians and sought to cultivate the minorities who lived in Hungary. If Conrad was a skilled linguist with eight languages under his command (he was learning English when he died), Franz Ferdinand of course knew German but little Hungarian and showed contempt for it as a language. More importantly, he left no doubt that he viewed the *Ausgleich* of 1867 as a mistake and that some effort to undo it, or at least mitigate some of its worst features, would be high on his initial agenda. Equally troubling and wildly at odds with Wilhelm II who saw István Tisza as the strongest, most impressive man in the monarchy, Franz Ferdinand ostentatiously refused to meet with the most powerful political figure in Hungary. This attitude, which reflected an almost absolutist view left over from earlier centuries, at one point prompted Conrad to label his patron a "despot." How this person would have navigated the political world that had emerged in both halves of the monarchy, especially after the electoral reform of 1907 in Austria, leaves even the most optimistic observer doubtful.

Bled provides a very useful, careful summary of the various plans associated with Franz Ferdinand and the possible reshaping of the monarchy. Though the concept of "trialism" long dominated interwar views of the archduke, Bled sees that tossed aside. Nor does he think the more federalized approach of Aurel Popovici, though considered at length, would have been adopted. Instead, Bled concludes that the initial plans called for trying to undermine certain pieces of the *Ausgleich* arrangement, seeking to avoid a confrontation but not afraid to have one if necessary. But above all, the *Thronfolger* did not want to see the monarchy at war and then come to the throne; that would almost certainly rob him of any chance to alter the constitutional situation. For him, peace had enormous domestic consequences.

Bled examines the archduke's daily life, his simple meals, and his devotion to his children who were, he notes, barely tolerated after Sarajevo by the Hofburg court. Strongly opposed to the "Secessionist" wave of modern art, he hoped he could shift the focus elsewhere. Nor did he ever neglect his hunting; his trophy count of animals stood at 274,889. If he preferred his Czech estate at Konopischt, he also saw, prudently as it turned out, that he could not be buried in the Kapuziner Crypt, traditional resting place of the Habsburg rulers in Vienna, if he wanted Sophie by his side. Thus he made arrangements at his estate at Artstetten, near Melk, for a final resting place, never dreaming that it would be used within a few years of his decision.

Conrad, his partner and adversary in strategic and military matters, not to mention war-peace decisions, got the war he wanted. In the first months of war he lost 200,000 men dead and wounded, another 100,000 captured by the Russians. In the south the Serbs dealt Potiorek two losses and brought his ouster. If there were gains, including Serbia and on the eastern front, 1916 saw the gains eroded. Then in November Franz Joseph died. The new emperor, Karl, for whom Conrad had only scorn, soon reciprocated and removed Conrad from his overall command on 1 March 1917, relegating him to the Italian front where he stayed until completely relieved in July 1918. Thereafter he would spend his time preparing, with the aide of many colleagues, his own version of the "Stab in the Back" with his erstwhile allies, the Germans, as the principal culprits.

What should scholars make of this odd couple? The two books are helpful introductions to the problem, though they prompt many critical questions for even this reviewer who has studied the problem for decades. First, the archduke serves as a useful reminder of just what made the monarchical system so out-moded. That someone like Franz Ferdinand, by virtue of lineage, could become the head of a state with fifty million citizens must necessarily make even a sympathetic person wince. That he might have sought to pursue his domestic objections against the Hungarians based on his simple prejudices and hatred suggest an illusionary world in which his wishes become reality. His stubborn willfulness, though a useful trait, was his Achilles heel. But so too was the system in which he operated. It must remain doubtful that he could have saved the monarchy that he would have inherited it; some part perhaps, but not the entire piece.

Conrad by contrast shifted his views constantly; he held to few fixed positions and did not let consistency bother him too much. The only fixed points were his desires for preventive war and for marriage to Gina. He must rank high in the pantheon of those leaders who brought the Great War; he promised much but delivered little. This reviewer remains amazed at how little he understood the power of the machine gun, at his careless recklessness with his alliance relationships to Helmuth von Moltke (his counterpart on the Prussian General Staff), and at his almost willful neglect of the threat posed by Russia. Still, compared to Franz Ferdinand, Conrad lived in a political world in which rough and tumble were part of the process. In that world he won and lost and his mental state often suffered; his bouts of self-doubt and depression, seen only by a few, could be seen in his endless letter writing and his total absorption in military matters. An early physical fitness buff and an artist of some skill, he found some relaxation from his suffering and his rebuffs. Yet, like Franz Ferdinand, if there were real setbacks, it was always someone else's fault.

Taken together, these two thoughtful studies suggest very strongly that Sigmund Freud could have gleaned a great deal of material for his theories from conversations with Franz Ferdinand and Conrad at Café Central. They were the odd couple whose lives and actions, even in death, would do much to shape today's contemporary world a century later.

Gerald Steinacher, *Hakenkreuz und Rotes Kreuz: Eine humanitäre Organisation zwischen Holocaust und Flüchtlingsproblematik* (Innsbruck: StudienVerlag, 2013)

Richard Wiggers

This year (2014) marks the 150th anniversary of the establishment of the International Committee of the Red Cross (ICRC) and the launch of the first Geneva Convention "for the Amelioration of the Condition of the Wounded in Armies in the Field" (1864). Since it was founded, the ICRC has come to represent the promotion of humanitarian principles at a number of different levels. Various national associations have been involved with first aid training, disaster management, blood collection, etc., while the international association is best known for the assistance and oversight it provides as it tries to ensure the humane and appropriate treatment of civilians and captured military personnel in times of international conflict.

There has recently been an extensive amount of research, scholarship, and debate regarding the role of the Vatican and the Catholic Church, as well as Switzerland and the Swiss banks, during the Second World War, focusing on the efforts by both to maintain their neutrality even in the face of the many crimes of the Nazi regime, including the Holocaust. This book explores the role of the ICRC in a similar light. In fact, it is the inherent tension between some of the very principles upon which the ICRC was founded and continues to operate today—the goal of humanitarianism versus the perceived need to protect impartiality and neutrality—that provides a great deal of the focus for this book.

The author, Gerald Steinacher, is currently an Assistant Professor of History at the University of Nebraska-Lincoln, and most recently authored *Nazis on the Run: How Hitler's Henchmen Fled Justice* (2011). His past research on the Holocaust, central Europe, and Italian fascism is clearly evident in this work. In summary, this publication actually combines three somewhat separate stories related to the Second World War and its aftermath, each of which involves both the ICRC and the Swiss government.

The middle two chapters (pages 71-106) focus on the evolution of the 1944 negotiations to rescue at least some of Hungary's Jewish population during the last stages of the war as the Red Army approached from the east and German troops moved in to occupy the territory of their former ally. The subtitle of the second of the two chapters in this section, "The Swedes are Coming," summarizes the author's main premise, namely that neutral and more distant Sweden was willing to more actively intervene to save Jewish lives while the equally neutral Swiss government and the ICRC officials were not. In the end it was the Swedes who arranged for as many as 21.000 concentration camp inmates (approximately 6.500 of them Jews) to be transferred to neutral Sweden, while their diplomat Raoul Wallenberg is credited with saving as many as 20,000 additional Jews within Hungarian territory (106).

The final two chapters (pages 107-152) touch upon a topic for which a vast and completely separate academic literature already exists, the escape from justice of alleged war criminals in the final stages and aftermath of the Second World War. Since the 1980s this has been one of the most extensively researched and debated aspects of the conflict and its aftermath. In this section of his book, Steinacher focuses on the collusion between individuals within both the ICRC and the Catholic Church—particularly those based in Rome and Genoa—in securing identity documents for those attempting to evade justice in the months and years immediately following the defeat of Nazi Germany. Some of the names of prominent Nazis who evaded postwar justice by fleeing to South America with at least some apparent assistance from the ICRC included Franz Stangl (a former commander of the extermination facility at Treblinka), Erich Priebke (one of the most notorious war criminals from the Italian theater of war), and Adolf Eichmann (a primary architect of the Holocaust).

In this section of the book in particular, much more background information and context would have been helpful for the reader, particularly in regards to the important role of the United Nations Relief and Rehabilitation Administration (UNRRA) and other organizations attempting to deal with the many millions of postwar refugees and displaced persons from all over Europe. The role of Allied intelligence organizations is also worth at least some mention here. While some U.S., British, Soviet, and other military and intelligence units were searching for alleged war criminals for postwar trials in Nuremberg and elsewhere, others were seeking intelligence assets and assisting some alleged war criminals in evading postwar justice. The incredible confusion and turmoil of the period immediately following the end of active hostilities in postwar Europe is barely addressed in these two chapters.

The core of Steinacher's book, and really the most intriguing part, is the first section of two chapters which address the tension between the ICRC commitment to humanitarianism and the determination to maintain neutrality for both the organization and for the host nation of Switzerland. As Steinacher notes, by the end of 1944 there were 27.000 Jewish and 20.000 non-Jewish refugees interned in Switzerland, and more than 40.000 interned military personnel from various nations (36). All this was taking place while the mountain-locked nation was completely encircled by Nazi Germany and its allies and conquered territories. Steinacher concludes that throughout World War II "the national interests of Switzerland trumped the neutrality and independence of the ICRC" (165), particularly when it came to reporting on and speaking out against the Holocaust.

Some of these revelations were addressed in a previous publication by Swiss historian Jean-Claude Favez in 1988. At the time, the book came out in French under the title *An Impossible Mission?*, and the English edition only appeared more than a decade later in 1999 as *The Red Cross and the Holocaust*. In the meantime in 1996, the ICRC released more than 25,000 relevant documents to the United States Holocaust Memorial Museum. On 27 January 2014, in fact, the following statement was published on the official ICRC website:

> 27 January is the anniversary of the liberation of Auschwitz in 1945. For the ICRC, it also marks a failure, the failure to help and protect the millions of people who were exterminated in the death camps. The ICRC has publicly expressed its regret regarding its impotence and the mistakes it made in dealing with Nazi persecution and genocide.
> (http://www.icrc.org/eng/resources/documents/misc/history-holocauste-020205.htm)

One of the main justifications given by ICRC supporters for the refusal to speak out in regards to the fate of Europe's Jews was its primary mission of caring for prisoners-of-war (POWs). In fact, throughout the Second World War ICRC officials focused the vast majority of their attention on caring for the prisoners-of-war of those nations who were signatories to the earlier Geneva Conventions. Throughout the conflict the ICRC made 8,000 visits to POW camps, and delivered 36 million packages (500.000 tones) of relief supplies and 120 million messages to military and civilian prisoners on all sides. In comparison, only 7.000 tones was delivered to concentration camp inmates, and millions of prisoners-of-war on both sides of the eastern front were also not covered because the Soviet Union had never ratified the 1929 Geneva Convention (47, 112-113). Interestingly, no significant mention is made by Steinacher of the extensive debate that took place among scholars throughout the 1990s regarding allegations that the western allies also denied POW status and adequate rations to captured German military personnel in postwar Europe, resulting in the deaths of thousands.

Another topic that could have been explored in greater detail was the preoccupation with maintaining a neutral stance for the ICRC and the tension between the national and the international agencies and personalities of the Red Cross. While Steinacher mentions the involvement of the Red Cross in the pre-war investigation of Italian war crimes in Abyssinia and in the German commission investigating the Katyn forest massacre of Polish POWs (63, 64), in both instances there were significant differences between many of the national Red Cross associations, which were willing to take a more critical position in the case of Italy and to participate in the Germany commission in the case of Katyn, and the ICRC based in Geneva which continued to pursue a strictly neutral position throughout.

In summary, this publication is a valuable contribution to an improved understanding not only of the ICRC on the 150th anniversary of its founding, but also of the complex relationship between it and both the national associations around the world, and the Swiss government that has hosted the organization since it was first founded.

Maria Fritsche, *Homemade Men in Postwar Austrian Cinema: Nationhood, Genre, and Masculinity* (New York: Berghahn, 2013)

Jacqueline Vansant

After seven years of Nazi rule and the loss of life and property in the war, Austria was struggling to recover and establish itself as a sovereign nation. Policy makers were also faced with the herculean task of the constructing of an Austrian identity. They saw their task in distancing Austria from Germany, promoting a harmonious society absent of the rancorous class conflict that had plagued the First Republic, and imbuing citizens with a sense of national pride. Although not an official platform, cinema played an important role in this endeavor. Based on her analysis of 140 out of the 212 films produced or co-produced by Austrian film companies during the years before Austria regained its independence in 1955, Maria Fritsche explores the ways postwar Austrian cinema, the country's most popular public entertainment, entered into discourses on nationhood and masculinity. She shows how constructions of gender in Austrian cinema dovetailed with official political goals and evolved with the ever-changing status of men and women in the ten years between the end of the war and Austrian independence.

In the "Introduction" and first chapter, Fritsche provides a sound theoretical and historical context for her explorations of the films. She includes a short discourse on the connections between cinema and societal trends, pointing out that cinema is both shaped by and shapes ideas circulating in popular discourse. She also presents a short history of cinema in Austria and underscores the continuities between filmmakers under National Socialism and postwar filmmakers. In Chapter One, "Popular Cinema and Society," Fritsche paints a detailed picture of the place of cinema in postwar Austria and its popularity. Moviegoing easily outstripped other forms of popular entertainment. In 1954 in Vienna alone "cinemas counted 48.3 million tickets sold" compared to 2.5 million for sports events and 2.67 for theaters (22). Despite the number of imports, with the United

States and Germany outnumbering domestic production, the homegrown films were very popular. Again, looking at the year 1953, Fritsche shows that six out of the nine most frequently screened films were Austrian films. If the play length was determined by popularity and box office take, the draw of the national industry is impressive indeed.

Building on scholarship on gender and nationhood, Fritsche argues that the concepts of masculinity and nationhood are inextricably bound in select Austrian films. In the remaining four chapters, each devoted to a popular Austrian genre—the historical costume film, Heimatfilm, the tourist film, and comedy—Fritsche presents each genre's general traits. She argues that within the conventions of the genre gender was constructed in a variety of ways that addressed questions of national identity and responded to the positions of men and women in the changing postwar situation. "[I]mages of hard, virile men," that had been discredited by the war and were viewed as less desirable "were largely absent from postwar Austrian films" (45.) If the immediate postwar situation presented Austria with a crisis of masculinity, as conditions improved and society stabilized notions of masculinity were bound to change, too. In general, the films distance Austria from Germany and promote a peaceful, harmonious society. They imply Austria's victim status and present a society absent of class conflict. While the early films implicitly praise independent women, this changes in the 1950s with the economic stabilization of society and the affirmation of traditional gender roles.

The historical costume film (45 films out of the 213) is the most obvious genre to connect masculinity to questions of national identity. In these films Fritsche identifies a "softer masculinity" that deviates from images of hard, virile men. The male protagonists are somewhat feminized in appearance and action. They embody culture, love music, and are well spoken and to some extent hedonistic. The military in these films is also "softened" or depoliticized and shown as spectacle rather than an instrument of force. The historical costume film served as a celebration of Austria culture and history, presenting a past Austrians could be proud of. The films skip over Nazi years and Austro-Fascism as well as the First Republic with its internecine battles between left and right. They favor two periods of Austrian history—the Metternich era (1809-1848) and the long rule of Emperor Franz Josef (1848-1916). Whereas the Metternich era is seen as a time of oppression and as Fritsche reads them, a displacement for the National Socialist "occupation," the films of Franz Josef's rule highlight the grandeur and promote the myth of a paternal monarch who holds the diverse empire together.

Fritsche then turns to the Heimatfilm (20 films out of 213) and shows how this genre, too, responds to Austria's troubled past. Despite the customary Alpine setting that could be German as easily as Austrian, the author maintains that the use of local dialects, identifiable *Trachten*, and actual place names in Austrian-made Heimatfilms allowed Austrian audiences to identify with the narratives. She argues that the subtext in the narratives served a cathartic function, obliquely addressing questions of guilt. In these film men are seen as victims. "Using the plot device of wrongful accusation, Heimatfilm does not allow men to redeem themselves by their own actions; they have to wait and exhibit patience until the course of the nation or the actions of other people bring their innocence to light" (106). "Falsely" accused of collaboration, the Austrian people, too, must be patient as the films suggest. The male protagonists' ability to deal with the challenges life has dealt them depends on a combination of traits very different from the softened masculinity in the historical costume film. In contrast to the positive emotionality of the historical costume film, in the Heimatfilm outward expression of emotion is viewed as a dangerous loss of self-control. Rather, physical and mental strength, rationality, and renunciation are desirable.

In the final two chapters, Fritsche examines the tourist film (12 films out of 213) and the most popular of the genres, comedy (65 films out of 213). As forward-looking genres, they respond more directly to modernity and societal changes in postwar Austria between 1946 and 1955. They are virtual seismographs for conservative gender trends resulting from the economic recovery in the 1950s. The tourist film welcomes the urban visitor, embraces modernity, and praises mobility in contrast to the Heimatfilm where nature is viewed as an exclusively male purview and outsiders are unwelcome. If the Heimatfilm deals with issues of guilt, the tourist film presents men finding stability in heterosexual relationships. It shows male protagonists as nonconfrontational and seeking harmony, a reflection of the consensus politics of the Second Republic. In turning to the last genre, comedy (65 films out of 213), Fritsche maintains that the recurring theme of mistaken identity argues for the promise of reinventing oneself and the nation. She shows that despite the appearance of bucking convention, the comedies present an improved patriarchy as the desired family unit. In most films, the fathers are seen as present, anti-authoritarian, and unaffected by the traumas of the war. Fritsche rounds off her study in the conclusion by reiterating the different constructions of gender in the various genres and over time. She also presents a brief overview of Austrian film industry since 1955.

Homemade Men in Postwar Austrian Cinema will be a welcome addition to personal and university libraries and will no doubt become a staple in classes on postwar Austrian film and culture.

Anton Pelinka, *Wir sind alle Amerikaner: Der abgesagte Niedergang der USA* (Vienna: Braumüller, 2013)

Marion Wieser

As Samuel P. Huntington put it in his essay "The U.S.—Decline or Renewal?" in 1988: "Decline has been on everyone's mind, and the arguments of the declinists have stimulated lively public debate." He identified five waves of declinism in the U.S. that retrospectively turned out to be wrong, from the launch of the Sputnik by the Soviets in 1957 to the economic crisis in the U.S. in the late 1980s. During the last 25 years, scholars as well as the media all around the globe have continued to debate about whether the United States remains a dominant power in the world, has already ceased to be one, or will actually soon be on the rise once again. There have been many more such "waves of declinism" since the publication of Huntington's essay. Currently, statements that the U.S. is a power in decline are highly persistent once again. Discussions of this sort became routine and are actually quite anticlimactic at this point. So, a book titled *We are all Americans: Rejecting U.S. Declinism*, written by Anton Pelinka, a well-renowned Austrian political scientist, seems to add yet another "grand strategy" book about American power and hegemony to an already long list of existing publications.[1] But this is not what this book does nor is it what it intends to do.

After dealing extensively with Europe, its political culture, current challenges, and possible future developments, in his book *Europa: Ein Plädoyer*[2], Pelinka, a longtime professor of political science at the University of Innsbruck and now professor at the Central European University in Budapest, turns his view across the Atlantic. With his new publication he wants to offer a representation of "the political science discourse on

---

1. To name a few publications in this regard: Paul Kennedy's *"The Rise and Fall of Great Powers"* (1987), Joseph S. Nye's *"Bound to Lead: The Changing Nature of American Power"* (1990), Torbjorn L. Knutsen's "The Rise and Fall of World Orders" (1999), or John J. Maersheimer's *"The Tragedy of Great Power Politics"* (2001).
2. Anton Pelinka, *Europa. Ein Plädoyer* (Wien: Braumüller, 2011).

America" (p. 7). At the same time he wants to share with the reader his profound and at times very personal political and historical thoughts on the debate about the state of American power, transatlantic relations, and identities on both sides of the Atlantic. This is reflected by the special structure of the book: each of the eight chapters is introduced by a short preface, many times including a personal reflection by the author on one of his personal experiences with the U.S., starting with his first encounter with Allied Forces as a young boy in Post-war Vienna, his first visit to the U.S. in 1967, and his many visits thereafter. These introductions are not always directly connected with the content of the respective chapter, yet they give the book the touch of a personal journal, full of thought-provoking reflections on politics, culture, history, and society in the U.S. and in Europe.

Pelinka begins with a summary and analysis of American foreign policy in the 20th century. And it becomes immediately apparent why Pelinka can easily be called a nonpareil when it comes to explaining in a short, compact, and easily intelligible manner complex political processes and historical developments. In his synthetic style, Pelinka concludes this chapter by bringing it all down to the following point: "In the 20th century Europe did not become a model for America. America became a model for Europe. And that is good" (p. 30). The second chapter focuses primarily on the U.S. and the role and influence religion plays in American politics. And whereas Pelinka—again—is able to summarize and touch upon most important aspects that characterize the U.S. on this topic, his conclusion falls a bit short. He argues that in Europe matters of separation between church and state, religion and politics, are widely settled today (p. 41). Undoubtedly, Europe has gone through a process of secularization over the last decades. The church, however, still plays a major role in politics in many European countries, certainly not as openly and in such an institutionalized way as it once used to, but still enough to be considered an influential political force.[3] Later in the chapter, even Pelinka acknowledges that there are "signs of a new renaissance of political religiosity" (p. 43), citing the mass murder by right-wing militant Anders Breivik in Oslo in 2011 and the controversies over building a new mosque in Cologne that started in 2009 and have continued up until today.

---

3. One only needs to look at countries like Italy, Poland, Malta, Ireland, or Austria for that matter, where the church did not really lose its political influence. Legislation concerning abortion, civil unions, same sex marriage, stem cell research, the building of mosques, or cultural integration of immigrants, and the ever-so-tiresome topic of church taxes in Germany and Austria are indicators that religious views and values still influence politics in many ways.

The third chapter is proof of Pelinka's in-depth knowledge about the U.S., where he writes about American nation building. He rightly highlights the significance of the American Civil War (1861-1865) not only for the abolition of slavery, but also for the following development of the United States, all the way up to the era of the Civil Rights movement until today. Similarly instructive are Pelinka's observations on the topic of immigration. To understand better what we see in Europe today in terms of xenophobia, the debates about multicultural societies, the closing of the borders, and stricter immigration laws, one can take a look at the U.S. in the 19th century and see how similar challenges were faced then in order to maybe find a way how to deal with them today. In light of the refugee crisis in the Mediterranean, the referendum to limit EU immigration in Switzerland in February 2014, and the deportation of over a thousand Syrians from Austria in 2013 alone, this is a very urgent problem for Europe as a whole.

The format of the book, with its personal introductory chapters and sometimes "journal-like flow of thoughts," may generate some confusion with regard to the target audience. It is definitely not a heavy read and not studded or overly cluttered with facts and footnotes. Most likely this book was written for a politically interested general public with some historical and political knowledge about the United States. This seems to be confirmed by chapter four, where Pelinka gives a twelve-page crash course on the functioning of the political system of the U.S., its institutions, and its system of checks and balances. A more expert audience will just skip this part. Sometimes Pelinka makes rather large jumps from one topic to the other, leaving the reader to wonder how the different parts would be connected. At times, he also tries a little too frantically to give specific examples and connect them with the broader topic of a chapter. For example, in chapter four he jumps from the political party system to the death penalty to racism and anti-Semitism, all undoubtedly important topics which would deserve their own time and space in a book like this. In some instances, the easy readability also leads to some repetitiveness (for examples see p. 78, 84, and 95). The many subheadings, formatted in the same font size as the main chapter titles, may also lead to some confusion for readers.

This aside, Anton Pelinka's book is a courageous book since it comes at a time when "US-bashing" (p. 122) is easier and more popular than ever, especially in light of the NSA scandal and the negotiations for a free trade agreement between the U.S. and the EU. Many in Europe—especially the political elite in Germany—are overly fond of talking about a transatlantic divide and of criticizing the U.S. for spying on their friends and allies. Of course, they imply that "we would never do such a thing" while they must be aware that this moral outrage is false and disingenuous.

This book holds up a mirror for us to understand better our criticism toward the United States and our own European identity. "Europe often thinks it is different from the U.S.," Pelinka points out, "but it is not" (p. 139). Chapter six deals extensively with Anti-Americanism in Europe and Pelinka concludes that Anti-Americanism can actually be considered "anti-cosmopolitan" because it reduces the world—and everything bad in it—to America (p. 124). In connection with the U.S. it is very easy to confound Anti-Americanism with legitimate critique. Pelinka does not get into that trap. He does not blindly defend the U.S. and everything for which it stands. He criticizes corruption, violence in schools, racism, the easy access to guns, the Iraq War in 2003, and other grievances and political decisions. This criticism turns into "Anti-Americanism" when it is only expressed in connection with the U.S. and overlooked everywhere else in the world (p. 129). Referring to Andrei Markovits' book *Uncouth Nation: Why Europe Dislikes America*, Pelinka argues that Europe needs a "defining other," not only to distinguish itself from the rest, but also to form a common identity out of the conglomerate of traditions, values, nations, and political views that form the European patchwork rug. What Europe and Europeans easily forget is that the U.S. shaped in great part the Europe of today, and that Europe and the U.S. have many similarities, share many common values (p. 137), and face many common challenges. In this sense—according to Pelinka—Europe suffers from a denial of reality (p. 139). What one could criticize is that Pelinka uses the term "Europe" mostly in a very broad sense throughout the book (with an exception on p. 172, where Pelinka refers to the lack of a common European foreign policy), too easily ignoring the many differences between the countries and nations that form Europe (in a geographical as well as a political sense).

This book is not a snapshot of transient political observations as is unfortunately often the case when Europeans write from afar about American politics or history. Pelinka shows that he has an in-depth knowledge about American history and politics on which he builds his observations. This does not mean that the reader necessarily has to agree with all his political conclusions, but his thesis that Europe and the United States resemble each other in many ways is correct and it is time that Europeans acknowledge that and admit that Europe still looks across the Atlantic with the wish to be—in many ways—just like the U.S.

Pelinka's advice for the West to function as an attractive model for the rest of the world is not to be a national or religious construct, but to be "transnational, post-ethnical and multicultural" (p. 51). The United States should define itself more through its global function and position to continue to cast a spell over the rest of the world and by doing so "Americanize the world." We are not living in a unipolar or bipolar world today. We are living in a multipolar, or even in a nonpolar international system, as Richard N. Haass described it in his essay "The Age of Nonpolarity" (2008).[4] Power is distributed among many different centers and between many different actors, be they states, cities, corporations, terrorist organizations, or other actors. But still within this system, the United States remains the most powerful force and no other rival has (yet) emerged who could really challenge this in the foreseeable future, not even China or India. In the end, the old saying "the condemned live longer" might actually apply to the United States.

---

4. Richard N. Haass: "The Age of Nonpolarity," *Foreign Affairs 87*, No. 3, May/June 2008, p. 44-56.

Robert Kriechbaumer, Franz Schausberger, eds., *Die umstrittene Wende: Österreich 2000 – 2006* (Vienna: Böhlau, 2013)

More than a decade since the inauguration of Austria's disputed "Wende" government, a new, extended volume delves into politics of the Schüssel years. As the editors, historian Robert Kriechbaumer and Franz Schausberger, a former ÖVP governor of Salzburg, set out in their opening essay, this book puts a premium on evaluating the government's policy record and, to a lesser extent, attempts to change the country's polity (p. 14-15). It also highlights conflicts between supporters and defenders of the February 2000 pact between party chairmen Wolfgang Schüssel (ÖVP) and right-wing populist Jörg Haider (FPÖ) and their struggles to frame a political narrative based on that partnership. The various studies devoted to this theme are amassed in the section on *Kulturpolitik*.

The second part of the preface is written by Dieter A. Binder, who calls the most antagonist actors in parties, press, and cultural life before the curtain. His drawing of demarcation lines as of winter 1999 and spring 2000 conveys the tenor that characterizes the few contributions on intellectuals' criticism which stand in contrast to the style, content, and conclusions of the majority of the essays on policies and reforms in this volume. The first stress the intensification of political conflict and dispute all the way up to hysteria. The latter more or less clearly resume predominance of business as usual.

Not all contributions to this volume reflect the book's title and allow for detailed (or any) account on forms of dispute and levels of conflict, however. Michael Neider's essay in the section on institutional reform serves a different purpose and offers a purely chronological listing of laws passed and enacted in the field of judiciary. A more analytical approach would have revealed the continuity of far-reaching interparty consensus on "grid and group" issues, which are indeed central to the structuring of party political space in many other countries, most prominently in the United

States. This applies to the bulk of governance of life issues (e.g. pro-life vs. pro-choice) and handling of nuclear power.

In part of one of the main analytical essays, devoted to the study of party competition and political culture, Wolfgang C. Müller and fellow Marcelo Jenny examine patterns of interparty relations and majority building in parliament. Based on a wealth of data on ballots and MPs' individual political attitudes and preferences, the authors resume "relevant change towards conflict or majoritarian democracy" (p. 80; all quotes in this review translated by D.W.). Yet, this displays little more than reinforcement of long-term trends. Eventually, as the authors add, the new, more conflictual pattern got suspended during the second Schüssel cabinet (after 2003).

Next, Schausberger turns to "second order" attributes of provincial elections (*Landtagswahlen*). Despite the fact that Austrian voters lack effective means to realize forms of divided government, some tend to blend national and regional/local politics in ways which lead them to protest vote to punish parties in government, cast a strategic vote, or simply abstain from ballots. This link was absent in many cases but of striking significance on a few occasions, notably in the autumn 2003 local and regional election in Upper Austria that was much influenced by pension reform and reduction of government share in Austria's largest steel group, *Voestalpine*.

Similar to Schausberger, Heinz P. Wassermann deals with political communication, adding information on the supply side of political reasoning as he tracks effort of branding and selling by the parties in government. Essentially, the article creates a twofold message. First, he documents substantial campaign effects that secured a hundred-year influx of voters to the ÖVP in 2002 but also made possible a last-minute swing favoring the SPÖ four years later (p. 165-80). Second, the incoming government's credo of dedication to a fresh and more cooperative style of governing, first of all in their internal relationship, was authentic and credibly delivered until Riess-Passer resigned as vice-chancellor in 2002 and it eventually gave way to routine politics during Schüssel's second term.

The remaining contribution to this section comes from Herbert Dachs, whose assertions are not quite distinct from those of Wassermann in his search for core elements and magnitude of "new governing." He provides a fair sketch of the need for political reforms, airing views of all parties represented in parliament and the corporatist actors. Readers may infer from his description that vigorous "speed kills" (coined by ÖVP party whip Andreas Khol) policy-making was replaced early on by the "time of harvest" politics due to a lack of internal homogeneity and the electoral cycle. Turning back to coalition bargaining in the aftermath of the 1999

GE, Dachs portrays the leaders of the ÖVP as sincerely convinced that Haider's electoral rise would have been unstoppable had the grand coalition status quo politics been prolonged. Whether one believes in the legend of dragon slayer or refuses this idea, politically viable alternatives would have probably paved the way to further FPÖ gains.

In the section on—largely failed—institutional reform, Peter Bußjäger, looking at relations between the Federal and *Länder* governments, concurs with the diagnosis of the rather limited scope of the "Wende." Once more analyses reveal a prevalence of deadlock over political change, with efforts made by both parties tending to centralize, yet not disentangle, legislative decision-making powers (compare Theurl on the health care sector, p. 328-29). This process was in part due to the effects of EU integration. Bußjäger, a promoter of more federalism, identifies provincial governors as able veto players within their parties and vis-à-vis the federal government.

The section on *Politikfelder* contains studies of fiscal and economic policies (Christian Dirninger), social policy (Guenther Steiner) and the health care sector (Engelbert Theurl). Here both the performance evaluations and the attributed level of political conflict are more diverse and mixed. The legislative imprint at the heart of redistributive efforts has been widely disputed. Key political actors such as the trade union ÖGB vividly, and to some extent, successfully opposed the government's plans to cut back on pension spending. The contributions of all three denote the predominance of fiscal considerations over aspirations to employ sector-specific reforms conducive to meeting good governance standards, in particular for the first Schüssel cabinet (explicit Steiner; in the same vein Stachel p. 341-342). Theurl's article is especially worth reading carefully for analytical reasons as its views on the accountability and decision-making capacity of key players are embedded into situational veto player analysis. Although the analyses are short on interparty competition and intraparty frictions (as everywhere in this volume except for Dachs, Müller and Jenny, and Bußjäger), they ably carve out the persistence of long-standing patterns in decision-making on "greed" issues—benchmarks of state centrism and operational clientelistic arrangements.

Binder (*Vorwort*), Kriechbaumer (sections *Politisches System und politische Kultur, Kulturpolitik*), and Ernst Hanisch (again *Kulturpolitik*) concordantly target intellectual criticism towards the "Wende'" government, albeit in different fashions. While Binder and Kriechbaumer castigate the indisputably misguided and obstinate criticisms of the spearheads of left-intellectual attacks on both coalition partners (protagonists/writers Robert Menasse and Marlene Streeruwitz and former general director of the Salzburg Festival Gerard Mortier), Hanisch faces up to more nuanced stances which necessarily result in a less entertaining while more intellectually stimulating endeavor. The latter entry contains an elegant attempt to carve out the political self-conception of intellectuals. In addition, Hanisch offers an accurate analysis of the Freedom Party's populist character, showing how Haider aroused indignation for his own (electoral) purposes. Summed up, the four contributions reveal some elements of *Kulturkampf* largely confined to political and cultural elites who, in the words of Kriechbaumer, contested for "interpretation of Austrian contemporary history" through empowerment of "historical loci, Ringstraße, Helden- and Ballhausplatz" (p. 201).

The dominant impression created by the contributions on foreign and security policy (Michael Gehler, Paul Luif, Gunther Hauser) is that application of foreign policy is overwhelmingly conditional on parties' domestic policy considerations. This applies to handling of major strategic decisions by all parties represented in government since the mid-1980s (SPÖ, ÖVP, and FPÖ/BZÖ), including the blatant double-talk on the compatibility of the country's neutrality with their (full) participation in the European Security and Defense Policy, and public relations concerning the EU's Eastern enlargement (for the interceptor purchase in 2002/03 see Luif 569-70; for the dispute on terminating compulsory military service in favor of having a professional army see Hauser 622-23). Government parties' maneuvering on both matters evolved into various degrees of political isolation. Notwithstanding Austria's pariah status in 2000-01, the country for Michael Gehler already had become a "case apart" as a "major contribution of internal European and integration politics" (p. 521). Gehler's article uniquely involves Schüssel's performance as minister and party chairmen before February 2000, a conjuncture that might explain the length of his entry (90 pages). He sees Schüssel's role as foreign minister (1995-2000) as burdened and eventually eclipsed by multi-tasking demands as he would also serve as chairman of his party (1995-2007) and vice-chancellor (1995-2000). Gehler concludes the foreign and EU integration policies enacted during Schüssel's term as chancellor made for "the least consensual of all governments in the Second Republic" (p. 545), characterized by "more controversy than consensus as well as more defeats and setbacks than successes and progress" (p. 549).

Following the bulk of policy analyses, Walter Reichel presents "The Schüssel Era as Reflected in Foreign Media," a mostly balanced foray into Western print media accounts on Austrian party competition during the Schüssel chancellorship. This is most of all notable for exposing the inclination of the international press to exaggerate and scandalize, and for providing readers the opportunity to share in the temptations experienced foreign observers of Austrian politics succumbed to when distorting Schüssel's story to somewhat lesser extent. Readers can feel the magic behind Schüssel's advancement in media reports, which in the beginning of his chancellory predominantly portrayed him as a coldhearted, ruthless power politician but later on recognized him as "dragon slayer" in light of the FPÖ's landslide defeat in the 2002 GE. Overall, this press review reflects a tendency of the media to personalize politics to an inaccurate degree.

The book completes with the printed interview some of the authors conducted with Schüssel in November 2010. While questions addressed to Schüssel typically were critical and to the point, some statements of the former chancellor would have required the "interviewers" to double-check with the responses. For instance, Schüssel promoted his 1999/2000 idea of exchanging portfolios held by years and decades by the very same party, addressed to then coalition partner SPÖ, as a necessary modicum of commitment to innovative governing (p. 801). The Social democrats showed unwillingness to agree, not least for the reason doing so would have handed over key ministries to their political rival. If realized, this arrangement would have reduced the largest party in parliament to the status of a junior coalition partner.

Or, alternatively, what are the precise implications of governing with chambers and trade unions in the shadow of the majority principle as Schüssel (p. 804-05) rejects the impression of having downsized and bypassed the legislative influence of established corporatist actors? Is it a case of swim or sink? Is it a relationship still based on cooperation and meeting each other at eye level in the mere absence of veto powers? Did the partial recovery of social partnership in the years past 2003 simply reflect changing power relations, perhaps coupled with electoral strategies?

Also, it seems then interviewers and later collaborators on this volume too quickly bought Schüssel's alleged discretion over personal matters including national listings for parliamentary candidates (p. 807-08) as these apparently reflected management of balancing the interests of the party's Land organizations and party factions/sub-parties (*Bünde*). The same applies to Schüssel rejecting the notion of any sincere considerations ("sandtable exercises"; 799, see also p. 802) of switching to the Freedom Party throughout the 1990s, a view adopted in Binder's contribution to the book (p. 21). At least, the People's Party repeatedly used the threat of turning to the right as a viable pledge in coalition negotiations which disabled the SPÖ from translating electoral gains and vote advantage into portfolio gains and advantage.

Altogether, policy-based analyses carve out both the merits and pitfalls of the Schüssel cabinets. Take Heinz Fassmann who makes a good case for migration policies, a controversial matter at both the elite and mass levels. Quite contrary to the level of public dispute, the essay, in looking at the legislative output since the mid-1990s, highlights continuity instead of rupture. In fact, years ago Haider made the same claim, announcing the agenda of his notorious 1993 "Austria First" initiative had been cleared primarily during the years of grand coalition government. More specifically relevant to the performance of the Schüssel cabinets, Fassmann attests to beneficial "differentiation of regulation on migration" (p. 711).

This volume offers thick descriptions of political ups and downs, attitudes, and records throughout the Schüssel years. Many of its contributions deserve credits for competent evaluation of arguments and performances and tentative conclusions. Nevertheless, the book also suffers from a number of asymmetries and imbalances. First of all, a volume devoted to the study of the Schüssel government must address the issue of political corruption as evident in recent and forthcoming court trials. Having said this, I hesitate to subscribe to the by-now-popular notion of a new era of political fraud established during the years of populist right executive representation. This readily underestimates the extent of corruption in prior decades of which one lacks valid and generalizable data.

Many other things we indeed know and which helped to assess government performances unfortunately remain largely left out. A few authors systematically portray the starting point of the "Wende" by offering detailed accounts on past policy choices and bringing in the perspective of path dependency (see Dirninger on privatization of enterprises owned by the state, p. 231). Peter Stachel exemplifies this task in his analysis of developments in higher education, summarizing "permanent reforms" instead of *Reformstau* for the years until 2000 (p. 363). It comes as a surprise that hardly anywhere in this volume do authors attempt to assess the performance of previous governments. Ironically, they leave defending the legacy of the 1987 to 2000 grand coalition cabinets to Schüssel himself, who acknowledged its merits primarily, but not solely, in relationship to European integration (p. 800, 834-35). Once more he would also portray himself, having served as a minister since 1989, as a supporter of this type of coalition government if it was geared toward realizing potential for political innovation.

On some aspects, in light of many prior attempts to deal with the Schüssel years academically, the book at hand offers roundabout statements based on compilations or condensed summaries of earlier studies (Müller and Jenny, Gehler, Luif). There might be a bit less to say on these years than suggested by the book's title. Finally, the structure of the book not always convinces and at times puzzles. Why have a section entitled *Politikfelder* followed by sections that refer to other policy domains (*Kulturpolitik, Außenpolitik*) if the detached article on migration and integration policy pops up in the institutional reform rubric later on?

Overall, the focus on intellectual disputes and on the early period of the "Wende" laid down in the Preface creates a picture that overstates the extent of the conflict that characterized party politics between the years 1999-2000 and 2006-07. While this reflects the editors' views, claiming the "Wende" years were "like no other epoch in the history of the Second Republic again brought about *Lager* alignment and societal fragmentation generated by ideological and verbal patterns of the past"(p. 10) runs against the essence of the overwhelming majority of articles on policies and institutional reform. Against the backdrop of preceding books on this topic, we see confirmed the predominance of continuity and adaptation over rupture and pendulum swings in the world of policy-making, resembling the style of consociational democracies as opposed to conflict or competitive Westminster democracies. As the government's mastermind Andreas Khol (ÖVP) already had declared in his widely noticed book *Der Marsch durch die Wüste Gobi* (March 2001), the "Wende" was not supposed to equal a turn toward conservatism on the scale realized in the cases of Thatcherism and Reaganomics.

Many reforms implemented by the Schüssel governments moved Austria closer to what can be labeled the European democratic average such as steps towards academic autonomy (*Hochschulautonomie*), the temporary introduction of student fees, the ongoing process of welfare retrenchment, and (almost) full participation in Common European Security and Defense Policy (CDSP). But internationalization also runs upstream and top-down and bottom-up processes merged at some point as shown in Ewald Hiebl's essay on media consumption, political campaigning, and deregulation on television.

The structural drivers behind de-Austrification and the convergence of democracies in general are as prominent as identifiable membership in the EU and other cases of supranational integration that bring about multi-level governance, and the pluralization of lifestyles and political attitudes in postindustrial society in a small open-trade country shaped by the forces of cultural and globalization.

Ludger Helms und David M. Wineroither, eds.,: *Die österreichische Demokratie im Vergleich* (Baden-Baden: Nomos, 2012)

Peter A. Ulram

In their introduction the editors describe the aim of this book to be "to undertake a more precise ascertainment of the place of the second republic within the family of consolidated liberal democracies" (p. 14) not least because many studies on Austrian democracy avoid a comparative view. The following eighteen contributions are divided into three sections: historical landmarks and theoretical perspectives, structure, process and content, and new challenges and the future of Austrian democracy. Most of these authors (mainly political scientists) are established and renowned experts in their academic fields and offer sound and valuable overviews of their respective subjects, sometimes allowing for novel insights and pointed statements.

Helmut Reinalter describes Austria's understanding of democracy in the eighteenth and nineteenth centuries as well as the social and political conditions that contributed to the monarchy's late democratic development. Oliver Rathkolb attempts to place its more recent history into a European context. The latter article, however, suffers from a problem that also effects some other contributions, namely the lack of a real comparative perspective. This is even more pronounced in the articles by Birgit Sauer, Gary S. Schaal, and Oliver W. Lembcke. Sauer's article views the Austrian democracy and state from a gender-critical perspective but leaves the reader wondering if there is a genuine difference in Austria's situation from that of other democracies and, if so, which ones. Schaal's article presents the pros and cons of "modern" democratic theories, concentrating on deliberative and alternative conceptions (especially post-democracy). Their remarks on the Austrian situation are not only very short but also based on rather debatable sources. More telling from a comparative perspective are Theo Öhlinger's reflections on the constitution: its principles, changes, interpretation, and the political background. His conclusion that the Austrian constitution is "de facto similar to the largely unwritten and flexible constitution of Great

Britain" and the "constitution" of the EU (p. 98) might seem surprising but is well argued.

The articles in the second section generally stand out due to their sound empirical foundations and comparative design. Ludger Helms and David M. Wineroither deal with the governmental area, attesting to the Austrian system both as an acceptable system and as a possible model role for reforms in other countries. Peter Bußjäger finds that the federal system—some problems notwithstanding—opens up a broad range of avenues for participation. Somehow less convincing are his examples of institutional innovations such as the lowering of voting age and the direct elections of mayors. Klaus Armingeon presents the changing structures and patterns of interest organizations and representation while David M. Wineroither and Herbert Kitschelt analyze the transformation of party competition using an elaborate conceptual scheme. Fritz Plasser and Gilbert Seeber compare democratic political cultures over time and among European democracies. These three contributions agree that Austria has moved toward the European mainstream and Western European standards in spite of its remaining national particularities. Herbert Obinger places Austria's public activities in the economic and financial field between the liberal and Scandinavian models, noting an increasing importance of international factors. Austria's media system is also said to inhabit an intermediate position between the democratic-corporatist press found in Western Europe and the media of Southern Europe, where political parties have a much stronger impact on the public media and close relationships are common between some media outlets and political power holders (Fritz Plasser and Günther Pallaver). David F. J. Campbell uses a set of indicators to measure the quality of democracy in forty democratic countries. Here, Austria scores high on political rights, civil liberties, income equality and sustainable development, medium on economic freedom, freedom of the press, gender equality and corruption, and low on migration issues. As to be expected, the assessments are heavily influenced by the kind of indicators chosen, and one could argue that two indicators for migration issues (vs. one each for political rights and civil liberties) are somewhat overrepresented.

That migration and integration pose an important challenge is pointed out by Sieglinde Rosenberger in the last section. Johannes Pollak and Sonja Puntscher Riekmann give detailed insights into the Europeanization of Austrian politics with special respect to the coordination of EU politics, noting a comparatively "stronger decentralized coordination sometimes leading to difficulties with making intersectorial package deals" (p. 357). Reinhard Heinisch traces the conditions for and the ups and downs of

Austrian neopopulism. Although he avoids the common superficialities often associated with the subject, his final judgment on the rise and activities of populism is unequivocal—both regarding the negative effects on the quality of democracy and the unresolved question of the FPÖ's ability to govern. Finally, Anton Pelinka looks on the reasons for the "political reform paralysis" in Austria. His essay blames not so much "the usual suspects" (governments of grand coalition and social partnership) but rather the new veto powers: federalism and mass media. While many observers will agree with these conclusions, there is practically no connection between his essay and the other contributions.

Summing up, the book excels in providing many informative and well-presented analyses but sometimes suffers from a lack of real comparative perspective. A few articles, especially those on recent democracy theories and on civic education (Wolfgang Sander), have their merits, but the reasons to include them in an anthology about essential features of Austrian democracy remain rather unclear.

Annual Review

Austria 2013-2014

Reinhold Gärtner

General Elections

The new Government

Never Ending Story: Hypo Alpe Adria

Withdrawal from Golan

Economic and Statistical Data

General Elections

The General Elections were held on September 29, 2013. The legislative period in Austria lasts for 5 years (since 2007) and in Austria as nowhere else in the world people at the age of 16 are entitled to vote (people at the age of 18 can be elected for the Austrian Parliament). The Austrian Parliament consists of two chambers, Nationalrat and Bundesrat, the members of the Nationalrat are elected every five years, and the members of the Bundesrat are delegated according to the parties' results in regional elections. The really important and influential body is the first chamber, the Nationalrat. A party has to get at least 4 per cent of the votes cast to get seats in the Nationalrat (or a direct seat in one of the 39 regional constituencies).

There were some questions to be answered with this election: First, could the SPÖ and ÖVP still get the outright majority (92 of 183 seats);

second, would the BZÖ, which had been quite successful in the 2008 election, manage the re-entry into the Nationalrat; third, could the FPÖ really challenge the first and second position of the SPÖ and the ÖVP; and finally, which of the new parties (especially Team Stronach and the Neos – Das Neue Österreich) could manage to jump over the 4 percent hurdle?

In the end, the SPÖ remained the strongest political party with 26.8 percent, followed by the ÖVP with 24.0 percent. Both parties obtained their worst result in the Second Republic but they managed to gain a small majority of 99 seats in the Nationalrat. The FPÖ came in third with 20.5 percent followed by the Grüne with 12.4 percent. Both, Team Stronach (5.7) and the Neos (5.0) could jump over the four percent hurdle; the BZÖ was disappointed with only 3.5 per cent. The BZÖ had not been able to compensate for the death of the former party-chairman Jörg Haider (who had died in a car accident in October 2008). Thus many surmise that the time of the BZÖ as a political party is over.

Though the FPÖ could win more than 20 percent (+ 3 percent in comparison to 2008) it could not really challenge the first or second place of the SPÖ and the ÖVP. The Grüne achieved their best result in a nation-wide election (beside the 12.9 percent they got in the European Parliamentary elections in 2004).

	2013		2008		+ / –	
	%	seats	%	seats	%	seats
SPÖ	26,8	52	29,3	57	-2,5	-5
ÖVP	24,0	47	26,0	51	-2,0	-4
FPÖ	20,5	40	17,5	34	+3,0	+6
Grüne	12,4	24	10,4	20	+2,0	+4
Team Stronach	5,7	11	--	0	+5,7	+11
Neos	5,0	9	--	0	+5,0	+9
BZÖ	3,5	0	10,7	21	-7,2	-21

Turnout: 74.9 per cent (78.8 per cent in 2008)

Interesting newcomers were two new parties: Team Stronach and the Neos – Das Neue Österreich. Team Stronach was founded by Frank Stronach, a successful entrepreneur (Magna International). He wooed away some former BZÖ-MPs and ran for regional elections in Carinthia, Tyrol, Lower Austria and Salzburg already in 2013. According to spring 2013 polls, Team Stronach should have been capable of getting some 10 percent of the votes cast, due to Stronach's inferior media performance and the incompetence of many of his candidates, the outcome in the elections was comparatively poor (5.7 per cent).

The really surprising fact was the showing of the Neos – Das Neue Österreich. A completely new party with Matthias Strolz as chairman managed to jump into the parliament straight away. Strolz had been active in the ÖVP, but he did not make a political career within this party. So Strolz (and former Liberals) founded a liberal party favoring free enterprise, a strictly pro-European Union attitude and also a rejection of right wing populism. The Neos seem to gain ground especially at the expense of the ÖVP. At the recent local council elections in Salzburg, the Neos got more than 12 percent and it is likely that they will get seats in the European Parliamentary Elections in Mai 2014.

The new Government

On December 16, 2013 the new SPÖ-ÖVP government was introduced. Within the ÖVP Andrä Rupprechter, Sophie Karmasin, Sebastian Kurz (former State Secretary in the Federal Ministry of the Interior) and Wolfgang Brandstetter were new Ministers, within SPÖ Johann Ostermayer (former State Secretary of the Federal Chancellor) received a ministerial appointment.

Federal Chancellor	Werner Faymann	SPÖ
Federal Ministry for Arts, Culture, Constitutions and Public Service	Josef Ostermayer	SPÖ
Federal Ministry for Agriculture, Forestry, Environment and Water Management	Andrä Rupprechter	ÖVP
Federal Ministry of Defense and Sports	Gerald Klug	SPÖ
Federal Ministry of Family and Youth	Sophie Karmasin	ÖVP

Federal Ministry of Science, Research and Economy	Reinhold Mitterlehner	ÖVP
Federal Ministry for Education and Women's Affairs	Gabriele Heinisch-Hosek	SPÖ
Federal Ministry for Europe, Integration and Foreign Affairs	Sebastian Kurz	ÖVP
Federal Ministry of Finance	Michael Spindelegger (Vice-Chancellor)	ÖVP
Federal Ministry for Health	Alois Stöger	SPÖ
Federal Ministry of the Interior	Johanna Mikl-Leitner	ÖVP
Federal Ministry of Justice	Wolfgang Brandstetter	ÖVP
Federal Ministry of Labour, Social Affairs and Consumer Protection	Rudolf Hundsdorfer	SPÖ
Federal Ministry for Transport, Innovation and Technology	Doris Bures	SPÖ
State Secretary within the Federal Ministry of Finance	Sonja Steßl	SPÖ
	Jochen Danninger	ÖVP

The former Federal Ministry of Science (Karlheinz Töchterle, ÖVP) was dissolved and the agenda given to the former Minister of Economy and Youth, Reinhold Mitterlehner. There was widespread protest against this decision. The Federal Ministry of Family and Youth was newly constituted.

Never Ending Story: Hypo Alpe Adria

In 2007 Hypo Alpe Adria, a bank in Carinthia was sold to the Bavarian Landesbank (BayernLB). The Governor of Carinthia at that time was Jörg Haider who expected some compensation for this sale for Carinthia. In 2009, though, Hypo Alpe Adria had to be nationalized because of the threat of bankruptcy.

Meanwhile, in various trials some former Hypo Alpe Adria managers have been sentenced but the real magnitude of the financial disaster is still not fully known. In March 2014 there were rumors of some € 17 billion of public funds which might be necessary to save the bank. The main argument against a bankruptcy is the fear of a loss of reputation for Austria as a reliable financial partner. The fact is that this legacy of Haider and his cohorts will be the most expensive burden Austria will have to cope with in the near future.

Withdrawal from Golan

"Is Austria more cowardly than the Fijis?" headlined the daily Kurier on June 19, 2013 after Austria had announced the withdrawal of its UN-troops from the Golan Heights in Syria – they were replaced by soldiers from the Fiji Islands.

Austrian "blue helmets" had been in Syria for 39 years but decided in 2013 to withdraw its troops because of the Civil War in Syria. In Austria, this decision was criticized as another sign of its diminishing foreign policy.

Economic and Statistical Data

Inflation was at 2.0 per cent in 2013 (compared to 2.4 per cent in 2012); HVPI was at 2.1 per cent (compared to 2.6 per cent in 2011). The public deficit amounted 2.5 per cent in 2012 (2.5 per cent in 2011) and public debts amounted to 77.1 per cent in the third quarter of 2013 (74.5 per cent in 3/2012).

In 2013, GNP was at € 36.980 per capita (compared to € 36.640 in 2012); economic growth was 1.1 per cent in 2013 (compared to 0.5 in 2012).

In 2013, imports amounted € 130.000 million (€ 92.500 million from the EU-28) and exports amounted € 125.400 million (€ 83.100 million to the E.U.). Imports from NAFTA were € 5.002 million; exports to NAFTA € 8.539 million.

In 2013 4.230.000 people in Austria were employed; the rate of unemployment was at 4.8 per cent in 3/2013 (on average 4.3 per cent in 2012).

At the beginning of 2013, 8.451.860 people were living in Austria, among them 1.004.268 foreigners (and among them 424.669 from EU/EWR/CH). In 2012 78.952 children were born alive in Austria and 79.436 people died. Life expectancy is at 78.0 years (men) and 83.3 (women).

List of Authors

Christina Antenhofer is an assistant professor for Medieval History at the University of Innsbruck.

Kurt Bednar has received degrees from the University of Vienna in both Law and History.

Peter Berger is a professor of history and head of the Institute for Economic and Social History at the Vienna University of Economics and Business.

Günter Bischof is the Marshall Plan Professor of History and the Director of CenterAustria at the University of New Orleans.

Wolfram Dornik is a researcher at the Ludwig Boltzmann Institute for Research on the Consequences of War in Graz and head of the Museum im Tabor in Feldbach.

Jason C. Engle is a graduate assistant at the Department of History at the University of Southern Mississippi.

Nicole-Melanie Goll is a research assistant of Contemporary History at the University of Graz.

Jonathan E. Gumz is a lecturer in Modern History at the University of Birmingham, UK.

Birgit Johler is a cultural scientist, museum curator and teaches at universities in Austria and Germany.

William M. Johnson retired in 1999 as professor of European History at the University of Massachusetts, Amherst, and resides in Melbourne, Australia.

Katharina Kober is a freelance historian in Vienna.

Marion Krammer is a photo- and media historian and researcher at the Department of Communication at the University of Vienna.

Günther Kronenbitter is a professor of Modern and Contemporary History at the University of Augsburg.

Richard Lein is an assistant professor at Andrássy University in Budapest.

Hannes Leidinger is a lecturer at the Institute for History at the University in Vienna.

Verena Moritz is a scientific project leader in the Austrian National Archives.

Hans Petschar is a historian and Director of the Picture Archives and Graphics Department at the Austrian National Library.

Barbara Sauer is a historian at the University of Vienna in a research and memory project on the Nazi-persecuted Austrian medical doctors.

Gerhard Senft is a professor at the Institute for Economic and Social History at the University of Economics and Business in Vienna.

Michael P. Steinberg is the Barnaby Conrad and Mary Critchfield Keeney Professor of History, Professor of Music and German Studies, and Director of the Cogut Center for the Humanities at Brown University.

Margarethe Szeless is a photo- and art historian and researcher at the Department of Communication at the University of Vienna.

Ulrike Tauss is a freelance cultural scientist in Vienna.

Peter A. Ulram is a Lecturer at the Department of Political Science at the University of Vienna.

Jacqueline Vansant is a Professor of German at the University of Michigan-Dearborn.

Joanna White is a freelance translator in London and carried out research into Shoah memorials as part of her postgraduate studies in Vienna.

Marion Wieser is the head of the New Orleans Office at the University of Innsbruck and a PhD candidate in Political Science.

Richard Dominic Wiggers is Executive Director for Research and Programs in the Higher Education Quality Council of Ontario.

Samuel R. Williamson, Jr. is President and Professor of History Emeritus of the University of the South.

David M. Wineroither is a Lecturer at the Department of Political Science at the University of Innsbruck.

Contemporary Austrian Studies

Günter Bischof and Anton Pelinka/Fritz Plasser/
Ferdinand Karlhofer, Editors

Volume 1 (1992)
Austria in the New Europe

Volume 2 (1993)
The Kreisky Era in Austria
Oliver Rathkolb, Guest Editor

Volume 3 (1994)
Austria in the Nineteen Fifties
Rolf Steininger, Guest Editor

Volume 4 (1995)
Austro-Corporatism: Past—
Present—Future

Volume 5 (1996)
Austrian Historical Memory &
National Identity

Volume 6 (1997)
Women in Austria
Erika Thurner, Guest Editor

Volume 7 (1998)
The Vranitzky Era in Austria
Ferdinand Karlhofer, Guest Editor

Volume 8 (1999)
The Marshall Plan in Austria
Dieter Stiefel, Guest Editor

Volume 9 (2000)
Neutrality in Austria
Ruth Wodak, Guest Editor

Volume 10 (2001)
Austria and the EU
Michael Gehler, Guest Editor

Volume 11 (2002)
The Dollfuss/Schuschnigg Era in
Austria: A Reassessment
Alexander Lassner, Guest Editor

Volume 12 (2003)
The Americanization/
Westernization of Austria

Volume 13 (2004)
Religion in Austria
Hermann Denz, Guest Editor

Volume 14 (2005)
Austrian Foreign Policy in
Historical Perspective
Michael Gehler, Guest Editor

Volume 15 (2006)
Sexuality in Austria
Dagmar Herzog, Guest Editor

Volume 16 (2007)
The Changing Austrian Voter

Volume 17 (2008)
New Perspectives on Austrians
and World War II
Barbara Stelzl-Marx, Guest Editor

Volume 18 (2009)
The Schüssel Era in Austria

Volume 19 (2010)
From Empire to Republic: Post-
World War I Austria

Volume 20 (2011)
Global Austria: Austria's Place in
Europe and the World
Alexander Smith, Guest Editor

Volume 21 (2012)
Austrian Lives
Eva Maltschnig, Guest Editor

Volume 22 (2013)
Austria's International Position
after the End of the Cold War